Storage Networking

An Introduction to Storage D… Applications, Management, a… Systems

Marc Farley

Cisco Press
800 East 96th Street
Indianapolis, IN 46240 USA

Storage Networking Fundamentals

Marc Farley

Published by:
Cisco Press
800 East 96th Street
Indianapolis, IN 46240 USA

Printed in the United States of America 2 3 4 5 6 7 8 9 0

Second Printing January 2007

Library of Congress Cataloging-in-Publication Number: 2003108300

ISBN: 1-58705-162-1

Warning and Disclaimer

This book is designed to provide information about storage technologies used in SAN and NAS network storage implementations. Every effort has been made to make this book as complete and accurate as possible, but no warranty or fitness is implied.

The information is provided on an “as is” basis. The authors, Cisco Press, and Cisco Systems, Inc. shall have neither liability nor responsibility to any person or entity with respect to any loss or damages arising from the information contained in this book or from the use of the discs or programs that might accompany it.

The opinions expressed in this book belong to the author and are not necessarily those of Cisco Systems, Inc.

Feedback Information

At Cisco Press, our goal is to create in-depth technical books of the highest quality and value. Each book is crafted with care and precision, undergoing rigorous development that involves the unique expertise of members of the professional technical community.

Reader feedback is a natural continuation of this process. If you have any comments on how we could improve the quality of this book, or otherwise alter it to better suit your needs, you can contact us through e-mail at feedback@ciscopress.com. Please be sure to include the book title and ISBN in your message.

We greatly appreciate your assistance.

Corporate and Government Sales

Cisco Press offers excellent discounts on this book when ordered in quantity for bulk purchases or special sales.

For more information please contact: U.S. Corporate and Government Sales 1-800-382-3419
corpsales@pearsontechgroup.com

For sales outside the U.S., please contact: International Sales international@pearsoned.com

Trademark Acknowledgments

All terms mentioned in this book that are known to be trademarks or service marks have been appropriately capitalized. Cisco Press or Cisco Systems, Inc. cannot attest to the accuracy of this information. Use of a term in this book should not be regarded as affecting the validity of any trademark or service mark.

Publisher	John Wait
Editor-in-Chief	John Kane
Executive Editor	Jim Schachterle
Cisco Representative	Anthony Wolfenden
Cisco Press Program Manager	Nannette M. Noble
Production Manager	Patrick Kanouse
Development Editor	Andrew Cupp
Project Editor	Marc Fowler
Copy Editor	Gayle Johnson
Technical Editors	Philip Lowden
	John Nelsen
	Guy Shimabuku
Team Coordinator	Tammi Barnett
Book and Cover Designer	Louisa Adair
Composition	Mark Shirar
Indexer	Larry Sweazy

CISCO SYSTEMS

Corporate Headquarters
Cisco Systems, Inc.
170 West Tasman Drive
San Jose, CA 95134-1706
USA
www.cisco.com
Tel: 408 526-4000
800 553-NETS (6387)
Fax: 408 526-4100

European Headquarters
Cisco Systems International BV
Haarlerbergpark
Haarlerbergweg 13-19
1101 CH Amsterdam
The Netherlands
www-europe.cisco.com
Tel: 31 0 20 357 1000
Fax: 31 0 20 357 1100

Americas Headquarters
Cisco Systems, Inc.
170 West Tasman Drive
San Jose, CA 95134-1706
USA
www.cisco.com
Tel: 408 526-7660
Fax: 408 527-0883

Asia Pacific Headquarters
Cisco Systems, Inc.
Capital Tower
168 Robinson Road
#22-01 to #29-01
Singapore 068912
www.cisco.com
Tel: +65 6317 7777
Fax: +65 6317 7799

Printed in the USA

About the Author

Marc Farley is well-known throughout the network storage industry for his objective and in-depth analysis of network storage technology. His writings include *Building Storage Networks*, First and Second editions, as well as numerous articles, technology white papers, and opinion pieces that have been published in the industry trade press. He regularly speaks at industry events and participates in online seminars and discussions.

Farley started working in network storage in 1991 as a systems engineer at Palindrome Corporation, a company that developed network backup systems for Novell NetWare environments. Since then, he has worked in a variety of marketing strategy roles on a wide variety of storage technologies, including storage routers, disk subsystems, file-level virtualization, and storage switches. Farley has a bachelor of science in physics from the University of Washington.

About the Technical Editors

Philip Lowden currently holds the position of customer support engineer for Storage Area Networking at Cisco Systems, Inc. Before this role, he worked four years at Cisco and six years at Electronic Data Systems as a senior UNIX systems administrator, performing production systems architecture and support duties on a variety of host and storage platforms. He was also an officer in the U.S. Air Force for six years. He holds a master of science degree in computer engineering from North Carolina State University, a bachelor of science degree in computer science from the University of Nebraska, and a bachelor of arts degree in English from Saint Meinrad College. He is a SNIA-certified FC-SAN Specialist. He is married and has two children.

John Nelsen is a member of the Cisco Infrastructure Architecture Team and a project manager within the Cisco Systems IT Enterprise Storage Solutions Group. Before joining Cisco, he worked for 10 years in the pharmaceutical industry. He has 20 years of experience in various IT architecture and operational roles. When he joined Cisco in 2000, his primary responsibilities included defining and selling a strategy to reduce storage TCO that was founded on the concept of a consolidated storage utility. Since gaining acceptance for the strategy in 2001, Nelsen has focused on defining the hardware and software technologies along with the business processes and projects required to build and implement a storage architecture that can support the storage utility. He received a bachelor of science degree from Allegheny College in 1984 and a master of science degree from North Carolina State University in 1988.

Guy Shimabuku is a senior engineer with the Architecture and Enterprise Services Group for Verizon. His primary function is evaluating storage and networking elements for Verizon's next-generation data centers. In addition, he manages a research laboratory that encompasses 125 TB of storage and 500 Fibre Channel ports serving 600 development servers. He is a graduate of California Polytechnic University School of Engineering and has been in the field of networking and data storage for 15 years. He has been published and interviewed in trade magazines for his work on testing and implementing broadband networks.

Dedications

To you, Dad. You are imprinted on everything I think and do. Even so, I'm doing fine. I still miss you terribly after all these years.

Acknowledgments

I'd like to thank several people who made major contributions to this book. Matt O'Keefe helped me immensely when I was just getting under way by pointing out weaknesses in my previous analysis of system storage processes. He also got me started on the more realistic and Byzantine analysis that runs throughout this book. Matt has contributed heavily to the development of open-source storage software for Linux and possesses major storage wisdom.

Toward the end of the project, I circled up with Bruce Thompson for a sanity check and some finishing touches. Bruce truly has an advanced view of storage, coming from many years of working through the strange and frustrating relationships between file systems, operating systems, and device drivers. When Bruce tells you how something works, you can take it to the bank.

Mike Workman is no longer involved in the day-to-day grindings of the disk drive industry; nonetheless, he is an undisputed authority on the subject. Sincere best wishes for you, Mike, and your team at Pillar. May your star rise and hover long. Big thanks also to my good friend John Groves, the SCSI I/O master in Austin. John and I like to talk about everything from music to politics to storage. But when it comes to storage I/O processes, John is the teacher and I am the student.

A heaping helping of gratitude to Steve Legg, a soft-spoken, hugely talented, and patient man if ever there was one. This is a person I want to take human being lessons from, but, in the meantime, I'll settle for insights on virtualization, clusters, and multipathing. Joel Harrison is one of those rare people who comprehends technology, industry, people, and organizations equally well with amazing deep-blue clarity and deft humor. He is a true master of the storage world.

Big thanks to James Long for his generous assistance with determining the contents and scope of the book when it was just a bunch of raw ideas. Also, an enormous debt of gratitude goes to Jim Schachterle for marshalling this project through the long journey with an author who seldom met deadlines. The technical editors, Phil Lowden, John Nelsen, and Guy Shimabuku, also deserve credit for their work reviewing the contents and pointing out things that needed to be set right.

Thanks also to John Howarth, Ron Riffe, Jeff Browning, Jeff Barnett, Joaquin Ruiz, Gordon Arnold, and Charles Potter for their help.

Contents at a Glance

Contents

Introduction

When I was a boy, my dad used to tell me, "A job is only worth doing if you do it right." I've since learned that for some projects "getting it right" involves many years, repeated attempts, and the ability to identify and throw away weak components that do not further the goals of the project.

For a couple years, I'd been feeling that I wanted to write another book that would take on more difficult topics and present them in a way that allows an experienced networking professional to gain a deeper understanding of storage technologies and processes. So when Cisco Press approached me about working on a new storage book, I was interested. Fortunately, their concept aligned with mine, which was to focus almost entirely on the storage technologies and ignore most of the networking content. I've always preferred the murky Neanderthal swamp of storage to the technology reservoirs of network standards anyway.

One of the most difficult things in discussing storage is terminology. The problem is that the terms used in storage often have a historical context that no longer fits with new architectures and environments. For example, the terms virtual disk, disk volume, and LUN are often used to refer to the same type of storage entity, but they can also refer to distinctly different things within the same expanded I/O system. These types of overlapping definitions cause no end of confusion in the industry. I knew from the outset that explaining storage better this time was going to require some different techniques, terms, and analysis.

There is a lot of literature in computer science where storage is simply referred to as "a disk drive" because of old, outdated assumptions embedded in operating systems. Historically, there had never been a reason to make a distinction between the file system's view of a collection of SCSI block addresses and the thing that an HBA device and driver software actually communicate with. However, when the downstream storage is virtualized in any number of ways—as it often is in a SAN—it becomes very useful to clarify the pieces of storage that come into play and their respective roles.

The concept of a "storage address space" is introduced early in the book (in Chapter 2, "Establishing a Context for Understanding Storage Networks") to refer to the flat, contiguous string of addresses where data is stored by a file system or database. Now the words "storage address space" might not be a phrase that leaps off the tongue, but I can assure you that if you start using them to refer to an abstract, addressable "chunk" of storage, many difficulties interpreting storage become much, much easier. No caveats or asterisks are needed to augment the term storage address space, like there are with more familiar terms like virtual disk, disk, and volume.

Throughout the book, a perspective on the relationships between host storage software, storage subsystems, and storage devices is included. This necessarily includes the relationship between the operating system kernel and the file system. A surprising thing about operating system/file system interactions is that very few people understand what goes on at any detailed level. This is not an environment based on object orientation or structured programming devices, but instead is an environment optimized by performance with cunning algorithms and shortcuts. Once things work well in an operating system, every attempt is made not to change it. Hence, the problem with carrying old assumptions forward, well past their appropriate age.

Another key to understanding storage is knowing SCSI protocols and processes. Chapter 6, "SCSI Storage Fundamentals and SAN Adapters," will be a pivotal chapter for many readers, and I expect it will be referred to often by readers working on concepts in later chapters. I hope my explanation of SCSI architecture is at the appropriate level and works for you. Like so many things, it is not necessary to know the details of a technology if a good architectural understanding exists and provides predictable operating principles.

The concept of a "layout reference system" is used in the discussions of file systems. Again, a good general term has not existed for the logical entity that describes the location of data in a storage address space. There is simply no reason to believe that I nodes or V nodes would necessarily have to be the technology used to track stored data in other, newer file systems. My apologies to file system developers. I am not trying to change what you do; I am only trying to explain it in an accessible, generic fashion, the same as I would do if I were trying to write a requirements document for a file system.

Trying to clarify old, existing constructs by inventing new generic terms carries some amount of personal risk, because it is not at all clear that people will accept them. But for this attempt it was clear that some new language and new analysis were needed to do the job "right." I didn't see any other way to make storage easier to think about and understand.

This book is the result of a great deal of work and a lot of help from many people who graciously pitched in. From my perspective, I can honestly say that no shortcuts were taken, no assumptions went unquestioned, and no conceptual coasting was done in writing this book. I look forward to hearing from readers in the years to come.

Who Should Read This Book?

This book was written for systems, networking, and storage professionals who want to gain an in-depth understanding of the processes and architectures used in storage. It is intended to be read by systems engineers and architects as well as network, systems, and storage administrators who are responsible for planning, implementing, and managing network storage solutions. It is not a cookbook, but an explanation of storage architectures, applications, and processes used in real-world environments.

How This Book Is Organized

Storage implementations combine many different technologies, and any in-depth discussion of a real-world storage implementation could use concepts from every chapter of this book. One could certainly read the book in chapter sequence, but it is much more likely that readers will first read the chapters that are most immediately applicable to specific tasks and responsibilities in their environments.

In general, the book is structured as follows:

- Chapter 1 discusses the rationale for network storage.
- Chapters 2 and 3 present a broad picture of how storage I/O processes work.
- Chapters 4 and 5 illustrate the functions and architectures of storage devices and subsystems.
- Chapter 6 is primarily about the architecture and protocols of SCSI. A brief discussion of HBAs and NICs appears at the end of this chapter.
- Chapter 7 examines the various storage interconnects used for device attachment.
- Chapters 8 and 9 discuss redundancy, mirroring and RAID.
- Chapters 10 and 11 present the processes used for remote copy and multipathing redundancy protection.
- Chapter 12 is about virtualization and volume management.
- Chapter 13 covers backup and recovery.
- Chapters 14 to 16 look at file system designs for network storage.
- Chapter 17 discusses data management.
- Appendix A contains answers and explanations for the Q & A review questions at the end of each chapter.
- Appendix B is a brief listing of INCITS standards pertaining to storage networking.
- The glossary defines key storage terms used throughout the book.

PART I

The Big Picture of Storage Networking

Upon completing this chapter, you will be able to

- Participate in discussions and analysis of data access architectures and requirements
- Describe the availability shortcomings of legacy storage architectures
- Analyze DAS storage for scalability and utilization problems
- Participate in planning sessions for justifying storage network solutions to replace DAS storage

CHAPTER 1

Data Access in the Internet Era

Storage networking promises to be one of the most dynamic areas in all of information technology for several years to come. If the evolution of other groundbreaking networking technologies provides any clues, we should expect network storage to radically improve the ways organizations leverage data. As an infrastructure element, network storage is being used to make applications and systems more scalable and robust.

The initial concept behind network storage is simple: extend legacy storage processes into a network-connected world. Eventually, these legacy storage processes will be replaced as new methods are developed, but to date the major benefits have been the result of applying network flexibility to storage applications.

One of the first challenges in implementing network storage is gaining a clear understanding of the intricacies and idiosyncrasies of storage. Many implementation details defy intuition and logic. Storage networking can be incredibly powerful, but its strength can't be fully realized without knowing storage in sufficient detail.

Many newcomers to network storage approach the topic having ample experience with networking technologies. There is no question that a strong networking background is helpful, but one should always be careful of extending Ethernet and TCP/IP data networking assumptions to storage networking. For instance, there are very different expectations for transmission quality in TCP/IP networks and in storage networks. Storage communications have always assumed reliable, in-order delivery with very few retries. Legacy TCP/IP networks, on the other hand, have been built with the assumption that most networks have imperfections and that packets will be lost or delivered out of order. Because it represents the integration of these different legacy communications systems, storage networking must find ways to bridge these different perspectives.

Information Technology (IT) professionals who find themselves in the role of planning for, architecting, implementing, and managing storage networks need to understand both parts of the storage networking equation, as the wrong assumptions can be very costly.

Availability Requirements for Network Storage

Many aspects of computing have changed since the massive buildup of the commercial Internet in the last decade. One of the most significant and painful changes has been the necessity for round-the-clock operations and the push for five-nines (or 99.999%) reliability. Most technology people would agree that living in a wired world is a great thing, but it does have its disadvantages—such as living with a pager as a required appendage for round-the-clock administrative actions and emergency troubleshooting.

In a short period of time, American society has gone online en masse to the point where we take data access for granted. Furthermore, it's amazing how intolerant our society has become regarding system and data access. If we can't get the data we want on demand—whether it is for personal or business use—we tend to become frustrated and look for other avenues to get what we want. This impatience with data access puts an incredible amount of pressure on IT professionals.

Data access represents only one of the management vectors involved with storage today. Another issue is the hoarding habits of technology users who want to make sure they have copies of any data that might be useful in the future. Systems and networks do not always work as expected when they are continually being stretched to their capacity. While storing oodles of data online could turn out to be as natural as any other form of human behavior, it's far from natural for systems administrators to enjoy wrestling with the aftermath of it every day.

Ready access to the endless amount of Internet-resident data makes it easy to see how today's enormous disk drives can actually be filled in a relatively short period of time. When things reach their limits, something has to give. Where storage is concerned, the resolution has historically meant data access was shut off while new equipment was installed and data was transferred between devices.

It should be obvious that there can be no access to data without some sort of storage connectivity between systems and storage. What might not be as obvious is the fact that storage connectivity needs to be incredibly accurate, reliable, and scalable.

A storage system that inadvertently corrupts or loses data is worthless. Likewise, a storage connection topology that injects transmission errors and does not provide seamless capacity scaling is also a liability. There is no way to achieve anything close to five-nines availability from storage topologies that encourage disconnections as a way of life.

In order to qualify for five-nines availability, a system and its storage has to run all year, with only 5 minutes allowed for maintenance or unpleasant surprises. To illustrate how challenging this level of high availability is, the International Engineering Consortium (IEC) has published information about system availability on its website. Table 1-1, with information from the IEC website, matches availability percentages (percentage of uptime) with the maximum amount of downtime allowed to meet those percentages.

Table 1-1 *Availability Percentages and the Corresponding Downtime Per Year*

Availability Percentages	Downtime Equivalents Per Year
99.0% uptime (two nines)	Up to 3.7 days of downtime per year
99.9% uptime (three nines)	Up to 9 hours of downtime per year
99.99% uptime (four nines)	Up to 53 minutes of downtime per year
99.999% uptime (five nines)	Up to 5 minutes of downtime per year

Considering all the systems and network equipment commonly used in a business, it is simply not realistic to think that they can all run with five-nines availability. And when one considers that Windows servers require rebooting for such things as device driver updates, a person can only wonder how anybody can expect to have a five-nines operation.

The answer lies with redundancy: in doing more with more. The term "N+1" refers to a distributed system that requires N individual systems to do the work, but has a spare (+1) system that can take over if something happens to one of the other N systems.

So, by using extra systems, extra network links, and network equipment, as well as using extra storage connections and devices, it is possible to provide continuous application services, even when individual pieces of the puzzle break or are replaced.

Traditional Client/Server Computing with Direct Attached Storage

This section takes a look at a legacy storage topology that worked for many years but is incapable of meeting today's high-availability system requirements. Before there was network storage, there was just plain old storage. Storage products were categorized by the computer platform they were designed for, such as IBM mainframe systems, Digital VAX systems, AS/400s, UNIX workstations and servers, PC servers and desktops, and Apple Macintosh computers. Historically, storage was usually sold as an integrated part of the system.

Open-systems machines were connected then as they are today, mostly over Ethernet and TCP/IP networks. File sharing, the first form of open-systems network storage, allowed workstation and desktop users to access data on file server systems. Client systems could be almost anywhere on a LAN and could access data from the file server. This way, storage on a UNIX server from one vendor could be used by users running many different kinds of operating systems. In other words, the cost of storage could be shared among many different platforms. A simple client/server file-sharing network is shown in Figure 1-1.

Figure 1-1 *Basic Client/Server File-Sharing Network*

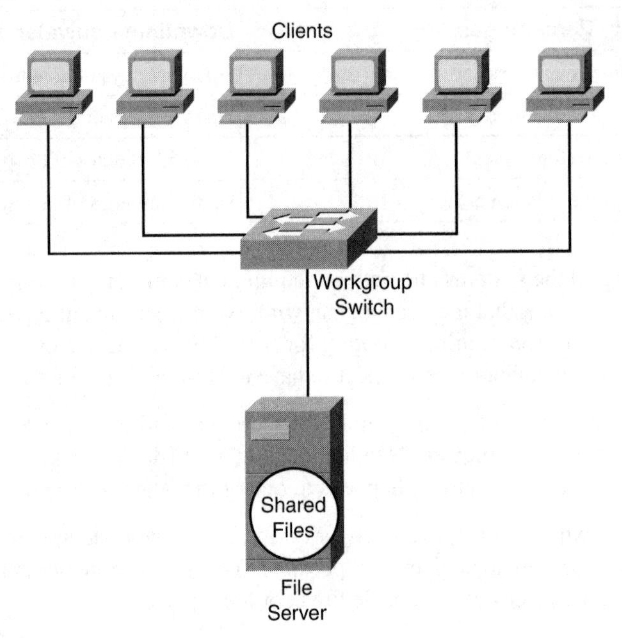

Introducing DAS

The acronym DAS stands for *direct attached storage* and reflects the legacy storage connection topology used in client/server file-sharing networks. The storage connectivity technologies in this environment have typically used either Small Computer Systems Interface (SCSI) or Advanced Technology Attachment (ATA), although there have been a few others over the years. With the advent of storage networking technologies, a term was needed to differentiate preexisting storage technologies from newer storage area network (SAN) and network attached storage (NAS) technologies; hence the term DAS was invented.

Connectivity Shortcomings of DAS

DAS uses a bus topology in which systems and storage are connected by a bus that commonly takes the form of a ribbon cable. Every entity on a DAS bus has a unique address from a limited number of possible addresses. Devices are connected to the DAS bus in sequential fashion, sometimes called a daisy chain, as illustrated in Figure 1-2.

Figure 1-2 *DAS Devices Connected on a Daisy Chain Bus*

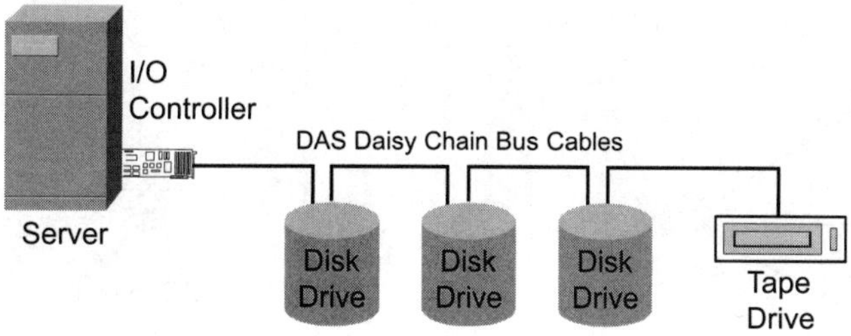

Data Availability Depends on Server System Health

Notice in Figure 1-2 that there is a single host system storage controller for all the devices on the bus. This is certainly a cost-effective arrangement, but it is hardly optimal for high availability. If the controller were to fail, data on any of the devices on the bus would not be accessible. More important, if the system were to fail for any reason, data on any of its buses would not be accessible until the system were recovered and made operational again. With a goal of high availability, single points of failure such as these are simply not allowable.

Figure 1-3 shows a client/server network with several clients accessing three different application servers, each with its own storage. Server 3 is in the process of being upgraded and has been shut down to complete the upgrade process. While the upgrade is being done, the application's data is temporarily unavailable.

Less dramatic than a system crash, but almost as frustrating to users, is the scenario in which storage workloads increase until they exceed the server's capabilities, creating an I/O bottleneck that can increase application response time. Referring to Figure 1-3 again, instead of Server 3 being down for system maintenance, it could still be running but not keeping up with its I/O workload, creating performance problems for the clients and applications that are using it.

Static Configuration of DAS Storage

In addition to the single point of failure problems and the bottleneck problems of DAS, the electric-connection nature of parallel DAS buses makes it almost impossible to change the configuration of the bus while the system is running. I've sometimes referred to this condition as "electric love" because the controllers and devices on the bus cannot stand to be separated, even temporarily, while the system is operational.

Without the ability to dynamically change the configuration of the bus by adding, for instance, more storage devices, it is impossible to make adjustments on the fly that could relieve I/O bottlenecks or create additional storage capacity.

Figure 1-3 *Data Accessed Through Server 3 Is Unavailable While the Server Is Being Upgraded*

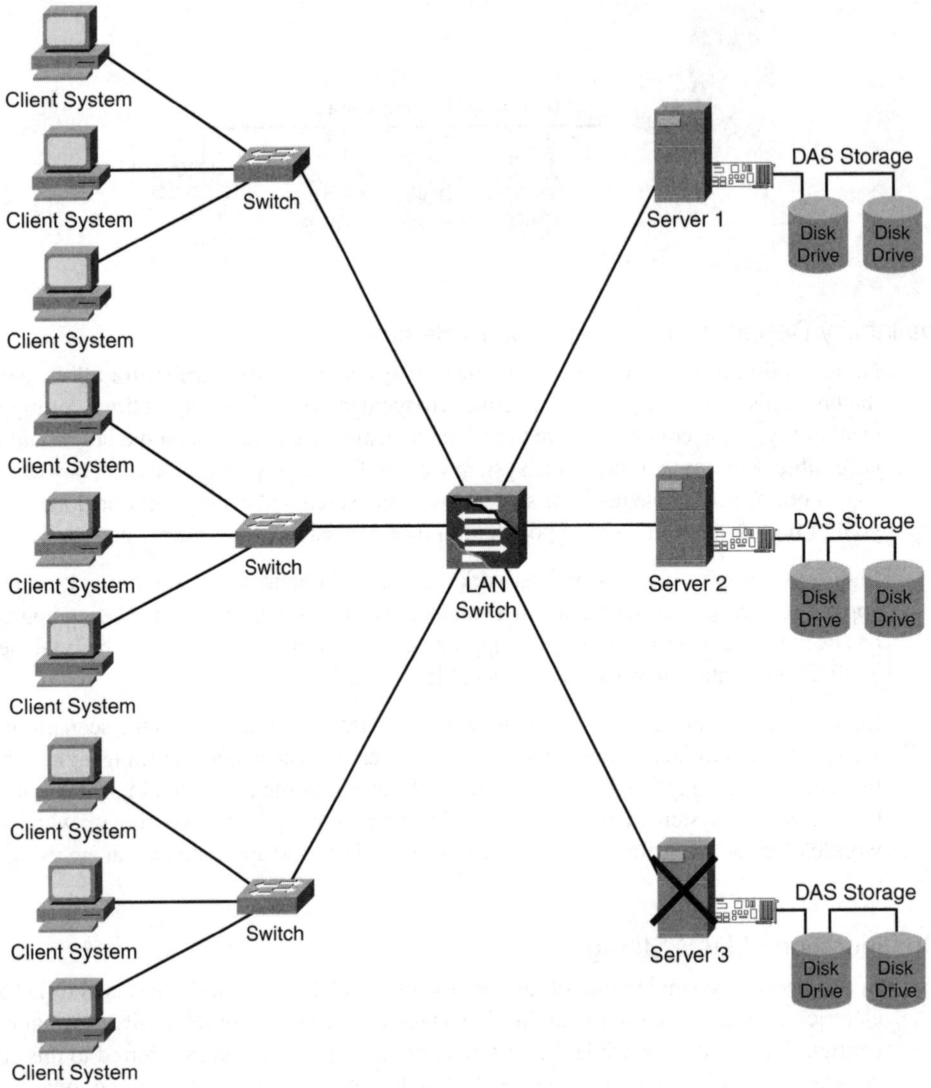

Distance Limitations of DAS

No discussion of DAS storage shortcomings would be complete without mentioning the distance limitations of DAS storage buses. DAS makes many different bus and cable lengths available, but they are all relatively short. The longest cable length for DAS storage is 30 meters, which used to be supported with differential SCSI. Today, low-voltage differential SCSI cables can be 12 meters long.

There are two fundamental problems with short cables. The first is disaster tolerance. A fire, flood, or any other site disaster that physically impacts a storage subsystem will also wipe out a redundant subsystem that is 12 meters away. There is no good way to achieve the required distances for data redundancy and business continuity using DAS.

The second problem with DAS cable lengths becomes painfully clear when positioning servers and storage in a crowded data center or server room. DAS's limited-distance connections force servers and storage to be positioned adjacently. As systems and storage are upgraded and new systems and storage are installed, the challenge of fitting all servers and storage close enough to each other can become an expensive and time-consuming exercise. Most IT professionals agree that spending time plotting the moves of servers and storage to accommodate cabling is a waste of time they would gladly avoid.

Business Issues with DAS

DAS worked well enough in the pre-Internet days, but today's high-availability environments suffer when using DAS-based storage. Storage has become an increasingly dynamic part of the information infrastructure, but the requirements for using and managing it have exceeded the capabilities of DAS static products.

High Cost of Managing DAS Storage

DAS is typically the least expensive storage to buy but the most expensive to own and manage. Considering that storage management costs exceed the cost of storage several times over, it is clear that DAS is on the wrong side of the value fulcrum.

DAS Capacity Fire Drill

Storage capacity limitations are familiar to almost all network administrators. A "disk full" message is not necessarily the worst thing that can happen in an administrator's day, but it's certainly not good news either. There is always plenty to do besides bailing out a bloated server system. The fact is, disk-full conditions occur with some regularity, and the larger a business is, the more frequently they occur.

When a server runs out of disk capacity, the first order of business is creating fresh capacity by deleting or removing data—a practice that certainly runs the risk of losing data. After that, a plan needs to be created for solving the problem, which includes analyzing the storage configuration and selecting replacement or additional products. If products need to be acquired, there might be paperwork to fill out, approvals to arrange, and budgets to exceed—which can lead to reworking the plan.

Finally, there is the storage upgrade process itself, which involves downing the server, installing new storage, restarting the server, copying and distributing data among the storage devices, and verifying that the whole thing worked as planned.

The disk-full condition in a DAS environment is just the first domino in a chain. There are risks and delays along the way with costs that should not have cropped up.

One of the primary issues with managing DAS storage is the lack of centralized management. As management can be performed only through the server that connects to the DAS system, the management of DAS storage is determined by the server's operating system, if it exists at all. With inconsistent management methods, the end result is that DAS storage problems can be more difficult to predict than one might expect, which means that unpleasant disk-full surprises are more likely to pop up.

Captive Resources and Storage Utilization

A common frustration with DAS storage is the inability to share storage resources between servers. Say you have two servers, Server A and Server B, both using DAS storage. The storage capacity on Server A cannot be used by Server B and vice versa. This makes it difficult and expensive to purchase storage collectively for all the servers together, because each system needs to have its own excess storage capacity. The utilization of storage resources cannot be balanced or spread among multiple servers. In other words, the cost of storage cannot be leveraged across all servers, but is isolated to each server and its applications. Unfortunately, it is nearly impossible to predict the amount of storage an application is going to need before it is installed. Some applications are never used as expected, while others that start out as simple utilities can grow into full-fledged workhorses.

Figure 1-4 shows two servers, each running two applications on separate I/O buses to reduce I/O bottlenecks. Of the two applications on Server A, one is growing faster than planned, while the other is growing slower than planned. Of the two applications on Server B, one is growing faster than planned, and the other is growing as expected.

Figure 1-4 *Inconsistent Utilization of DAS Storage*

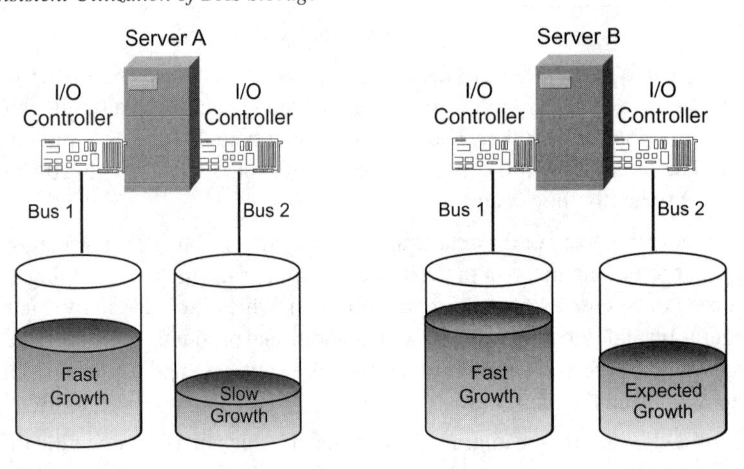

The situation in Figure 1-4 poses some difficult challenges. It might be possible to allocate some of the storage from the slower-growing applications to the fast-growing applications. This type of solution could possibly work, but it could also trigger other problems, such as I/O bottlenecks. Regardless, the solution is only a Band-Aid, as there is still an excellent chance that some data growth will continue to be faster than expected, and the applications will be more likely to run out of storage space.

Even though there are two separate I/O buses on each server, it is not possible to add storage while the system is running. If the I/O bus needs to be changed, the entire system must be shut down. Therefore, a capacity-full situation with either application creates a data availability problem for both applications running on the server.

Performance and capacity of slow-growing applications seldom create operational problems, but there might be other financial issues to deal with. As more companies look for ways to run more efficiently, storage resources that are less than 50% utilized might be viewed as overly expensive. Requests for more budget resources to address storage problems when current storage resources are underutilized are not always warmly received by financial managers.

In the final analysis, DAS products are simply not capacity-efficient. Companies wind up buying far more storage than they need to.

Limited Scalability with DAS

Another serious problem with DAS storage is the lack of scalability, which comes from having a small address space. While most networking technologies can accommodate thousands or even millions of entities, DAS storage is limited to a few hundred.

The SCSI bus has been implemented with a variety of address spaces. Today, SCSI adapters for systems typically support one or two buses with a total of 16 target addresses. In turn, each one of these supports up to 15 subaddresses, which expand the addressability a great deal, but it is still small by networking standards.

Whether or not the address space allows enough storage devices to be connected, there are still other matters that must be considered, such as the way fairness algorithms are implemented in SCSI. Without plunging in too deeply at this point, all entities on the bus *arbitrate* to determine which entity will gain control of the bus and transfer data. The bus address determines the priority that is used to resolve concurrent arbitration attempts from multiple bus entities. While this is sometimes referred to as a fairness algorithm, there is nothing fair about it, as the entities with the lowest-priority addresses get serviced the least.

In fact, the target addresses with the lowest priority could potentially have 15 devices with subaddresses needing to transfer data over the bus. If these devices are unable to gain control of the bus, a situation called *device starving* can occur, which has the unpleasant side effect of ruining the performance of applications needing services from those devices.

Exasperation with DAS Backup

There is no question that on a day-to-day basis, backup and recovery operations are among the most problematic in many IT organizations. Backup processing in a DAS environment can be almost impossible. IT workers that say they do not have problems with DAS-based backups are probably either lying or don't know what they are talking about. Servers with DAS storage can be backed up either over a LAN or to locally attached DAS tape devices. Backing up over the LAN enables backup to be centrally managed but creates significant network congestion. The cruelest part is that backup over the LAN often cannot complete in the allotted time for the most important servers, which means that full recoveries are jeopardized and made even more stressful than they already are. The alternative is to use a decentralized backup approach that backs up servers to their own DAS tape equipment. This provides optimal performance, but the complexity of distributing hundreds of tapes on a daily basis is error-prone as well as time-consuming.

New SAN-based backup architectures that supercede DAS backup capabilities are badly needed for this all-important systems management application.

Network Storage Architectures That Overcome DAS Limitations

The Internet makes it clearly evident that we live in the Information Age, where data access is paramount to the success of an organization. It has become obvious to many that the most valued asset in their entire IT infrastructure is their data. The efficiencies of conducting automated business functions depend on having data stored and providing access to it. In some cases, an organization's data was collected over decades, and it represents unrecoverable business intelligence that cannot be replaced.

One-to-Many Relationships with DAS

The primary problem with DAS storage is that there are single points of failure, which can block access to data. Bus topologies for data access have not been able to reflect the seminal role data has in the overall scheme of data processing.

DAS uses a one-server-to-many-storage relationship structure, in which a single server controls one or more storage devices, as shown in Figure 1-5.

Figure 1-5 *One-to-Many Relationship Structure of DAS*

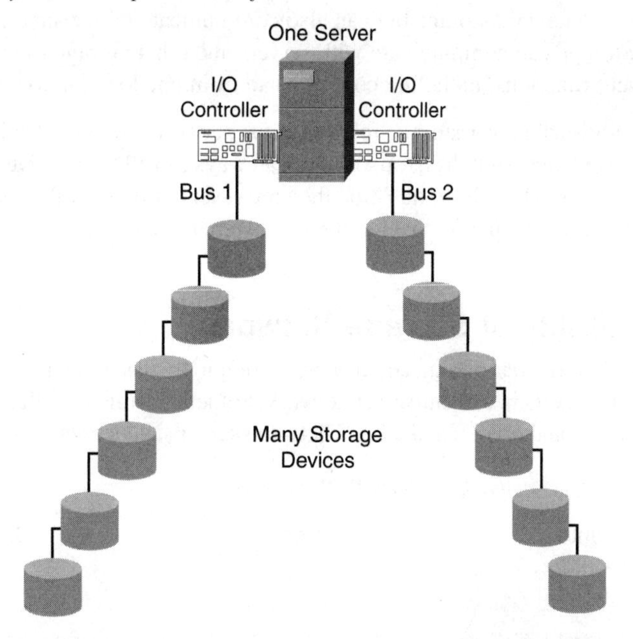

A subtle detail in DAS's relationships is that a single bus controller manages all bus activity. In general, storage entities on a DAS bus do not communicate directly with other storage entities. Even though the technology might support storage-to-storage communications, those implementations are not common.

Many-to-Many Relationships with Storage Networking

If data is the most important asset, the connectivity providing access to it must also be highly valued. Communication topologies for data access need to be flexible, resilient, scalable, and secure.

In traditional client/server environments, server systems have been the center of attention. Client systems located throughout the organization can access applications running on centralized servers. However, with the DAS one-server-to-many-storage relationship structure, there is no way to build a flexible connectivity infrastructure between servers and storage that provides the necessary options for alternative paths to data.

The missing link is clear: The communication topology between servers and storage has to change.

Network storage changes the relationships between servers and storage by creating peer-level communications between all entities in the network, servers and storage alike. Whereas DAS uses a one-to-many relationship structure, network storage has a many-to-many relationship structure where multiple servers and multiple storage devices can all communicate with each other.

This new arrangement creates all kinds of new opportunities for storage applications. Servers can communicate with storage but can also communicate with each other over a storage channel. Storage can communicate with servers and other storage to provide a variety of management functions, including copying data from one location to another.

Beyond traditional server/storage relationships, network storage introduces new network entities into the mix. Switches, routers, and gateways can all have active roles as peers in storage communications. There is no question they are essential parts of the plumbing, but they might also be used as active participants in the management of storage.

Connection Flexibility of Storage Networks

When SANs were first introduced, they were commonly described as the storage network "behind" the servers in a client/server network. Sometimes this was illustrated by placing a LAN between clients and servers and a SAN between servers and storage, as shown in Figure 1-6.

Figure 1-6 *A LAN "Front End" and a SAN "Back End" Network*

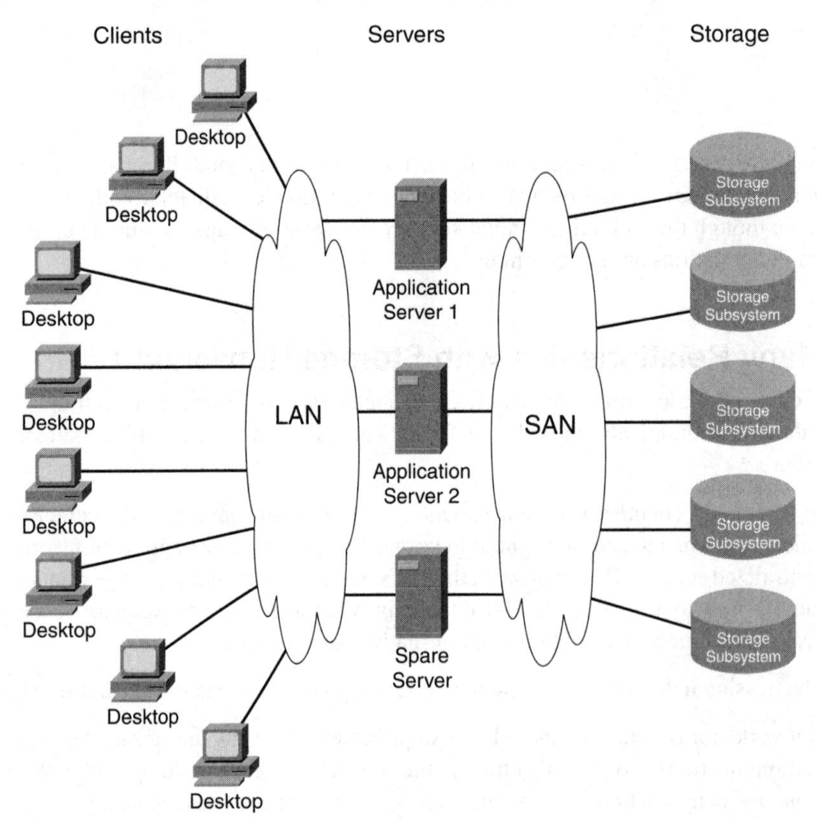

One of the main differences between the simple SAN model illustrated in Figure 1-6 and the DAS data-access model is the presence of a spare server in the SAN model. The spare server is the "+1" part of an N+1 deployment. If an application server needs maintenance or fails, the spare server can assume its IP address and take its place in the client/server network.

More importantly, where data access is concerned, avoiding the problems of DAS-style "electric love" that necessitate downtime, the spare server simply logs in to the proper storage and immediately starts accessing data. In the case of failures, there will be some necessary data integrity checking to perform first, but there is no need to power off the storage or the spare server to make wiring changes.

The concept of a spare server can easily be extended to incorporate server upgrades. A server system lacking CPU resources for an increasing workload can be replaced with a different, more powerful machine. The new system can noninvasively be plugged into the storage network and tested before it connects to the storage. Depending on the capabilities of the operating system, the cutover from the old server to the new one can take seconds, as opposed to hours. Figure 1-7 shows a new server taking over for an aging server that is being retired.

Figure 1-7 *Upgrading Servers in a Storage Network Environment*

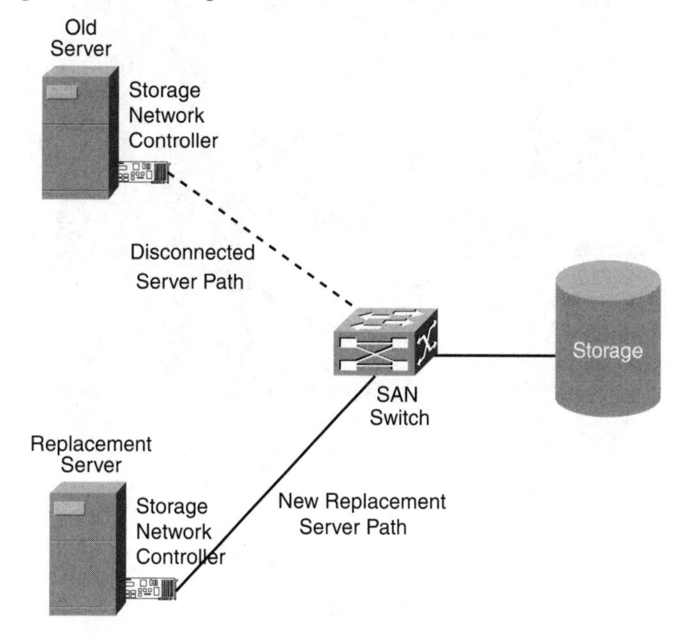

Similarly, storage can also be upgraded. New storage can be connected to the storage network for testing and prepared for use. The process of upgrading storage is more complicated than upgrading a server because the data has to be moved from one storage location to another. While there are several ways to accomplish this, the key point made here is nothing has to be powered off and no cabling changes have to be made during the cutover process.

Architectures for Data-Centric Computing

In today's computing environment, it is virtually assured that systems and storage products will come and go, but the data itself will remain useful and important for a much longer period of time.

One of the most significant contributions storage networking has made is the introduction of new data-centric computing architectures. Whereas client/server computing uses an application-centric architecture, with many client systems accessing centralized application servers, storage networking facilitates data-centric architectures with multiple servers accessing centrally located storage subsystems.

Figure 1-8 depicts a data-centric computing architecture implemented with a storage network.

Figure 1-8 *A Data-Centric Computing Architecture*

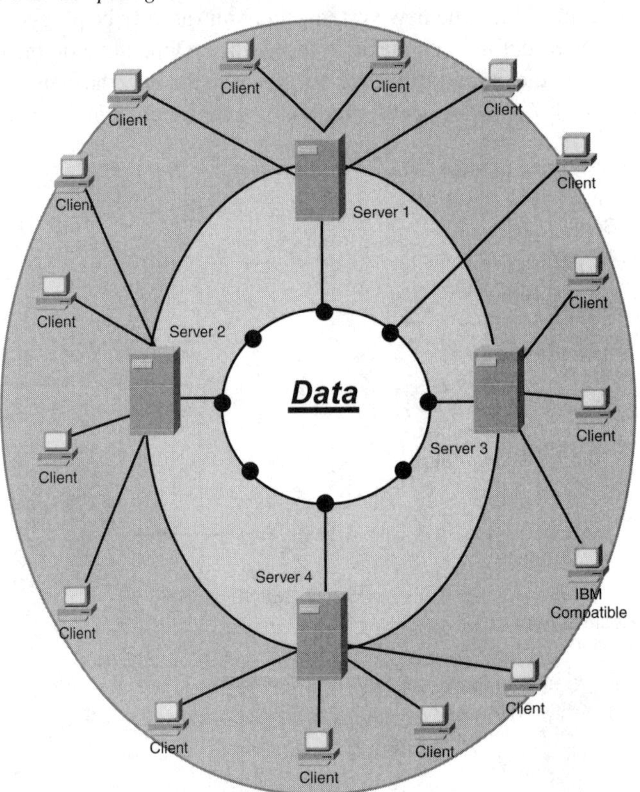

One of the most important aspects of Figure 1-8 is the presence of multiple access points for storage and systems in the storage network. Obviously, if there is going to be many-to-many connectivity, the individual components have to be able to support it. These access points can be physical network ports with unique addresses, such as network interface cards (NICs) and host bus adapters (HBAs), or they could be logical in nature, such as service access points (SAPs), subaddresses, and virtual network addresses.

With plentiful connection options, it is possible to build storage networks in which data—and the access to it—are given the highest emphasis through the architecture. Data-centric computing is not possible without robust, fault-tolerant, multiported storage that can easily be connected to many different servers simultaneously.

The Mighty Notebook Weighs In

Sometimes it's easier to understand concepts like "data-centric computing" by changing the context a bit. This time, notebook computer storage is used to illustrate data-centric computing.

Notebooks are self-contained, complete computing solutions that give you everything you need. The problem is that strange things happen to notebooks. They become lost, get stolen, get dropped, and become moody from travel abuse. If access to data is the goal, it's clear that the notebook's data needs to be protected in a way that makes it readily available.

A system-centric storage approach would back up the notebook's data to one or more CDs that are kept with the laptop. Obviously, if you lose your notebook, there is a good chance that the CDs and your data will also be lost. In the best-case scenario, a physically damaged notebook can be replaced with another using the first machine's hard drive. It's also possible that you might be lucky enough to restore data from CDs that survived. Otherwise, you might be out of data and out of luck. In any case there is a definite loss of productivity (and opportunity).

The data-centric model does not assume that data is part of the notebook, but exists to be processed by applications running in a system. The data could be stored on an external disk or memory device. In fact, multiple copies could be made on multiple devices for safety and convenient access. Now, if something destroys the notebook, the data is still immediately available on any machine that has the software that can use it.

Of course, most of us do something like this with our own notebooks and desktops (we *DO*, don't we?). The rationale for building storage networks and data centric computing environments is the same—it's just that the scale and stakes are different.

By contrast, if the data-centric approach is taken, the notebook's data could be stored on a small, portable, external disk drive with a universally common interface such as USB. This way, when the notebook goes AWOL, the data can still be accessed almost immediately—all that is needed is any compatible computer with the same applications and a connecting port for the external disk drive. This other system could be located at work, home, school, a friend's house, or a commercial business that has systems available for use, such as a Kinko's Copy Center or an Internet café.

The real power of the external drive is that it provides almost limitless connection options to systems. A USB portable disk drive can connect to millions of computers around the world.

Obviously network storage subsystems designed for data center environments are not portable, nor do they use USB as an interface. But they can have the same powerful ability to connect storage to many potential servers that could be called upon to work with data stored within.

Enterprise Storage

Data-centric architectures were initially promoted by EMC, IBM, and Hitachi as a benefit of large storage subsystem products classified as enterprise storage products.

Enterprise storage is a product concept that is something like a data "fortress." It has broad connectivity to support many servers in addition to having many redundant components and technologies for withstanding component failures and environmental problems. Data is stored with redundant protection within the enterprise storage subsystem.

Enterprise storage subsystems are discussed in greater detail in Chapter 5, "Storage Subsystems."

Redundancy and Data-Centric Topologies

This chapter closes with a glimpse of a topology that provides redundant data access paths to centralized storage. Figure 1-9 shows a data-centric environment with storage at the center of the infrastructure.

Figure 1-9 *A Topology for Centralized Storage with Redundant Paths*

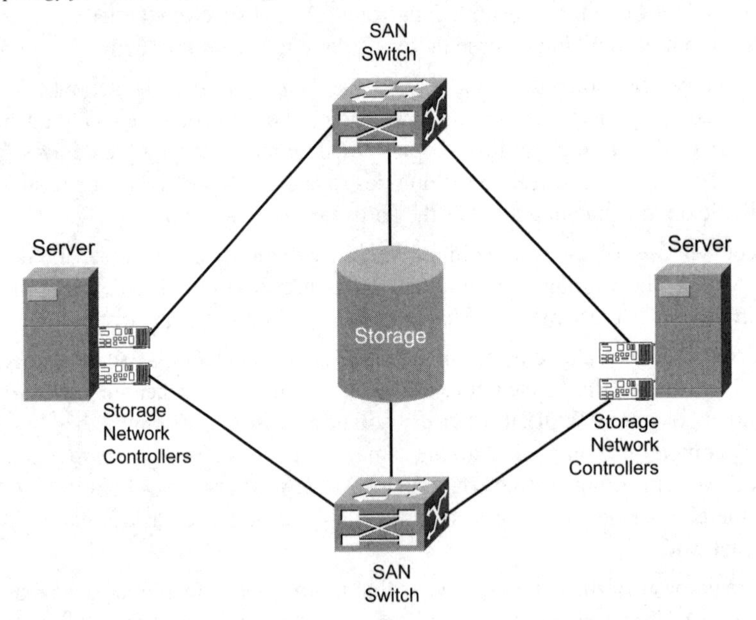

Both servers in Figure 1-9 have the ability to access centralized storage—and all the data stored there—through two different paths. Chapter 11, "Connection Redundancy in Storage Networks and Dynamic Multipathing," covers redundant pathing in much greater detail.

In general, the *potential* for any-to-any data access is the desired goal, not necessarily the reality, of universal storage connectivity. As long as a connection can be created instantaneously when it is needed, the storage network is doing its job. In practice there are many reasons to restrict access between servers and systems that have nothing to do with each other under normal operating conditions.

Summary

As computing environments have changed with the advent of the Internet, storage requirements have also changed to increase the availability of data. Five-nines availability is not easy to achieve, considering that it allows a maximum of only 5 minutes of downtime a year. Even four-nines availability is very difficult, allowing less than an hour per year—including the time needed for normal system maintenance.

Legacy DAS storage connectivity architectures have been exposed as being too inflexible and costly for businesses that have adopted the Internet as a major element of their businesses. Companies need storage network solutions to improve the availability, scalability, and utilization of their storage resources.

Connectivity options with storage networks vastly exceed those of DAS storage buses. Sharing storage resources allows administrators to respond faster to capacity-full situations while simultaneously increasing the utilization of storage products.

One of the primary differences between legacy DAS storage and SAN technology is the ability to create data-centric storage topologies where data is viewed as the center of the network. This type of topology can be supported with multiple access paths to create centrally managed storage with excellent data availability capabilities.

Q & A

1. How much downtime is allowed per year to have five-nines availability?
2. Before SANs and NAS, what was DAS called?
3. DAS is used by which storage technologies?
4. True or false: DAS allows storage devices to be connected and disconnected while the system is operating.
5. What is the relationship between host systems and storage using DAS?
6. What is the relationship between host systems and storage using network storage?
7. True or false: Upgrading storage and servers is easier with network storage than it is with DAS.
8. Where is storage located in a data-centric architecture?

Upon completing this chapter, you will be able to

- Analyze storage networking products and designs according to their connecting, storing, and wiring capabilities
- Describe the role of connecting in a storage network, and make basic distinctions between storage buses and storage networks
- Participate in discussions about storage products and implementations, locating the basic functions, roles, and locations of storage controllers, as well as identifying storage address spaces used by host systems to store data
- Describe the relationship between filing systems and operating systems and the role of space allocation performed by filing systems
- Explain the difference between block I/O and file I/O in storage networks, and describe how SAN and NAS can be analyzed as applications for storing and filing in a networked environment

CHAPTER 2

Establishing a Context for Understanding Storage Networks

People who come to storage networking with experience in Ethernet and TCP/IP networking have a tendency to start analyzing storage network architectures using the familiar protocol stack method that has been so effective in data networking. While protocol stacks obviously exist in storage networks, the stack approach does not necessarily reveal anything very useful or relevant for storage processes because so much of the interesting stuff in storage happens at the network application layer.

Much of this chapter explores a "three-legged stool" analysis for storage networking technology. This analysis breaks the subject into three distinct functional areas that divide the work of storage I/O processes and form a complete, functioning system:

- Connecting
- Storing
- Filing

The end of this chapter covers the major product groups for storage networking, storage area networking (SAN), and network attached storage (NAS). It also applies the analysis model to show how the basic functions are typically implemented in storage network solutions.

The Three Primary Functions of Storage Networking

Storage processes can be broken into the three different functional areas shown in Table 2-1. The fastest way to gain in-depth understanding of network storage is to know what each of these three functional areas does and what products typically provide them.

Table 2-1 *The Three Primary Functional Areas Involved with Storage Networking*

Functional Area	Description
Connecting	Provides the transmission of data between systems and storage.
Storing	A lower-level application with specialized commands and control protocols for system/device interactions.
Filing	Directs the placement of data objects in storage and is responsible for presenting data to applications and users.

NOTE Readers who are familiar with my writing on this subject might notice a change with the use of the word "connecting" to replace the word "wiring." Connecting more accurately conveys the breadth of hardware and software that were intended to be included together. The word "wiring" has strong connotations for many people that limit its interpretation to physical cables. It does not communicate the larger sphere of technologies containing such things as switches, routers, gateways, routing algorithms, addressing schemes, and network management.

Connecting

There has always been some way to connect systems to storage products. Essentially, this means providing some sort of data transmission system between storage devices or subsystems and the system processor.

For the most part, storage has used either bus connecting technologies for DAS storage or network connecting technologies for SAN storage. The sections that follow briefly examine these two connecting technologies.

A Quick Look at Buses Used for Connecting DAS Storage

Bus technologies used with DAS storage are constructed from a collection of copper wires working in parallel, each transmitting a single bit of information at a time. Data transmitted over a bus is first disassembled from bytes into bits by the sender, transferred over the bus as binary signals (either a 0 or a 1), and then reassembled into bytes again by the receiver. All information is transferred in parallel, including application data, addresses, and communication protocols.

The process of disassembling data, transferring it over a parallel bus, and reassembling it at the receiving end is shown in Figure 2-1.

Figure 2-1 *A Byte of Data Transmitted Across a Parallel Bus*

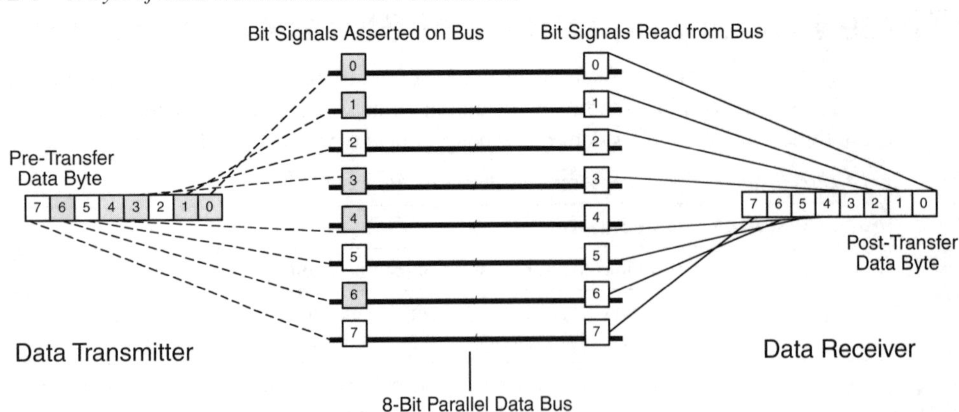

NOTE When we discuss storage data transfers, it seems logical to picture storage data "moving" from one place to another, but of course nothing physical actually travels anywhere. Serial network transmissions work by signal propagation, similar to an analog telephone call. You hear somebody talking, but it is a representation of what he said, not the actual acoustic phenomenon.

Parallel bus transmissions, like those in Figure 2-1, are different. A DAS storing controller creates signals by changing the voltage on the eight data lines. The receiving node measures the voltage across these lines in parallel as an actual byte of data.

The physical characteristics of a bus, such as length, are heavily constrained by the requirement for precise time synchronization in sending and receiving each bit accurately. As a result, buses have inverse relationships between transmission rates and length—the faster a bus is, the shorter its maximum length can be.

Buses tend to be finite in scope with few degrees of freedom—and therefore they have limited failure modes. Data on a DAS storage bus is guaranteed to be received in the same order it was sent. This is called *guaranteed in-order delivery*. The primary advantage of bus technology is the reliability of the connection. The primary disadvantage of buses is that they are rigid and inflexible. In addition to their physical limitations, they have limited addressing schemes that do not accommodate key concepts like bridging and routing. Bus environments also lack basic management concepts such as domains, naming, and authentication.

The Small Computer Systems Interface (SCSI) bus has been used for two decades to connect storage and other peripherals such as scanners and printers to computer systems. Another common bus has been the Advanced Technology Attachment (ATA) bus, which has been used over the last decade as a way to connect desktop and laptop storage to PC systems.

SCSI bus cables come in two varieties: internal and external. Internal SCSI cables are assembled as ribbon cables, and external SCSI cables are fairly thick and heavy multistrand cables within a common shield. ATA cables are available only as internal ribbon cables. Both SCSI and ATA cables have fairly large connectors containing many pins or connecting sockets.

NOTE ATA is also often referred to as Integrated Device Electronics (IDE). The terms have been used interchangeably by many, but ATA is more accurate as it refers to the name used in standards documents.

Readers wondering about Serial ATA (SATA) as an exception to the discussion here will find it discussed in Chapter 7, "Device Interconnect Technologies for Storage Networks."

A Quick Look at Networks Used for Connecting SAN Storage

Unlike bus technologies, which have many parallel wires for transmitting binary signals, network technologies typically have four or fewer wires that serially transmit data as frequency modulated signals. Network cables can be made with fiber-optic technology, twisted-pair wiring, and coaxial cable as well as using wireless transmission. In practice, most storage network implementations use fiber-optic transmission technology due to its superior distance and bandwidth capabilities.

Networks also have much richer connection possibilities than buses. For starters, most modern networks have multifaceted topologies that enable highly scalable implementations. In addition, many types of technologies are used to transmit data between different physical networks, such as bridges, gateways, and routers, which increase a network's scalability. Perhaps most importantly, networking technologies usually have important management characteristics such as large address spaces, naming abstractions, and sophisticated measurement and alerting mechanisms.

For all their advantages, the fact that networks have so much more functional breadth than buses also means that they have many more variables and, therefore, potential problems. This is why products with advanced management functions are so important in storage networks.

As mentioned at the beginning of this chapter, one of the difficulties newcomers have in understanding storage networking is related to the assumptions they make based on their experience with TCP/IP and Ethernet data networks. In general, the design of data networking products assumes there might be delivery problems in the network and that data could be transmitted over different network paths. The bottom line is that in-order delivery of data is not guaranteed, as is the case with bus connectivity. The requirement for in-order delivery turns out to be extremely important for storage applications and is discussed more in Chapter 3, "Getting Down with Storage I/O," and Chapter 10, "Redundancy Over Distance with Remote Copy."

Fibre Channel networking technology has been the most common connecting technology used for SANs. The most recent connecting technology to be introduced is iSCSI, which is implemented on top of TCP/IP, meaning it can run on any physical network that supports TCP/IP. TCP/IP Ethernet networks are by far the most common for connecting systems to NAS storage appliances.

The Logical Side of Storage Connections

The connecting component of a storage network has logical aspects as well as physical. These logical processes incorporate such things as access algorithms, including fairness and congestion control, addressing and naming, network configuration and domain management, network operations management and other topics such as link aggregation and virtual networking. In essence, any technology used in a network for storage networking is part of the connecting component in a storage network.

This is a very rich topic with many interesting nuances. For the most part, this book focuses on storing and filing technologies in storage networks and does not address connectivity topics. Readers interested in exploring the connecting components of storage networks should seek other books that focus on such topics as storage protocols (FCP, iSCSI, and FC/IP), Fibre Channel, Ethernet, TCP/IP, and network switching technologies.

Storing

The second primary functional area in storage networking is *storing*—an area that is explored extensively in this book. Storing encompasses many types of storage technologies, including host-based volume managers and disk managers, storage subsystems, host bus adapters, storage devices, and storage virtualization.

Storing has its technology roots in the interactions between DAS storage devices and host computer systems over a bus. The storing methods used to configure and use storage devices have become standard functions in nearly all major operating systems. Although storing technology has changed a great deal over the years, especially since the advent of network storage, these old and simplistic operating system methods still determine how storage works.

Role of the Storage Controller

The physical electronic device or circuitry that actually performs storing functions is called a *storage controller*. Storage controllers are present in all storage products and are responsible for the detailed operations of reading, writing, and transmitting storage data.

Storage controllers are present in the following products:

- Host bus adapters (HBAs)
- Storage devices such as disk, tape, CD, and DVD drives
- Storage subsystems
- Storage appliances
- Storage routers, gateways, and channel extenders
- Switches with integrated storage functions

Storage controllers are often implemented in products that span both the connecting and storage functions. For instance, an HBA is used to formulate storing commands for storing devices and subsystems, but it also manages the transmission of those commands and storage data over the bus or network that connects them. Sometimes this is evident by the presence of multiple device drivers—there might be one device driver for the storing function plus another driver for the connecting function.

Initiators, Targets, and Command/Response Protocols

Storing processes are characterized by the interactions between controllers. Unlike peer-to-peer and client/server networks, where most entities have the same general capabilities, the functions available in a storage controller typically depend on the role it is designed for.

In a client/server or peer-to-peer network, almost all systems have the capability to act as either a server or a client. However, in storage networks, controllers are designed to function specifically as an *initiator* or a *target*.

Initiators are usually implemented as HBAs. HBA initiators receive requests for storage services through their device driver/kernel interface and then issue storing commands to satisfy those requests. A target is a controller in a storage device or subsystem that performs the actions requested by the initiator.

NOTE It might be easier to understand the relationship between initiators and targets by using the terms *master* and *slave*. It's not necessarily technically accurate, but it's one of the fastest ways to appreciate the fundamental difference between storage networking and data networking architectures. Readers should know that there is a great deal of subtlety involved in the relationships of initiators and targets. Chapter 6, "SCSI Storage Fundamentals and SAN Adapters," discusses this topic in much more detail.

The protocols used for storage are referred to as command/response protocols and reflect the roles of initiators and targets. It is important to understand the nature of these protocols, as they influence the operation of the underlying network. For instance, a network technology might support full-duplex, bidirectional communications, but if the application protocol (in this case, the storing protocol) does not, the full capabilities of the network might not be able to be realized.

Block I/O

Storing processes store data in blocks, which are the basic storage capacity elements in storage networks. Block I/O is the process of writing and reading data in these granularly-sized amounts. Block I/O commands specify the type of operations to perform, the *block address* to work with, and the storage or control data being transferred. The size of a data block is determined by the file system or database system that manages the complete block storage address space.

The Storage Address Space

We are accustomed to talking about data storage in terms of disk drives. While it is true that nearly all online data is stored on disk drives, the storage element where data is directed and stored in storage networks is usually much more complex than a single disk drive. In a storage network environment, storage is created by merging and segmenting storage from multiple disk drives or storage subsystems. In these cases we often say that the storage is a "virtual disk."

Unfortunately, the familiar terms disk, disk drive, virtual disk, virtual storage, exported storage, and logical unit number (LUN) are all used to refer to storage elements that provide the exact same fundamental storage function. Newcomers to storage are often confused by the lack of a single term that describes the architectural role of a data storage receptacle. This makes things unnecessarily awkward when discussing storage processes.

To keep things simple, this book uses the term *storage address space* to refer generically to all the various storage elements that are used for online data storage. A storage address space is defined herein as a sequence of contiguous, regularly sized storage blocks between a starting address and an ending address. From a host system perspective, a storage address space is the storage resource that a filing system manages.

Compare the following two sentences:

> Data is written to a storage address space.
> Data is written to either a physical disk or a virtual disk.

These two sentences say the same thing, but the first is much more straightforward and easier to grasp.

Figure 2-2 represents an address space made up of 20 contiguous blocks.

Figure 2-2 *A (Very) Simple Storage Address Space of 20 Contiguous Blocks*

1	2	3	4	5	6	7	8	9	10	11	12	13	14	15	16	17	18	19	20

Storage Address Space Manipulation

Storage address spaces are commonly manipulated in a variety of ways by storing products. On the simplest level, a disk partitioning process can create a single address space on a disk drive. Slightly more complex, a disk can be partitioned to create multiple logical drives, each with its own independent address space. Conversely, multiple disk drives can be combined to create a single larger address space. These three types of address space manipulation are shown in Figure 2-3.

Figure 2-3 *Basic Storage Address Space Manipulations*

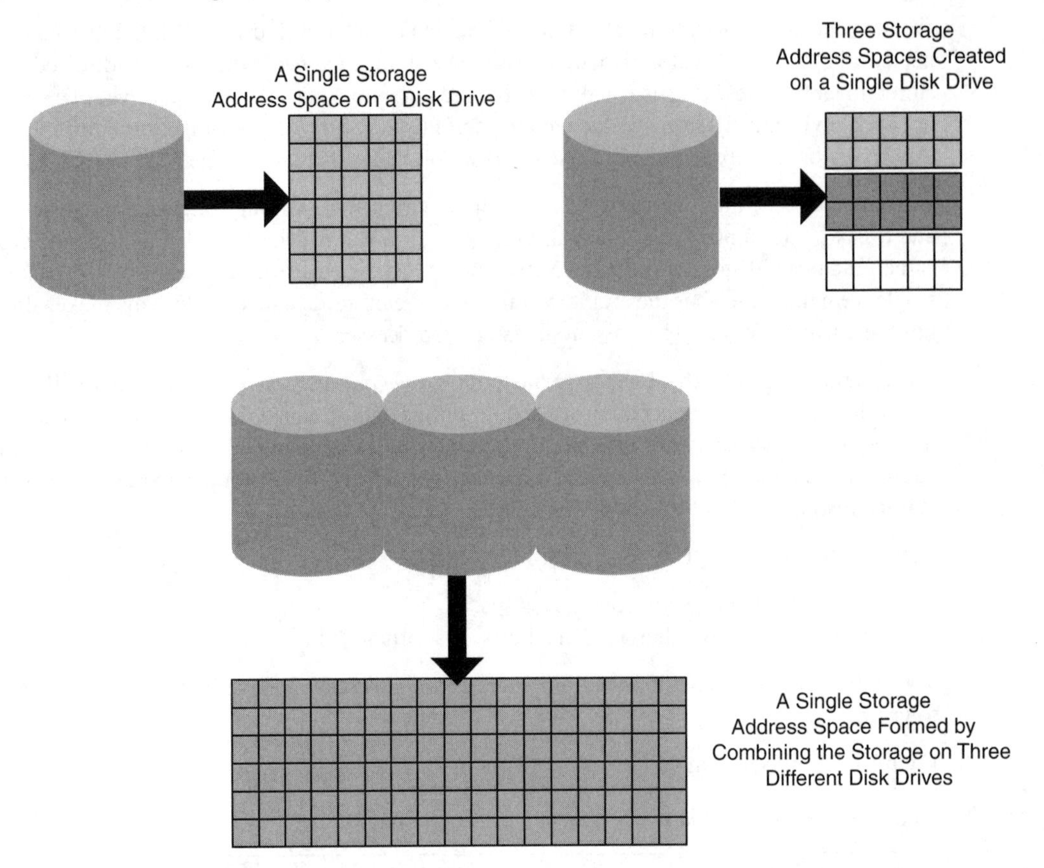

Several address space manipulation techniques are commonly used in storage management applications, such as mirroring and RAID. These forms of address space manipulation are covered in Chapter 8, "An Introduction to Data Redundancy and Mirroring," and Chapter 9, "Bigger, Faster, More Reliable Storage with RAID," respectively.

Volumes, Exported Drives, and Virtual Storage

Storage address spaces can be created by several different types of storage products. Some of the most common terms used for storage address spaces are covered in Table 2-2.

Table 2-2 *Common Terms Used for Storage Address Spaces*

Storing Product	Term Used for Storage Address Space
Host system volume management software	Volume
Disk subsystem	Exported drive or virtual disk
SAN virtualization system	Virtual disk

Filing, File Systems, and Operating Systems

The last of the three fundamental storage network functions is *filing*. In general, filing's role is to organize how data is structured in a storage address space as well as to represent it to applications and users. In practice, two types of filing products are in the market: file systems and databases.

File systems are closely associated with operating systems and have very close interactions with them. Considering how much storage activity there can be within a system, it is imperative that the file system and operating system work very well together without errors.

In most cases, they appear to be part of the same product, but that does not have to be the case. It is possible to use file systems that are not part of the operating system as long as the operating system supports third-party file systems. Most modern operating systems do, including most UNIX systems, Windows server systems, and Linux.

Space Allocation

One way to understand the differences between filing systems (including databases) and operating systems is to separate them by the system functions they manage. Operating systems manage the sequence of processing events in the system. In other words, they schedule all work in the system and establish the proper environment for each task. Filing systems manage the placement of data in storage address spaces.

In general,

- Operating systems manage time
- Filing systems manage space

One of the primary responsibilities of the filing function is *space allocation*. This involves figuring out what storage blocks to use when new data is being written or when data is changed or updated, as well as what to do with blocks that might be freed when objects are changed or deleted. While storing functions perform the actual operations of reading and writing data, filing functions determine what those operations should be.

One of the challenges in space allocation is creating a system that provides consistent performance over an extended period of time as data objects are created, updated, and deleted.

In order to achieve consistent performance, the filing system spreads data over the storage address space, providing a level of fairness to all data and its associated applications.

Filing's Role in Access Control and Security

Another key role of filing is access control. Filing systems often have attributes or access control lists (ACLs) that determine who has the authority to access data objects. To date, storing-level processes do not have the ability to provide access control, as storing level processes have no contextual information about data objects.

NOTE DAS storing products never had to have access control capabilities, because all security functions were provided by the filing system and other system security functions. However, with SANs, it has become necessary for storage subsystems to provide some amount of access control to protect data resources. One storage technology used for access control is called LUN masking, and it is described in Chapter 5, "Storage Subsystems." Access controls for storage is an area that undoubtedly will see a great deal of development in the years to come.

File I/O

As described previously, storing functions work with storage address spaces made up of contiguous, fixed-length block locations. To maintain performance expectations, filing systems logically fragment this neat and orderly structure by scattering data objects throughout the address space. Fortunately, the details of this data scattering are masked from users and applications by the file system.

File systems provide friendlier and more intuitive structures for accessing data, such as a directory tree and filenames. Applications are developed to access data through these structures using published interfaces that are easily invoked in the application's code. This type of data access is called *file I/O*.

While applications are abstracted from storing-level details, they know everything about the byte structure within their data files. For example, the header information in a file might be 100 bytes and the data might be 2000 bytes. Applications today have many different types of data within their files, and it is essential that they are able to access the various discrete sections of files efficiently and accurately.

Therefore, file systems allow applications to locate data within the file by its *byte location* or *byte range* within the file. Byte ranges can be expressed by the number of bytes from the beginning or end of a file as well as by offsets of bytes from these locations. For example, an application might issue a request to read 50 bytes of a file starting at the 50th byte, as shown in Figure 2-4.

Figure 2-4 *An Application Accesses Bytes 50 to 99 in a File*

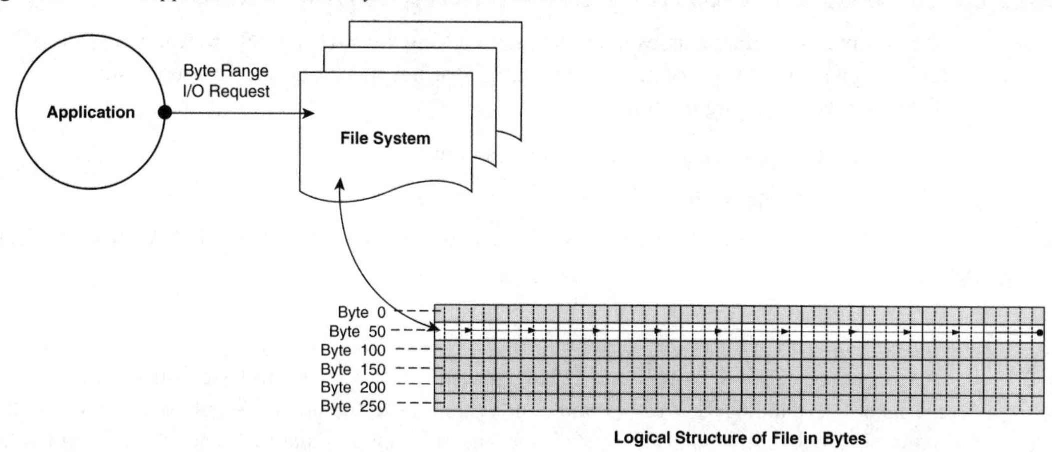

The file system bears the responsibility of converting these byte-range requests to detailed storing data access operations.

File Systems and Storing Applications

File systems contain the mappings of data objects into storing address spaces. This mapping function might also include the ability to translate file byte range requests into storing requests. Notice that while the byte range request might be for contiguous bytes, the lower-level block storing addresses are probably not contiguous.

So, a question arises: Why aren't file systems considered storing applications? The reason is because I said so, and it's my analysis! There has to be a separating point somewhere, and this is where I drew the line. Mapping a data object to a bunch of storage addresses does not involve storing processes by my way of thinking.

File systems make use of lower-level storing interfaces and functions that are provided by the operating system. The operating system kernel passes storage I/O requests to the proper storage device drivers that formulate the I/O requests into storing commands that are transferred to storage over a bus or network. The file system knows absolutely nothing about storing commands or devices; it only knows about a flat storing address space—and what files are stuffed into which blocks within that storage address space.

This file system perspective of storage is the rationale behind using the term storage address space as a generalization for the wide variety of disks, disk partitions, volumes, and virtual storage.

SAN and NAS as Storing and Filing Applications

The two major product classes in storage networking are SAN and NAS. Analyzing these technologies within the system of connecting, storing, and filing, they can be easily differentiated by stating the following:

- SAN is the application of storing over a network.
- NAS is the application of filing over a network.

SANs are used to convey storing commands and data over a network, while NAS conveys filing commands.

NOTE When storage networking was first getting started, there was enormous confusion over the merits of SAN and NAS: Was one inherently superior to the other?, Would one win out in the market in the long run?, and all sorts of other meandering speculations. The whole thing wasted an obnoxious amount of time.

It really bugged me that so many people were spinning their wheels on discussions that would not be resolved due to the lack of a fundamental functional analysis. That's what led me to develop the three-legged stool analysis of connecting, storing, and filing. For the most part, when people understand this analysis, their confusion over SAN and NAS positioning melts away.

In the remainder of the chapter, we'll look at how connecting, storing, and filing work together in storage networking processes.

If there were a "stack" for storage processes, it would look like Figure 2-5, where connecting is the bottom-most layer, storing is in the middle, and filing is at the top-most layer.

Figure 2-5 *The Storage Process "Stack"*

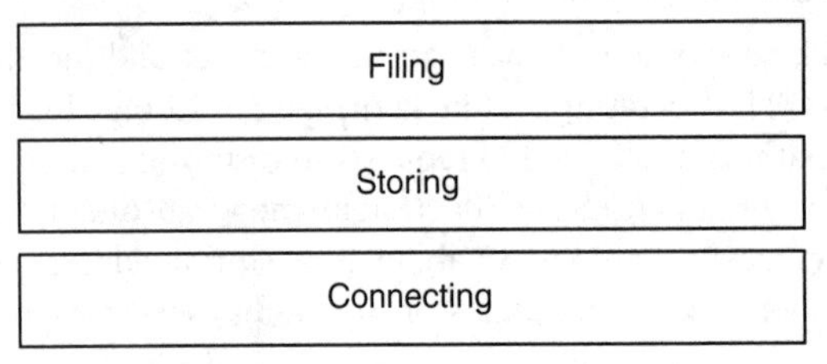

For people familiar with networking stacks, Figure 2-6 shows the traditional TCP/IP network stack alongside the storage process stack. Notice that most of the interesting parts of the TCP/IP stack are part of the connecting component of the storage process stack.

Figure 2-6 *A Comparison of the Storage Process Stack and the TCP/IP Protocol Stack*

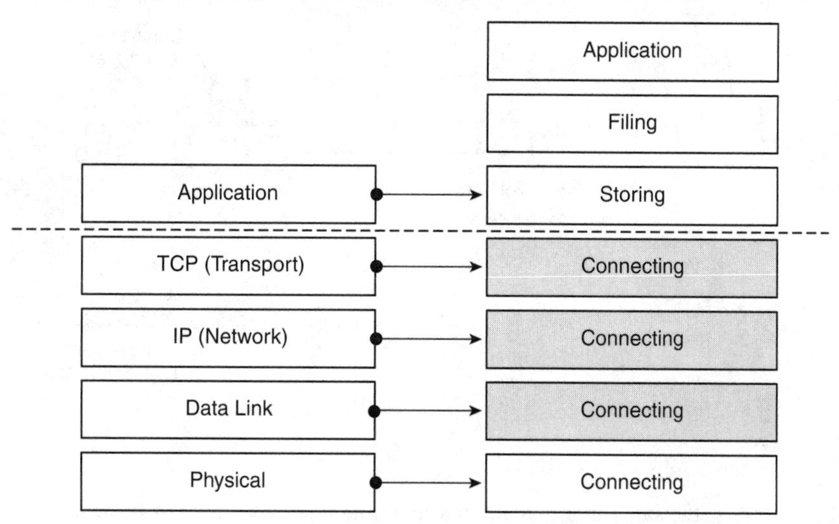

Now we'll start connecting various products and show their relative function within the storage process stack. Figure 2-7 shows a host bus adapter on the left connected to a disk subsystem on the right. The connecting function is provided by the SCSI bus and the communication function in the HBA and subsystem controller. The storing function is at a higher level in both controllers. In Figure 2-7 both the HBA and the disk subsystem controller have dual roles.

Figure 2-7 *Storage and Connecting Processes Between an Interacting HBA and a Disk Subsystem*

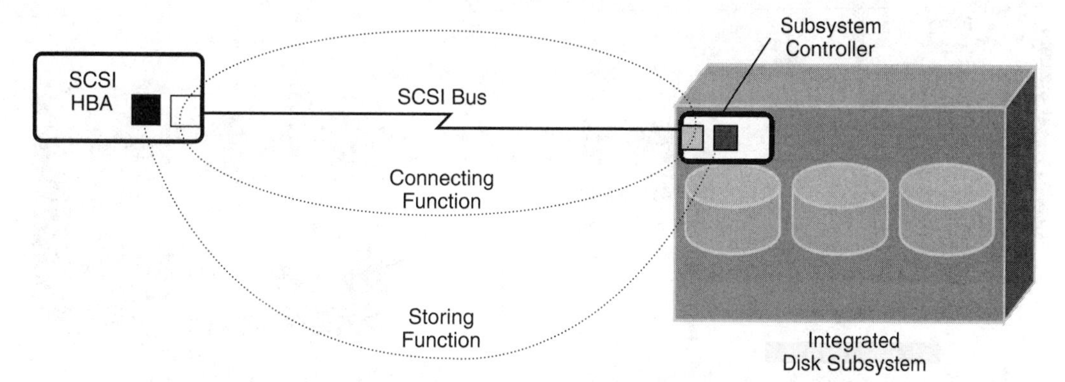

Figure 2-8 is the exact same figure but with a SAN switch between the HBA and the disk subsystem. Notice the changes in this figure from the last: the SAN switch and SAN cables replace the SCSI connection between the HBA and the subsystem. In Figure 2-8, the switch has only a connecting role.

Figure 2-8 *A Storage Switch and Cables Replace the SCSI Bus in Figure 2-7, Making a SAN*

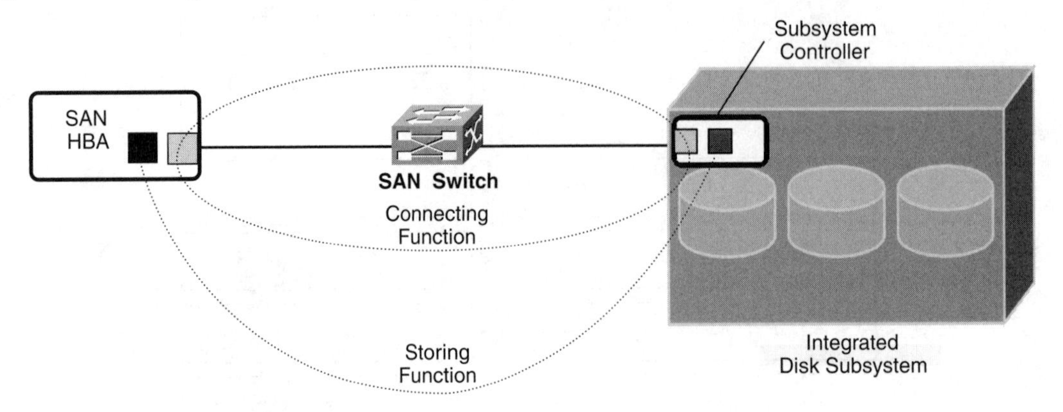

Figure 2-9 is the same figure again, but this time it shows the HBA residing in a host system along with application and file system software. Notice that there is now a filing function on the left, but not on the right.

Figure 2-9 *An Expansion of Figure 2-8, Adding the Host System and a File System*

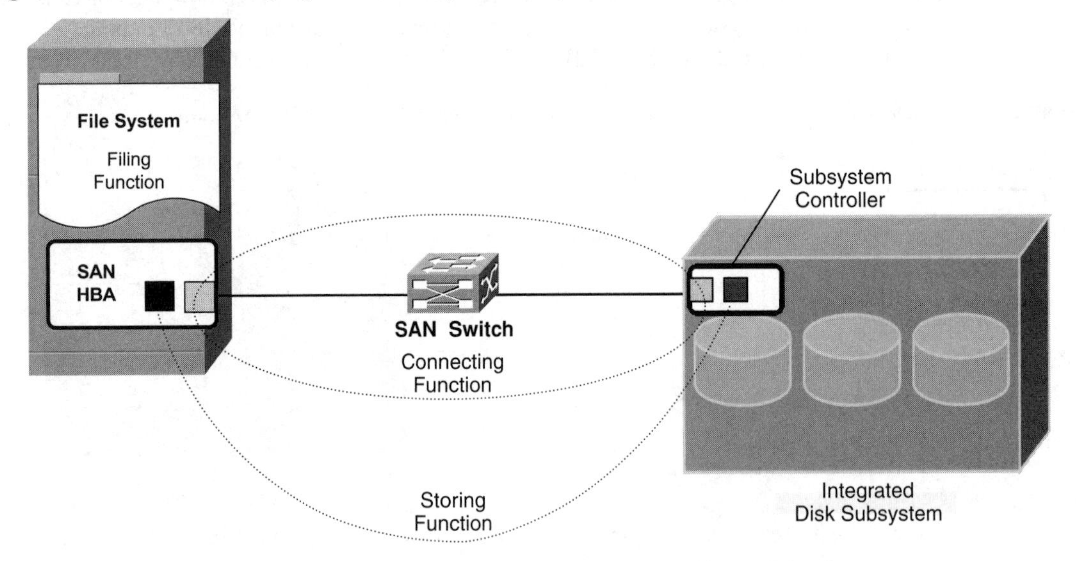

Figure 2-10 converts the system we have been building with this sequence of figures by turning the system from Figure 2-9 into a NAS appliance system with an integrated storage subsystem. This system also has a network interface card (NIC) for communicating with client systems over a LAN.

Figure 2-10 *Enlarging the Figure to Include NAS*

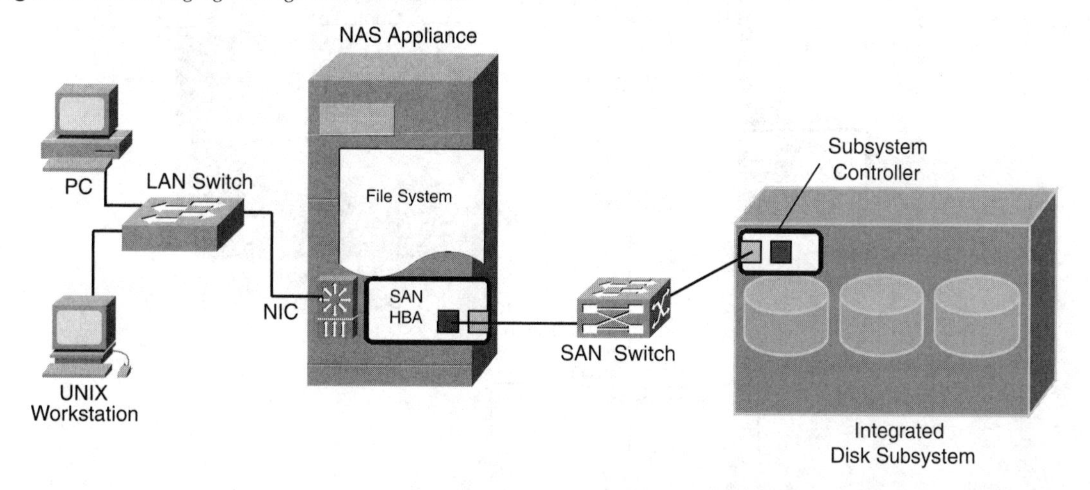

The connecting functions in Figure 2-10 are suddenly much more interesting than in the previous figures. Historically, the connecting technology on the LAN (NAS) side of the drawing has been a different technology from the connecting technology on the SAN side of the drawing.

However, as both filing (NAS) and storing (SAN) functions are at the application layer of the underlying connecting network, there is no reason why the two connecting functions (LAN and SAN) could not use the same technology. In fact, they could even be the same physical network, as shown in Figure 2-11.

NOTE This example is not intended to suggest that putting SANs and LANs on the same physical network is the preferred way of doing things. But it does help drive home the point that connecting, storing, and filing are, in fact, three independent and orthogonal functions.

Figure 2-11 *A LAN with NAS Connected to a SAN, All Using the Same Connecting Technology*

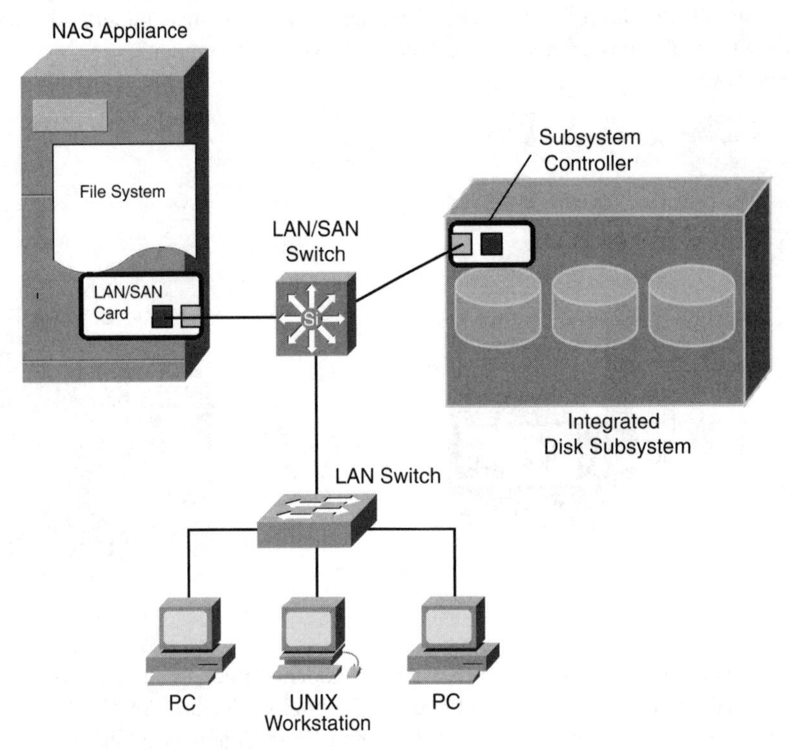

Summary

This chapter presented readers with the fundamental analysis tools that run throughout the book. As with any complex topic, storage networking has many possible interpretations. It's important to find a stable analysis method that can be used for a wide breadth of products and network designs.

The three functional areas of connecting, storing, and filing can be ascribed to any element of a storage network. It is a powerful analysis, because there is very little overlap between them, which limits confusion to a great extent. It can even be used to clarify the long-standing confusion regarding NAS and SAN.

Another major tool introduced in this chapter was the term *storage address space* as a generalization of all sorts of storage receptacles, including disk drives, disk partitions, disk volumes, virtual disk, exported storage, and LUNs. Using this term simplifies discussions of storage processes immensely without obscuring the nature of how storage works. A storage address space is the element that a filing system uses and manages.

There is a great deal of flexibility in how storage networks can be constructed. The architectural diagrams at the end of the chapter are graphical depictions of the fundamental approaches that can be used. It is hoped that these diagrams will speak volumes to readers who think visually.

Q & A

1. What are the three primary components of storage networking?
2. True or false: Buses guarantee the order of delivery.
3. Which of the following is not part of the storing component: volume management, virtualization, zoning, host bus adapters, or block I/O?
4. True or false: Disk drives do not need a controller.
5. What is the difference between initiator and target controllers?
6. What kinds of storage devices and subsystems create storage address spaces?
7. What are the primary two things filing is responsible for?
8. Explain the different roles of file systems and operating systems.
9. What is the application difference between SAN and NAS?
10. True or false: Storing and filing have to use different networks.

Upon completing this chapter, you will be able to

- Participate in discussions and planning sessions regarding the requirements and design goals of storage network designs
- Identify all the various hardware, software, and networking components involved in I/O transmissions in a storage network
- Discuss the role of the operating system in I/O processes, including the difference between user space and kernel space operations and how they impact storage processes

CHAPTER 3

Getting Down with Storage I/O

It's difficult to understand the details of storage networking without understanding the big picture of how data gets from an application to storage media and back again. This chapter explores the basic requirements for storage I/O that create the operating environment and then steps through an end-to-end analysis of storage I/O processes in the I/O path. Having a basic understanding of fundamental I/O processes gives readers a context for understanding the details that follow in later chapters.

Requirements for Storage I/O

Storage networks have unique requirements for performance, reliability, and integrity that differentiate them from other types of networks. This section analyzes the requirements for each of these three categories.

Performance Requirements

There are two meaningful performance areas in storage networking: bandwidth and latency.

Bandwidth

Bandwidth is the total amount of data traffic that a network can accommodate. It is typically measured in megabits per second or megabytes per second.

Bandwidth measurements are meaningful for host bus adapters (HBAs), network links, switching hardware, and storage controllers. In general, 100 Mbps and 1 Gbps are commonly used with network access server (NAS) products. 1 Gbps, 2 Gbps, and 4 Gbps are typical for Fibre Channel storage area networking (SAN) products. Both SAN and NAS are likely to adopt 10 Gbps technology within a year of each other.

A choke point in a network is a hardware or software function that constrains performance. The following four components in storage network are potential choke points:

- HBAs
- Network links

- Switching hardware
- Storage controllers

If bandwidth is inadequate through any of these potential choke points, the storage network will not be able to provide the expected results. The choke points for a storage network are shown in Figure 3-1.

Figure 3-1 *Bandwidth Choke Points in a Storage Network*

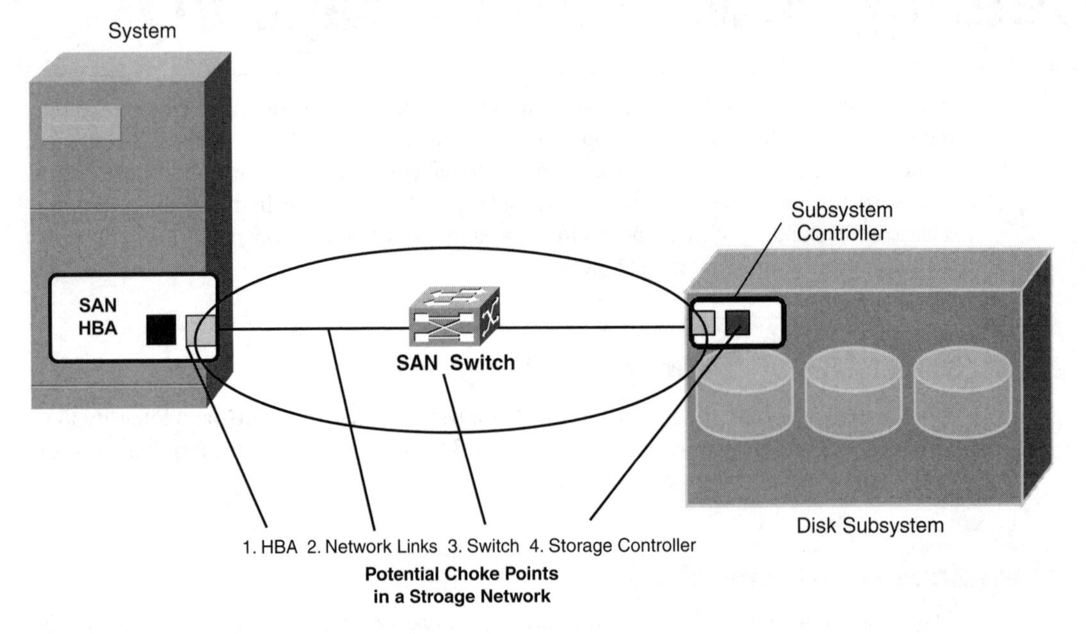

Of the potential choke points shown in Figure 3-1, the two that are most likely to be problematic are (1) links between switches and storage and (2) storage controllers. The reason for this is the high degree of session multiplexing that occurs. This topic is addressed in more detail in Chapter 5, "Storage Subsystems."

Latency

Latency is the transmission delay that occurs in sending, receiving, or forwarding a network transmission. A good analogy for network latency is a water pipeline with a storage tank in the middle, as shown in Figure 3-2. The volume moved through the pipeline per second is equivalent to bandwidth, while the time the water is held in the storage tank is equivalent to latency. The larger the water tank, the greater the latency for water flowing through it.

Figure 3-2 *Latency in a Pipeline*

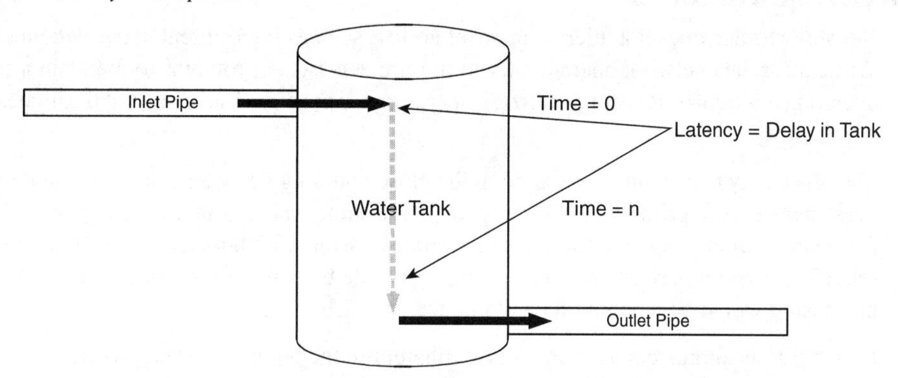

Sometimes networking professionals have difficulty reckoning latency issues in storage networks because latency is not often a critical issue for data networks. Rest assured, the situation is completely different for storage networks, especially SANs. Storage I/O transmission latency can have a direct impact on systems performance due to the need to ensure data integrity, as discussed in the next section.

Latency requirements depend on the applications being used. Transaction processing applications have the most demanding latency requirements, while other applications, such as e-mail, are relatively unaffected by it.

Fibre Channel SAN switches are typically designed to have 1 to 3 μ sec (microseconds) of latency. By contrast, many data networking switches do not even list latency measurements in their specifications because they have not been important to the market. Latencies for Ethernet switches are typically in the hundreds of microseconds.

NOTE

Some (still) believe Gigabit Ethernet will not effectively support storage I/O because Ethernet latencies are too high. But latency requirements are mostly valid for a small percentage of applications. The problem is that latency-sensitive applications tend to be the most important applications running in the data center, and they do not tolerate slack performance.

Obviously, Gigabit Ethernet switches can be built with lower latencies (and higher costs) if needed, but they can also be used (latency warts and all) to support the enormous volume of applications that do not have much sensitivity to latency.

Reliability Requirements

Network storage does not tolerate poor reliability, such as intermittent network connections. While most data network operators try to minimize network problems to maintain a smoothly operating environment, storage network operators cannot afford anything but the highest degree of reliability.

The sensitivity to reliability is rooted in the close coupling between storage I/O and system performance. As a primary system function that is almost always in use during system activity, there is very little tolerance for delays or retransmissions. Without a high level of connection reliability, system performance and reliability would be completely unpredictable. Automated processing would be anything but automatic.

Reliability in storage connections is also inherent in the nature of storage writes. Data that is being written by an application probably does not exist anywhere else, and there may be no other opportunities to store it properly. Re-creating it may not be possible, depending on the application.

From a historical perspective, DAS storage was designed with the assumption that bus connections were *always* available and latency was *never* an issue. Storage network technology does not necessarily improve connection reliability over storage buses, but it certainly can be equivalent, and it extends to much greater distances. In addition, using multiple connections over a storage network improves the overall reliability and availability of the system.

Network storage allows the concept of service level agreements (SLAs) to work with storage. The reliability of DAS storage usually depends on the reliability of the products forming the bus and attached to it, such as the HBA and the devices or subsystems connected to it. With storage networks, reliability is also an element of the network design—a dimension that never existed with DAS storage. SLAs can be established for storage networks that define multiple tiers of network reliability for different types of applications.

NOTE The requirements for NAS storage are more varied than for SANs. Realistically, low-end NAS products used as departmental file servers work well enough with average LAN connections. However, high-end NAS products that support mission-critical applications should run only over high-speed LANs with optimal reliability.

Integrity Requirements: Write Ordering and Data Consistency

One of the most challenging aspects of storage networks is the requirement for data integrity. This does not mean that storage networks need to have better transmission integrity for their payloads than data networks. Instead, data integrity in storage networks refers to the sequence in which data is written to storage media compared to the way writes were issued by the system. Data must be written to storage media in a way that does not distort an application's intended order of write I/Os. In other words, write ordering cannot be violated.

The term *data consistency* is used to refer to the complete and proper writing of storage data to storage *media*. In a nutshell, data consistency is a concept where the intended results of all data processing operations are reflected correctly in stored data. Under normal I/O operations, this is never a problem. However, data consistency is an issue when disasters occur and when creating point-in-time copies of data (see Chapter 17, "Data Management") or when making remote copies of data (see Chapter 10, "Redundancy Over Distance with Remote Copy").

To illustrate the concept of data consistency, consider a hypothetical situation where an application writes data in sequence to two different storage locations and their respective system cache memory locations, as pictured in Figure 3-3. After the first write is made to system cache (1), the system attempts to write the data to storage (2), but something goes wrong and the write does not complete. Shortly thereafter, the application reads the first piece of data from cache memory (3), processes it, and writes new, dependent data to its cache memory location (4). Shortly thereafter, the system writes the dependent data successfully to storage (5). At this point the data is inconsistent because the dependent data is stored on media, but the original write that was used to create the dependent data is not on media. The data is inconsistent until the original data is written to media (6).

Figure 3-3 *Dependent Data Written to Media Out of Order*

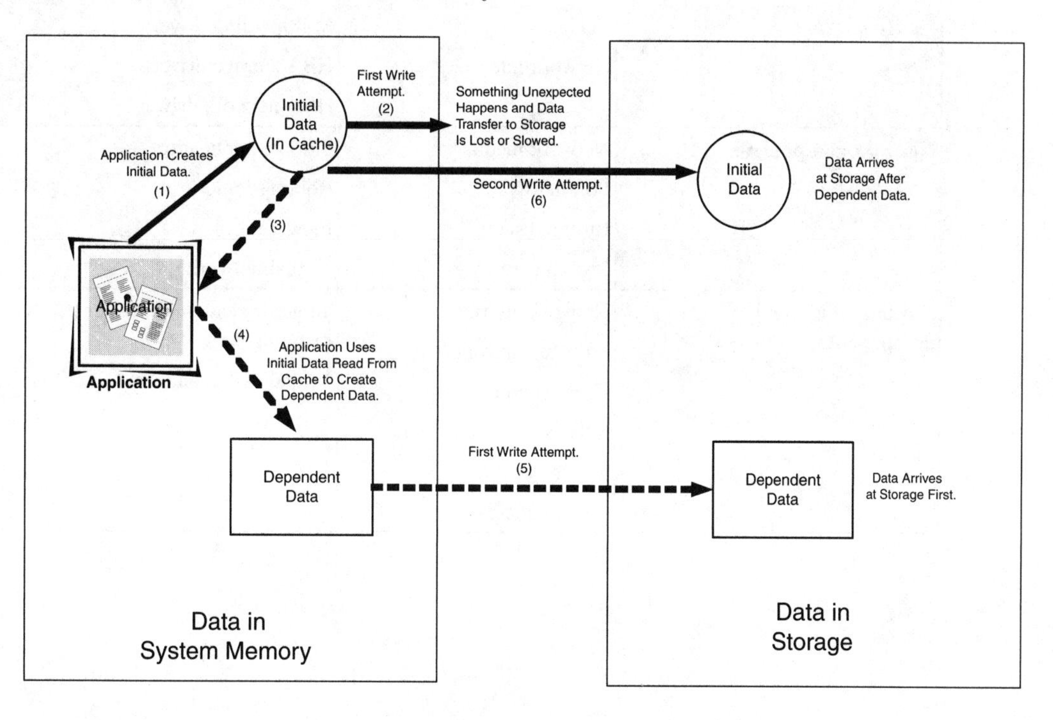

The I/O Path

Storage data is typically created by an application running on a system processor and then is transferred over the *I/O path* to its location on storage media. The remainder of this chapter describes the various hardware and software elements that storage data encounters on the I/O path. We'll begin by breaking down the entire end-to-end path and then take a second look at some of the more interesting aspects of host system software elements.

The I/O path can be conceived of as a set of distinct hardware and software elements, each with its own role, that acts on storage data as it moves from point to point along the I/O path.

Table 3-1 shows a generic "top-down" listing of the various hardware and software elements that comprise the I/O path.

Table 3-1 *Hardware and Software Elements in the I/O Path*

Component	Hardware	Software
Host system components	Processor	Application
	Memory	File system
	Memory bus	Volume manager
	I/O bus	Multipathing driver
	Network interface	HBA storage driver
		HBA network driver
Network components	Network media	Storage application
	Port hardware	Routing logic
	Buffer system	Flow control
	Switch core	Virtual network
Storage subsystem components	Network interface	Target/logical unit number (LUN) mapping
	Storage controller	Virtual disk manager
	Cache memory	
	Subsystem bus/network	
	Storage device	
	Storage media	

Host System I/O Path Elements

Host systems have many key software and hardware I/O path elements. Some of the elements, such as the system processor and memory, are used by virtually all functions in the system. Others, such as the file system and volume manager, are dedicated to storage I/O tasks.

Core System Hardware: Processors, Memory, and Memory Bus

Most of the action in a system happens within close proximity to the system CPU(s). This is where the software I/O path elements such as file systems, volume management software, multipathing drivers, and HBA device drivers run.

There are three core hardware system components of interest to storage networking:

- System processors
- System memory
- System memory bus

Figure 3-4 represents the three hardware inner-system components: processor, memory, and memory bus.

Figure 3-4 *Processor, Memory, and Memory Bus*

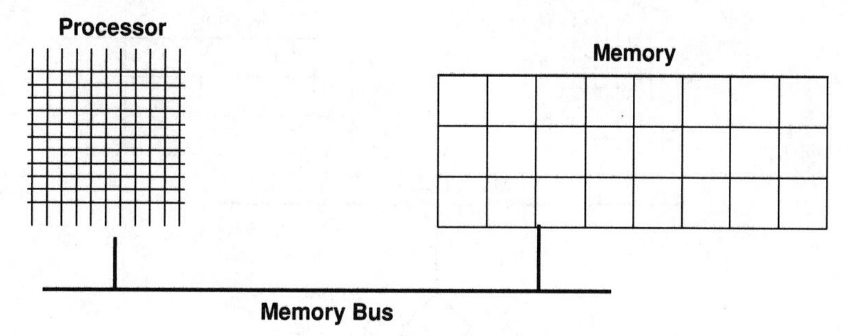

System Processors

The I/O path starts in a system processor when an application creates data that it needs to store. While many computer designs have a single CPU, many systems can use two, four, eight, or more to increase system performance. The number of processors does not materially change the I/O path, but it certainly affects the performance of system software components along the way.

System Memory

System memory chips are high-speed semiconductor devices having transfer rates in the range of nanoseconds. They are the fastest storage devices in a system and are typically used as cache or buffers for temporary data storage. The fast RAM used for system memory is volatile storage, which means the data is lost if the power is removed from the memory device. In general, it is a good idea to make sure there is plenty of memory in systems, especially those providing network services, such as NAS servers.

The System Memory Bus

Between the system and system memory is a high-speed bus for transmitting data from memory to the CPU and back. The system memory bus is not much of a variable when it comes to storage networking processes; it usually cannot be upgraded, expanded, or replaced.

System I/O Hardware: The I/O Bus and Host Bus Adapters

Systems communicate with storage through their I/O bus and an attached HBA. Storage data being transmitted from a system to storage is first transmitted from system memory over the system memory bus to the I/O bus to an HBA and then out to a storage network, as shown in Figure 3-5. A bridge controller chip manages the interface between the system memory bus and the I/O bus.

Figure 3-5 *The Complete System Hardware I/O Path Picture*

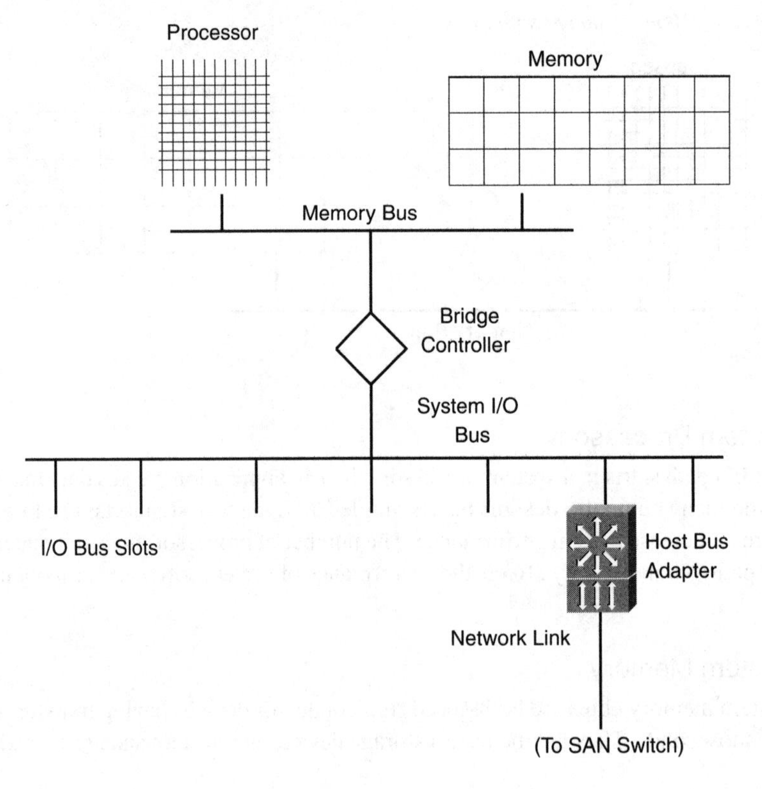

The I/O Bus

The I/O bus is a way to attach a variety of peripherals to a system. Like the system memory bus, the system I/O bus cannot be changed or upgraded. Unlike the system memory bus, which normally has plenty of bandwidth for its work, the system I/O bus has lower performance capabilities that limit the total amount of data that can be transferred at any given time through the system. When calculating storage I/O workloads, remember that storage data crosses the I/O bus both on its way in and out of the system.

NOTE Eventually I/O bus technology will probably be replaced with some sort of I/O networking technology, but I'm not holding my breath considering the delays and disappointments that have occurred in the development of InfiniBand technology. Tired of using convoluted terms like "I/O bus/network," I'm more than happy, for now, simply to refer to I/O connecting stuff in a system as the I/O bus until something else comes along that actually has more market traction.

Host Bus Adapters

The last piece of system hardware in the I/O path is the HBA. It performs the same types of actions that network interface cards do in other types of networks, except that they also have a storing level component for managing the exchange of storage information. From a purist's networking perspective, the HBA is a specialized network interface card (NIC) with application level functions built in. The term *storage NIC* is sometimes used to refer to an HBA for iSCSI SANs.

Host System Storage Software: File Systems, Volume Management, Multipathing Drivers, and HBA Device Drivers

Although they are often sold as separate software products, file systems, volume managers, multipathing software, and HBA device drivers work transparently together as the software elements that control the I/O path.

NOTE The high-level overview of the I/O path that follows completely ignores the most important software in the machine—the operating system. Obviously, keeping the OS out of the discussion is *just not right!* Unfortunately, adding the operating system to high-level I/O path discussions clarifies nothing because the OS has no specific defined storage I/O role. Instead, it works closely with *all* the other host software elements in the I/O path. The section "The Operating System's Role in the I/O Path" near the end of this chapter takes a look at the role the OS has in storage I/O processing.

File System

File systems are filing entities, managing the placement of data in storage address spaces. The I/O path starts when an application makes a file I/O request (also called a *file system call*) to a file system. The file I/O request specifies the name of the file as well as optionally indicating which bytes within the file to work with. File systems do a number of things, but where the I/O path is concerned, their job is to translate relative byte locations within a file to block addresses in a storage address space. Figure 3-6 is similar to Figure 2-4 in the previous chapter, but Figure 3-6 shows a file system receiving a file I/O request for a range of bytes within a file and converting it to a request for blocks of data.

Figure 3-6 *A File System Converts a Byte-Range Data Location to Its Associated Block Addresses*

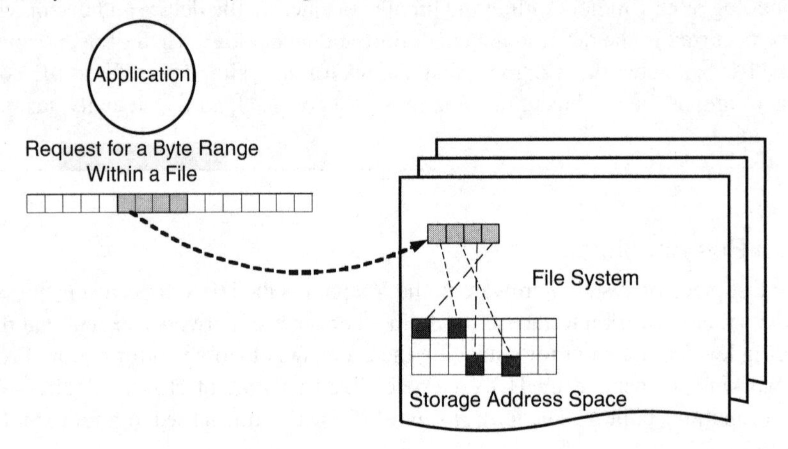

While most file systems are sold as part of operating system software, they can also be purchased separately or as part of a storage network solution. Systems can have multiple different file systems running concurrently, accessing data on different storage address spaces. The characteristics of the file systems installed in a system have an enormous impact on the system's network storage capabilities.

When the file system is done processing the file I/O request, it passes it as a block I/O request to the next stop in the volume management process—the volume manager—as shown in Figure 3-7.

Figure 3-7 *A File I/O Request Is Processed by the File System and Is Passed Down the I/O Path to the Volume Management Function as Multiple Block I/O Requests*

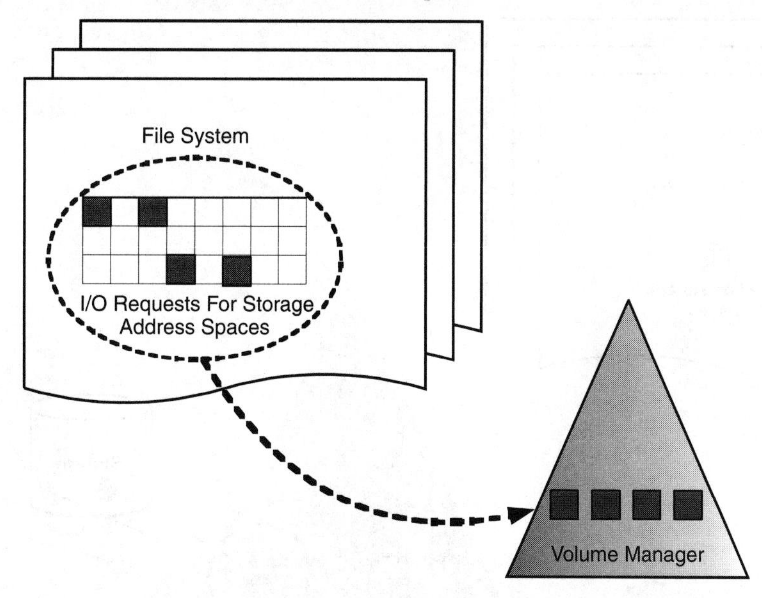

Volume Managers

Volume managers are responsible for creating storage volumes by manipulating storage address spaces. These volumes are typically identified by users and applications as drive letters such as C:\ or D:\. Like subsystem controllers and storage virtualization products that manipulate storage address spaces, volume managers aggregate, subdivide, and mirror storage resources in the SAN. Volume managers are optional, but all systems have a program that creates disk partitions, such as DOS's simple FDISK function.

The volume manager creates one or more downstream (toward storage media) block I/O requests from a single upstream I/O request that it receives from the file system. Figure 3-8 shows a volume manager creating three downstream block I/Os from a single upstream I/O created by a file system.

Figure 3-8 *A Volume Manager Creates Three Downstream Block I/Os for a Block I/O Request It Receives from a File System*

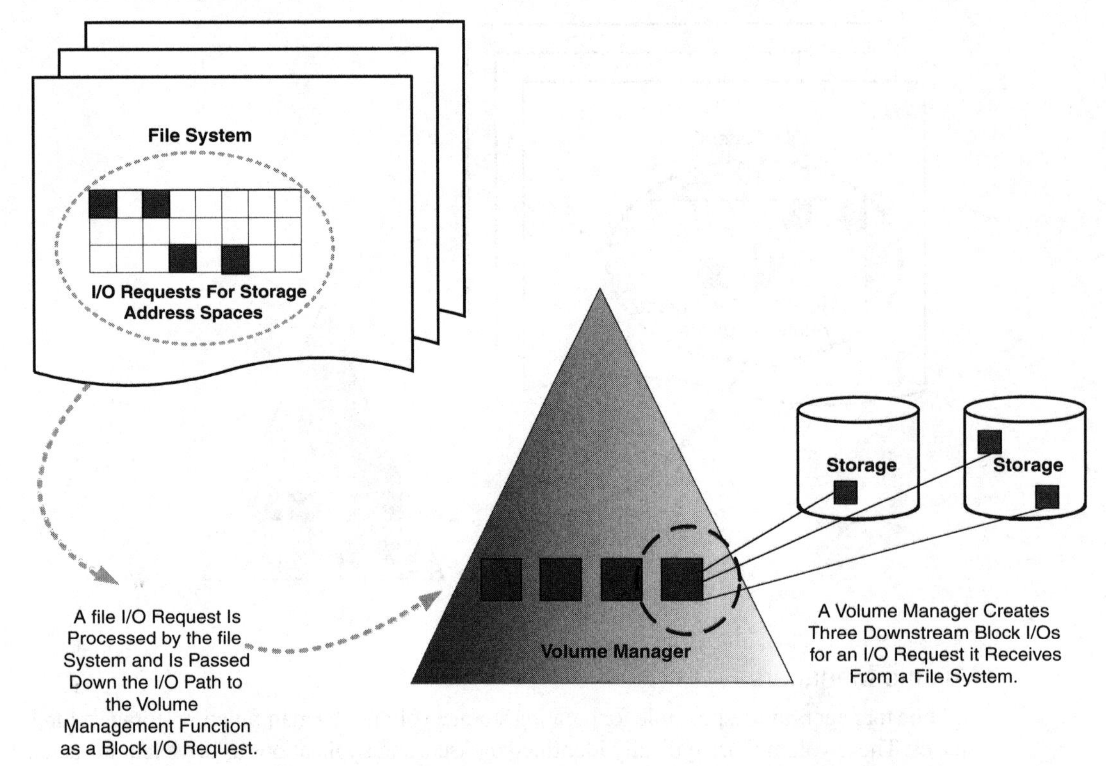

NOTE The terms *upstream* and *downstream* are used in this book to refer to the general direction of an I/O process. Upstream refers to a process where a command or data is being transferred to an initiator. Downstream refers to a direction away from an initiator.

When the storage I/O request has been processed by the volume manager, the next stop along the I/O path is multipathing software drivers.

Multipathing Drivers

High availability for storage I/O dictates redundant paths, including redundant host initiators in the SAN. Software that manages the configuration and use of redundant paths in a SAN is called multipathing software. Multipathing is usually implemented as an upper-layer storing device driver that determines which connections are used for storage transmissions. Chapter 11,

"Connection Redundancy in Storage Networks and Dynamic Multipathing," discusses this important topic in detail.

NOTE

For the most part, multipathing is primarily used to change the HBA that is used, regardless of the nature of the connection failure. Multipathing uses storing level addresses, particularly the host initiator and the storage target addresses.

The *network path* used for storage I/O is also part of the I/O path. However, the network path is determined by routing algorithms in network switches and routers and is independent of the storage connection selected by multipathing software. Multipathing and network routing work together but function like ships passing in the night that have little knowledge of the other's mission. If you want to improve the world a tiny bit, think of ways to collaborate timeout values between the storing and connecting worlds so that network switches can correct link errors before SCSI errors force multipathing changes.

HBA Storing Drivers

The HBA's storing drivers are usually referred to by their corresponding technology, such as "the SCSI-layer driver." After the block I/O addresses have been identified by the file system, translated by the volume manager, and passed to the appropriate HBA by multipathing software, a storage-level HBA driver formulates the storage command or data transfer payload that will be transmitted to the target device or subsystem.

HBA Network Drivers

The last piece of host software to see data transmission on the way out of the system—and the first to see it on the way back in—is the HBA's network driver. This software participates in the actual transmission of signals over the network or bus.

The Host Software Stack

It's possible to think of storage software as a stack of functions, as shown in Figure 3-9. The top-left corner of Figure 3-9 shows the top of the stack, starting with an application that creates and uses data. The next level down is a file system that determines where the data is stored and how it is accessed. Next comes the volume manager, which creates storage address spaces in the host using downstream device and subsystem storage. Finally, the bottom of the stack is the device driver level, which has an optional multipathing component as well as required storage and network components.

Figure 3-9 *The Storage Software Stack*

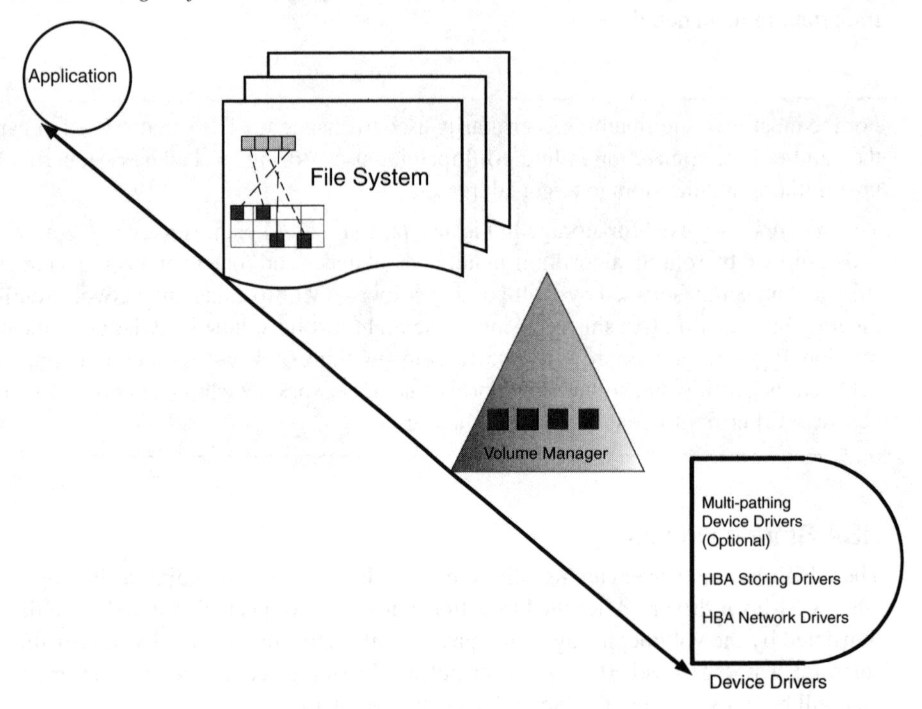

The Complete Host System I/O Path

Figure 3-10 shows the combined picture of host I/O path elements. The top-left corner of Figure 3-10 shows the hardware elements that surround the processor, including memory and the system memory bus. The top-right corner of the figure shows the software elements that run in the system CPU and use memory resources to accomplish their tasks. The remainder of the figure is the same as Figure 3-5, except for the dotted line between the device driver software on the far upper-right corner and the host bus adapter at the bottom. Device driver software runs in the system processor, but it interacts with the host bus adapter using interfaces provided by the operating system.

Figure 3-10 *Combined Host System Hardware and Software Elements of the I/O Path*

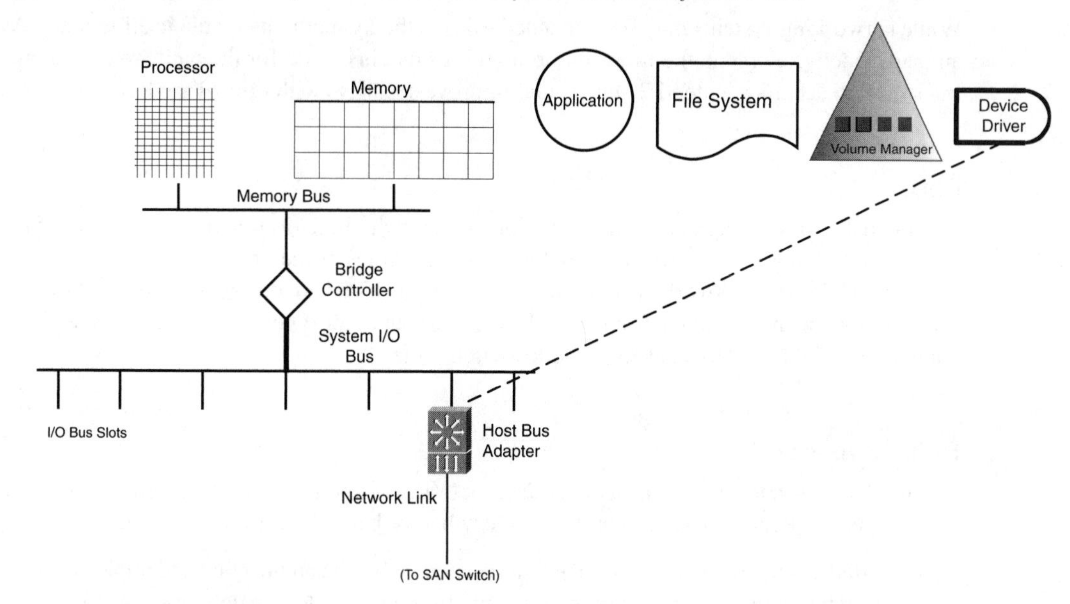

Network Systems and Components in the I/O Path

Networking products provide the connecting function in a storage network and obviously have key roles in the I/O path. As the technology continues to develop and mature, many expect networking systems to assume larger roles that will include enhanced management capabilities as well as storing and filing functionality.

Network Hardware

Networking technology has both hardware and software components; we'll look at network hardware first. The network hardware covered in this section is as follows:

- Network media
- Ports
- Buffer memory
- Switching core

Network Media

While networking systems may see expanded roles in the I/O path, the media itself will not. As an inert, inactive element, the most important things media can do for the path are to increase transmission accuracy, extend distance, and improve security (with optical media).

Ports

The I/O path goes through networking equipment (switch, director, router, etc.) by way of its ports. Network ports may have specific definitions and roles or may be available for a variety of functions. Ports in network switches tend to be very fast and are designed to forward storage transmissions with a minimal number of delays. Ports in other types of devices, such as SAN appliances, might use HBAs as opposed to switch ports.

Buffer Memory

Storage data that is forward by a switch, router, or bridge—or otherwise processed by a network system—is temporarily placed in buffer memory before being forwarded to the storage target.

On the surface, buffer memory seems like a simple matter, but the architecture and implementation of queues in buffer memory can make significant differences in storage network capabilities and management. A single buffer in a switch can impact many different I/O paths for many different pairs of targets and initiators.

NOTE One could say that buffer memory is just a part of a switch's port and is not worth singling out as a separate I/O path element. But that would be slighting buffers unfairly. Buffers and queuing in network switches are a subsystem within the switch, implemented in association with ports.

Switching Core

Storage network switches and directors (large, high-availability storage switches) are among the most important products in the I/O path. A switch's performance and availability capabilities depend on the design of its core switching technology, which is the primary I/O path element in a switch.

Network Software

As storage networks grow in size and complexity, networking software becomes increasingly important as a way to safely and accurately configure, change, and manage a storage network. Some of the network software elements directly involved in the I/O path are routing logic, flow control, virtual networking, and storing applications.

Routing Logic

The implementation of routing algorithms is among the most important part of any network, including storage networks. In addition to simply determining how to route storage I/O traffic from ingress to egress ports, routing algorithms can also determine the prioritization of traffic if failures occur in the network. Prioritization of multiple I/O paths is highly desirable in large storage networks.

Flow Control

Flow control is the ability to adjust the data rate for a transmitting network node. It does not impact the addressing, commands, or payloads of storage I/O, but instead changes the frequency at which transmissions are made on the I/O path. Considering how heavy and irregular storage I/O traffic can be, it may be desirable at times to throttle back certain nodes and reduce network congestion. As a rule of thumb, storage networks work best when unnecessary data retransmissions can be held to a minimum.

NOTE This last sentence would be a "duh!" for all networks. By the way, flow control can also be implemented in the HBA and network device driver code, as it is with Transmission Control Protocol (TCP). However, in Fibre Channel SANs, most connections are Class 3 and do not support end-to-end flow control—which means if meaningful flow control is going to happen, switches need to be involved.

Virtual Networking

Virtual networking technologies such as virtual LANs (VLANs) and virtual SANs (VSANs) are closely related to routing in that they can also be used to determine where to forward incoming frames through a switch. However, virtual networking is much more than a different way to implement frame forwarding; among its virtues are strong I/O path segregation and the ability to assign quality of service (QoS) levels to I/O paths.

Storage Applications

There is considerable potential for running storing or filing applications within a switch or other storage network system. If so, these applications would affect the I/O path in much the same way as the host software processes discussed previously. Additional hardware components, such as memory, would also be required to support application processes.

For example, a network switch could provide a security function that would restrict access to downstream subsystems without proper credentials. Another storage application that could run in a network system is storage virtualization, the subject of Chapter 12, "Storage Virtualization: The Power in Volume Management Software and SAN Virtualization Systems."

The Complete Path Through Network Systems and Components

Figure 3-11 illustrates network I/O path elements. On the upper-left corner of this figure is the network media. Below that is the network port and the buffer memory, which is used to temporarily hold storage transfers that are en route. The bottom layer of this drawing shows the switching core elements, including the core hardware on the left and the primary supporting software functions of routing, flow control, and virtual networking on the right. Storage applications are also shown on the right, although these are not likely to run in the core function of a switch, but rather through an add-on module of some sort that interfaces with the switch.

Figure 3-11 *Network I/O Path Elements*

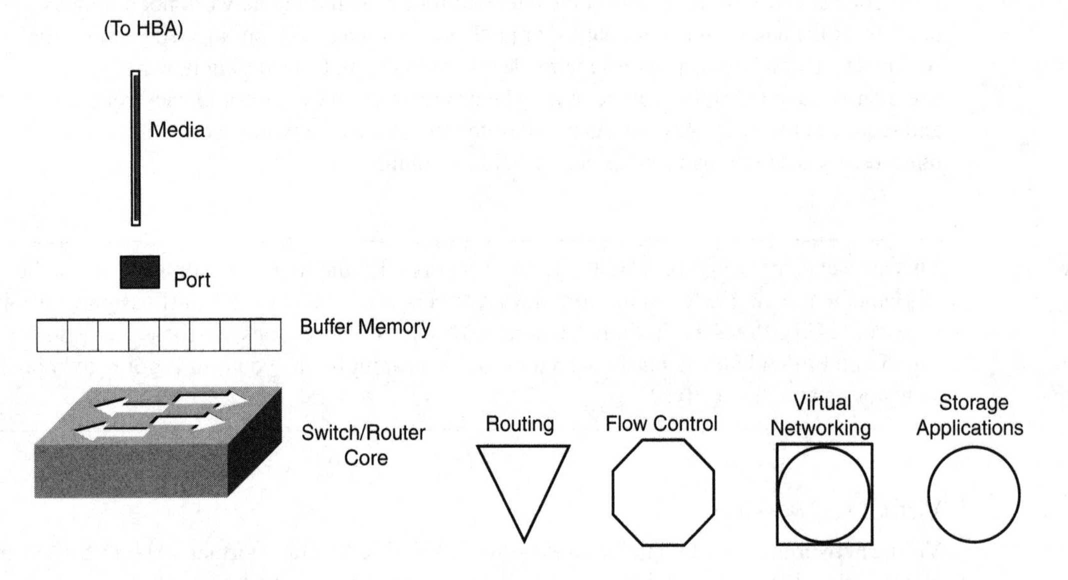

Storage Subsystem Hardware

The last part of the I/O path left to examine is within storage subsystems. While this topic is the subject of Chapter 5, it needs to be discussed briefly here to complete the overall picture of the I/O process and path.

Storage subsystem hardware has six basic I/O path elements:

- Network ports
- Storage controller
- Cache memory
- Internal interconnect
- Storage devices
- Storage media

Subsystem Network Ports

Storage subsystems can have one or more ports with multiple virtual disks that are made accessible, or *exported*, through each port. Subsystem ports can be implemented as circuits built from chip components, but they are more likely to use HBAs. After storage transmission is read by the subsystem port, it is copied to the storage controller for further processing.

Storage Controller

Controllers in storage subsystems may be implemented with off-the-shelf products or with unique, proprietary designs. The subsystem controller interprets incoming storage I/O commands and then issues downstream commands to storage devices inside the subsystem.

Cache Memory

Memory is much faster than magnetic storage, such as disk and tape drives. As a result, storage subsystems often have cache memory to improve system performance by decreasing I/O response times. The subsystem controller is responsible for determining what data to place in the cache, what data to write to disks, and what data to delete from the cache.

Internal Interconnect

All subsystems have some type of interconnect, such as a storage bus or private network, for transmitting storage data from the subsystem controller to storage devices. High-availability subsystems provide redundant internal connections between the subsystem controller and the subsystem's internal storage devices.

Storage Device

The basic building block of network storage is the disk drive. It has its own connection ports and a controller for internal operations and logic. Although far fewer tape drives than disk drives are installed, they are used almost universally as a storage device for backup and recovery.

After a disk or tape drive receives a storage I/O command from the subsystem controller, it performs the action requested and reads or writes data through an internal connection called the *read/write channel*. The read/write channel connects the device's controller with the recording heads that are ultimately responsible for creating and detecting the magnetic signals on metallic media that we refer to as stored data.

Storage Media

The I/O path ends at the storage media, where data is persistently stored. When writing data, the recording heads in a storage device induce a magnetic signal to be imprinted on the moving magnetic surface of storage media. Data resides on storage media as magnetically imprinted "1 and 0 bits." When reading data, the signals are detected as voltage changes as the media moves past the head.

The Complete View of Storage Subsystem I/O Path Elements

Figure 3-12 shows the storage subsystem I/O path elements discussed earlier. I/O operations begin with the connection port on the left of Figure 3-12 and then are processed by the subsystem controller. The subsystem's cache might be used, depending on I/O details and the design of the subsystem. The controller creates one or more downstream I/Os that are transmitted across the subsystem's interconnect to storage devices, and from there the device transfers them across its read/write channel to media where the data is stored.

Figure 3-12 *Storage Subsystem I/O Path Elements*

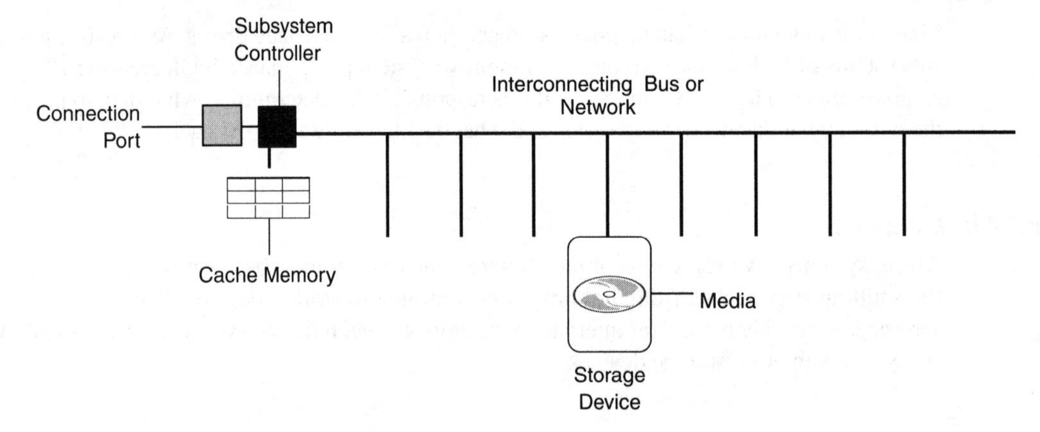

The Operating System's Role in the I/O Path

NOTE The conceptual I/O path model shown in this chapter is fairly compact, allowing people to easily understand how storage data transmissions work. More importantly, the conceptual model allows people to design effective storage network architectures.

But that does not mean it answers questions about how things *really* work in host software. The unfortunate fact is, relatively few people understand the OS inner workings of the I/O path. Experts in the field, whom most of us would consider "computing geniuses," spend their working lives in and around this topic and are often perplexed by the complexity involved.

Nonetheless, I believe some insight into and appreciation of this greater complexity is useful. Readers are advised that storage I/O, like sausage and legislation, may be best understood by the results, rather than the makings.

If the CPU is considered the brains of the system, the operating system is its consciousness. As the controlling logic that manages access to the CPU, memory, and communication resources and schedules all work in the system, the operating system has a profound impact on the storage I/O capabilities of a system.

Operating system processes separate their work into two primary processing environments:

- User space (also referred to as running in protected mode on Intel-compatible processors)
- Kernel space (also referred to as running in real mode on Intel-compatible processors)

User space is the system environment provided by the operating system for all processes that are not involved in running the system. This includes application software as well as many system functions. User space processes do not access system hardware or firmware, but rely on the operating system kernel for these actions. Each user space application is given its own *context* (virtual address space and state) by the operating system. Storage networking software that runs primarily in user space includes such products as backup/recovery and storage resource management.

Kernel space is the processing environment where the operating system manages system hardware and firmware resources. Kernel processes are sometimes referred to as *primitives*. There is typically a single context for all kernel space functions, and kernel processes need to start and finish quickly. File systems and device drivers run primarily in kernel space as high-priority, high-performance system subroutines.

Operating systems have a variety of interfaces that applications and system software use to pass control messages and data from one process to another. Transitions between user space and kernel space take a lot of CPU resources, and vigorous attempts are made to minimize them.

File System Integration

File systems are the transition operator between user space file I/O requests and kernel space block I/O storage services. In other words, file systems are smack in the middle of many of the user space/kernel space transitions that go on in a system. Keeping in mind that such transitions are relatively expensive and that attempts are made to minimize them, it turns out that the file system and operating system have to be tightly integrated.

The most intricate interfaces in a system are those between the operating system kernel and the file system(s). A single storage I/O request from an application may generate many exchanges between the kernel and the file system, some in user space and some in kernel space, but all require fast code execution without errors or bugs. A great deal of operating system and file system development efforts are spent fine-tuning and testing file system/kernel interactions.

The I/O Operation

It's convenient to talk about the "I/O operation" as a compartmentalized process with a consistent data structure that is passed from process to process with clearly defined abstraction boundaries between them. In fact, nothing could be further from the truth. I/O operations are much more like spaghetti structures with many different processes that access data as lists of addresses on disk or pointers to memory addresses.

NOTE In fact, the OS gets involved immediately with every I/O operation. In the I/O path model discussed earlier, the first interaction in the I/O path was between the application and the file system. However, this was a bit misleading for the sake of brevity. The application actually makes the file system call to the OS, which passes the call to the file system.

Installable File Systems

Historically, file systems were implemented as part of the operating system, but over time most operating systems externalized subsets of their file system functions through programmatic interfaces. File systems that use these interfaces are called *installable file systems (IFSs)*. Installable file systems allow existing operating systems to support new storage devices when they are introduced to the market, such as when DVD-RAM drives were introduced. More importantly for storage networking, installable file systems can provide higher levels of data availability through clustered or distributed file systems.

An example of an IFS is a NAS client. NAS access depends on a special type of file system technology loaded on client systems that redirects file I/O from client systems over a network to a remote file system running on a NAS server.

Figure 3-13 shows how a NAS IFS in a client redirects file I/O over a network to a remote system.

Figure 3-13 *A File I/O Request Is Redirected by a NAS Client IFS to a Remote NAS Server*

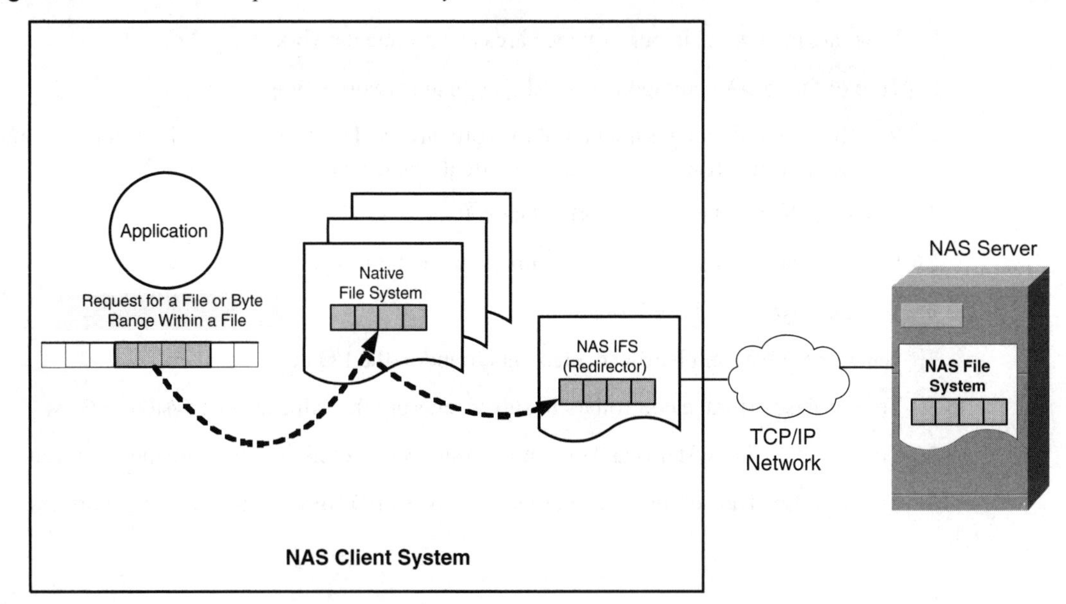

IFS implementations may be used for a wide variety of purposes. Where storage networks are concerned, these tend to involve methods of sharing access to data among clustered or distributed systems.

Summary

This chapter discussed the general environment for storage I/O processing as well as the path used for storage I/O transmissions. The environment for storage processing is not very forgiving due to the need to preserve system performance and the need for data consistency.

The concept of an I/O path was discussed, including the numerous software, hardware, and networking elements involved in data transmissions between applications to storage media. As this type of analysis indicates, many intervening components can have an impact on I/O processing.

Readers now have the background needed to understand the more detailed discussions in the remainder of the book. Analyzing storage using the global context laid out in this chapter is a valuable skill that can help clarify discussions of storage processes and networks at any level.

Q & A

1. What are the two main performance areas in storage networks?
2. True or false: DAS storage is less reliable than network storage.
3. Which of the following is not part of the software used in the I/O path: file system, volume manager, storage resource manager, multipathing drivers, or SCSI driver?
4. What are the two layers most HBAs need?
5. Name the host system hardware components in the I/O path.
6. What is flow control used for?
7. Name the subsystem hardware elements found in the I/O path.
8. True or false: Storage controllers in subsystems are the same as host system HBAs.
9. True or false: File systems and operating systems do not have to be from the same vendor.
10. True or false: The volume manager usually writes I/Os directly to disk device drivers.

PART II

Working with Devices and Subsystems in Storage Networks

Upon completing this chapter, you will be able to

- Participate in discussions with vendors, work colleagues, and other professionals about the advantages and disadvantages of disk drive implementations being used in or planned for storage networks
- Analyze and compare the specifications and capabilities of different disk drives and their suitability for different types of applications
- Discuss and plan deployments of tape drives for storage networks

CHAPTER 4

Storage Devices

Storage devices perform the fundamental function of storage networks, which is the reading and writing of data stored on nonvolatile media. They operate in the microscopic realm, combining advanced magnetic physics, chemistry, and electronics. Demands to increase capacity and performance continue to force the industry to conduct fundamental scientific research on the microscopic characteristics of materials.

Storage devices are the building blocks of storage in disk subsystems as well as being used as standalone products in server systems. This chapter mostly examines disk drive technology as the device that is used far more than any other. Tape drives are looked at at the end of the chapter.

Disk Drives

Several types of storage devices are used in storage networking, but by far the most important is the disk drive. If Harry Truman worked in the storage network industry, he would have said the buck stops at the disk drive. By now we have almost come to take disk drives for granted as ubiquitous gadgets that are readily available at volume discounts. The fact is, disk drive technology is as impressive as any other technology in all of IT, with amazing capabilities and physical characteristics.

In the sections that follow, we'll examine the various subassemblies that make up a disk drive, discuss the strengths and limitations of these amazing machines, and point out what they mean for storage network applications.

Major Parts of a Disk Drive

Disk drives are constructed from several highly specialized parts and subassemblies designed to optimally perform a very narrowly defined function within the disk drive. These components are

- Disk platters
- Read and write heads
- Read/write channel

- Arms and actuators
- Drive spindle motor and servo control electronics
- Buffer memory
- Disk controller

Now we'll discuss each of these subassemblies briefly.

Disk Platters

The physical media where data is stored in a disk drive is called a *platter*. Disk platters are rigid, thin circles that spin under the power of the drive spindle motor. Platters are built out of three basic layers:

- The substrate, which gives the platter its rigid form
- The magnetic layer, where data is stored
- A protective overcoat layer that helps minimize damage to the disk drive from microscopically sized dust particles

The three different layers within a disk platter are illustrated in Figure 4-1, which shows both the top and bottom sides of a platter.

Figure 4-1 *Material Layers in a Disk Media Platter*

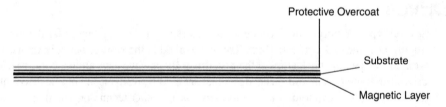

Substrates are made from a variety of materials, including aluminum/magnesium alloys, glass, and ceramic materials. Considering the microscopic nature of disk recording and how close the heads are to the surface, they must be amazingly flat and relatively inelastic to thermal expansion and contraction. In addition, they have to be almost completely uniform in density and free from material defects that could result in balance imperfections, which cause vibration and friction (heat) problems when spinning at high revolutions per minute (rpm).

The magnetic layer in most disk drives today uses thin film technology, which is very smooth and only a few millionths of an inch in thickness. The thin film layer is made by spraying vapor molecules of the magnetic materials on the surface of the substrate. The magnetic characteristics of the magnetic materials give the platter its areal density—the measurement of how many bits can be written per square inch.

The protective overcoat layer provides protection from microscopic elements such as dust and water vapor, as well as from disk head crashes. Considering the physics involved in high-speed disk drives, this coating is necessarily thin and provides, at best, light-duty protection. The best way to protect disk drive platters is to operate them in clean, dust-free, temperature-controlled environments.

Storage capacity of a single platter varies from drive to drive, but recent developments in commercially available products have resulted in platter capacities in excess of 100 GB per platter.

Disk drives are usually made by arranging multiple platters on top of each other in a stack where the platters are separated by spacers to allow the disk arms and heads to access both sides of the platters, as shown in Figure 4-2.

Figure 4-2 *Disk Platters Connected to the Spindle Motor in a Stack*

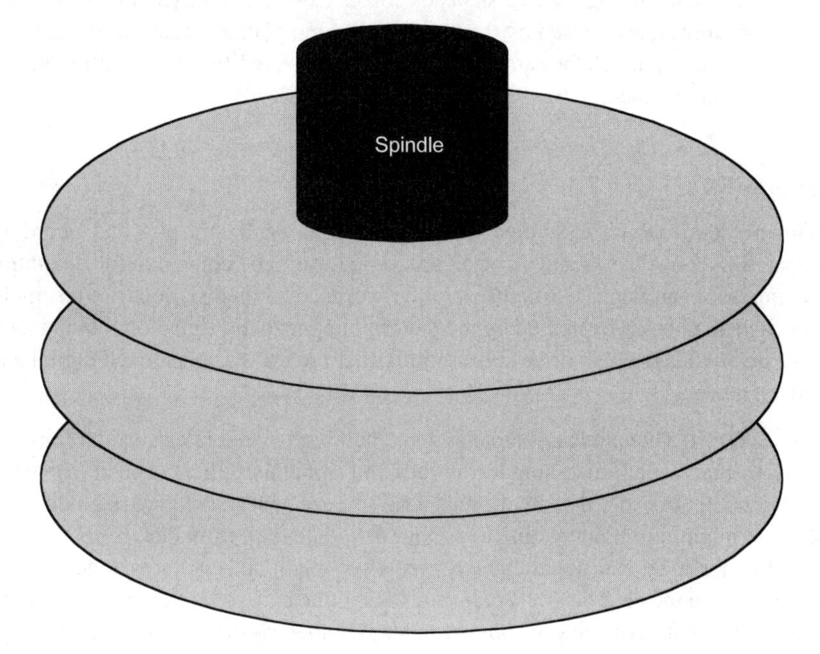

Read and Write Heads

The recording heads used for transmitting data to and from the platter are called *read and write heads*. Read/write heads are responsible for recording and playing back data stored on the magnetic layer of disk platters. When writing, they induce magnetic signals to be imprinted on the magnetic molecules in the media, and when reading, they detect the presence of those signals.

The performance and capacity characteristics of disk drives depend heavily on the technology used in the heads. Disk heads in most drives today implement giant magnetoresistive (GMR) technology, which uses the detection of resistance variances within the magnetic layer to read data. GMR recording is based on writing very low-strength signals to accommodate high areal density. This also impacts the height at which the heads "fly" over the platter.

The distance between the platter and the heads is called the *flying height*, or head gap, and is measured at approximately 15 nanometers in most drives today. This is much smaller than the diameter of most microscopic dust particles. Considering that head gap tolerances are so incredibly close, it is obviously a good idea to provide a clean and stable environment for the tens, hundreds, or thousands of disk drives that are running in a server room or data center. Disk drives can run in a wide variety of environments, but the reliability numbers improve with the air quality: in other words, relatively cool and free from humidity and airborne contaminants.

The reference to "flying" with disk heads comes from the aerodynamic physics at work in disk drives: air movement caused by the rapidly spinning platters passes over the heads, providing lift to the heads in much the same way airplane wings are lifted by the difference in air pressure above and below them.

Read/Write Channel

While we tend to think about data purely in the digital realm, the physical recording is an analog signal. Somehow, the 0s and 1s of digital logic have to be converted to something that makes an impression on magnetic media. In other words, data on disk does not resemble written language at all but is expressed by the pattern of a magnetic signal on moving media. The *read/write channel* is the disk drive subassembly that provides a specialized digital/analog conversion.

The read/write channel is implemented in small high-speed integrated circuits that utilize sophisticated signal processing techniques and signal amplifiers. The magnetoresistive phenomenon that is detected by the read heads is very faint and requires significant amplification. Readers might find it interesting to ponder how data read from disk is not actually based on detecting the magnetic signal that was written to media. Instead, it is done by detecting minute differences in the electrical *resistance* of the media, caused by the presence of different magnetic signals. Amazingly, the resistance is somehow detected by a microscopically thin head that does not make contact with the media but floats over it at very high speeds.

Arms and Actuators

The read and write heads have to be precisely positioned over specific tracks. As heads are very small, they are connected to disk arms that are thin, rigid, triangular pieces of lightweight alloys. Like everything else inside a disk drive, the disk arms are made with microscopic precision so that the read/write heads can be precisely positioned next to the platters quickly and accurately.

The disk arms are connected at the base to the drive actuator, which is responsible for positioning the arms. The actuator's movements are controlled by voice-coil drivers; the name is derived from voice coil technology used to make audio speakers. Considering that some speakers have to vibrate at very high frequencies to reproduce sounds, it's easy to see how disk actuators can be designed with voice coils to move very quickly. The clicking sounds you sometimes hear in a disk drive are the sounds of the actuator being moved back and forth.

Drive Spindle Motor and Servo Control Electronics

The drive platters rotate under power of the drive spindle motor, which is designed to maintain constant speeds with minimal vibration over long periods of time, sometimes measured in the tens of thousands of hours.

Most drive failures are related to motor failures. This is not to say the motors are poorly designed or designed to fail, because they clearly are not. However, they are always moving toward higher speeds with less power consumption and less noise, and the tolerances are thin.

The actual spindle that the platters connect to is directly fixed to the motor's drive shaft. The spindle looks a bit like the inner core of some old 45-rpm record players, except the platters do not drop or slide over the core, but are fixed in place. Separator rings are used to space the platters precisely so their surfaces can be traversed by the disk arms and heads accurately.

Among the many parts of a disk drive, the bearings in the motor see constant wear and tear. While many other things can make a disk drive fail, it is inevitable that the bearings will eventually wear out.

The speed of the spindle motor must be constantly monitored to make sure it remains consistent hour after hour, day after day, month after month. The type of technology used to maintain constant speed is called a *servo-controlled closed loop*, and it is used for many different applications to fine-tune automated systems. Disk drives are designed with sophisticated feedback control circuits that detect minute speed variations in the rotating platter by reading tracking and timing data on the disk. If the speed varies too far one way or another, the servo feedback circuit slightly changes the voltage supplied to the spindle motor to counteract the change.

Buffer Memory

The mechanical nature of reading and writing data on rotating platters limits the performance of disk drives to approximately three orders of magnitude (1000 times) less than the performance of data transfers to memory chips. For that reason, disk drives have internal buffer memory to accelerate data transmissions between the drive and the storage controller using it.

Buffer memory might not have a significant performance impact for a single disk drive system, such as a desktop or laptop system, but buffer memory can make a big difference in storage subsystems that support high-throughout applications. When multiple drives are assembled together in an array, the controller, such as a subsystem controller, can overlap I/Os across multiple drives, using buffer memory transfers whenever possible. The drive can make internal transfers of data between buffer memory and its media platters while the subsystem controller is working with another drive. In general, buffer memory in disk drives can improve I/O performance for applications that read and write small chunks of randomly accessed data. Alternatively, streaming applications with large files stored in contiguous storage locations do not realize many benefits from buffer memory.

Buffer memory sizes have increased over time, although not at the same rate as the areal density of platters. Today, disk drives typically have buffer capacities between 2 MB and 16 MB.

Disk Controller

Disk drives all have internal target controllers that respond to commands from host or subsystem initiators. In addition to interoperating with the external initiator, the storage controller in a disk drive is responsible for executing the command within the drive. The software component of a disk drive controller is referred to as firmware and is typically stored in e-prom chips in the drive's circuit board.

Processor chips used as disk drive controllers are constantly being improved with faster cores and more memory. Strangely enough, one of the challenges for disk drive manufacturers is how to make the best use of the additional intelligence at their disposal. It's a tougher question than it first appears because disk drives have traditionally been used as relatively stupid slave devices responding to I/O requests from host and subsystem controllers. Storage applications such as NAS can be added to disk drives, but that creates competition between the disk drive manufacturers and their customers—the system and subsystem vendors. So far, the disk drive manufacturers have been at the wrong end of the pecking order and their attempts to integrate higher-level storage functions in the drives have mostly failed.

Instead, what has been successful is the use of processor intelligence to increase reliability and ease of use. If you stop to consider how much easier it is to install disk drives today than it was ten years ago, the improvement has been remarkable. When you think about these improvements in terms of installed capacity, the advancements have been truly incredible. For example, the reliability provided by a handful of today's high-capacity disk drives used together to form a terabyte (TB) of storage is far, far better than the reliability of the approximately 500 disk drives that were needed ten years ago to build the same terabyte of capacity. Obviously, improvements in areal density make this possible, but a significant amount of work has also been done in the drive's internal controllers.

Data Structures on Disk Drives

The mechanisms of disk drive technology are only half of the story; the other half is the way data is structured on the disk. There is no way to plan for optimal storage configurations without understanding how data is structured on the surface of disk drive platters. This section discusses the following data structures used in disk drives:

- Tracks, sectors, and cylinders
- Disk partitions
- Logical block addressing
- Geometry of disk drives and zoned-bit recording

Tracks, Sectors, and Cylinders

Disk platters are formatted in a system of concentric circles, or rings, called *tracks*. Within each track are sectors, which subdivide the circle into a system of arcs, each formatted to hold the same amount of data—typically 512 bytes. Once upon a time, the block size of file systems was coupled with the sector size of a disk. Today the block size of a file system can range considerably, but it is usually some multiple of 512 bytes.

Cylinders are the system of identical tracks on multiple platters within the drive. The multiple arms of a drive move together in lockstep, positioning the heads in the same relative location on all platters simultaneously.

The complete system of cylinders, tracks, and sectors is shown in Figure 4-3.

Disk Partitions

Disk partitions divide the capacity of physical disk drives into logical containers. A disk drive can have one or more partitions, providing a way for users to flexibly create different virtual disks that can be used for different purposes.

For instance, a system could have different partitions to reserve storage capacity for different users of the system or for different applications. A common reason for using multiple partitions is to store data for operating systems or file systems. Machines that are capable of running two different operating systems, such as Linux and Windows, could have their respective data on different disk partitions.

Disk partitions are created as a contiguous collection of tracks and cylinders. Visually, you can imagine partitions looking like the concentric rings of an archery target with the bull's-eye being replaced by the disk motor's spindle. Partitions are established starting at the outer edge of the platters and working toward the center. For instance, if a disk has three partitions, numbered 0, 1, and 2, partition 0 would be on the outside and partition 2 would be closest to the center.

Figure 4-3 *Cylinders, Tracks, and Sectors in a Disk Drive*

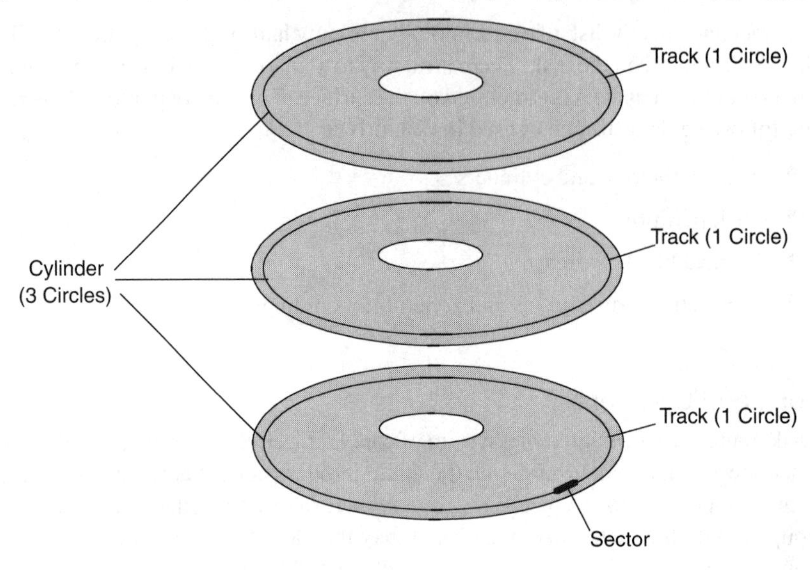

Logical Block Addressing

While the internal system of cylinders, tracks, and sectors is interesting, it is also not used much anymore by the systems and subsystems that use disk drives. Cylinder, track, and sector addresses have been replaced by a method called logical block addressing (LBA), which makes disks much easier to work with by presenting a single flat address space. To a large degree, logical block addressing facilitates the flexibility of storage networks by allowing many different types of disk drives to be integrated more easily in a large heterogeneous storage environment.

With logical block addressing, the disk drive controller maintains the complete mapping of the location of all tracks, sectors, and blocks in the disk drive. There is no way for an external entity like an operating system or subsystem controller to know which sector its data is being placed in by the disk drive. At first glance this might seem risky—letting a tiny chip in a disk drive be responsible for such an important function. But, in fact, it increases reliability by allowing the disk drive to remap sectors that have failed or might be headed in that direction.

Considering the areal density and the microscopic nature of disk recording, there are always going to be bad sectors on any disk drive manufactured. Disk manufacturers compensate for this by reserving spare sectors for remapping other sectors that go bad. Because manufacturers anticipate the need for spare sectors, the physical capacity of a disk drive always exceeds the logical, usable capacity. Reserving spare sectors for remapping bad sectors is an important, reliability-boosting by-product of LBA technology. Disk drives can be manufactured with spare sectors placed throughout the platter's surface that minimize the performance hit of seeking to remapped sectors.

Geometry of Disk Drives and Zoned-Bit Recording

There is no way to escape radial geometry when working with disk drives. One of the more interesting aspects of this radial geometry is that the amount of recording material in a track increases as you move away from the center of the disk platter. Disk drive tracks can be thought of as media rings having a circumference that is determined by the mathematical expression $2\pi r$, where r is the radius for the track. The amount of recording material in a track is determined by radial length. This means that the outermost tracks can hold more data than the inside tracks. In fact, they can hold a lot more data than inside tracks.

To take advantage of this geometry, disk drive designers developed zoned-bit recording, which places more sectors inside tracks as the radius increases. The general idea is to segment the drive into "sector/track density" zones, where the tracks within that zone all have the same number of sectors. The outermost zone, zone 0, has the most sectors per track, while the innermost zone has the fewest.

Logical block addressing facilitates the use of zoned-bit recording by allowing disk drive manufacturers to establish whatever zones they want to without worrying about the impact on host/subsystem controller logic and operations. As platters are never exchanged between disk drives, there is no need to worry about standardized zone configurations.

Table 4-1 shows the zones for a hypothetical disk drive with 13 zones. The number of tracks in a zone indicates the relative physical area of the zone. Notice how the media transfer rates change as the zones move closer to the spindle. This is why the first partitions created on disk drives tend to have better performance characteristics than partitions that are located closer to the center of the drive.

Table 4-1 *Disk Drive Zones*

Zone	Number of Tracks	Sectors in Each Track	Media Transfer Rate in Mbps
0	1700	2140	1000
1	3845	2105	990
2	4535	2050	965
3	4365	2000	940
4	7430	1945	915
5	7775	1835	860
6	5140	1780	835
7	6435	1700	800
8	8985	1620	760
9	11,965	1460	685
10	12,225	1295	610
11	5920	1190	560
12	4320	1135	530

Disk Drive Specifications

Disk drive specifications can be confusing and difficult to interpret. This section highlights some of the most important specs used with disk drives in storage networking applications, including the following:

- Mean time between failures
- Rotational speed and latency
- Average seek time
- Media transfer rate
- Sustained transfer rate

Mean Time Between Failures

Mean time between failure (MTBF) indicates the expected reliability of disk drives. MTBF specifications are derived using well-defined statistical methods and tests run on a large number of disk drives over a relatively short period of time. The results are extrapolated and are expressed as a very large number of hours—usually in the range of 500,000 to 1.25 million hours. These numbers are unthinkably high for individual disk drives—1.25 million hours is approximately 135 years.

MTBF specifications help create expectations for how often disk drive failures will occur when there are many drives in an environment. Using the MTBF specification of 1.25 million hours (135 years), if you have 135 disk drives, you can expect to experience a drive failure once a year. In a storage network environment with a large number of disk drives—for instance, over 1000 drives—it's easy to see that spare drives should be available because there will almost certainly be drive failures that need to be managed. This also underlines the importance of using disk device redundancy techniques, such as mirroring or RAID.

Rotational Speed and Latency

One of the most common ways to describe the capabilities of any disk drive is to state its rotational speed in rpm. The faster a disk drive spins, the faster data can be written to and read from the disk's media. The performance differences can be enormous. All other things being equal, a 15,000-rpm disk drive can do more than twice the amount of work as a 7200-rpm disk drive. If 50 or more disk drives are being used by a transaction processing system, it's easy to see why somebody would want to use higher-speed drives.

Related to rotation speed is a specification called rotational latency. After the drive's heads are located over the proper track in a disk drive platter, they must wait for the proper sector to pass underneath before the data transfer can be made. The time spent waiting for the right sector is called the rotational latency and is directly linked to the rotational speed of the disk drive.

Essentially, rotational latency is given as the average amount of time to wait for any random I/O operation and is calculated as the time it takes for a platter to complete a half-revolution.

Rotational latencies are on the range of 2 to 6 milliseconds. This might not seem like a very long time. But it is very slow compared to processor and memory device speeds. Applications that tend to suffer from I/O bottlenecks such as transaction processing, data warehousing, and multimedia streaming require disk drives with high rotation speeds and sizable buffers.

Table 4-2 shows the rotational latency for several common rotational speeds.

Table 4-2 *The Inverse Relationship Between Rotational Speed and Rotational Latency in Disk Drives*

Rotational Speed	Rotational Latency (in ms)
5400	5.6
7200	4.2
10000	3.0
12000	2.5
15000	2.0

Average Seek Time

Along with rotational speed, seek time is the most important performance specification for a disk drive. *Seek time* measures the time it takes the actuator to reposition the read/write heads from one track to another over a platter. Average seek times represent a performance average over many I/O operations and are relatively similar to rotational latency—in the range of 4 to 8 milliseconds.

Transaction processing and other database applications that perform large numbers of random I/O operations in quick succession require disk drives with minimal seek times. Although it is possible to spread the workload over many drives, transaction application performance also depends significantly on the ability of an individual disk drive to process an I/O operation quickly. This translates into a combination of low seek times and high rotational speeds.

Media Transfer Rate

The *media transfer rate* of a disk drive measures the performance of bit read/write operations on drive platters. Unlike most storage specifications, which are listed in terms of bytes, the media transfer rate is given in terms of bits. The media transfer rate measures read/write performance on a single track, which depends on the radial length the track is positioned at. In other words, tracks in zone 0 have the fastest media transfer rates in the disk drive. For that reason, media transfer rate specifications are sometimes given using ranges.

Sustained Transfer Rate

Most I/O operations on a disk drive work across multiple tracks and cylinders, which involves the ability to change the location of the read/write heads. The sustained transfer rate specification takes into account the physical delays of seek time and rotational latency and is much closer to measuring actual user data performance than the media transfer rate.

That said, sustained transfer rates indicate optimal conditions that are difficult to approach with actual applications. There are other important variables such as the size of the average data object and the level of fragmentation in the file system. Nonetheless, sustained transfer rate is a pretty good indication of a drive's overall performance capabilities.

Optimizing Disk Drive Performance in Storage Networks

Given that disk drives are relatively slow, people have developed several methods and techniques to increase their performance. The performance enhancements discussed in this section include

- Limiting drive contention
- Short-stroking the drive
- Matching rotation speeds
- Aligning zones

Limiting Drive Contention

Multiple applications that are actively performing I/O operations on a single disk drive can generate a significant amount of seek time and rotation latency, causing performance to deteriorate. Therefore, it makes sense to understand which applications are accessing each disk drive in order to avoid contention for a drive's slow mechanical resources.

Disk bottlenecks can occur in storage area networking (SAN) environments where many disk drives provide storage to many systems and applications. Without good planning, it's possible for different partitions on a single disk drive to be assigned to different applications requiring higher I/O performance levels. In that case, the two applications would wind up competing for the use of a single actuator and a single rotating spindle.

One of the best ways to limit contention for a disk drive is to limit the number of partitions it has. For example, administrators could configure some percentage of high-speed drives to have two partitions—one for a high-performance application and the other for a lower-performance application. Unfortunately, the enforcement of this objective would have to be a manual task, as the technology for automating it is not yet available. A facility that allowed automated disk partition policies to be applied to drives might be very useful. The intelligence to do it is in the drive, but the requirement to provide it is not yet obvious to disk drive manufacturers.

NOTE Most applications have minimal storage I/O requirements and place a minimal load on disk drives. These "I/O-lite" applications probably don't need to be monitored for disk drive contention problems. These applications also do not deserve to hog the best parts of high-speed disk drives. Most administrators are not used to creating partitions and letting them sit idle, but that could be done to reserve a percentage of the "choicest cuts" of some drives in case they are needed by a high-performance application in the future. The question is, if an application does not require optimal I/O performance, why allocate a high-performance disk partition to it?

Short-Stroking the Drive

A technique known as short-stroking a disk limits the drive's capacity by using a subset of the available tracks, typically the drive's outer tracks. This accomplishes two things: it reduces seek time by limiting the actuator's range of motion, and it increases the media transfer rate by using the outer tracks, which have the highest densities of data per track.

Short-stroking is normally done by establishing a single partition on a drive that uses some subset of the total capacity. For instance, you can establish an 80-GB partition on a 200-GB disk drive to increase performance.

Matching Rotation Speeds

There is a tendency in storage networking to treat all storage address spaces equally, which makes them easier to manage. This approach is likely to work very well for the majority of applications, but it falls short for those applications that need the highest performance.

An obvious difference between disk drives is their rotational speed. It would not be a good idea to match slow-speed drives with high-speed drives in support of a high-throughput transaction processing application.

The same concept applies to drive buffer memory. You would not want to use drives with insufficient buffer capacity, slowing down an otherwise fast configuration.

Aligning Zones

The performance differences across different zones on disk drives could be significant for certain applications that expect consistently high I/O rates, such as data warehousing processing. For example, a disk partition on the outside of a disk might have almost twice the performance of a partition on the inside of a disk. In effect, this is the same situation as wanting to match the rotational speeds of disk drives used for high-performance applications, except this variable adds the element of matching the zones or the relative position of the partitions on a drive.

Tape Drives

Tape drives are used universally for backup and restore operations. While there are far fewer tape drives than disk drives, the function they provide is very important. The primary difference between tape and disk storage is that tape media is removable, which means it can be transported for safekeeping from disasters as well as being a mechanism for sharing data over the "sneaker net."

NOTE Sneaker net is certainly not the only way tapes have been used to share data. Companies have used courier services, air cargo, and even refrigerated trucks to move tapes from one site to another to share data.

One of the less-obvious differences between disk drives and tape drives is their read/write ratios. While disk drives are most often used to read data, tape drives are usually used to write data.

This section discusses topics concerning tapes and tape drives:

- Tape media
- Caring for tape
- Caring for tape heads
- Tape drive performance
- The tale of two technologies

A Look at Tape Media

The media where data is stored on a tape drive is—surprise!—magnetic tape. The result of a great deal of chemicals, materials, and manufacturing technology, magnetic tape is pretty amazing and very durable, as long as it is not abused. Magnetic tape is constructed in four basic layers:

- Backing
- Binder
- Magnetic material
- Coating

The backing of a tape is the foundation material that gives the tape its inherent flexibility and strength. In addition, backing provides a magnetic barrier so that signals from one section of tape do not "print through" onto adjacent sections of the tape when tapes are rolled up tightly and stored for long periods of time.

Tape binder is the flexible glue-like material that adheres to the backing as well as the magnetic material.

The magnetic materials in tape are where the action is, of course, and where data is written and read. The magnetic properties are provided by fine metal oxides, which are smooth to the human eye but somewhat jagged and rough at a microscopic level.

The coating layer levels the surface of the tape and provides a smoother surface for running over the tape heads. Without the coating layer, wear and tear on tape heads would be excessive.

Caring for Tape

In general, tapes deteriorate slowly over time. They develop cracks in the surface, they tear along the edges, and the metal oxides corrode. It is important to use and store data tapes under conditions of moderate temperature and low humidity. This includes tapes that have not been used yet but are being stored for future use. Tape deterioration that starts before data is written to it can lead to data loss later, even if the tapes are well taken care of after they have been used.

Caring for Tape Heads

Unlike disk drive heads that float at microscopic levels above the platter, tape heads are designed to be in contact with the tape when reading or writing data. As a result, tape heads eventually wear out over time due to the constant friction of regular operations.

Tape heads should be cleaned after every 30 hours of use. Unlike disk drives, which have limited exposure to airborne particles, tape drives are exposed when tapes are removed and inserted. This makes it practically impossible to keep particulate matter away from the tape heads, and that's why it's important to operate tape drives in a clean environment. Also, tapes shed fine pieces inside the tape drive as they are run through the tape transport, especially when they are new. This material sticks to the tape heads and reduces their effectiveness. Dirty tape heads are often reported by backup software as tape failures, even though there might be nothing wrong with the tapes you are using.

Tape Drive Performance

Tape drives have wide performance ranges based on two variables:

- A sufficient amount of data being transferred
- The compressibility of data

Streaming and Start-Stop Operations

Unlike disk drives, tape drives run at different speeds. A drive's streaming transfer rate represents the speed at which data is written from buffers onto tape. Obviously, this implies that a sufficient amount of data is being written into the drive's buffers by host or subsystem controllers.

Start-stop operations occur when there is insufficient data to maintain streaming mode operations. Start-stop speeds are typically far less than streaming speeds because the tape has to be stopped, rewound slightly, and started up again. Unlike analog recording, where it is no problem to have "dead air," digital recording cannot have undefined gaps. Therefore, if there is no data to record, the tape drive must stop and reposition the tape appropriately for when there is more data to write. This starting and stopping is obviously detrimental to performance. Larger buffers can help, but they do not solve the problem of having too little data to write.

Compression

Tape drives typically incorporate compression technology as a feature to boost data transfer rates. Compression can increase performance several times beyond native (uncompressed) data transfer rates, but that depends on how much the data can be compressed. Different types of data vary a great deal in this respect; multimedia data might not compress at all, and database data might compress many times. Tape drives in storage networks should be able to support native streaming transfer rates of at least 10 Mbps.

The Tale of Two Technologies

The history of tape technology is littered with many obsolete technologies that faded fast. People have protested about the interoperability and compatibility problems of tape technologies for many years, and the situation is no different today. Tape drives used in storage networks can be divided into two broad technology areas, with two contestants in each area—all of them being incompatible with the others.

In the sections that follow, we will briefly look at both technologies.

Linear Tape Technology

Linear tape reads and writes data just as it sounds—by placing "lines" of data that run lengthwise on the tape media. Linear tape drives use multiple heads operating in parallel, reading and writing data simultaneously. They tend to have very high transfer rates and capacities.

Tape used in linear tape drives is .5 inches wide, leaving a great deal of room for capacity improvements over time. Linear tape cartridges have only one spool to hold tape. When the tape is loaded, the outside end of the tape is fed into the drive and wrapped around a take-up spool inside the drive.

There are two primary, competing linear tape technologies:

- Super digital linear tape (SDLT)
- Linear tape open (LTO)

SDLT has its technology roots in the digital linear tape technology developed by Digital Equipment Corporation many years ago for its VAX line of computers. LTO is a relatively new type of tape technology that was jointly developed by IBM, HP, and Seagate.

Helical Scan Tape Technology

Helical scan tape technology was originally developed for video recording applications. Most helical scan tape drives used for data storage applications use 8 mm tape, which is approximately .25 inches wide. Helical scan drives write data in diagonal strips along the tape.

In general, helical scan tape cartridges are much smaller than linear tape cartridges, even though they have two reels, unlike linear tape. Data density with helical scanning technology is typically better, although helical scan tape cartridges usually hold less data than linear tape cartridges.

Two primary helical scan technologies are used in storage networking environments: Mammoth-2 and AIT-3. Mammoth tape technology was developed by Exabyte Corporation in the mid-1990s in response to DLT's growing popularity and success. At this point it seems to have been eclipsed in functionality by AIT, LTO, and DLT as the preferred technologies for storage network environments.

Sony's Advanced Intelligent Tape (AIT) was also developed as a new data recording technology in the mid 1990s in response to the need for higher reliability, performance, and capacity. AIT included many innovations, including a memory chip embedded in the tape cartridge that could be used by storage applications.

Comparing Tape Technologies

Table 4-3 compares the leading tape technologies used in storage networks.

Table 4-3 *Comparison of Tape Technologies Used in Storage Networks*

Technology	Linear or Helical	Capacity (Native/Compressed)	Maximum Transfer Rate (Native/Compressed)
Mammoth-2	Helical	60 GB/150 GB	12 Mbps/30 Mbps
AIT-3	Helical	100 GB/250 GB	12 Mbps/30 Mbps
SuperDLT	Linear	110 GB/220 GB	10 Mbps/20 Mbps
LTO Ultrium	Linear	340 GB/680 GB	20 Mbps/40 Mbps

Summary

Device technology continues to evolve and is being heavily pushed by the requirements of storage networks. In general, bare devices are not addressed individually in a storage network but are part of larger subsystems that provide centralized management for a larger number of resources.

That said, understanding the capabilities and shortcomings of these devices is important to maintaining a well-run SAN environment—especially where high-performance I/O operations are required. The rotational speed of a drive, its average seek time performance, the relative location of the tracks being used, the number of applications sharing space on the drive, and the amount of buffer memory are all contributing factors that need to be considered for I/O performance tuning in a SAN.

Tape drives have made tremendous strides in the last five years. Capacities and transfer rates have increased by a wide margin, pushed by the enormous amount of data that is being stored. While there are some who believe tape is a dead and dying technology, it is not likely to go away anytime soon because its portability works so well for disaster recovery situations and the ability to restore historical versions of data.

Q & A

1. Which of the following is not part of a disk drive: platters, arms, controller, or fan?
2. What is the flying height of modern disk heads?
3. True or false: The clicking sound coming from disk drives is caused by the head touching the media.
4. What does logical block addressing provide?
5. Where is disk throughput greater: inside tracks or outside tracks?
6. What is MTBF used for?
7. True or false: Multiple applications can access different partitions on a disk drive without regard for performance.
8. How often should tape heads be cleaned?
9. True or false: Data compression always cuts the time it takes to run backup in half.
10. What are the two major types of tape technologies used in UNIX and Windows environments?

Upon completing this chapter, you will be able to

- Identify the major architectural components used in a storage subsystem
- Participate in discussions with coworkers, vendors, and analysts about the strengths and weaknesses of designs used in storage subsystems
- Analyze the functions and features provided by a storage subsystem, including its capabilities for high-availability environments
- Participate in planning exercises concerning the connections used between systems and storage subsystems

CHAPTER 5

Storage Subsystems

Storage networks tend to be designed using storage-centric architectures. Obviously, the storage at the core of such designs should be flexible, scalable, and robust. In most storage networks this is accomplished by implementing *storage subsystems* that combine storage devices with intelligent storage controller, network, and power technologies. Just as computer systems span an enormous range of prices and capabilities, storage subsystems range from fairly simple products that resemble enhanced storage devices to those with enormous processing power and sophisticated data protection applications and management capabilities. This chapter examines the technologies, architectures, and implementations that are commonly found in this important product category.

NOTE The analysis in this chapter views storage subsystems primarily as *storing* products, meaning that network-attached storage (NAS) systems are not explicitly discussed. For those NAS lovers out there who feel shortchanged, don't feel slighted. NAS systems are often used as core infrastructure storage products, and they all use some type of disk subsystem for their storage. The topics discussed in this chapter apply to the storage part of NAS servers the same way they apply to storage area network (SAN) subsystems.

Subsystem Architecture

Most subsystems share the following functional elements:

- **Controller hardware and logic**—Performs most of the storage functions in a subsystem, including the execution of storage commands received from host systems as well as subsystem-based storage applications
- **External storage network ports**—Connects to host systems as well as optional data network ports for management connections
- **Memory**—Used for caching storage data
- **Internal connection technology (including the bus or network technology)**—Used to connect network ports with controllers and memory, as well as the device interconnect technology used to connect storage devices
- **Storage devices**—Where data is eventually stored

Sometimes the term *front end* is used with storage subsystems to indicate functions that process data at or near the point it is received by the subsystem. For example, the front end of a subsystem might include a number of access control functions and possibly caching functions. The term *back end* is used to indicate functions relating to device operations. An example of a back end is a Small Computer Systems Interface (SCSI) bus controller.

Figure 5-1 shows the basic architectural elements of most storage subsystems.

Figure 5-1 *Basic Architecture of a Storage Subsystem*

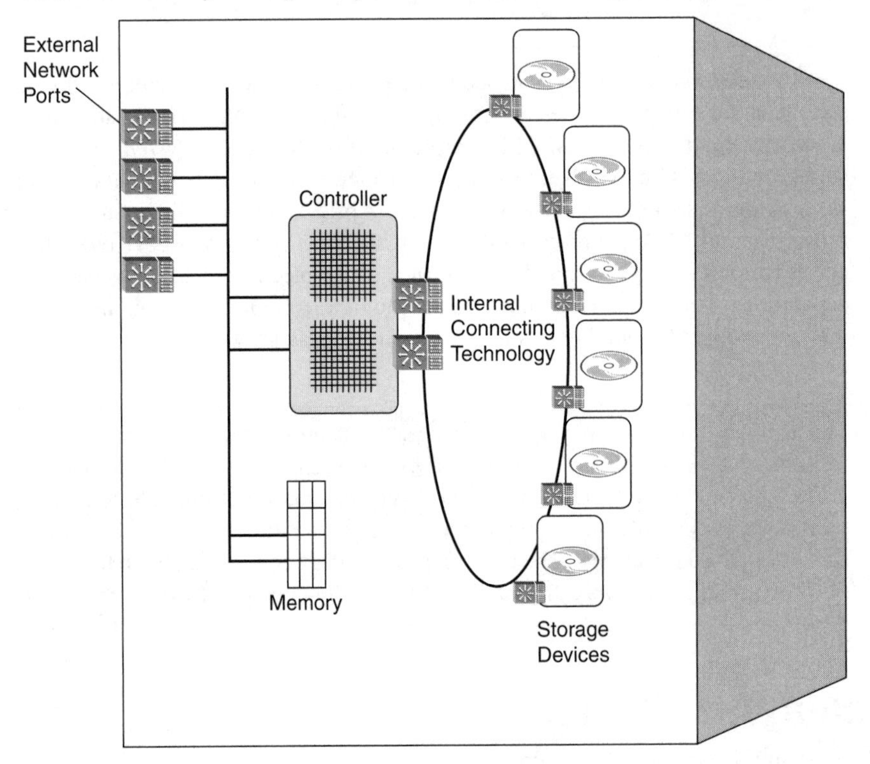

Subsystem Controllers

The controller design of a subsystem determines most of its capabilities. Subsystem controllers can be implemented many different ways—from relatively simple, inexpensive single-board designs to highly intricate switched architectures. Many types of processors are used, including those designed for real-time applications, such as the Intel i960 or StrongArm processors, systems processors, such as the Power PC and Pentium, or embedded processor cores that are integrated into custom designs, such as those from MIPS Technologies.

While there are many possible subsystem designs, most of them can be placed within three categories:

- **Integrated controller/adapters**—These are subsystem controllers implemented as adapter cards that manage the actions of smaller storage subsystems. These integrated controllers usually hold some fixed configuration of cache memory and are limited in scalability by the number of external network and internal storage ports.
- **System-based controllers**—These are characterized by specialized, standalone systems complete with processors, high-speed cache memory, and a system bus or internal loop network connecting the various subsystem elements. These subsystems typically have multiple processors to provide scalable performance and high availability.
- **Switching-based controllers**—These are the most recent innovation in subsystem design. These subsystems have integrated high-speed switching cores and backplanes instead of shared media buses or loop networks. Controller processors and logic are located within processing modules or "blades" that fit into rack slots.

NOTE In this chapter, the term *controller* refers to the complete set of functions and processors that drive the subsystem. The word controller might seem a bit puny when referring to all the stuff that goes into a large enterprise subsystem, but there needs to be a way to discuss the functional role of the controller succinctly. Controller uses the perspective of an I/O operation, in which a host I/O controller (that is, an adapter) communicates with a storage subsystem controller.

Subsystem Internal Connectivity

Controller designs are necessarily closely integrated with the internal connectivity technologies used in a storage subsystem. The internal communications technologies in storage subsystems often include a system bus for connecting controller processors, ports, and memory, as well as a device interconnect technology such as SCSI or Fibre Channel (see Chapter 7, "Device Interconnect Technologies for Storage Networks").

Some of the internal connection technologies used in storage subsystems include the following:

- **System I/O buses such as Peripheral Component Interconnect (PCI), PCI Extended (PCI-X), and proprietary bus implementations**—System buses are normally used for front-end connections, although they can also be used on the back end to connect devices.
- **Direct attached storage (DAS) storage buses such as SCSI, Advanced Technology Attachment (ATA), Serial ATA (SATA), and Serial Attached SCSI (SAS)**—These are used for back-end communications within a subsystem.
- **Fibre Channel (FC) loop networks**—FC loop can be used for front-end connectors between network ports and controllers as well as for connecting storage devices in the back end. FC loop technology can also be used to connect external expansion cabinets that expand the storage capacity of a subsystem.

- **Switched connections**—This can include almost any type of switchable communications technology, including FC, Ethernet, dense wavelength division multiplexing (DWDM), SATA, SAS, and proprietary switching technology. High-speed processors are used at the front and back ends to provide an interface between the switched technology and its adjacent element.

Whereas the controller design determines the functions and applications supported by a subsystem, the subsystem's internal connection technology determines its scalability, performance, and availability characteristics.

For instance, the address space of switched topologies tends to be far greater than that of buses and loops, which means it is easier to accommodate large numbers of devices in a subsystem. In addition, switched technologies tend to have much better bandwidth characteristics than shared media technologies, such as buses and loops.

Aggregating Devices in Subsystems

The primary characteristic of storage subsystems is their ability to aggregate multiple storage devices into a single manageable system. While there are many possible configurations and feature sets for storage subsystems, the aggregation of devices typically results in some or all of the following key advantages:

- **Data redundancy**—Data is written to multiple devices, allowing continuous operations should an individual device fail.
- **Capacity scaling**—Aggregating a large number of physical devices enables the creation of large virtual devices.
- **Integrated packaging**—Devices installed in a single enclosure or in linked, modular enclosures are more easily added, removed, and managed.
- **Hot swapping**—Devices can be removed and replaced without interrupting production operations.
- **Managed, shared power**—Devices receive power from conditioned, redundant power supplies.
- **Consolidated communications**—Devices are connected via a single communications system that manages storage traffic for all devices.

NOTE The subsystem characteristics discussed in this chapter involve mainly disk drives. They are by far the most common type of device, and disk subsystems are by far the most common type of subsystem. But disk drives aren't the only kind of subsystem—tape, optical, and solid-state subsystems also exist. This chapter could deal with disk drives or storage devices, but either way, the discussion can be misleading. If you interpret *storage device* to mean *disk drive,* you won't be far off.

High Data Availability with Redundant Subsystem Designs

A number of different problems can obstruct data availability, including device failures, connectivity failures, and power failures. While it is not necessary to have high availability storage to achieve high availability for data, most storage network architects prefer to increase their odds by using subsystems designed for high availability. In general, high availability is equated with redundancy for all components in the I/O path.

Redundant Storage Devices

One of the most common and powerful forms of redundancy is mirroring data on a pair of disk drives. Mirroring in a subsystem is a simple concept: the subsystem's controller duplicates every I/O operation it receives from a host system to a pair of internal disk drives. Figure 5-2 illustrates disk mirroring in a storage subsystem controller.

Figure 5-2 *Disk Mirroring in a Storage Subsystem*

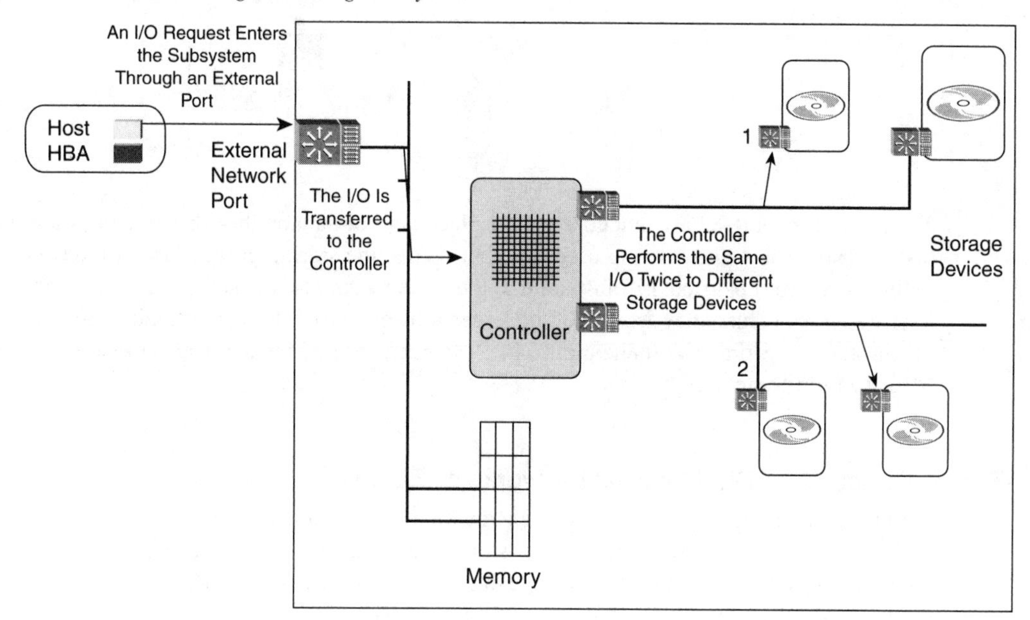

Although it is a simple concept, this relatively simple idea has some interesting and unexpected angles that are discussed in greater detail in Chapter 8, "An Introduction to Data Redundancy and Mirroring."

Another form of storage redundancy commonly used in storage subsystems is based on parity RAID (redundant array of independent disks), the topic of Chapter 9, "Bigger, Faster, More Reliable Storage with RAID." In essence, the subsystem controller performs a function similar to disk mirroring, except that with parity RAID the operations are not duplicated. Instead, the operations are segmented to form multiple I/O operations, as shown in Figure 5-3.

Figure 5-3 *Storage Subsystem Controller Performing RAID Operations*

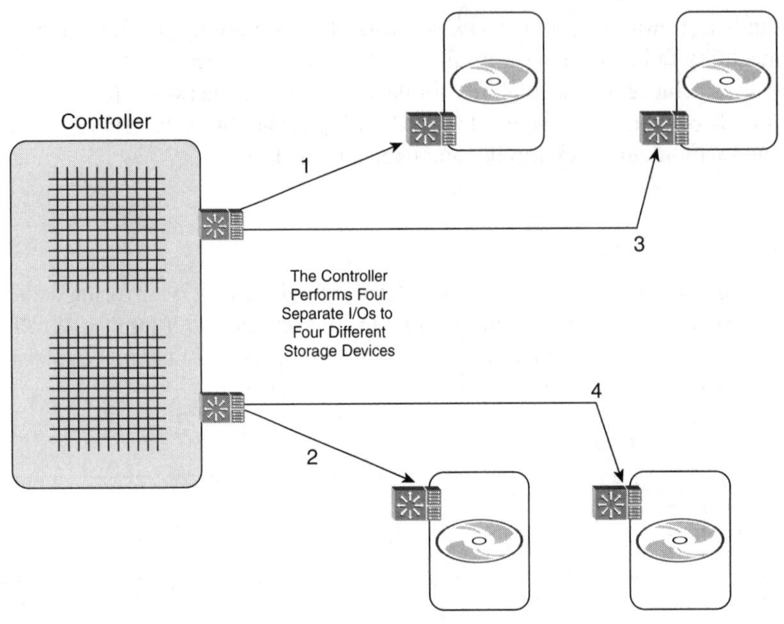

The file system or database that controls the placement of data on disk drives is unaware that disk mirroring or RAID is being used. In other words, the storing process used for device redundancy in a subsystem is transparent to the systems that use the subsystem. Mirroring and RAID used for redundancy are part of the larger subject area of storage virtualization, the topic of Chapter 12, "Storage Virtualization: The Power in Volume Management Software and SAN Virtualization Systems."

Dual-Ported Devices and Dual Internal Networks or Buses

Traditionally, storage devices were designed with a single connecting port for communicating with host systems. However, some newer storage devices designed for storage networking applications, such as FC disk drives, have dual ports that provide redundant protection from failures to device connectors, controller connections, or controllers.

NOTE The road maps for SATA and SAS disk drive technologies also include dual-ported products. Perhaps by the time you read this book, dual-ported SATA and SAS drives will be available. As one familiar with self-induced hypoxia from holding my breath waiting for technologies to appear, I find it more pleasant now to write about actual shipping technologies as opposed to those with high dew points.

If dual-ported devices are used in a subsystem, it is possible to have redundant network or bus connections between subsystem controllers and storage devices. The idea is similar to multipathing in a storage network (see Chapter 11, "Connection Redundancy in Storage Networks and Dynamic Multipathing"), but the redundancy occurs within the confines of a subsystem. If one of the connections fails, the other can be used, as shown in Figure 5-4.

Figure 5-4 *Redundant Connections to a Dual-Ported Device*

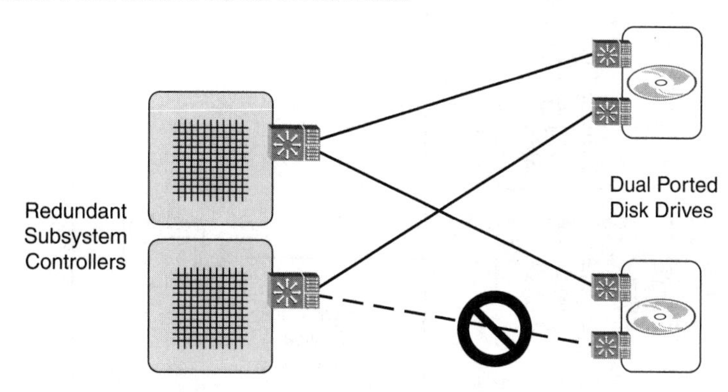

The presence of multiple networks or buses does not necessarily mean the storage subsystem provides connection redundancy. For example, a subsystem could have four independent parallel SCSI buses with multiple single-ported devices connected to each bus. Even though there are multiple buses in the subsystem, there is no connection redundancy because the devices have only a single port.

Redundancy in Storage Controllers and Processors

Another potential point of failure is the storage controller. There are several ways multiple storage controllers can be implemented to achieve redundancy, including the use of multiple modular controller cards. For example, each controller card could have its own integrated external network port, run its own copy of the controller logic, and connect to other controller cards over a system bus, as shown in Figure 5-5.

When you are using multiple controller modules, and one of them fails, all storage access must be routed through one of the other controller modules. Obviously, the redundant module must be able to access the devices where the data is stored. More importantly, the redundant controller must be able to assume storage work that is already in progress.

Another approach for controller redundancy is to use multiple processors within a single controller design. In this case, all processors are capable of performing storage I/O work, and if one of the processors fails, the other processors are assigned its tasks.

Figure 5-5 *Redundant Controllers Implemented on Multiple Controller Cards*

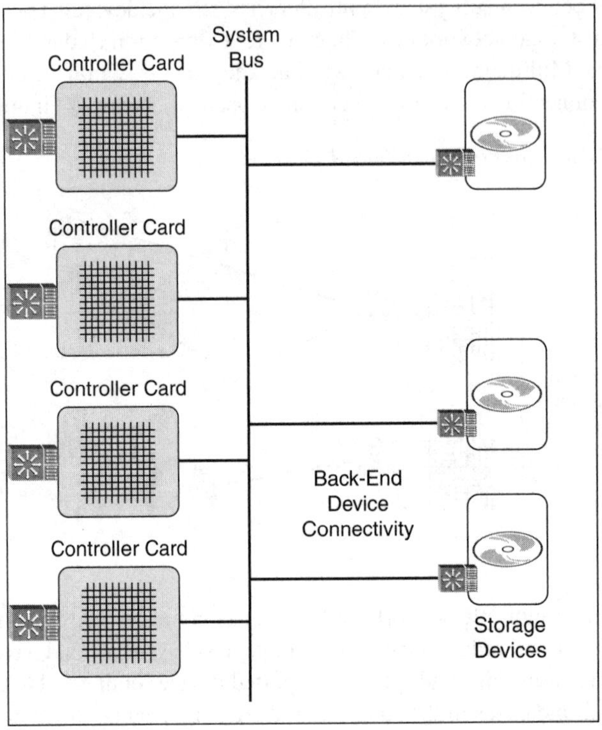

NOTE Storage subsystem controllers can be made with custom silicon or general-purpose (off-the-shelf) components. Although custom silicon is designed to deliver faster performance than general-purpose components, the redundant data protection is exactly the same for both. In other words, the redundant protection offered by disk mirroring or RAID does not depend on the cost of the controller doing the work, as long as the controller is functioning properly.

There are many differences between controller implementations, such as how they work with cache memory and how they connect to storage devices. The intrinsic nature of data redundancy on storage media, however, is independent of the controller implementation and its cost.

Redundant Cache Memory

I/O write data stored in a subsystem's cache memory that has not been written to disk is at risk of being lost before it is stored in nonvolatile storage. Therefore, subsystem designs might include mirrored cache memory so that a failure or loss of power to one of the caches will not cause data to be lost. The topic of redundant cache and the mechanisms to ensure data integrity during failure scenarios are advanced topics that are beyond the scope of this book.

Battery backup systems and subsystem control logic are used to ensure that data is not lost from cache memory should a problem interfere with writing cached data to storage. If power is lost or if the connection between cache memory and storage media should break, the data in the redundant cache would be used to write data to disk.

Redundant Network Ports

In general, subsystem network ports are host bus adapters (HBAs) with modifications for the requirements of subsystem operations. The HBAs used for subsystems are sometimes called Fibre adapters (FAs). They can differ considerably from host HBAs in the number of ports on a single board, the amount of memory, and available processing power.

Just like HBAs in host systems, the HBAs/FAs in subsystems can fail too. To counteract this, subsystem designs enable host/subsystem communications to be shifted to an alternate HBA/FA.

Redundant Power and Cooling

Like most computer and network products designed for high availability, storage subsystems typically have redundant power supplies to maintain uninterrupted power delivery to storage devices and all other components in the subsystem. These power supplies usually are designed to share the power load during normal operations and have the ability to provide consistent power levels during and after the failure of the other power supply.

Should a power loss occur, subsystems with battery backup power enable the subsystem to continue processing I/Os from host systems. The basic idea is to provide a window of coverage that allows the subsystem to process I/Os for a limited period of time and flush data from cache memory to nonvolatile disk storage.

It's never a good idea to cut off power to a storage subsystem through anything other than a planned orderly shutdown process. Therefore, it is recommended that subsystems without integrated battery backup power be connected to suitable uninterruptible power supply (UPS) systems.

Most storage subsystems are also designed with redundant fans that can provide the necessary airflow to maintain acceptable operating temperatures in a subsystem should one of the fans fail. Sometimes fan failures are not taken as seriously as disk drive failures, because no data is stored in a fan. However, devices that run hot are more likely to fail than those that run within the vendor's recommended specifications.

Capacity Scalability

Another important benefit of device aggregation is the increased scalability of block storage address spaces. By combining the storage address spaces of multiple devices, it is possible to create virtual devices that are many times larger than a single storage device and have the redundancy advantages discussed previously. Large subsystems can contain over 1000 drives with a total aggregate capacity larger than 150 TB. This gives administrators the ability to create multiple large virtual storage devices for a number of applications and systems while maintaining spare storage capacity that can be used where and when it is needed.

Capacity Scaling with Striping

The most common way to aggregate devices to achieve higher storage capacities uses a technique called *striping*. Striping writes and reads data across multiple storage devices in rapid succession. The storage capacities of the individual devices are aggregated to form a larger storage address space.

A simple analogy for data striping is a paint sprayer that sprays paint across multiple boards lined up in sequence. As the sprayer moves across the boards, a small amount of paint is deposited on each.

Unlike spray painting, the process of striping data is precise. Data striping segments data into regularly sized *stripes,* which are then transmitted to multiple storage devices in rapid succession.

Similar to mirroring and RAID, which were discussed earlier in this chapter, disk subsystem controllers receive storage commands from a host system and then parcel them out to individual devices. The file system or database that is responsible for using the storage is not aware that the subsystem is aggregating data by striping it. Figure 5-6 shows four disk drives aggregated by striping to form a virtual device with a larger storage address space.

In practice, striping is almost always accomplished through RAID technology to achieve the protection of data redundancy.

Capacity Scaling with Concatenation

Another way to scale storage capacity by aggregating devices is called *concatenation*. In a nutshell, concatenation fills each device, more or less in sequence. In other words, data is not subdivided into small pieces and scattered across multiple devices, as it is with striping; instead it is written together on a single device. Concatenation is not nearly as popular or commonly used as striped RAID, considering it lacks the redundancy and performance advantages of striped RAID.

Figure 5-6 *Four Devices Aggregated by Striping to Form a Larger Virtual Device*

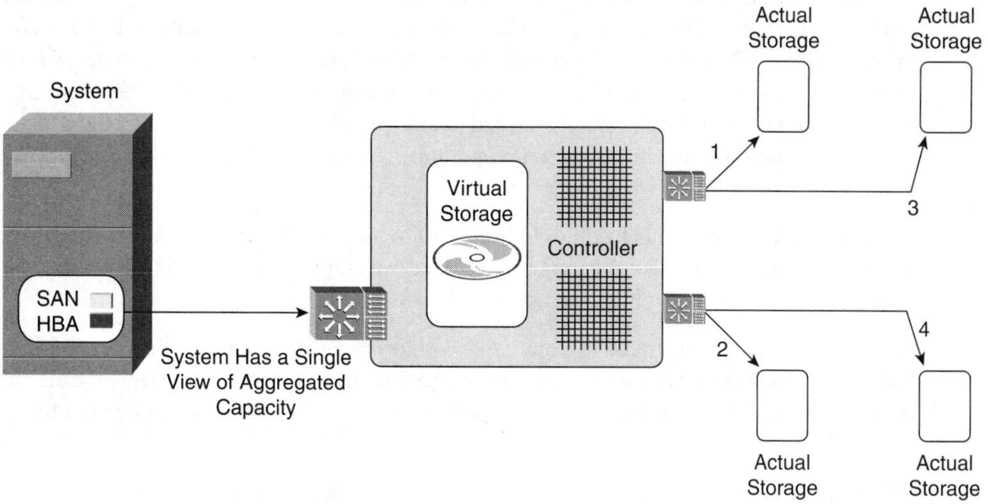

Performance Advantages of Subsystems

The electromechanical nature of storage devices limits their performance at orders of magnitude lower than microprocessor and memory devices and, thereby, creates I/O bottlenecks. Server systems and the clients that connect to them can be particularly affected. Subsystems address the performance limitations of storage devices through three different mechanisms:

- Parallelism through overlapped I/Os on multiple devices using data striping and mirroring
- Disk caching with high-speed memory
- Write-back caches

Parallelism and Overlapped I/Os

Because disk drives are inherently much slower than processors and memory devices, increasing storage I/O performance depends primarily on the ability to perform storage work in parallel on multiple devices. Parallelism with storage depends on the ability to use *overlapped* I/Os on multiple devices.

Overlapping is a technique where multiple commands and data transfers are distributed on multiple devices simultaneously. Figure 5-3, which shows RAID operations between a subsystem controller and four disk drives, also shows the basic concept of overlapped I/Os. The amount of overlapping and parallelism achieved depends to a large degree on the type of device interconnect used in the subsystem. The topic of device interconnects is the subject of Chapter 7.

Overlapped I/Os are accomplished through two different approaches: striping and mirroring. Striping naturally provides the mechanism for parallel operations. The subsystem controller initiates buffer-to-buffer data transmissions with each drive, starting multiple I/O operations on multiple drives. Each drive performs the command and signals the controller when it is done or has data to transmit. The controller aggregates the responses from all drives before completing the operation with the host system. For read operations, this means assembling the data in order and transmitting it to the host. For write operations, it means acknowledging the successful completion of the host's write command.

Systems with requirements for high I/O rates often have storage configurations that stripe data over a large number of disk drives. Large database systems, in fact, might stripe data over hundreds of disk drives configured as several virtual devices.

Mirroring, which is illustrated in Figure 5-2, also provides parallelism for read operations. The subsystem controller can split read requests and send them to different drives. By distributing read requests on the two different drives in a mirror, read performance can be effectively doubled.

Mirroring does not provide parallelism for write I/Os because mirroring needs to create duplicate data on both disks in a mirror. Therefore, all writes must be written to both drives.

Caching and I/O Performance

Another common technology for improving storage I/O performance is *disk caching*. The basic idea of disk caching is simple: data that will probably be needed in the near future is stored in memory by the subsystem controller, where it can be retrieved quickly (within several nanoseconds), as opposed to taking several milliseconds to retrieve from disk. Whereas disk striping and mirroring cannot overcome the relatively lengthy delays caused by disk seeks and rotational latency, disk caching can overcome the delays, because it circumvents disk accesses altogether.

The general architecture for a caching controller includes a high-speed memory bus and RAM. An index is created in memory that maps to sections of the storage address space that the cache is associated with. When data from a specific storage location is loaded in the cache, the memory index is updated to indicate that the data is in cache.

All storage I/O requests are first processed by the caching process in the controller that checks the index. If the data is in cache, it is accessed there instead of on disk. The term *cache hit* refers to the occurrence of data being read from cache, and the term *cache miss* refers to the occurrence of data having to be read from a disk drive. Figure 5-7 illustrates the operation of a disk cache, including a cache hit and cache miss.

Figure 5-7 *Comparing a Cache Hit and a Cache Miss*

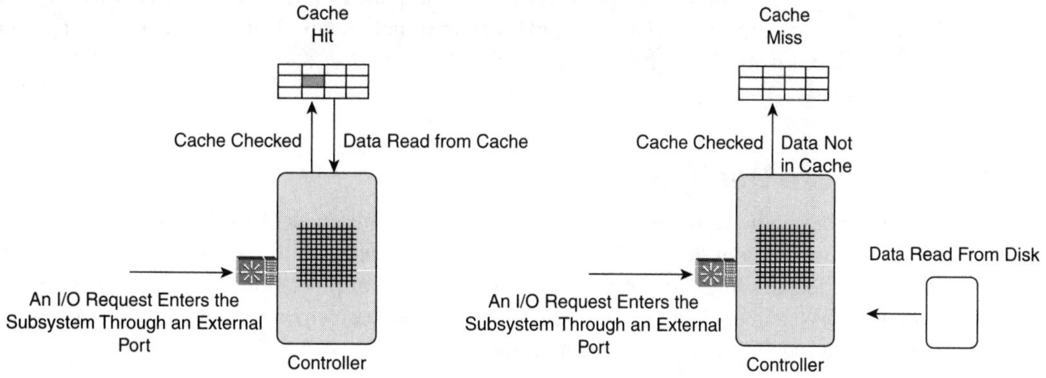

The effectiveness of disk caching depends to a large degree on the predictability of the I/O operations issued by the application that is reading and writing data. In general, caching is more effective for applications that read and write to certain blocks frequently. Applications that read and write large amounts of data sequentially, such as multimedia streaming and data warehousing, are not likely to benefit as much from disk caching.

Write-Through and Write-Back Caches

While caches can provide valuable performance benefits, they might introduce a risk of losing data if power is lost or the subsystem fails before the data in cache is written to permanent storage on disk.

Write-through caches eliminate the risk by always writing data to disk before acknowledging completion of the I/O operation. The write-through cache might write data into cache memory, but it also writes it to disk. The term *write-through* is used because the data is written through the cache function all the way to the disk. The I/O path to disk is not altered by the caching function. Some subsystems place the cache in the data path between the controller and disk drives. In that case, their write operations are always of the write-through variety.

Write-back caches are optimized for performance. They acknowledge the completion of a write operation after the data is written to cache and before it is written to permanent storage on disk. The term *write-back* refers to the fact that data is first written to cache memory and later written back to disk.

Obviously, it is important to have battery backup power for cache memory if the write-back cache is being used; otherwise, data could easily be lost during a power outage. Some subsystems have integrated battery backup within the enclosure or controller, and others might rely on external UPS systems.

NOTE The memory used in disk subsystems for caching is some of the most expensive memory sold. Therefore, it's a good idea to understand whether or not the applications you are buying cache for will benefit from the cache.

Modular Enclosure Designs

Storage subsystems facilitate the management of large numbers of storage devices by incorporating modular designs for fast servicing and manageability of all components. Storage devices, especially high-performance devices, use a lot of power and create a lot of heat. Storage subsystem enclosures are engineered to provide an environment that meets the power and cooling requirements of a large number of devices.

Hot Swapping

Most storage subsystems today are designed to allow the servicing of redundant components. *Hot swapping* refers to the ability to remove and replace (*hot swap*) components without having to shut down the subsystem.

The technology that supports hot swapping includes the following:

- **Component monitoring and analysis** to identify devices that might be operating near or past their limits or have failed altogether. This includes relatively unintelligent devices, such as cooling fans, and also includes more intelligent devices, such as disk drives.
- **Management interfaces for alerts and management,** including various forms of administrator notification, logical indicators within management consoles, and physical indicators, such as lights or audio signals.
- **Logical and algorithm adjustments** that are needed to maintain data integrity. For example, when disk drives fail, the subsystem controller has to adjust its RAID or mirroring operations to operate in *degraded* or *reduced mode* without the missing device. This topic is discussed in much more detail in Chapter 9.
- **Physical cabling and connectors** that facilitate removing and inserting components. Electrical circuits and connection buses/networks need to be able to operate without interruption while components are removed and inserted.

NOTE This matter of removing and inserting components transparently can be surprisingly convoluted and difficult. FC loop technology provides an example of how getting this wrong more or less sank a whole segment of the industry. Devices inserted or removed from FC loops force the devices on the loop to reestablish their prioritization and addresses. As it turned out, this process did not work nearly as well as expected and, in some instances, caused the complete failure of the SAN. This completely unacceptable situation drove the market toward switched topology networks (referred to as *fabrics* in the FC community). Today FC loops are mostly limited to internal subsystem connections in which the subsystem manufacturer can completely control the environment.

Not all subsystems support hot swapping. Instead, they might support the removal and replacement of components only if all I/O activities are stopped. This is known as *warm swapping*. It is obviously not quite as convenient as hot swapping, because it might force administrators to shut down applications to ensure that no I/O activities are taking place.

Hot Spares

In addition to device redundancy and hot swapping, many subsystems also provide *hot-spare* devices that are waiting and ready to step in when a production device fails.

Hot-spare devices are connected to the same power circuits and subsystem controllers as the other disk drives in the subsystem. They are powered on and identified as usable devices by the subsystem's controllers, but they are not used for storage until another device fails.

In the case of disk subsystems, the subsystem controller recognizes the disk failure and ceases operations with the failed disk. At that point, any mirrors and RAID arrays that were defined on the failed drive are operating in *degraded* or *reduced mode*. The controller then begins to activate the hot spare by recreating the same partitions on the hot spare that had been defined for the failed drive. After the partitions are recreated, they are ready to be repopulated with data from the other partitions on functioning drives.

The data repopulation process, also known as a *data rebuild,* can be started at any time. Most subsystems give administrators a choice between starting data rebuilds immediately when the hot spare is ready or at a later time chosen by the administrator. Chapter 9 discusses the data rebuild process in greater detail.

Storage Enclosure Services

The storage industry has created a standard for management of the environmental characteristics of storage subsystems called SCSI enclosure services (SES). SES is a fairly large specification with many different parts. Viewed primarily as an optional specification, vendors have implemented different aspects of this extensive standard. Although SES does not impact the interoperability of a storage subsystem in performing its primary functions, the subsystem's ability to be managed by third-party management software might be related to the extent to which it supports SES.

Modular Cabinet Components

Some storage subsystems are designed for modular configuration and scalability. This can include external connectors and cabling intended to expand the storage capacity of the subsystem with devices located in an expansion cabinet, as shown in Figure 5-8.

Figure 5-8 *Single Subsystem Connected to an Expansion Cabinet to Increase Storage Capacity*

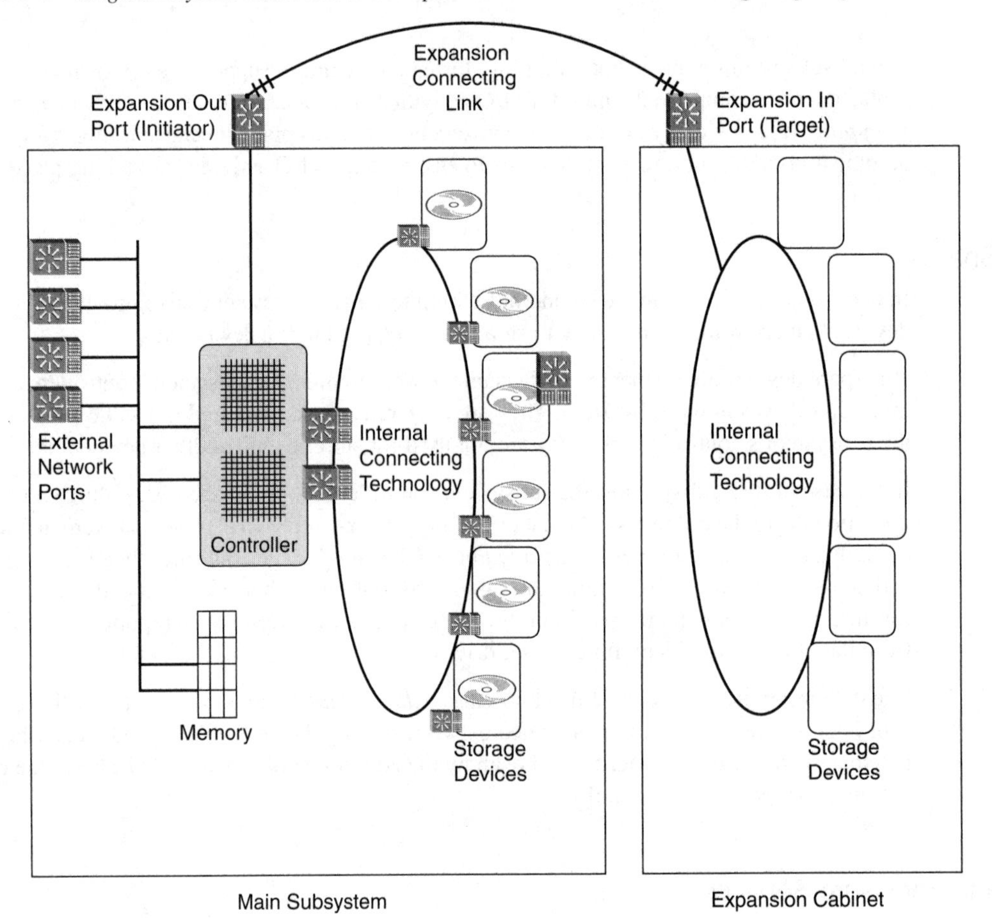

A subsystem controller in an existing subsystem enclosure would typically manage the devices inside the expansion cabinet. However, it is certainly possible to add additional controllers in expansion cabinets to achieve performance scaling as well as high availability features. Such designs would be much more complicated than a simple expansion cabinet and would likely require clustering technologies and traffic in addition to storage I/O traffic.

Common Functions of Storage Subsystems

Storage subsystems vary considerably in their designs and the choice of technologies that are inplmented in them. Yet, most storage subsystems share common characteristics and functions. The management techniques for accessing these functions may differ from product to product, but the architectural underpinnings are consistent. For instance, storage address space management is a basic function that can be controlled and managed many different ways.

One of the most important functional areas in storage subystem is the way the subsystem accommodates connections to multiple host systems and multiple HBAs in those systems. The sections on multiplexing I/Os and LUN masking are intended to give readers insight into ways enterprise subsystems can support a large number of host systems.

Storage Address Space Management

Of all the functions storage subsystems provide, the most important is managing the block storage address spaces of the storage devices that are part of the subsystem.

The techniques of mirroring, RAID, and striping, previously discussed in this chapter, are all examples of managing a storage address space. While it is easiest to discuss these types of storage virtualization techniques using an entire disk drive as the smallest granular address element, in fact storage address space manipulations are actually performed on logical partitions of disk drives.

Disk drives in a subsystem are partitioned into logical entities that are combined with other logical entities on other disk drives to form mirrors, stripes, and RAID arrays. A disk drive can have one or more partitions. Figure 5-9 shows a collection of five disk drives in a subsystem. The disk drives have been partitioned and combined to form six different virtual devices for use by host systems.

Figure 5-9 *Disk Drive Partitions Forming RAID Arrays and Mirrors*

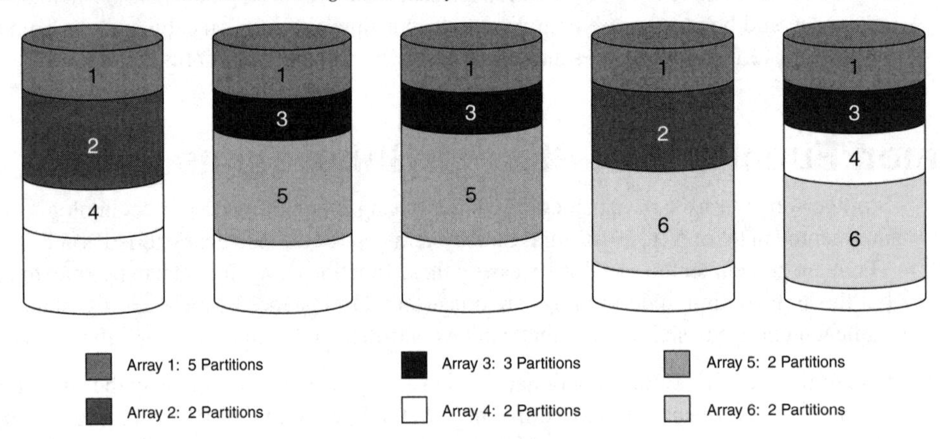

Differentiating Arrays and Subsystems

The term *array* is often used incorrectly to refer to a disk subsystem, as in "We just purchased a new array for our Oracle systems." Although the context makes this statement clear enough, the term *array* refers to the combination of multiple storage address spaces configured for use with striping and mirroring technology (in other words, as a RAID array). A single subsystem can have multiple RAID arrays of different sizes and levels running concurrently.

The word *subsystem* is preferred when discussing a storage product built by integrating controllers, power supplies, networking interfaces, cache memory, internal buses, and disk drives. With DAS technology, the difference between RAID and subsystems was not as significant as it is with storage networking. In a storage network, a RAID array can be constructed from elements on different subsystems. A simple example of this is an array of subsystems, like the one shown in Figure 5-10.

Figure 5-10 *Array of Subsystems*

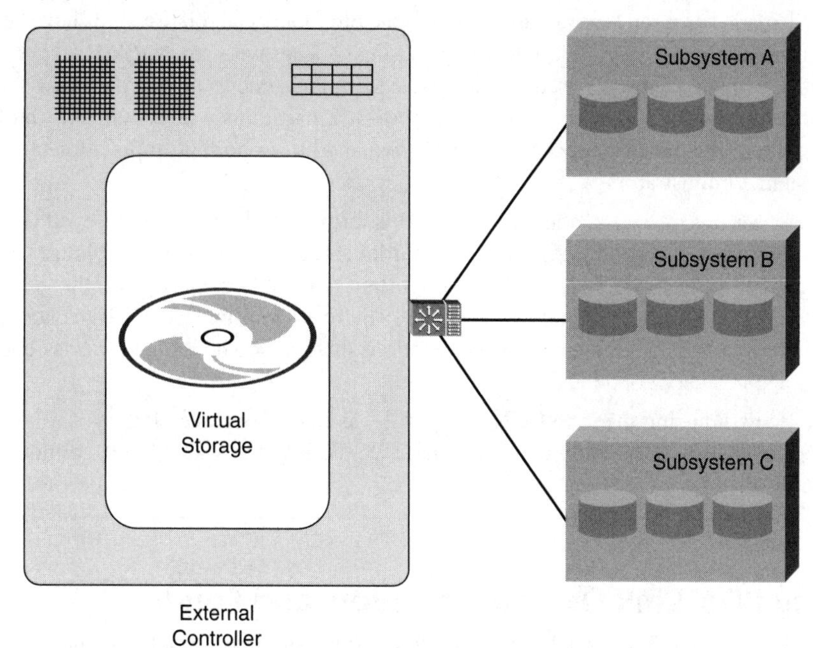

Accessing Exported Storage with LUN Addressing

The storage address spaces that are made available to systems are sometimes referred to as *exported storage*. In other words, systems use the storage that is exported by subsystems in a storage network.

Exported storage is often referred to by the SCSI term *logical unit number (LUN),* as in the sentence "I have three LUNs larger than a terabyte." Technically, LUNs are used to access storage devices and resources and are responsible for interpreting and exchanging SCSI protocol information with host controllers. The term LUN is *not* intended to be synonymous with exported storage. For instance, LUNs are also used to access storage devices that do not contain storage address spaces, such as robotic controllers in tape subsystems.

NOTE Misusing the term LUN is an excellent example of the sort of terminology sloppiness that makes storage networking more difficult than it needs to be. Storage professionals have been known to explain that LUN is another word for virtual disk. Well, they're not the same thing at all. There is a huge difference between the way storage resources are accessed and their characteristics and functions. Calling exported storage a LUN is akin to saying that a phone number is the same thing as a house.

The problem is that the technology has evolved from physical entities to logical constructs that have made some old terms obsolete, while the old functional relationships have been preserved. For example, the aggregation of storage address spaces with parity RAID arrays forms "virtual disks," because they are used by the host system the same as physical disks. Of course, the virtual disk RAID array is an aggregation of disk partitions with redundancy built in. It is considerably more complex than a disk drive and has important implications for database and system administrators.

Which brings us back to the term *LUN*. This term actually works pretty well to identify a specific storage resource exported by a particular subsystem, as in the phrase "Sunshine, LUN 14" or "Stormy, LUN 32." It is important to be able to clarify whether you are talking about "this LUN 12" or "that LUN 12" when there are multiple LUN 12s to choose from in your environment. Developing naming conventions that include how LUNs are assigned to exported storage is a very good idea.

Try to avoid using the term LUN generically, as in the sentence "Put five LUNs together in a blender and mash them up with some fried WAN links to make a big#$! remote LUN sandwich."

Multiplexing I/Os, Link Oversubscription, and Fan-In

At first thought, it's normal to suppose that a subsystem port would expose a single LUN for host systems to use, but this is not the case. In most cases there are several LUNs, representing several different storage address spaces being accessed through a single port.

The fact is that gigabit-speed SAN connections and subsystem ports have more bandwidth than most systems can utilize; in fact, they have more bandwidth than several PC-based systems typically need and can support. If subsystem ports were dedicated to specific host-LUN connections, they would be idle most of the time.

Therefore, it is common for switch-to-subsystem links to carry multiple host-LUN connections simultaneously. This is called *oversubscribing* the link or *fan-in* and is illustrated in Figure 5-11.

The amount of fan-in for any subsystem port depends on the I/O capabilities of the subsystem controller and the characteristics of the applications using it. Applications with light I/O requirements, such as most Windows servers, might be able to oversubscribe 15 or more host-LUN sessions. Other applications with heavy I/O requirements might limit oversubscription to four to six sessions; or they might even be assigned as a dedicated link.

Figure 5-11 *SAN Fan-In: Multiple Host-LUN Connections on an Oversubscribed Switch-to-Subsystem Link*

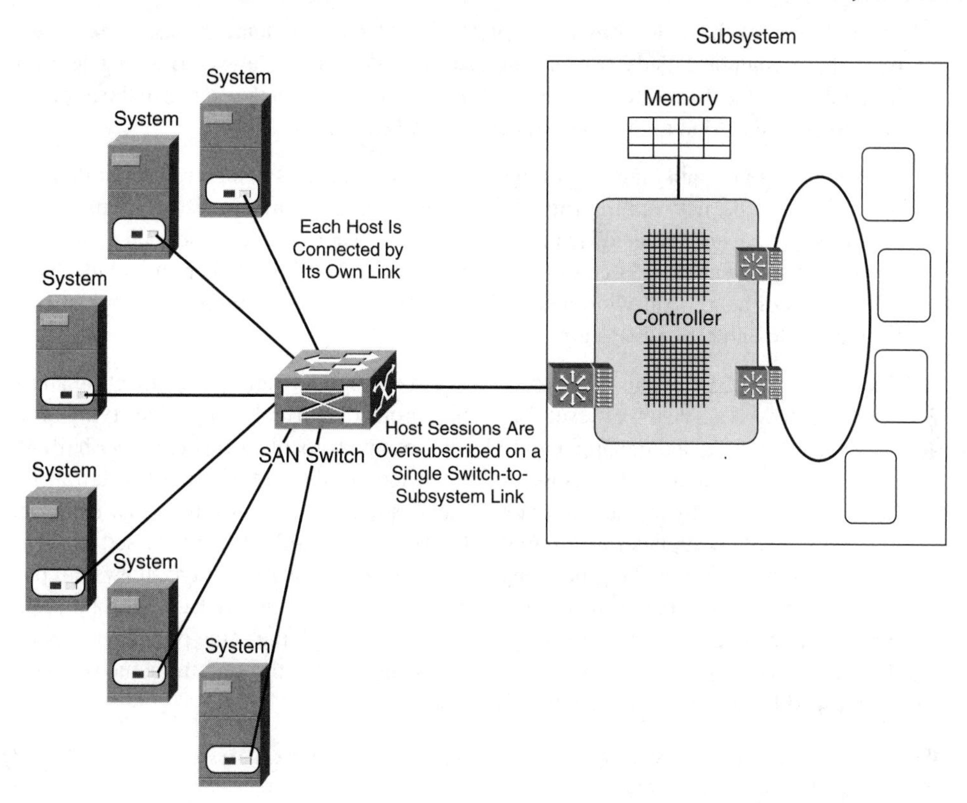

NOTE

There are no set rules of thumb for oversubscribing switch-to-subsystem links. Some of the variables besides the application include the networking technology used and the capabilities of the subsystem. When planning to oversubscribe a switch/subsystem link, however, you should watch out for a few surprises.

First, you should plan for backup traffic, which is probably much heavier than the day-to-day I/O traffic that the applications generate.

Second, consider how oversubscription works with traffic management plans, including multipathing, zoning, or virtual SANs/virtual LANs (VSANs/VLANs). Obviously, if you plan to segregate the I/O traffic in the SAN, make sure you don't also plan to multiplex primary and secondary paths over a single switch-subsystem link.

LUN Masking

Most subsystems have the ability to prevent unwanted or accidental access to exported storage through a technique called *LUN masking*. LUN masking offers a way to segregate traffic at the location where the data is stored, which is a pretty good idea, but the details of the implementation need to be understood to avoid unexpected mistakes.

LUN masking in a subsystem is similar to filtering by routers in a network, but there are some tricky details. Like network filtering, the subsystem is configured to discard transmissions from host systems that are "masked" from accessing them. There are no prescribed methods for LUN masking implementation. For example, a subsystem could keep either an include-list or an exclude-list of host world-wide-names that it would use to determine if I/O operations would be allowed to enter the subsystem.

The tricky part of LUN masking is rooted in the orthogonal nature of connecting and storing functions in SANs. The lower-level connecting protocol carries half the identifying information needed for filtering, and the application layer storing protocol carries the other half. More explicitly, the host address that is located in the source_ID field of the network transmission header is processed by the network port logic. Also, the LUN subaddress that is located in the header of the SCSI application command descriptor block (CDB) is processed by a part of the storage controller logic. The processing would not be an issue if storage subsystem ports were not oversubscribed, but they are, and host systems that access certain LUNs through a particular port should be masked from accessing other LUNs through the same port. Figure 5-12 illustrates how two different host systems accessing storage through the same subsystem port are masked from accessing each other's storage.

Figure 5-12 *LUN Masking: Two Host Systems Accessing Data Through a Single Subsystem Port Are Masked from Accessing Each Other's LUNs*

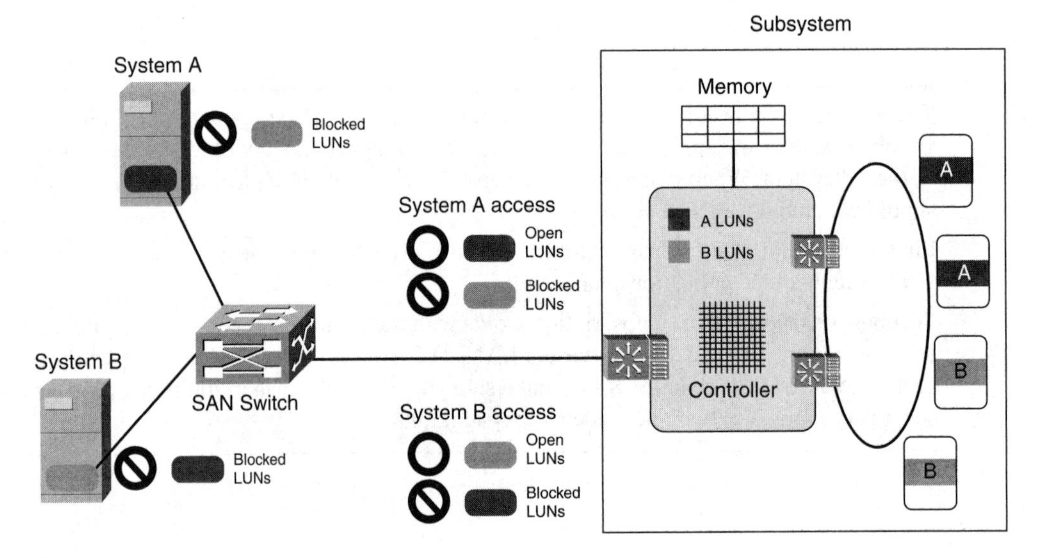

LUN masking is sometimes implemented in a way that spoofs host systems from discovering that masked LUNs even exist. This technique is rooted in the SCSI protocol discovery process, in which a host system discovers all available target addresses (and LUNs) by issuing a SCSI inquiry command to all addresses. The protocol is designed so that all SCSI targets acknowledge the inquiry, sending back ID information including product name, firmware release levels, and attached LUNs. LUN masking spoofs hosts by not acknowledging certain LUNs to certain hosts. Systems that do not discover LUNs do not use them.

This approach is a bit like trying to stop telemarketing phone calls by having an unlisted number and using caller ID to screen calls before answering. However, this approach does not prevent access from systems to storage for other commands that the systems could conceivably send. Any entity on the SAN with access to a subsystem port has the ability to send any SCSI commands to it.

NOTE

It's a good thing SCSI-based LUN masking exists, but the situation could be much better than it is. In fact, there might never be a good solution for access control using SCSI discovery mechanisms because they were never designed for shared storage environments.

This is one of the reasons I get excited about virtual networking technologies for SANs. Similar to the way VLAN or VSAN switches work, subsystems could assign virtual networking IDs to storage address spaces and discard incoming transmissions that lack proper credentials. A consistent mechanism for traffic segregation among switches and subsystems would be truly valuable. It's certainly not strong security, but it's much better than spoofing the discovery process and letting everything else fly through unchecked.

Integrating virtual networking in a storage subsystem would require new designs that incorporate switching technology. OK, so what? Isn't this why the whole thing is called storage *networking,* anyway?

The SMI Standard and Container Management

The Storage Networking Industry Association (SNIA) began in the late 1990s as an association of storage networking vendors working on several fronts to advance the technology and markets for storage networking. From its inception, one of the primary goals of SNIA was finding ways to manage heterogeneous storage environments. The group's work has resulted in the Storage Management Initiative (SMI), which was defined by the release of its first specification (SMI-S) in the spring of 2003.

SMI divides management tasks into three areas: storage resource management, container management, and information management. Storage address space management is considered part of container management in SMI. Besides subsystem controller technology, SMI's container management also includes volume management software, RAID technology, and storage virtualization.

SNIA's SMI is based on the object-oriented Common Information Model (CIM) of the Distributed Management Task Force (DMTF). SMI provides the underpinnings for consistent management methods through consistent programmatic interfaces that are exported by SMI-compliant entities in a storage network. One of the most important advantages of SMI is that it does not require third-party management agents to be loaded.

Of course, the software behind the interfaces has to be developed and tested across the entire industry—a process that will take several years and much hard work. Nonetheless, SNIA's goal is to attain basic SMI interoperability throughout the industry by the end of 2005.

Redundant Access to Subsystem Storage

A single exported storage address space can be accessed through two different subsystem ports to achieve redundant paths. For example, a single address space can be accessed with the same LUN ID through both ports in a dual-port subsystem. In other words, port redundancy in a subsystem is achieved by configuring LUN access through multiple subsystem ports.

The assignment of LUNs to primary and secondary ports can be done any number of ways, depending on the amount of storage traffic generated by applications and host systems. Of course, it is important to verify that the primary and secondary ports being used are actually on two different HBAs/FAs to avoid a single point of failure in the connection path. The topic of connection redundancy in SANs is explored in Chapter 11.

JBOD

Much of this chapter has focused on discussing disk storage subsystems that incorporate storage address space management as a key feature. A lower-cost alternative is *JBOD,* short for just a bunch of disks. JBOD does not provide redundancy, address space management, caching, or storage applications. It simply provides power and packaging benefits and centralized access to a collection of disk drives.

JBOD cabinets have a number of physical ports, and the disks inside are made available through LUNs assigned to those ports. JBOD subsystems export storage as raw disks without first partitioning them or creating redundancy with disk mirroring or RAID arrays. Redundancy is achieved through the use of host-based volume management software or through virtualization modules running in network switches and storage appliances.

Hot swapping might be supported if the JBOD cabinet has been designed to support removing and inserting devices while operating. System administrators are responsible for ensuring that all I/O operations are stopped to affected JBOD disk drives before removing and replacing disk drives.

Tape Subsystems and Disk Subsystems for Backup

Another important application for subsystem technology is the automation of storage for backup and recovery. Backup and recovery is one of the primary ongoing storage applications in most Information Technology (IT) organizations. As the amount of data has increased, many organizations are finding it necessary to automate backup tasks to reduce errors and improve administrator efficiency. The application of backup is discussed in Chapter 13, "Network Backup: The Foundation of Storage Management."

Backup and recovery in storage networks uses three basic types of storage subsystems, each with its own variations:

- Autoloaders
- Libraries
- Disk subsystems

Autoloaders

The basic idea of a tape autoloader is to provide automated tape changes for one or two tape drives. Autoloaders are relatively small subsystems with small footprints and the ability to store up to 20 tapes. A robotic mechanism changes the tapes as needed under the control of backup software. Autoloaders are intended to be dedicated to large servers or shared among small groups of smaller servers.

Autoloaders typically have parallel SCSI interfaces and do not have integrated SAN interfaces, which means they need to be connected to some form of SAN/SCSI router to use them on the SAN. As SCSI routers add significant cost relative to the cost of an autoloader, autoloaders have not been as widely deployed in SANs as tape libraries.

Libraries

Tape libraries pick up where autoloaders leave off and grow to be fairly large in some cases. Tape libraries for storage networks can hold up to 16 tape drives and store thousands of tapes. Tape libraries are commonly used in SANs to centralize backup operations. They offer significant management advantages over manual tape administration methods and can contribute significant savings to backup administration.

Unlike autoloaders, libraries are available with SAN interfaces—either through the use of embedded HBAs or by implementing SAN/SCSI storage routers. In addition, libraries usually have embedded bar code readers to identify tapes quickly as opposed to having to load tapes into tape drives so that the software can identify them.

Libraries might also have the ability to initiate data transfers by functioning as data movers for serverless backup products.

Disk Subsystems

Disk subsystems are becoming much more commonly used for backup to increase backup performance. Disk storage can be used the way disk drives normally are or can be made to operate as virtual tape libraries using device and media emulation techniques. After copies of backup data are written to disk storage, tape equipment is often used to make redundant and historical copies of the data. Some backup subsystems integrate disk and tape in a single backup subsystem. This approach can significantly simplify the restore process compared to using nonintegrated disk and tape subsystems.

The entire topic of backup and recovery is covered more extensively in Chapter 13.

Summary

Storage subsystems are like enclosed networks within the broader storage network. An amazing set of components, functions, and features are available in storage subsystems in SANs. The sophistication of large storage subsystems is truly impressive.

This chapter gave an overview of the structures, functions, and characteristics of these essential SAN machines. While the descriptions are generic in nature, the principles described can be used to analyze and discuss a wide variety of storage subsystem technologies.

Q&A

1. List four types of connecting technologies used in storage subsystems.
2. Name two types of device redundancy.
3. True or false: Disk drives can have only a single connecting port.
4. How is battery backup used in a subsystem?
5. True or false: Temperature is never a problem for disk subsystems.
6. What form of device redundancy does not increase capacity?
7. Name two ways in which performance can be boosted in disk subsystems.
8. What is the difference between hot swapping and hot sparing?
9. Explain the difference between a subsystem and an array.
10. True or false: LUN masking blocks I/Os.

Upon completing this chapter, you will be able to

- Discuss the relevance of SCSI technology for storage networking
- Analyze SAN system and subsystem designs using the SCSI architecture model, including the roles of initiators and targets
- Explain the difference between a SCSI logical unit and a LUN and what both of them do
- Illustrate how tagged command queuing and extended copy functions work
- Describe the role HBAs have in SCSI processes in storage networks

CHAPTER 6

SCSI Storage Fundamentals and SAN Adapters

In hindsight, it's relatively easy to analyze storage as having three distinct functions: filing, storing, and connecting. However, those distinctions were not always obvious due to the close integration of the storage and connecting functions. For example, Small Computer Systems Interface (SCSI) storage technology was initially developed as a combination of storing and connecting functions. When you bought SCSI products, you assumed they were going to connect to a parallel SCSI bus using standard SCSI connectors. Over time, there got to be many different bus and connector options to choose from, but the perception remained that the storage and the connection were the same intermingled technology. Today, with a number of bus and network connectivity options to chose from, it's much easier to see that SCSI storage processes and the underlying bus or network are distinct, independent technologies.

There is no way to understand the workings of network storage without knowing something about the architecture and logic operations of SCSI. SCSI processes are used in virtually all storage area network (SAN) implementations as the application layer that does storing work.

This chapter examines the logical architecture and structure of SCSI, including a discussion of the roles host bus adapters (HBAs) and storage controllers have in SCSI.

NOTE Another protocol used in SANs is FICON (short for *FI*ber *CON*nection). FICON is the newest version of IBM mainframe I/O technology designed to run on Fibre Channel (FC) networks. FICON's origins begin with the legacy mainframe Enterprise System Connection (ESCON) protocol that was introduced by IBM in 1991 as the first commercial implementation of a storage I/O network over fiber-optic cabling. ESCON works well but is limited by a transfer rate of 17 MBps and requires a relatively high number of physical connections and paths between systems and storage. FICON, as a protocol for FC networks, can take advantage of FC's greatly improved data transfer rates as well as its multiplexing capabilities. The result is faster performance along with much simpler, consolidated configurations.

Mainframe systems have a completely different storage I/O architecture than open-systems computers. The controller designs, transmission mechanisms, and data structures are all different from those used in SCSI. Therefore, FICON has a unique set of requirements and operating characteristics. As such, FICON is considered an advanced topic that is not covered in this book.

The Architecture and Logic of SCSI

The SCSI communications architecture is a logical system of commands and responses exchanged between systems and storage, encompassing such things as addressing, naming, and error-correction procedures. The primary role of the SCSI architecture is to provide a reliable abstraction layer between systems and storage devices. Without a storage abstraction layer, every application would need to incorporate details about the operations of every storage device used with it. This situation would clearly be unacceptable, so it was necessary for the computer and storage industries to develop standard interfaces for both systems and storage devices. SCSI was developed as a standard storage abstraction for open-systems computers.

History of SCSI

SCSI began its development in 1981 with work done by Shugart Associates and NCR Corporation, which were both looking for ways to connect disk drives to systems. SCSI was originally called SASI, for Shugart Associates Systems Interface. In December of 1981, the ANSI standards organization created the X3T9.2 technical committee for the continued development of this work, and it was renamed SCSI. The first SCSI standard was approved and published in 1986. At the time, the protocol and the interconnect were tightly integrated as a single combined technology.

Since then SCSI has undergone two major expansions. SCSI-2 expanded the width of the SCSI bus and increased its clock speed. SCSI-3 articulated the architectural structure of SCSI communications, separated the various technology elements, and created multiple, separate committees to work on these elements in parallel.

The T10 SCSI Standards Committees

The ongoing standards work in SCSI is performed by the T10 Technical Committee of the International Committee for Information Technology Standards (INCITS). Readers interested in reading draft standards documents should visit the T10 website at http://www.t10.org/.

SCSI-3 Connection Independence

The most significant change between SCSI-2 and SCSI-3 was the abstraction of logical storage functions from the underlying connection technology. This separation allows SCSI processes to be transmitted as an application over virtually any kind of network. In general, you can assume the use of SCSI-3 logic, processes, and protocols in any type of network storage implementation. The SCSI-3 standards documents make it clear that SCSI protocols are intended to be implemented independently of the connecting technology.

SCSI Architecture Model

One of the key elements of the SCSI protocol is the communications architecture for exchanging storage commands and data, which is defined by the SCSI Architecture Model (SAM). This section covers the following topics from the SCSI architecture model:

- Initiators and targets
- Initiator and target ports
- SCSI remote procedure call structure
- Overlapped I/O
- Asymmetrical communications in SCSI
- Dual-mode controllers
- No guarantee for ordered delivery
- SCSI ports, IDs, and names
- SCSI logical units
- Tasks, task sets, and tagged tasks
- SCSI nexus and connection relationships
- Tagged command queuing

Initiators and Targets

The SCSI protocol is based on using distributed communications between *initiators* and *targets*. In general, initiators are implemented in HBAs and systems, and targets are implemented in devices and subsystems, but there is no reason to limit one's concept of storage I/O to systems and storage. Initiators and targets can be implemented many different ways as long as the roles of both are clear.

The initiator controller issues a command, and the target controller acts on the request and makes a response. Figure 6-1 shows an HBA initiator issuing a command to a disk drive controller target.

Figure 6-1 *An HBA SCSI Initiator Communicating with a Disk Drive SCSI Target*

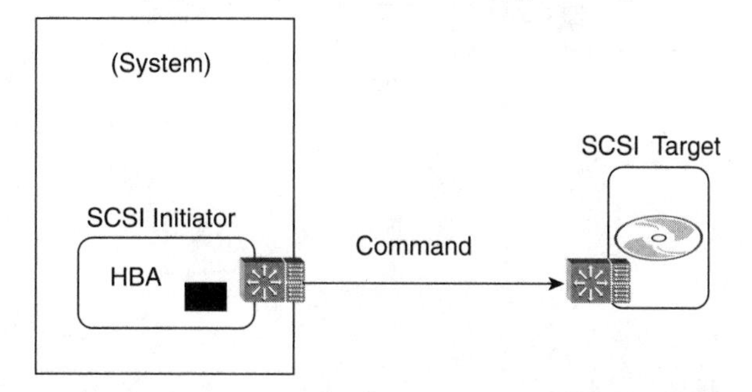

NOTE The SCSI specification is the ultimate source of clarity and confusion about SCSI. Written by engineers, it contains more than a few sentences like this one: "An initiator device name is a name (see 3.1.64) that is a SCSI device name (see 4.7.6) for a SCSI initiator device." As many times as I read this sentence, I cannot help but feel like a wiener dog chasing my own tail.

In an attempt to clarify some of the geek-speak in the SCSI spec, I've changed some of the terms to be more intuitive. For instance, I use the word *controller* where the standard language uses *device*. I simply prefer to call something that processes commands a controller as opposed to calling it a device, as the SCSI standard does. I also prefer to use *connecting technology* or *network* as opposed to *service delivery subsystem*.

The standard also refers to initiators and targets as clients and servers. While the communication model of client/server computing is used, SCSI components don't resemble what most people think of as clients and servers—especially in an environment that includes network attached storage (NAS) clients and servers.

Initiator and Target Ports

In the SCSI architecture model, the network ports that are part of initiator and target controllers are considered to be part of the connecting network and not part of the initiator or target controller function. This might seem counterintuitive, but it is the correct functional distinction. Network ports and the low-level drivers that control the formation and recognition of protocol data units (PDUs) and network operation are not involved with the storage processes of SCSI. They have connecting roles, but not storing roles. Figure 6-2 shows the same HBA and disk drive as Figure 6-1, but it identifies the communication ports as part of the connecting network, not part of the SCSI logical process.

Figure 6-2 *Communication Ports in SCSI as Part of the Connecting Network*

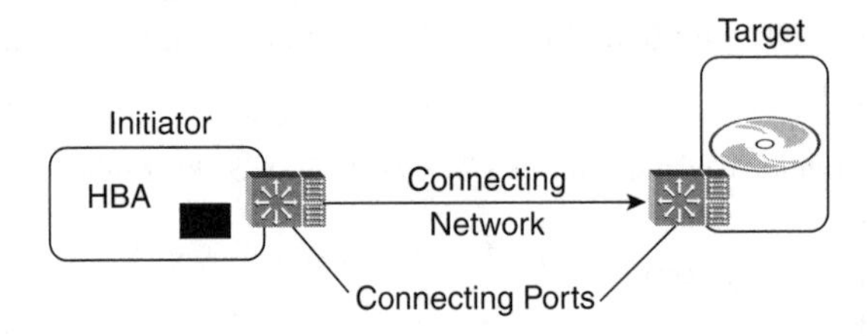

SCSI Remote Procedure Call Structure

The SCSI architecture model specifies a pair of controllers exchanging information as a sequence of commands and responses. Initiator-target communications use remote procedure calls, where the initiator transmits a command including the data being transmitted and any associated execution parameters. This command is addressed to a specific target controller ID. The target processes the command and responds with any requested outgoing data and any accompanying information about the command's completion status, including errors or failures.

The communication between the initiator and the target is asynchronous, which means the command is sent and then both the initiator and target disengage and go about conducting their respective tasks. When the target has a response to send to the initiator, it notifies the initiator, and they reconnect to manage the data transfer.

SCSI was designed with the assumption that a host system would be multitasking. Therefore, there is an inherent understanding in the SCSI communications model that targets might have multiple tasks to perform and might be busy doing other work and, therefore, cannot respond to new commands immediately.

When the initiator finishes transferring a command to its network port, the command is said to be *pending*. Any data transfers that accompany the command (READ or WRITE commands) are processed, and the command is completed when the target sends a response to the initiator. The response can be a command completion confirmation or a status message, such as an error or failure. Figure 6-3 illustrates the sequence of the SCSI command/response mechanism.

Figure 6-3 *Command/Response Sequence in SCSI*

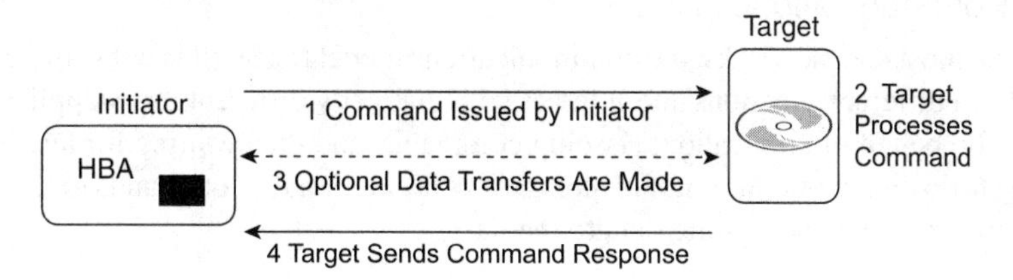

The initiator does not maintain constant contact with the target after sending the command so that it can be available for other work. This means the responses from targets are processed as interrupts from an HBA's device driver. Considering the number of interrupts that occur from storage I/O processes and the necessity to handle these interrupts correctly and quickly, it is easy to appreciate the interaction between the operating system kernel and the HBA's device driver software. This is why it is so important to check the OS support for storage HBAs and the various device drivers that are available. Unless an OS level is explicitly named in a device driver's support list, it should be assumed that the HBA and driver will not work in the system.

NOTE

Storage device driver development tends to be more of a black art, or alchemical process, than it is a clinical, predictable or scientific process. Experience working with devices and operating system kernels counts big time.

One of the challenges is the rate at which target-side responses occur, which determines the rate of host I/O interrupts. Target-side variables include cache size, RAID level, device capabilities, and file system fragmentation in addition to the application mix. The fact is, it is extremely difficult, if not impossible, to replicate actual scenarios in a development or test environment. That's one of the reasons things sometimes go awry.

Overlapped I/O

The SCSI communications architecture allows I/Os to be overlapped over the connecting bus or network. In other words, when a host initiator is finished issuing a command to one target, it can issue another command to the same or other targets before receiving a response for the first command. Responses from targets for different I/Os can be received in whatever order they finish processing.

For instance, an initiator can send a command to a tape drive that takes several minutes to complete and subsequently complete thousands of commands sent to disk drives that take only a fraction of a second each. Overlapped I/Os provide a high degree of parallelism for I/O communications and enable SCSI communications to be very efficient.

Asymmetrical Communications in SCSI

Unlike most data networks, the communications model for SCSI is not symmetrical. Both sides perform different functions and interact with distinctly different users/applications. Initiators work on behalf of applications, issuing commands and then waiting for targets to respond. Targets do their work on behalf of storage media, waiting for commands to arrive from initiators and then reading and writing data to media.

NOTE

If you think it seems goofy to say the user at the target side is storage media, you're right—it struck me as goofy, too, when I stumbled across that analysis. However, media *is* the thing at the end of the line on the target side. SCSI communications are asymmetrical, because there is something intelligent (a processor running applications) at one end and something unintelligent (media) at the other end.

So, while it is possible to put intelligent processors in storage subsystems and devices, the SCSI protocol was developed to manipulate unintelligent media with block storage addresses. The ramification of all this is that an "intelligent" storage controller on the target side of the exchange is limited to manipulating commands and addresses and is not capable of working with data objects.

There are huge differences between typical host HBA processes and storage target processes in devices or subsystems. The HBA needs to carefully manage operating system details, while the target has to manage the details of communications with multiple external initiators as well as internal storage targets. It might be tempting to describe a subsystem port as an HBA located in a subsystem, but that is not really true. The two implementations are very different.

Dual-Mode Controllers

Controllers can be designed to implement both initiator and target functions. Dual-mode controllers are useful for implementing the SCSI EXTENDED COPY command, discussed later in this chapter. Dual-mode controllers might also be implemented in SAN routers and virtualization appliances, as discussed in Chapter 12, "Storage Virtualization: The Power in Volume Management Software and SAN Virtualization Systems."

The simplest way to picture a dual-mode controller is a circuit board with two different physical ports—one port functioning as an initiator and the other port as a target. A storage subsystem could hypothetically use this type of design.

Another implementation model for a dual-mode controller is to use a single network port that operates as both an initiator and a target. Obviously the controller in this case needs to differentiate between the two different roles.

No Guarantee for Ordered Delivery

It is often also assumed that SCSI provides in-order delivery to maintain data integrity. In-order delivery was traditionally provided by the SCSI bus and, therefore, was not needed by the SCSI protocol layer. In SCSI-3, the SCSI protocol assumes that proper ordering is provided by the underlying connection technology. In other words, the SCSI protocol does not provide its own reordering mechanism and, therefore, the network is responsible for the reordering of transmission frames that are received out of order. This is the main reason why TCP was considered essential for the iSCSI protocol that transports SCSI commands and data transfers over IP networking equipment: TCP provided ordering while other upper-layer protocols, such as UDP, did not.

SCSI Ports, IDs, and Names

SCSI controllers can communicate over multiple networks simultaneously through different ports. They can also communicate through multiple ports connected to a single network. With this kind of flexibility built into the architecture, there obviously needs to be a way to identify ports distinctly to ensure safe, consistent operations.

The SCSI standard provides a mechanism for identifying controllers and their ports. All controller ports must have a unique identifier (port ID) on each network they are connected to.

For example, the port ID on the SCSI bus is a number between 0 and 15. The port ID on a FC fabric network is a 24-bit network address.

In addition to the port ID, there is also a port name that identifies each port uniquely. In FC, this port name is known as the worldwide name (WWN), which is a 64-bit hexadecimal value that is assigned to each port when the controller is being manufactured. These worldwide name values provide a mechanism to identify and address initiators and controllers in a SAN.

NOTE Naming in storage networking can be confusing. In addition to the port name, there is also an optional node name, known as the worldwide node name (WWNN), which sometimes forces the use of the acronym WWPN to differentiate the port name from the node name.

The idea of identifying the node could be useful as a way to identify a system or subsystem uniquely, but there are several tricky issues involved. For example, the WWNN is intended to identify a system, but it is generated by the HBA, not by the system itself. The problem is that a system might have multiple HBAs for different purposes, and those HBAs could each have a different WWNN. There might be cases when it would make sense to have a single WWNN for all the HBAs in the system, but there might be other cases where it is preferable to have different WWNNs.

Before SANs, there was not a big need for naming controllers, because the address space was limited to fewer than 16 controllers on a parallel SCSI bus. The parallel SCSI method of setting numerical values or physically positioning jumpers obviously could not work in a SAN environment with millions of addresses.

The situation becomes clear when considering a recovery from a disaster such as a large-scale loss of power, where it is paramount to quickly and accurately recreate storage configurations. Without a way to uniquely identify storage resources, it could be extremely difficult to quickly and accurately recreate the logical structure of the SAN. In other words, it's essential to have a persistent method of discovering and addressing storage resources. The combination of WWNs and the use of name services in SAN switches provides this mechanism.

SCSI Logical Units

SCSI targets have *logical units* that provide the processing context for SCSI commands. Essentially, a logical unit is a virtual machine (or virtual controller) that handles SCSI communications on behalf of real or virtual storage devices in a target. Commands received by targets are directed to the appropriate logical unit by a *task router* in the target controller.

The work of the logical unit is split between two different functions—the *device server* and the *task manager*. The device server executes commands received from initiators and is responsible for detecting and reporting errors that might occur. The task manager is the work scheduler for the logical unit, determining the order in which commands are processed in the queue and responding to requests from initiators about pending commands.

The *logical unit number (LUN)* identifies a specific logical unit (think virtual controller) in a target. Although we tend to use the term LUN to refer to a real or virtual storage device, a LUN is an access point for exchanging commands and status information between initiators and targets. Metaphorically, a logical unit is a "black box" processor, and the LUN is simply a way to identify SCSI black boxes.

Logical units are architecturally independent of target ports and can be accessed through any of the target's ports, via a LUN. A target must have at least one LUN, LUN 0, and might optionally support additional LUNs. For instance, a disk drive might use a single LUN, whereas a subsystem might allow hundreds of LUNs to be defined.

The process of *provisioning* storage in a SAN storage subsystem involves defining a LUN on a particular target port and then assigning that particular target/LUN pair to a specific logical unit. An individual logical unit can be represented by multiple LUNs on different ports. For instance, a logical unit could be accessed through LUN 1 on Port 0 of a target and also accessed as LUN 12 on port 1 of the same target. Figure 6-4 shows a two-port subsystem with a single logical unit being accessed this way.

Figure 6-4 *A Single Logical Unit Being Accessed Through Two Different Subsystem Ports Using Two Different LUNs*

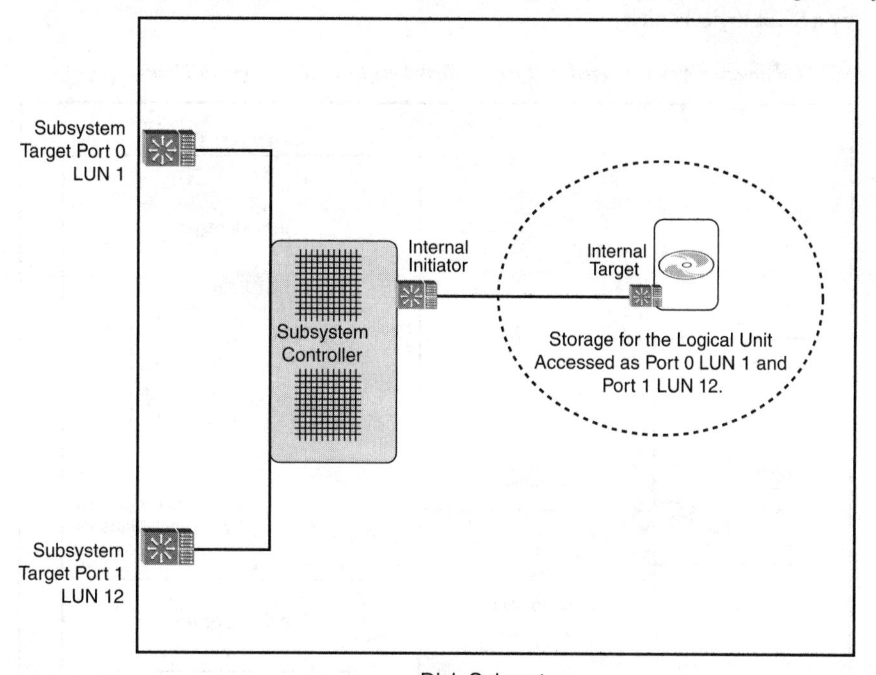

NOTE I've always thought the word "provisioning" was a bit off the mark for this, given its preexisting usage in data networking. The storage process described above always seemed much more like network protocol "binding" than it did network provisioning. Here is a definition for storage provisioning: it is the process of binding a virtual storage machine to a specific set of storage resources and making them available by one or more LUN IDs across one or more target ports.

Tasks, Task Sets, and Tagged Tasks

Commands in logical units are managed as *tasks*. SCSI tasks are placed in one or more queues, which are called *task sets*. The device server executes the tasks, and the task manager does what it sounds like—manages the various tasks in task sets. The use of multiple queues in SCSI provides both prioritization and optimization of storage I/O. SCSI queue management provides a multitasking environment for storage I/O processes to match the I/O requirements of multiprocessing servers.

SCSI's queuing capabilities are much more flexible than simple first-in, first-out (FIFO) or last-in, first-out (LIFO) queues, where low-priority applications can create I/O system bottlenecks. Instead, SCSI's queuing accommodates many different application I/O requirements simultaneously. This is one way the SCSI architecture supports high-throughput, multiprocessing computing environments. Figure 6-5 shows how multiple commands are managed as tasks in multiple task sets by a SCSI logical unit.

Figure 6-5 *SCSI Commands Are Managed as Tasks in Task Sets by a SCSI Logical Unit*

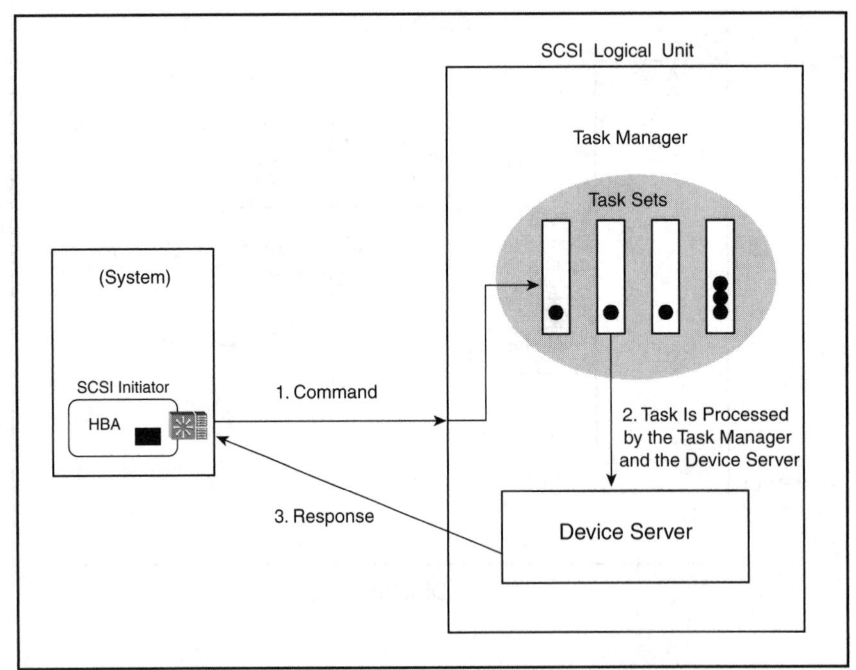

Tasks are further designated as being tagged or untagged. Tagging allows a group of commands to be transferred from an initiator to a logical unit using a sequential identifier for each command. Tagged commands and their associated tasks are placed together in a task set where the task manager can change the order in which they are processed. As each task completes, the logical unit responds to the initiator using the tag to identify the task. Tagging is used by multitasking applications that can have many independent I/Os, such as database applications.

SCSI Nexus and Connection Relationships

If you have been reading between the lines in the preceding sections, it might have occurred to you that there are multiple ways initiators can identify the communications they have with storage. The *nexus object* describes the initiator/storage communication relationship.

There are three nexus objects in SCSI:

- Initiator/target (an I_T nexus)
- Initiator/target/LUN (an I_T_L nexus)
- Initiator/target/LUN/tag (an I_T_L_Q nexus)

The type of nexus object used determines the number of concurrent commands that can be pending at any time. An I_T nexus allows only a single command between an initiator and a specific target. An I_T_L nexus allows a single command between an initiator and a specific logical unit. An I_T_L_Q nexus allows many possible commands to be pending, as long as the commands are tagged.

NOTE The SCSI nexus defines the SCSI path elements that are used for storage I/O processes, including multipathing. This definition of *path* is not necessarily intuitive to many networking people, who are accustomed to thinking about paths in TCP/IP networks. The underlying connecting bus or network is transparent to SCSI logical processes, which means that the SCSI path *cannot* include the network. The SCSI nexus entities, therefore, define the complete SCSI path.

Tagged Command Queuing

The most important feature of tagging in SCSI is *tagged command queuing (TCQ),* a mechanism that allows the logical unit's task manager to reorder tasks to optimize the performance of a storage device or subsystem.

Tagged command queuing was developed to optimize the performance of mechanical components in disk drives, particularly the disk arms and actuators. The basic idea is to reorder a group of commands to reduce the overall latency involved in seeking tracks on disk platters.

Assume there are 20 tagged tasks in a task set, each with a directive to read or write data across a random distribution of tracks on disk media. Without the ability to rearrange tasks, the seek time latency would be the average seek time for the drive. Using command queuing, the tasks could be structured so the actuator moves the minimal amount for each task as it moves from one task's track to the track of its nearest neighbor. Figure 6-6 contrasts the impact on seek times between targets that use tagged command queuing and those that do not.

Figure 6-6 *Differences in Seek Processes Used for Tagged Command Queuing and Untagged Commands*

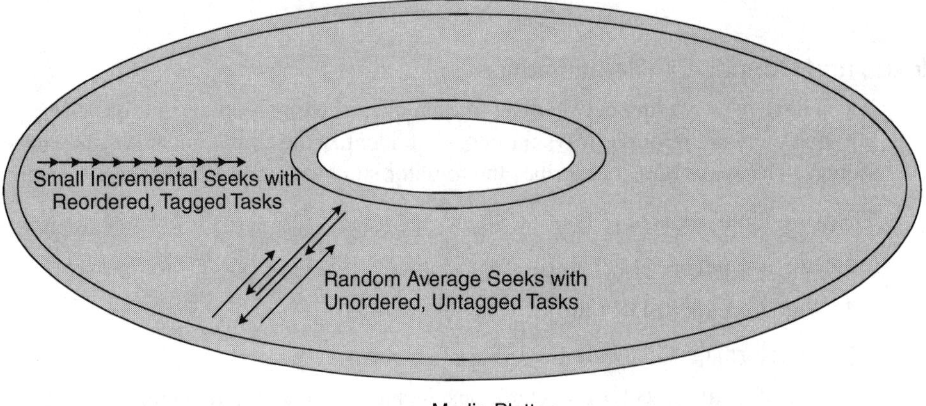

Tagged command queuing significantly reduces seek time latency for disk I/O operations. The degree of improvement depends heavily on the queue depth (the number of tasks in a task set). In general, the greater the queue depth is, the shorter the average seek time will be and the better storage performance will be.

SCSI Command Basics

SCSI has a rich command language that is used to move data between systems and storage quickly and accurately. Unlike commands used with systems and networking equipment, SCSI commands are rarely, if ever, entered from a command line or graphical user interface (GUI) by an administrator. Instead, SCSI commands are implemented programmatically and are embedded in software products, such as file systems and backup software. The sections that follow give a very abbreviated view of this deep and rich subject, including the following topics:

- Command descriptor blocks (CDBs)
- Types of SCSI commands
- Basic SCSI commands
- SCSI reservation
- Extended copy and third-party copy

Command Descriptor Blocks

Protocols provide a defined format for communications, allowing sending and receiving nodes to agree completely on what is being communicated. The format of the information that is exchanged is called a protocol data unit (PDU).

The PDU for SCSI commands is called a *command descriptor block (CDB)*. Initiators create CDBs, and the device server running in the logical unit interprets them. When the logical unit has finished processing the command, it responds by returning a status code for the command, along with any accompanying data, to the initiator.

Unlike most networking protocols, which have regularly-sized packet or frame sizes, SCSI CDBs do not have a prescribed, consistent length. Some commands are short, while others can be long. Implementations of SCSI-3 such as the Fibre Channel FCP protocol, define the way SCSI CDBs are mapped into their corresponding fixed-size network PDUs.

SCSI status codes have meanings that do not necessarily coincide with human intuition. A response signaling that a task has completed simply means that the task has finished processing; it does not necessarily mean that the intent of the command completed successfully. Only experienced storage and systems administrators who know what the status codes mean should attempt to use them when troubleshooting system I/O problems.

Types of SCSI Commands

There are several different types of commands in SCSI, reflecting the diversity of systems and devices it supports. In fact, multiple subcommittees in the T10 organization work on different subsets of the total specification. Some of the various types of commands in SCSI are as follows:

- **Primary commands (all devices)**—Considering the wide variety of functions afforded by SCSI and the mission-critical nature of storage, SCSI systems can be sizable and complex. Not surprisingly, the commands used to maintain a well-oiled SCSI environment have a great deal of depth. Primary SCSI commands are those that can be used by any system, device, or subsystem, including disk drives, tape drives, CD drives, printers, scanners, plotters, etc.
- **Block commands (storage devices such as disk drives)**—While there are many parts to storage and SCSI, the commands used to operate disk drives are the most critical and the most heavily used. SCSI block commands are primarily concerned with the operation of disk drives, but they also work with other block-storage rotating-media devices, such as CD and DVD drives. A related set of standards called reduced block commands is maintained for commands written for logical block devices that do not allow direct manipulation of their contents, but maintain a logical mapping of their contents.
- **Streaming commands (sequential access devices)**—Streaming commands control sequential-access devices. In general, sequential-access devices like tape drives are not considered random-access devices even though they can locate data anywhere on tape

media. Printers and plotters are other examples of streaming devices. There are two types of commands for streaming devices—those that contain positioning information and those that do not.

- **Media changer commands (removable media with robotics)**—The commands used to place and move media within automated changers as well as to insert and remove media from devices within changers constitute media changer commands. These include tape and optical media changers. At some point, they will likely also include the ability to change removable hard disk drives.
- **Enclosure services (cabinet/environmentals)**—SCSI devices are often enclosed in subsystem cabinets with many other devices. These cabinets necessarily have power and cooling systems to maintain the proper environment for reliable device operations. SCSI enclosure services commands are used to provide management operations and visibility to these important elements.

Basic SCSI Commands

The SCSI commands used most often for storage I/O transmissions are the READ and WRITE commands. READ commands request data to be sent by a logical unit in a storage target to the initiator, where it is then sent to a requesting application. WRITE commands request that data that is sent from the initiator to the logical unit be written to storage media. The intent of these commands is not just to transfer data between initiators and targets but to ensure that it reaches its eventual destination. There are several variations of both READ and WRITE commands.

Three other commonly used SCSI commands are MODE SENSE, MODE SELECT, and REPORT LUNS. The MODE SENSE and MODE SELECT commands are used together by applications to determine what operating capabilities (modes) a storage device or logical device has and to choose to use one of those modes. For instance, a MODE SENSE command could be used to discover the ways a tape drive can handle end-of-tape conditions. MODE SELECT could then be used by a backup application to work in the optimal fashion with the software's logic.

The REPORT LUNS command is used by an initiator when it attempts to discover what LUNs are available through a specific device port. After receiving the REPORT LUNS command, a target responds with an inventory of all the available LUNs exported through the port the command was received on. The REPORT LUNS command is at the core of how LUN masking works in SAN storage subsystems, as discussed in Chapter 5, "Storage Subsystems." By not including certain LUNs in the inventory that is returned to the initiator, the initiator will not discover them and try to use them.

While there is a lot of flexibility in how storage devices are designed, all SCSI targets are required to support four commands: INQUIRY, READ CAPACITY, REQUEST SENSE, and TEST UNIT READY.

The SCSI INQUIRY command is used to discover what the configuration is for a target and logical unit, including such things as manufacturers and product identification, version numbers, and information about its command support. READ CAPACITY is used by a system to discover the block size and the number of blocks used in a storage address space. The REQUEST SENSE command is used to query about command status, and the TEST UNIT READY command is a way to determine if a device and its media are available to commence operations.

SCSI Reservation

Certain SCSI commands reserve storage devices for the use of specific applications servers. This feature is particularly useful for backup applications where it is desired to reserve the use of tape drives and tapes for the highest-priority servers. This mechanism also includes a way to remove reservations.

The SCSI reservation mechanism was not used much prior to the advent of SANs. However, with the potential for many servers to back up data over a SAN to centralized backup storage, it became obvious that the SCSI reservation mechanism could be useful. This topic is discussed more in Chapter 13, "Network Backup: The Foundation of Storage Management."

Extended Copy and Third-Party Copy

A relatively new SCSI command that is primarily applicable to SAN environments is the EXTENDED COPY command. EXTENDED COPY allows dual-mode SCSI controllers to act as "proxy" initiators that copy data on behalf of another initiator. A controller supporting this function receives an EXTENDED COPY command from an initiator and then issues READ and WRITE commands to specified logical units for a specific block range of data. The terms *third-party copy, x-copy,* and *e-copy* are all used to refer to the function provided by the EXTENDED COPY command. Figure 6-7 illustrates the mechanism used for EXTENDED COPY.

In Figure 6-7, an initiator in a system sends an EXTENDED COPY command to a dual-mode storage controller. Acting as a SCSI target, this controller receives and interprets the EXTENDED COPY command and then proceeds to execute its initiator role by reading data from the source target and writing it to a destination target. The network ports on the dual-mode controller are not shown. There could be a single port or multiple ports. The actual port configuration does not impact the SCSI function, which is independent of the connecting technology.

The EXTENDED COPY command was designed to enable the transfer of data between different types of storage devices, such as disk, tape, and optical devices/subsystems. But it can also be used to transfer data between different virtual storage resources within the same subsystem.

Figure 6-7 *SCSI EXTENDED COPY Processing*

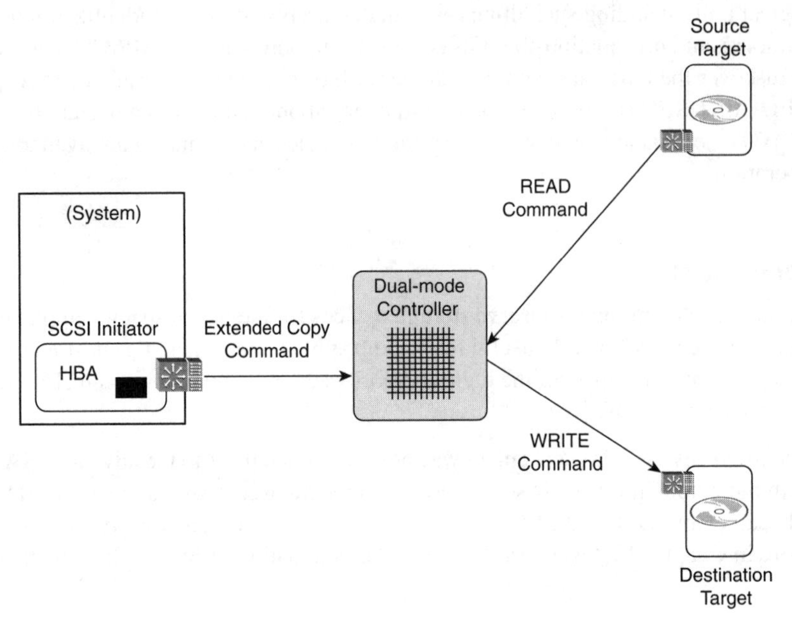

Intuitively, EXTENDED COPY would seem to make a lot of sense for performing backups in a SAN. Using EXTENDED COPY allows systems to be bypassed while transferring large amounts of backup data. However, the concept is far simpler than the implementation due to the necessity of synchronizing host system software operations to ensure data integrity. The topic of third-party copy backup is discussed in more detail in Chapter 13.

HBAs and Network Storage Interfaces

While it is true that storing and connecting functions are independent, there obviously has to be some sort of connecting interface that storage data passes through on its way between systems and storage. The connecting interface for SANs is a network adapter. Storage adapters in host systems are usually HBAs. This section discusses the use of HBAs as SCSI initiators, the qualification process for HBAs within the industry, the use of multiple HBAs in systems, and adapters used in devices and subsystems.

NOTE An interesting marketing problem is brewing with product naming due to the emergence of iSCSI. There are a few approaches to implementing a network adapter for iSCSI, including the ability to use an off-the-shelf network interface card (NIC). In that case, why would you call something that already has a name and a product class (NIC) by another name (HBA)? The answer is that you wouldn't.

But what about a NIC that has been reengineered for the needs of iSCSI SANs? It still functions as a NIC in an IP network, but its primary application is for storage. The terms *iSCSI HBA* and *iSCSI NIC* have been used and are likely to last due to their relative simplicity. The acronym *SNIC* (storage networking interface card) has been suggested. The desire of some vendors to amplify their TCP offload technologies has given rise to other names, such as *TOE adapter, NAC* (network accelerator card), and *TNIC*. I'm glad not to be a marketing person this go-round, trying to figure out what to call them, as long as we don't call them *TOE snacs*.

HBAs as SCSI Initiators

Regardless of the connectivity used, an HBA's primary function is to communicate storage data. It receives requests from system applications, such as file systems and databases, to transfer data to and from storage using READ and WRITE commands. It also performs various management functions for applications using commands such as REPORT LUNS, INQUIRY, REQUEST SENSE, MODE SENSE, and MODE SELECT. HBAs need to be able to handle a large number of commands, operating parameters, and responses used in SCSI implementations.

As mentioned previously, an HBA is much more than a hardware implementation; it is a combination of hardware and device driver software. Using a top-down I/O stack approach, the first interaction an HBA has is between its system device driver and the operating system of the host system. Due to the nature of multitasking operations and SCSI's command/response protocol, the interactions between the operating system and the HBA system driver are interrupt-driven. Whenever there is something to deliver to the host from the HBA, an interrupt is generated and the host system makes the necessary context switches to accommodate it. These exchanges need to be as efficient as possible without errors in order to meet system performance expectations. HBA vendors list the operating systems and versions their products support; it should not be assumed that they will work with versions that are not explicitly named.

The HBA must operate with system hardware, and, therefore, HBAs are designed to work with specific system I/O bus technologies. Over the years, there have been many different system buses, including the S-Bus, Microchannel, Industry-Standard Architecture (ISA)/Extended Industry-Standard Architecture (EISA), and protocol control information (PCI). Today, most systems use the PCI bus. Care should be taken to understand the various PCI technologies in systems to make sure there is not a mismatch.

Besides working with SCSI storage data and the host operating system, HBAs also participate as citizens on the connecting bus or network. This means that network device driver software is also involved. The HBA and network driver put SCSI commands and data into a network PDU (or send them over bus lines in the case of parallel SCSI) and then manage the network transmission to a device or subsystem in the SAN. Conversely, the HBA spontaneously receives transmissions from SAN target ports that it must route correctly to the proper requesting application.

There are, of course, other networking elements to consider with HBAs, including transmission media, signaling, and network protocols. Readers interested in SAN transmissions should look for details in other books and writings on SAN networking technologies, including those covering FC, Ethernet, and TCP/IP.

Qualification of HBAs by System and Subsystem Vendors

Due to the critical nature of their mission, and the fact that the engineering work is difficult, SAN products receive a great deal of testing from vendors selling SAN solutions. In general, the selection of an HBA for a SAN is not really an exercise in open-systems economics. The HBAs people usually buy are the ones that a systems or subsystem vendor has qualified and sells.

NOTE SAN system and subsystem vendors so far have been able to dictate which HBAs are used by their customers by withholding support for configurations using unqualified HBAs. People tend to look at this situation and wonder why SANs have to have tightly controlled qualification lists when other networks like Ethernet can have widespread interoperability almost immediately after a new technology is introduced.

The situation is not as one-sided as it seems. There are big differences between the nature of the data transmissions in SANs and LANs. Say what you want, LANs are not even close to being as critical a component as SANs are. Things can go haywire with LANS, and it causes pain but usually not the loss of data and employment. Because SANs can be complicated and nobody really wants a million degrees of freedom in something complicated where there is a lot at stake, it is much safer to go with a prescribed solution that is blessed by a SAN vendor.

That said, the situation will likely change over time as SAN standards mature and stabilize. When? Who knows? iSCSI SANs will likely influence attitudes and practices as Ethernet and TCP/IP networks are already universally interoperable.

Multiple SAN, Multiple HBA Configurations

High-availability systems often use multiple HBAs for high availability. The topic of multipathing is covered in Chapter 11, "Connection Redundancy in Storage Networks and Dynamic Multipathing." But that doesn't address the situation where more than one HBA is in a system to connect to different storage resources without regard for redundancy. An example of such a configuration includes a separate SAN connection to a backup SAN populated with tape subsystems and devices, as opposed to disk.

In general, there is nothing wrong or dangerous in doing this as long as some common sense is used. Things are simplest if the HBAs are the same product with the same version of driver and firmware code. However, you could be in a situation where you want a system to connect to storage subsystems sold by different vendors, without a single HBA qualified by both subsystem vendors. In this case, you need to proceed with caution in testing the dual-HBA configuration. Check with HBA vendors' technical resources about any known compatibility problems, and test the configuration on a test system before adding a second, different HBA to a production system.

SAN HBAs coexist with parallel SCSI HBAs in many systems. It is common for the boot drive that stores the operating system to be a SCSI disk while the application data is stored in the SAN. As it is with any system, the configuration of the boot drive should be fairly uncomplicated.

Device and Subsystem Network Controllers/Adapters

The product scenario for device and subsystem SAN network controllers is considerably different from HBAs. With HBAs there might be some leeway about the manufacturer or product, but with a subsystem you get the controller that is integrated with the subsystem. Subsystem controllers might have two or three options determined by the number of target ports in a configuration, but the controller is not sold by another vendor.

System HBAs and subsystem controllers appear to do the same things from a network perspective, but from a SCSI perspective they are considerably different. For starters, HBAs implement only SCSI initiator functions, whereas subsystems (and even some devices) implement both initiator and target functions. While the HBA initiator works through details of the operating system kernel, the target works through the details of connecting to multiple logical units and their device servers, task managers, queues, and storage media—including memory cache. More importantly, there are usually several systems working with a single subsystem concurrently in a SAN, while systems are less likely to be communicating with multiple subsystems. The dynamics of the SCSI work are completely different.

Summary

SCSI technology is fundamental to storage networking. While the physical SCSI bus is not commonly used to transport data in SANs, it is still used in NAS systems and server systems for local storage. More importantly, the logic of SCSI can be thought of as the storage application in SANs.

This chapter discussed the logical structures of SCSI, describing the key elements that are involved, including initiators, targets, logical units, LUNs, device servers, and task managers. The client/server nature of SCSI communications was discussed, along with some insight into how this impacts server operating system processes. Other topics included worldwide names used in SANs and advanced SCSI features, such as tagged command queuing and extended copy operations.

Q & A

1. The SCSI-3 standard is used for which SAN implementations?
2. What is the standards organization for SCSI?
3. True or false: Target and initiator ports are part of the logical processing of SCSI.
4. True or false: SCSI guarantees in-order delivery.
5. Where are SCSI logical units implemented?
6. Name the two main functions in a logical unit.
7. What are queues in SCSI called?
8. What is the standard size of SCSI CDBs?
9. What is a SCSI nexus?
10. Explain how TCQ increases performance.

Upon completing this chapter, you will be able to

- Participate in discussions with colleagues about the relative strengths of and differences between the various storage interconnect technologies used in storage networking
- Characterize the applications best suited for different types of storage interconnects
- Make recommendations for areas to test when evaluating disk subsystems with different types of storage interconnects
- Explain the difference between ATA and SATA technologies

CHAPTER 7

Device Interconnect Technologies for Storage Networks

Most people think of storage networks primarily as being storage connectivity over a network. However, when you look under the covers of network storage subsystems, you find out that they also depend on short-distance storage interconnect technologies that connect storage devices to controllers. In other words, storage area network (SAN) and network attached storage (NAS) networks can be thought of as the *external* network connections while interconnects are the *internal* storage connections. Figure 7-1 illustrates.

Figure 7-1 *External Storage Networks and Internal Storage Interconnects*

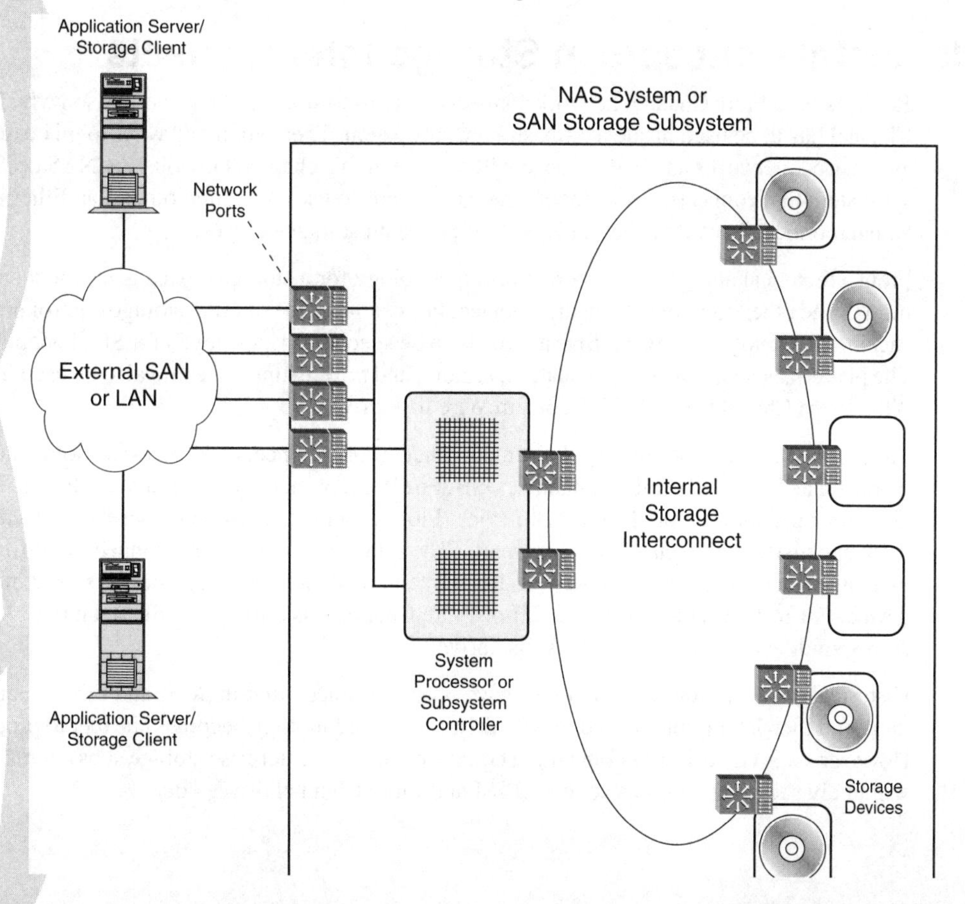

Several different storage interconnect technologies are used with SANs and NAS, including parallel Small Computer Systems Interface (SCSI), AT Attachment (ATA), Fibre Channel, and Serial ATA (SATA). In addition to these, it now appears likely that another interconnect, Serial Attached SCSI (SAS), will be added to the list in the next couple of years.

This chapter looks at the major interconnects used in storage networks and highlights their differences so readers can analyze how to most effectively use them.

NOTE USB and FireWire are interesting interconnect technologies, but they have not really had any impact on storage network products yet. FireWire especially has interesting networking capabilities, but like USB it is being implemented in products with external connections to desktop systems, not servers. As the lines between technology classes blur over time, it is still necessary to make meaningful distinctions between a high-end storage subsystem and a DVD drive. So, USB and FireWire fans, I'm sorry, but your technology didn't make the cut for this book.

Fundamental Concepts in Storage Interconnects

Just because a Fibre Channel network connects systems to storage, there is no reason why Fibre Channel has to be used inside a SAN storage subsystem. There are many ways to mix external and internal networks and buses, as we will explore in this chapter. Obviously, a NAS or iSCSI subsystem that connects to an Ethernet network needs to use something other than Ethernet as an interconnect, because Ethernet is not used (yet) on storage devices.

From a technical analysis, the interconnect technology for a storage device is independent of most of the other components inside a device. For example, the internal storage controllers and caching technology of a SCSI drive are likely to be specifically developed for SCSI operations. The platters, heads, disk arms, actuators, motors, and power supplies could also be used in any ATA, Fibre Channel, SATA, USB, or FireWire disk drive.

Storage devices are classified by their interconnect. For instance, disk drives are sold and marketed as SCSI, ATA, Fibre Channel, USB, FireWire, or other types of drives. Device prices also depend somewhat on the class of device. Fibre Channel and SCSI devices are typically more expensive than their ATA counterparts. The relative cost of an interconnect used for a particular device is commensurate with the cost and quality of other components used in a device. For instance, the cost of a SCSI or Fibre Channel disk drive is higher than the corresponding cost of a typical ATA disk drive.

Historically, innovations in disk drives have been introduced first in SCSI and Fibre Channel disks and then later implemented in ATA drives as the technology becomes cheaper to produce. However, as SATA drives become more commonly used in enterprise storage subsystems, they will likely see innovations as soon as SCSI and Fibre Channel drives do.

The interconnect technology used in a storage system or subsystem has a major impact on its performance capabilities. Obviously, the data transfer characteristics of an interconnect have a direct impact on the performance of a device or subsystem. What is less obvious is the fact that the protocol used by an interconnect also has an enormous impact on the performance of the device. SCSI's tagged command queuing (discussed in the preceding chapter) makes an enormous difference in the overall performance of disk drives and subsystems.

Interconnects also directly influence the scalability of a storage subsystem. Obviously an interconnect with a limitation of two devices per controller port cannot scale to the degree of an interconnect that supports hundreds or even thousands of devices.

Legacy DAS Interconnects

Two legacy direct attached storage (DAS) interconnects are commonly used in SAN and NAS products:

- Parallel SCSI
- ATA

The parallel SCSI bus, which began its history as part of the same technology as SCSI logic and protocols, is the leading interconnect for server systems and UNIX desktops. It has excellent performance characteristics and a great deal of versatility to support a wide range of functions and devices. Parallel SCSI is relatively expensive compared to ATA.

ATA was invented as an inexpensive disk interconnect for PC desktop computers. It is much more limited than parallel SCSI in both expandability and device support, but the cost of ATA technology is lower than any other storage interconnect technology.

Parallel SCSI and ATA are examined in the sections that follow.

The Parallel SCSI Bus: the Legacy Server Storage Interconnect

The parallel SCSI DAS bus is the legacy storage interconnect technology for open-systems servers. There have been many different versions of parallel SCSI over the years. The current technology is low-voltage differential (LVD) SCSI.

NOTE Most of the time the word *SCSI* is used to refer to parallel SCSI. In fact, the word *parallel* is not often used with SCSI in product descriptions or most conversations. So why use it here? For clarity, mostly, but also to help drive home the point that there is a huge difference between the logical stuff of *storing* and the physical stuff of *connecting* that coexists in the wide world of SCSI technology.

Parallel SCSI was invented as a single-controller interconnect technology. More than just a storage bus, parallel SCSI is used for several different types of devices, including scanners and printers. Its versatility helped establish it as an all-purpose interconnect, although today it is thought of primarily as a storage interconnect.

While parallel SCSI has excellent performance characteristics, it has many shortcomings as a way to connect enterprise storage. The cable distances are very short compared to SAN network distances, and the number of connected target addresses limits the scalability and therefore the storage capacity of the SCSI bus. In addition, parallel SCSI was never designed for dual-controller, high-availability environments, although it could be accomplished through specially designed controllers and subsystems. The typical parallel SCSI implementation involves a single server with one or more HBAs providing connections to storage. In this configuration, the server is a potential bottleneck and a single point of failure.

Parallel SCSI Bus Connections

Parallel SCSI buses are formed by the collection of cables and devices that are connected. There are different physical approaches to making these connections, but the fundamental idea is that every device on the parallel SCSI bus connects to the same set of wires. Each device has a unique address that is independent of the physical location on the bus. In that sense, the parallel SCSI bus is similar to other familiar buses, such as system buses.

Configuration changes to parallel SCSI buses require the bus to be powered down, which for many systems means that the system itself must also be powered down. This obviously limits its use for high-availability environments where data access is expected on a 24/7/365 basis. Maintenance for high-availability systems using parallel SCSI storage normally has to be done during weekend hours, when data access needs are reduced. Unplanned maintenance events, such as unexpectedly running out of disk space, can create an administrative emergency for data center managers.

SCSI buses have limited lengths that need to be carefully considered. LVD SCSI has a maximum bus length of 12 meters, encompassing both internal and external cables. Most previous versions of the SCSI interconnect had shorter connection lengths, some as small as 1.5 meters. The exception, differential SCSI, allowed bus lengths up to 25 meters. Historically, the variations in the different versions of parallel SCSI were a source of frustration and unnecessary costs.

NOTE For a technology that was supposed to be a standard, parallel SCSI over the years hardly resembled one, with a constant parade of connecting interfaces that always seemed to be changing. Normally standards are supposed to result in lower commodity pricing in things like cabling, but in the case of parallel SCSI, the cables and connectors are comparatively very expensive. Even today, with a relative stabilizing in the LVD bus, retail prices for cables range from $20 to $50, depending on the number of connectors on them. The fact is, the cost of a cable can be equal to or even greater than the cost of a device. Similar cables for ATA drives have fewer connectors but have retail costs between $3 and $15.

The cost of cabling was only part of the frustration with parallel SCSI. Adapters to connect devices with older interfaces to newer buses typically cost between $15 and $25. The cost of terminating resistors for the bus is also high. A bus terminator for differential SCSI costs $50 or more. To make matters worse, often the connector would not specify whether it was differential or single-ended SCSI, even though the parts were not interchangeable.

So why did people use parallel SCSI if it was such a pain in the backside? Because it was the fastest interconnect available. In many cases it was the only thing fast enough for high-performance applications. The need for speed was at the heart of the cabling/configuration problems. SCSI had to evolve in response to faster and faster system requirements. In the same time that system CPUs went from 25 MHz to more than 2 GHz, the SCSI interconnect has gone from 10 MBps to 320 MBps. Even though the performance improvement of parallel SCSI does not match the performance of CPU processors, it has not become a bottleneck. That honor still belongs to electromechanical devices such as disk drives.

Parallel SCSI Addresses, Arbitration, and Priority

Every controller and device on a parallel SCSI bus has a unique address. Today's LVD parallel SCSI bus has a maximum of 16 total addresses, including an address for the initiator. Addresses are assigned several different ways, depending on the product, including device management software, device driver settings, switches, and jumpers. If two entities are assigned the same address, the bus won't operate.

Initiators and targets gain access to the parallel SCSI bus through a process called *SCSI arbitration*. If only one entity arbitrates for control of the bus, it gets to control the bus for a short period of time. If more than one entity arbitrates, the entity with the highest priority gets to control the bus. The priority of an entity on the parallel SCSI bus is determined by its address.

For historical compatibility reasons, the highest-priority address on an LVD SCSI bus is 7. This is usually assigned to the HBA. The next-highest-priority address is 6, followed by 5, and then 4, and so on until address 0. Then the addresses and priorities resume again at address 15, followed by 14, on down to address 8. The priority scheme for parallel LVD SCSI is illustrated in Figure 7-2.

Figure 7-2 *SCSI ID Priorities*

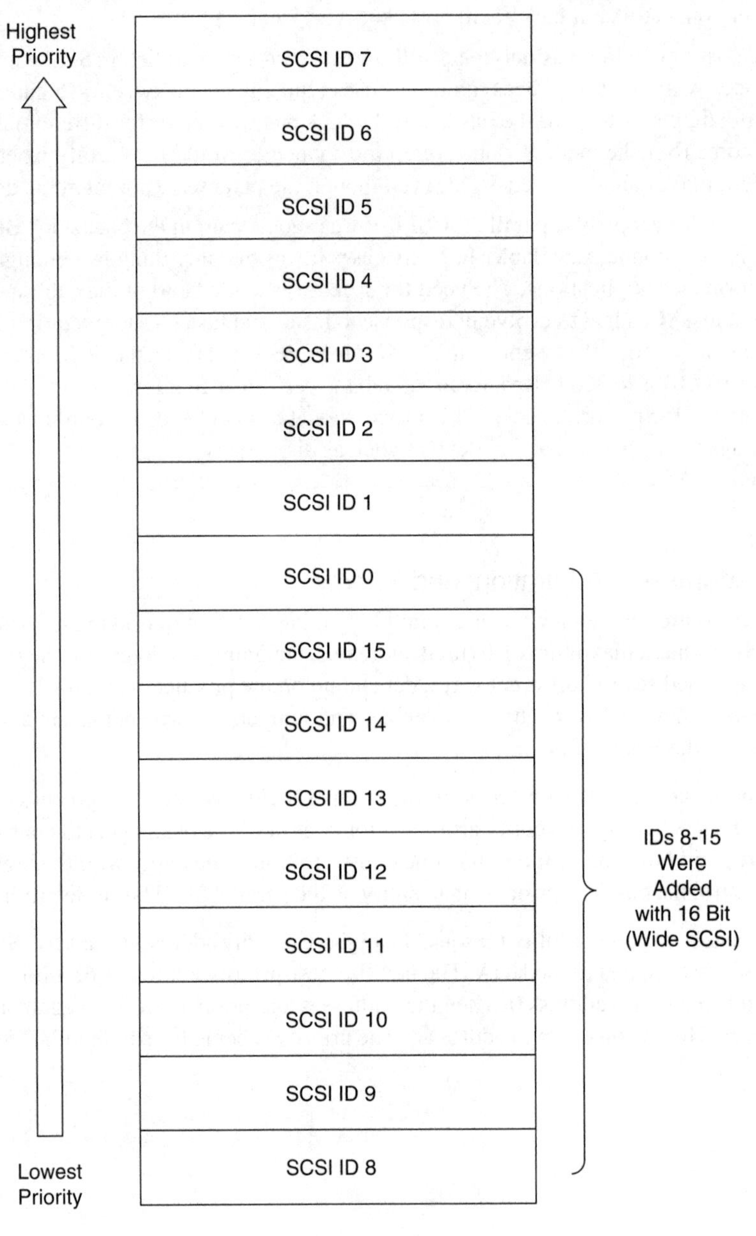

A Comparison of Single-Ended, Differential, and LVD SCSI Buses

Parallel SCSI technology changed a great deal in its short history to meet rapidly changing requirements. Performance improvements were usually offset by shorter cable lengths. The original parallel SCSI bus used an electrical system called single-ended SCSI (SE SCSI), which was relatively inexpensive to design and implement but had constrained bus-length distances. A second type of electrical system for SCSI was added later, called differential SCSI, which was more expensive but allowed bus length distances up to 25 meters. LVD SCSI is the current electrical system, and it has a maximum supported bus length of 12 meters.

LVD SCSI was designed to work with SE SCSI devices. It is possible to connect both SE and LVD devices on an LVD SCSI bus operated by an LVD HBA. Operating in this SE compatibility mode, the bus has the distance characteristics of an SE SCSI bus.

Many different names have been used for parallel SCSI buses over the years. The terms fast, ultra, ultra2, and ultra3 refer to bus transmission speeds, while wide refers to the bus width and the number of supported targets on the bus. The various versions of parallel SCSI and their characteristics are listed in Table 7-1.

Table 7-1 *Relative Speeds and Cable Lengths for Various SCSI Types*

SCSI Bus Version	Transfer Rate in MBps	Maximum Number of Devices	SE Maximum Length (in Meters)	Differential Maximum Length	LVD Bus Lengths
SCSI-1	5	8	6 m	25 m	—
Fast SCSI-2	10	8	3 m	25 m	—
Fast Wide SCSI-2	20	16	3 m	25 m	—
Ultra SCSI*	20	8/4	1.5 m/3 m	25 m	—
Wide Ultra SCSI*	40	16	—	25 m	—
Wide Ultra SCSI*	40	8/4	1.5 m/3 m	25 m	—
Ultra2 SCSI	40	8	—	—	12 m
Wide Ultra2 SCSI	80.	16	—	—	12 m
Ultra3 SCSI	160	16	—	—	12 m
Ultra 320	320	16	—	—	12 m

*Single ended Ultra SCSI and Wide Ultra SCSI have two different maximum bus lengths that correspond to the maximum number of devices. Eight devices can be connected to a bus up to 1.5 meters long and four devices can be connected on a bus up to 3 meters long. The case of connecting sixteen devices is not supported because it is not practical to connect sixteen devices on a bus that is shorter than a meter.

Parallel SCSI Applications

SCSI uses the SCSI communications architecture described in the preceding chapter, including the implementation of logical units, LUNs, device servers, task managers, tagged command queuing, and overlapped I/O. As a result, the parallel SCSI bus is well suited for implementation with multitasking, multiprocessing, and multiuser applications. Historically, parallel SCSI has been used effectively for any application that requires fast performance, including transaction processing systems, scientific and engineering applications, and enterprise-level data sharing (NAS). Parallel SCSI disk drives have also been successfully used for many years for film, multimedia, and graphics applications.

Parallel SCSI Storage Network Configurations

Many network storage configurations are used with the parallel SCSI interconnect. The following sections look at two basic options:

- Internal SCSI disks within a system
- SCSI JBOD or redundant array of inexpensive disks (RAID) subsystems

Internal SCSI Disks

Just because a system is on a storage network, it does not mean that all the storage it uses has to be external. For example, a NAS server system can store data for client systems on internal SCSI disks, and that is definitely something we think of as network storage. To achieve higher availability, these disks can be mirrored or configured for use as a RAID array. An example of a NAS server with internal SCSI disks is shown in Figure 7-3.

Mirrored SCSI disks are often used as boot disks for application servers that store their application data on a SAN. For example, database log files may be stored on mirrored high-performance SCSI disks, while data files are stored on SAN-based RAID arrays. Figure 7-4 shows a system connected to a SAN where the operating system is running on SCSI disks inside the system unit and where application data is being stored on a SAN.

Figure 7-3 *A NAS Server Storing Client Data on Internal SCSI Disks*

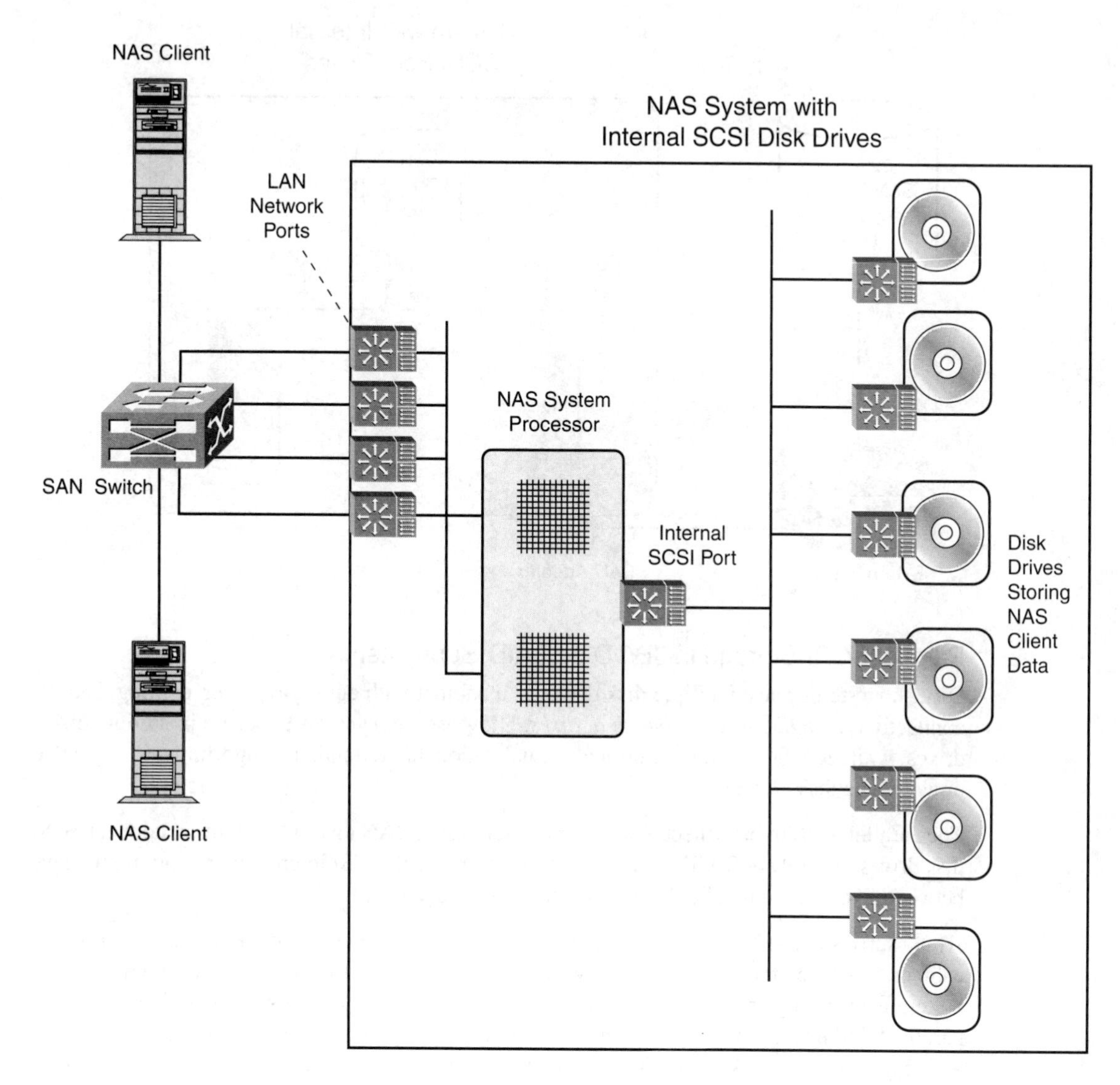

Figure 7-4 *A System with Internal SCSI Boot Disks and Application Data Stored in a SAN*

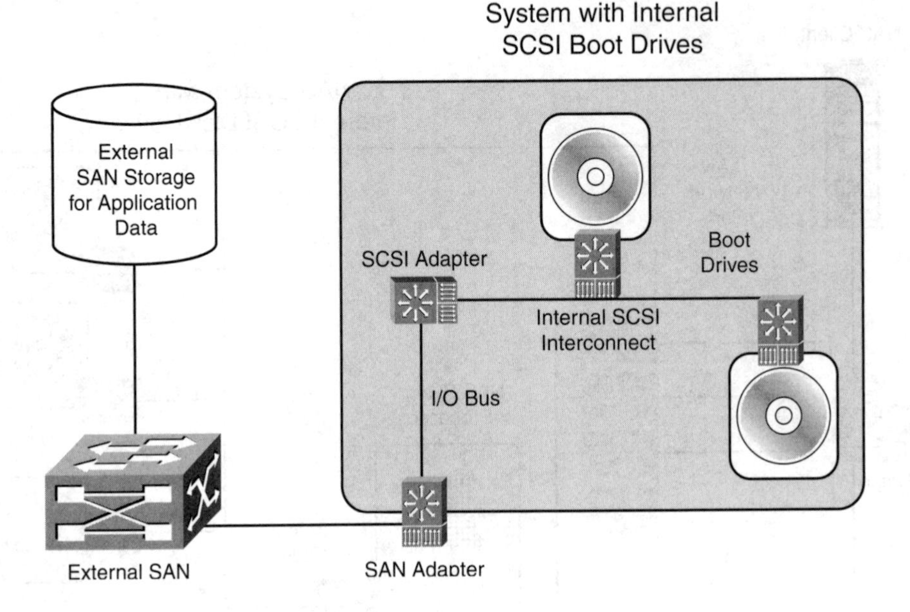

Parallel SCSI Storage in JBOD or RAID Subsystems

Disk subsystems place multiple disk drives in a cabinet with common power, cooling, and connectivity. *JBOD*, or *just a bunch of disks,* allows server systems to access individual disk drives, while RAID provides additional virtualization and redundancy algorithms to segregate or aggregate disk storage.

The parallel SCSI interconnect is sometimes used inside SAN disk subsystems to connect SCSI disk drives to JBOD or RAID controllers. Subsystems with SCSI interconnects commonly have between five and ten parallel SCSI disks in a single enclosure.

JBOD subsystems often allow disk drives to be removed and replaced without opening the cabinet. RAID, on the other hand, allows disk drives to be removed and replaced while the system is operating and data is being accessed—a process called hot swapping. However, the parallel SCSI interconnect—including power connections—was not designed for easy removal and replacement of disk drives. Therefore, parallel SCSI RAID disk subsystems are usually designed with special backplanes and drive trays that allow disk drives to be removed and replaced easily. Essentially, the backplane of a SCSI disk subsystem replaces the cables and connectors of a parallel SCSI bus. Figure 7-5 illustrates the connectors used with device trays and backplanes with parallel SCSI.

Figure 7-5 *Backplane and Disk Tray Connectors for Parallel SCSI*

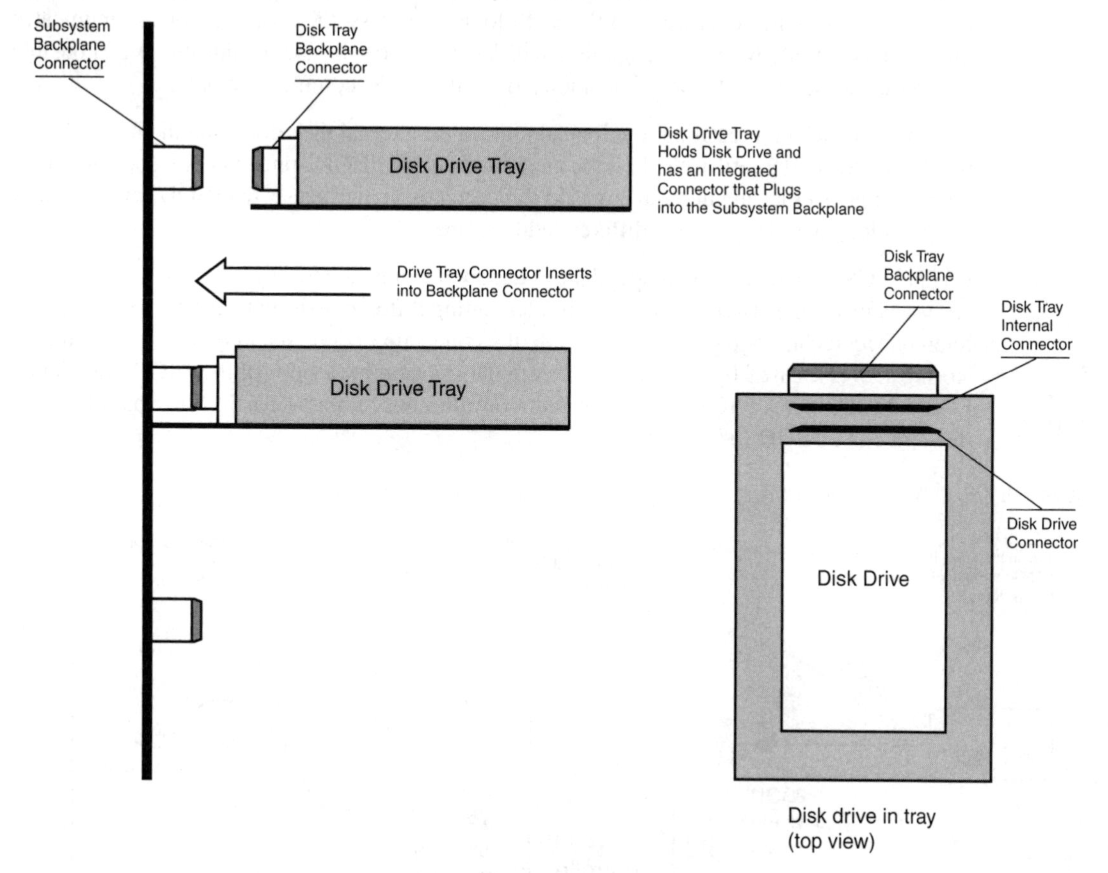

NOTE The trickiest part of this type of design for SCSI RAID is not the physical connectors, but the electrical "buffering" that needs to occur so that the removal or insertion of a new device does not cause errors on the bus, loss of data, or crashing systems. If you are not sure whether it is safe to remove a disk drive from a cabinet, don't do so until you find out or have a chance to quiesce the system.

Host systems access storage in a SAN disk subsystem by the target/LUN addressing combination. The number of LUNs that can be accessed through a single subsystem port depends on the design and implementation of the subsystem controllers. For example, a small subsystem might limit the number of LUNs per port to eight, while a larger subsystem might allow 128 or more.

JBOD subsystems allow access to individual disk drives without applying storage virtualization techniques. From the perspective of the SCSI logical process, the host initiator communicates more or less directly with a logical unit in a disk drive. The subsystem controller is responsible for converting serial SAN communications to parallel SCSI communications.

The external LUN representing the logical unit for an internal disk drive and the internal parallel SCSI bus target/LUNs do not have to match. The JBOD controller is responsible for mapping the external and internal target/LUNs correctly. In that sense, the JBOD controller acts like a bridge, manipulating two different address spaces.

Logical SCSI processes are independent of the connecting technology used, including scenarios involving JBOD subsystems implementing different external network and internal interconnect technologies. Therefore, while the connecting addresses may be different, the storing addresses used by SCSI processes are the same on both sides of the JBOD boundary. Figure 7-6 illustrates a SCSI logical connection from a host initiator in a SAN to a parallel SCSI disk drive in a JBOD subsystem.

Figure 7-6 *A SCSI Connection Using a JBOD Subsystem with Parallel SCSI Disks*

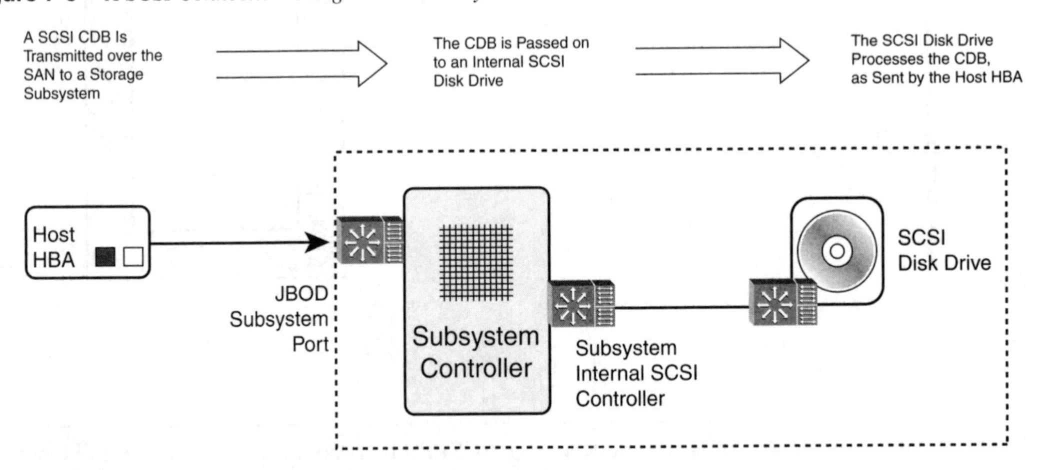

> **Author's Disclaimer**
>
> As in all things storage, there are several different ways to implement SCSI, and the preceding description of JBOD is simply one of them.

In contrast, RAID subsystems implement virtualization techniques that subdivide and aggregate storage on internal disk drives. With virtualization, the SCSI address spaces used by the internal storage controllers likely won't be the same as those used by host systems. Readers interested in virtualization will find much more information in Chapter 12, "Storage Virtualization: The Power in Volume Management Software and SAN Virtualization Systems."

The SAN host initiator establishes a connection with a logical unit in the subsystem controller. Then an internal initiator in the controller completes the operation by establishing internal connections to one or more disk drives over the SCSI interconnect.

SCSI communications between a host initiator and a SAN RAID subsystem with an internal parallel SCSI interconnect are pictured in Figure 7-7.

Figure 7-7 *A SAN RAID Subsystem with Parallel SCSI Disks*

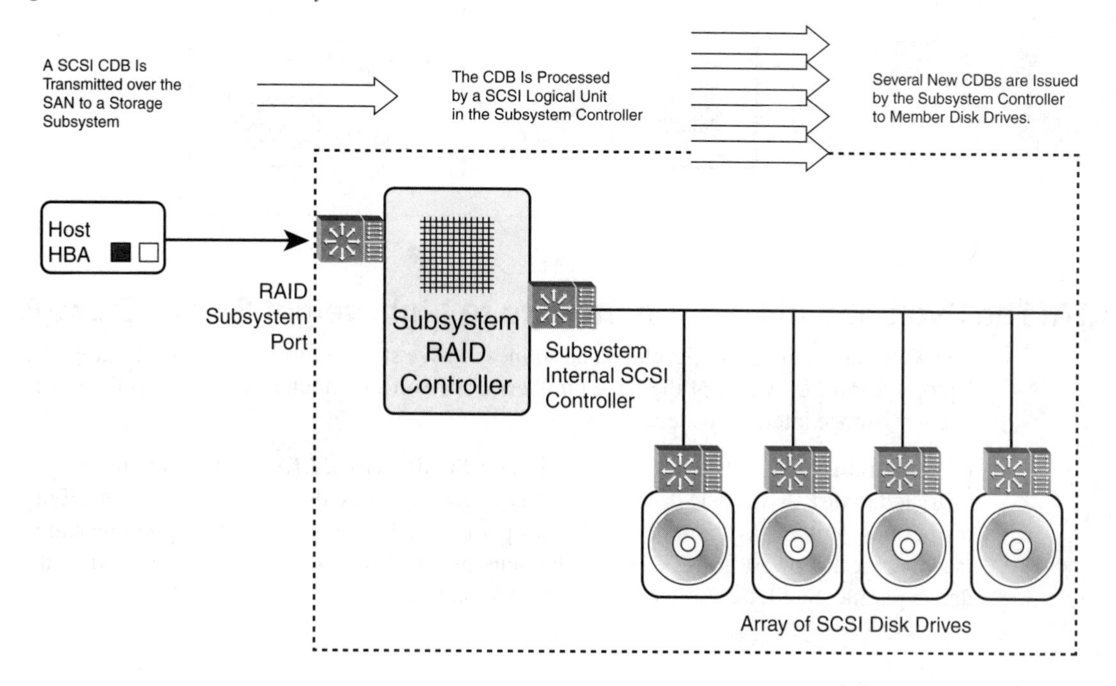

Dual-Controller Parallel SCSI Connections

Disk subsystems with internal parallel SCSI interconnects can support redundant paths to internal disk drives by connecting multiple controllers to internal SCSI buses. While it is not advisable to combine multiple controllers with off-the-shelf components on a parallel SCSI bus, it should not pose a problem as an engineered solution from a reputable storage products company. Figure 7-8 shows a disk subsystem with redundant internal connections over a parallel SCSI interconnect.

Figure 7-8 *A Disk Subsystem with Redundant Internal Parallel SCSI Connections*

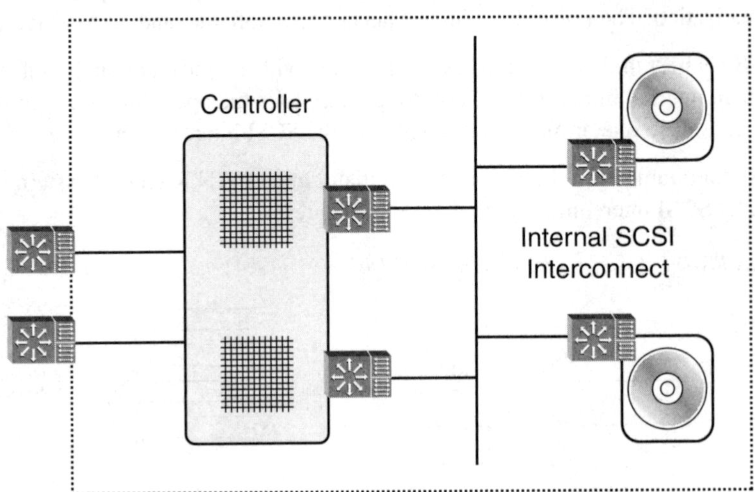

ATA: The Evolution of Desktop Storage to Lightweight Server Storage

The ATA interconnect was developed as an inexpensive storage interconnect for desktop and laptop systems. By virtue of the large numbers of personal computers sold, ATA is the most popular storage interconnect ever.

Unlike parallel SCSI, which can be used for non-SCSI devices, ATA functionality has been restricted to disk drives, CD drives, and DVD drives. ATA has almost ridiculous connectivity restrictions, with a maximum of two devices per bus, reflecting its intent to support desktop machines at the lowest possible cost. Cable lengths are also far less than parallel SCSI, and unlike parallel SCSI, there are no external cable options.

A Short History of ATA

The ATA interconnect is also referred to as Integrated Device Electronics (IDE). The technology has its roots in a project led by Compaq Computer along with Western Digital and Control Data's Imprimus disk drive division to create a PC hard drive with an integrated storage controller that served as an extension to the PC's IDE I/O bus. Products based on this work were introduced by Compaq in 1986, and in the years that followed, the approach was adopted and expanded upon by the rest of the industry. Eventually, the host system ATA controller circuitry was integrated on PC motherboards to eliminate the cost and footprint of a host adapter.

The first ATA standard, titled the *AT Attachment Interface for Disk Drives,* was submitted to the ANSI T13 standard organization in 1990 and approved in 1994. Between 1990 and 1994, the disk drive industry created multiple proprietary extensions to the fledgling standard with names such as Fast ATA and Enhanced IDE.

A revision to the original ATA specification, ATA-2, was published in 1996. This revision incorporated many of the proprietary extensions, including faster data transfer capabilities and several key usability features such as support for logical block addressing (LBA). A year later, the ATA-3 revision was published. It included Self-Monitoring Analysis and Reporting Technology (SMART), which is used to predict failures in disk drives.

Concurrent with the development of ATA-2, an industry consortium called the Small Form Factor Committee developed a specification titled the ATA Packet Interface (ATAPI) for CD-ROMs (also known as SFF 8020), which was published in 1996. ATAPI was needed due to shortcomings in the ATA specification for supporting CD drives and other storage devices, such as tape drives. Essentially SFF 8020 defined a new protocol for non-disk drive operations over the ATA interconnect. Designed to use ATA controllers and cables, the ATAPI interface borrows heavily from SCSI for its logical structure.

In 1998, the ATAPI specification combined with the ATA standards work in the ATA/ATAPI-4 standard. Another major breakthrough was the introduction of Ultra DMA transfer modes, which raised the maximum transfer rate to 33 MBps. To support the higher transfer rates, cyclic redundancy check (CRC) was introduced to ensure data integrity. In addition, an 80-conductor cable, which added ground conductors to the existing signal conductors, was specified to support higher transfer rates.

In the year 2000, the transfer rates were doubled with the addition of two additional ultra DMA transfer modes. The current version is ATA/ATAPI-6, completed in 2002. It incorporates yet another transfer mode, which is capable of transfer rates up to 100 MBps. In addition, the LBA scheme was increased to accommodate higher-capacity drives.

Table 7-2 lists the standards history of ATA/ATAPI.

Table 7-2 *ATA/ATAPI Standards Evolution*

Interface Standard	Year Published	Maximum Transfer Rate	Key Features Introduced
ATA-1	1994	8 MBps	—
ATA-2	1996	16 MBps	Block I/O, logical block addressing
SFF 8020	1996	16 MBps	Packet protocol for CD and tape devices
ATA-3	1997	16 MBps	SMART predictive failure
ATA/ATAPI-4	1998	33 MBps	ATAPI, Ultra DMA , CRC, 80-conductor cable
ATA/ATAPI-5	2000	66 MBps	Additional Ultra DMA transfer modes
ATA/ATAPI-6	2002	100 MBps	Expanded LBA, additional Ultra DMA transfer mode

ATA products are often referred to as Ultra ATA/*XX,* where *XX* is the maximum transfer rates of one of the ATA/ATAPI standards. For instance, an Ultra ATA/66 disk drive indicates that the drive is expected to be more or less compliant with the ATA/ATAPI-5 standard. New drives and motherboards are constantly being introduced with capabilities that anticipate unfinished standards. The industry uses these Ultra ATA names that indicate their transfer capabilities, which is what most people are most interested in.

ATA Connections

ATA buses are referred to as channels. An ATA channel can communicate with one or two devices. Obviously that limits the number of devices that can be assembled in a system. While it is certainly possible to put additional ATA controller adapters in a system, only so many slots are available. In addition, the ATA interconnect cannot be extended outside the system, as it can with parallel SCSI. In short, ATA was not designed to scale.

All ATA PC system connectors (not including laptops) have the same 40-pin form factor. However, that does not mean that all *cables* are the same. Only 80-connector cables built for Ultra DMA operations support high-speed transfers. The 80-connector cables also have 40-pin connectors to be backward-compatible. Disk drives sold today come with the 80-connector cable, and replacement cables are inexpensive and readily available.

The two devices connected to an ATA channel are configured as a *master* and a *slave*. Essentially, this is an arcane type of addressing and does not indicate a dependency between the devices. The determination of master or slave is made by positioning electrical jumpers on a set of pins on the drive. The jumpers can also be positioned to allow the master/slave selection to be made based on which connector a drive is attached to (this is called cable select). Cables sold with modern ATA hard drives are color-coded, as mandated by the standard, to facilitate their installation. The blue connector is intended to be used at the host controller connection, the black connector is to be used for a master drive, and the gray connector in the middle of the cable is to be used for a slave drive.

ATA Interconnect Performance

While the ATA interconnect has made rapid improvements in transfer rates over the years, approaching the transfer rates of parallel SCSI, the overall throughput of an ATA system is far less than a comparable SCSI system due to the lack of multitasking capabilities. Although the ATA standard has supported command queuing and overlapped I/O since the ATA/ATAPI-4 specification, these features have been mostly ignored by disk drive manufacturers.

Realistically, command queuing and overlapped I/O are not essential features for most single-user systems. In an industry where cost savings are paramount, adding unnecessary features with extra cost is considered bad business. That said, the lack of performance features for ATA interconnects certainly limits their applicability for storage networking. Storage networks are built on the premise that multiple users and systems can access a centralized storage infrastructure. If the disk interconnect in a storage infrastructure cannot deliver data fast enough, it will become a bottleneck at some point.

Another important consideration with ATA disk drives for storage networking is their expected duty cycle. While parallel SCSI and Fibre Channel disk drives are designed to run without pause for several years, desktop drives are not. That is not to say that ATA drives will all fail from round-the-clock use, but it is probably realistic to assume their failure rates will be higher than other more-robust drive designs. ATA drives are not poorly made, and shortcuts are not taken in reliability, but some additional technologies are used in SCSI and Fibre Channel drives to increase their reliability that are not used in ATA drives.

ATA Network Storage Applications

The ATA interconnect is obviously not optimized for storage network environments, but that does not mean it has no place in NAS or SAN products. In fact, ATA drives are already being used successfully in both NAS and SAN subsystems, and it is expected that they will continue to see more frequent use. But, unlike parallel SCSI, which works for practically any application, the selection of ATA in network storage needs to be more carefully evaluated to avoid unexpected performance problems.

Servers with relatively light I/O requirements can utilize ATA drives effectively. E-mail servers and file servers for small office environments usually have light I/O requirements, as do many general-purpose Windows servers. There is no reason to overspend on storage for systems that do not need the performance.

ATA drives can be characterized as having excellent capacity and mediocre performance. This combination is well suited for secondary storage applications such as disk-based backup, data archiving, hierarchical storage management (HSM), and Information Life Cycle Management. In general, these are not multitasking applications that need advanced I/O functions, but they do tend to consume lots of storage capacity.

ATA Storage Network Configurations

ATA disk drives are used in both NAS and SAN subsystems. In this section we'll look at using ATA drives in

- ATA-based NAS systems
- ATA-based SAN subsystems

NAS Server with Internal ATA Disks

Many NAS products have been designed with ATA disks in order to reduce costs. The design of these products is similar to any other NAS system: there are Ethernet ports for communicating with client systems and ATA interconnect ports to read and write data on internal disks. The ATA disks should be mirrored or striped with RAID to avoid risking data loss. When measuring the capacity of the system, be sure to calculate the usable capacity and not the raw capacity of the disks.

NAS systems tend to grow. As users get used to them, they store increasing amounts of data on them, and therefore it's essential to provide a cushion for capacity growth. Unfortunately, ATA-based NAS systems may not be able to grow as fast as user capacity demand. The limitations of ATA connectivity are not conducive to expansion.

Storage controller manufacturers began developing and selling ATA RAID a couple years ago, including integrated RAID on some PC motherboards. In general, ATA RAID is a very good idea in order to get redundant data protection along with some additional performance benefits. However, with only two devices per channel, it's not possible to create anything but small arrays with a handful of member disks. Still, a small array (including mirroring) is far better than no array at all. ATA RAID controllers are available with four channels supporting eight drives in an array, which is probably more than enough for small servers. Check with the NAS vendor about its disk/controller configuration to understand the expandability of its product.

Figure 7-9 shows a simple NAS system with mirrored internal ATA disks.

Figure 7-9 *A NAS System Built with an ATA Interconnect*

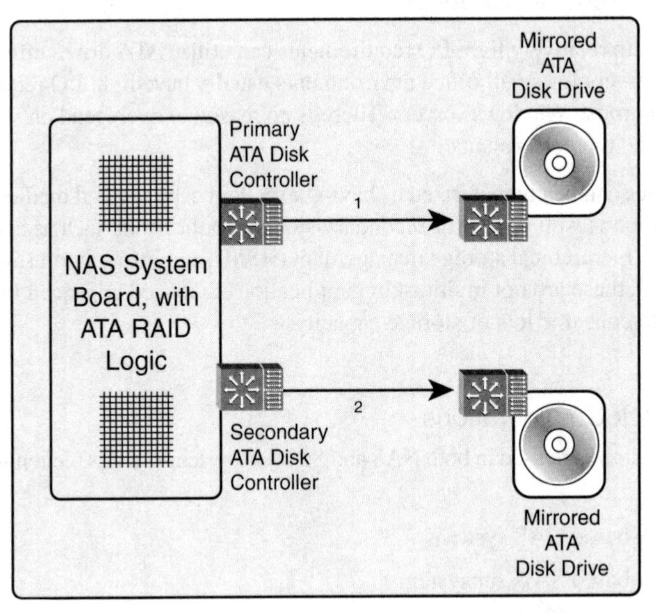

Storage manufacturers can do many different things when building their solutions. It is certainly possible to design large capacity NAS with ATA drives. The engineering effort involved is greater, but there are many possible ways to structure the connectivity to a large number of ATA drives. Network Appliance is an example of a company that has successfully designed and sold large-scale ATA-base NAS systems.

ATA-Based SAN Subsystems

ATA-based subsystems have also been introduced in recent years. Again, the idea is to use inexpensive ATA disk drives for servers with relatively light I/O requirements.

The same performance and capacity scaling issues just discussed for ATA-based NAS apply to ATA-based SAN disk subsystems. ATA's two device limit per channel can be offset by using specialized connecting backplanes and controllers. Considering that most SAN disk subsystems have specialized backplanes and controllers already, this is not a major change. The difference is the use of the ATA interconnect channels, controllers, and protocol, which is different than the SCSI protocol used for SAN data transmissions.

ATA-based SAN subsystems have external SAN ports to communicate with host system initiators. The controller assumes the role of all targets and logical units, including the logical unit's device controller and task manager. As SCSI logical operations and ATA operations are different, the internal ATA drives are virtualized by the subsystem controller. Commands are transferred to an ATA controller function, which issues commands to internal ATA drives. From the perspective of the ATA disk drives, the subsystem controller looks more or less like a controller in a PC system. That does not mean that the controller needs to contain PC components, but it has to replicate their role of the PC controller.

Figure 7-10 shows a basic ATA-based SAN disk subsystem.

Figure 7-10 *A Basic ATA-Based SAN Disk Subsystem*

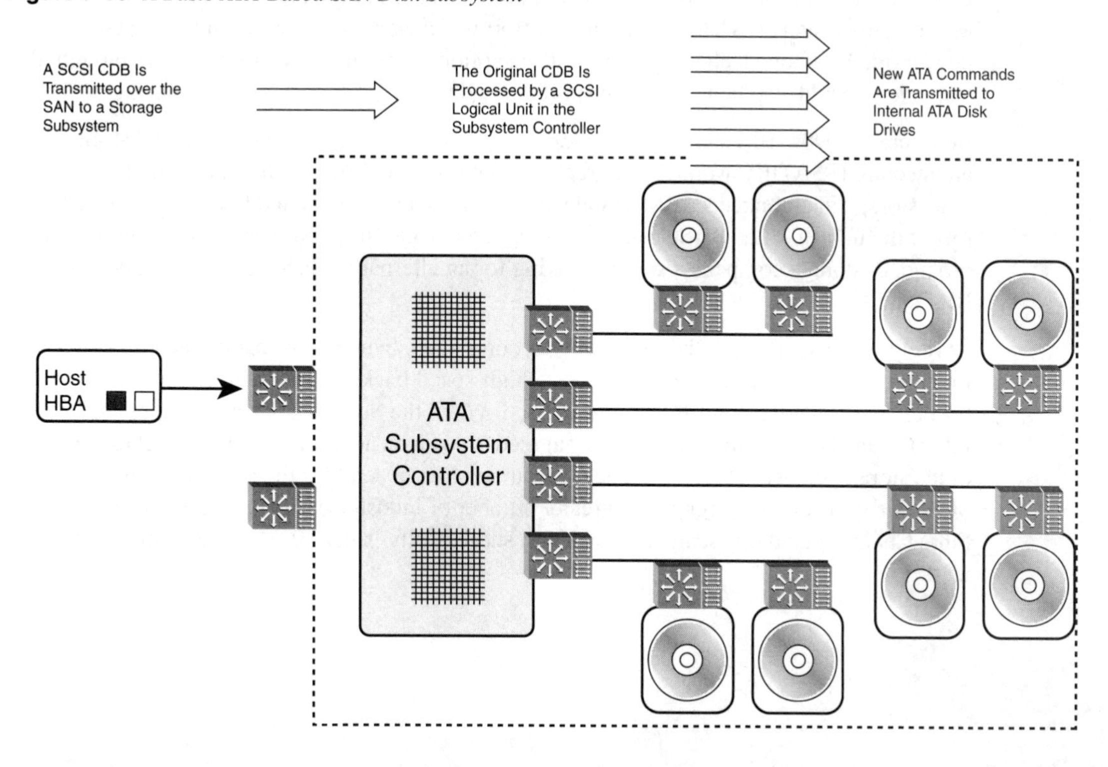

Serial Storage Interconnects

Two major serial interconnects are used for storage today: Fibre Channel and SATA. In the rest of this chapter we'll explore how these interconnects work in storage networking products.

Fibre Channel Loops as an Interconnect for Network Storage

While most people think of Fibre Channel strictly as a storage networking technology, it has been implemented very successfully as a device interconnect inside Fibre Channel SAN subsystems. This section does not discuss Fibre Channel as a networking technology, but looks at its use as an interconnect technology.

Fibre Channel Topologies

Fibre Channel has three topologies: fabric, loop, and point-to-point. The most common Fibre Channel topology used in disk subsystems is the loop technology. Fibre Channel disk drives have interfaces designed to operate in loop topologies.

A Brief History of Fibre Channel

Fibre Channel was initially a joint research project started in the late 1980s by IBM, Sun Microsystems, and Hewlett Packard in an effort to develop a new switched high-speed networking backbone technology. From its inception, some of the early developers thought the technology could also be used to transport storage traffic.

In the early 1990s IBM started to develop a new storage interconnect called serial storage architecture (SSA) that would have greater scalability and throughput than parallel SCSI and other storage interconnects. IBM's goal was to own the technology and license it for a fee to the rest of the industry. Led by Seagate technology, the leader in SCSI disk drives, a number of prominent storage companies started looking for an alternative technology to compete with IBM's SSA.

At roughly the same time, the research effort on Fibre Channel was losing traction. Gigabit Ethernet was emerging as the next obvious high-speed backbone technology, and the chances for Fibre Channel were not looking very good. When the Seagate consortium approached the Fibre Channel organization, they jointly agreed to work on adapting Fibre Channel to the needs of the storage industry. Fibre Channel's arbitrated loop resembles the operations of parallel SCSI fairly closely. By engaging a greater number of industry partners around the new, open Fibre Channel standard, Seagate was able to successfully isolate IBM's SSA initiative in the market.

NOTE In my humble opinion, Seagate's efforts to work with the floundering Fibre Channel industry were pure genius. One of the main reasons its strategy worked was the fact that Fibre Channel was already on its way to becoming a standard, even though it did not have strong market backing. Regardless, a standard is a standard, and using an open industry standard gave Seagate and its allies an incredibly powerful marketing weapon against IBM with its proprietary technology—which was very good technology, by the way.

The first Fibre Channel standards were published in 1994. Unlike the SCSI and ATA standards bodies, the Fibre Channel standards organization was fairly broad from the beginning. Most of the standards have very little to do with storage operations. Instead they deal with such topics as network signaling, switch operations, fabric services, and network addressing methods. Appendix B, "INCITS Storage Standards," lists many of the various subject areas under development by the INCITS T11 committee at http://www.t11.org.

Fibre Channel Interconnect Connections

Unlike parallel SCSI and ATA, the Fibre Channel *interconnect* was never designed to use cable connections. Instead, the physical interfaces on Fibre Channel disk drives were designed to connect directly to connectors on backplanes inside subsystems. Fibre Channel disk interfaces include both data and power connections in a single integrated connector, facilitating accurate removal and insertion. The electrical engineering challenges involved with hot swapping devices on Fibre Channel are far less than on parallel SCSI or ATA interconnects.

Whenever the device is removed from or added to the loop, the loop must reinitialize to establish addresses and priority. The loop topology in Fibre Channel is called an *arbitrated loop,* which means the devices on it arbitrate for access, just as they would on a parallel SCSI bus, as discussed in the earlier section "Parallel SCSI Addresses, Arbitration, and Priority."

With any arbitration scheme, there has to be a way to break deadlocks between competing devices. Similar to parallel SCSI buses, Fibre Channel loops use address priorities to break these deadlocks. However, unlike parallel SCSI, there are several ways addresses can be assigned in a Fibre Channel loop. The Fibre Channel loop initialization process (LIP) is designed to ensure loop addresses are correctly established. Considering that Fibre Channel disk drive interfaces were designed to plug into subsystem backplanes, Fibre Channel HBAs are not designed to attach to internal drives within a computer system. That is one of the reasons why internal parallel SCSI disks are often used to store the operating system on servers that use the SAN for application data only.

NOTE Depending on the HBA, you might actually be able to connect a few Fibre Channel disk drives inside a server system. Some HBAs have a little three-pin connector on them for connecting a set of wires to a small surrogate backplane doohickey called a riser card. It merges the signal from the HBA with a standard PC power connector on one side and connects to the disk drive with the standard backplane connector on the other side. Oh yes, you'll also need a terminator to stick on the riser card. Oh yes, you can also chain these things together to make a loop. Oh yes, you will never get any support for any of this, but it might be a lot of fun if you don't have anything better to do with your time.

The Fibre Channel loop topology supports a maximum of 127 target addresses. Given SCSI's target/LUN addressing, there can theoretically be more than a thousand devices on a single loop. This would probably not make sense for any application, but it points out the scalability advantages of Fibre Channel compared to other interconnects.

Fibre Channel disk drives are *dual-ported,* which means they can connect to two different internal controllers for high availability. This feature is not obvious when looking at the drive because both ports are incorporated into the drive's single connector.

Fibre Channel Performance and Applications

Fibre Channel disk drives have unrivaled performance characteristics, having the fastest rotational speeds and the lowest seek times. While most Fibre Channel disk drives have 3.5-inch form factors, the fastest 15,000 rpm drives are sometimes designed for smaller 2.5-inch form factors. This is done to keep the drives from overheating.

Applications for the Fibre Channel interconnect are similar to parallel SCSI—transaction processing, science and engineering, enterprise-level data sharing, and film, multimedia, and graphics applications.

Fibre Channel Interconnect Configurations

Because Fibre Channel drives are not designed to be connected inside systems, the only meaningful configuration for the Fibre Channel interconnect is inside a SAN disk subsystem.

NOTE Of course, it is possible to use Fibre Channel to connect storage to a NAS system. The issue is whether this connection should be called a SAN or an internal storage interconnect. I would argue that a NAS system with a Fibre Channel "back end" uses a SAN and not an interconnect, but this is simply word shuffling. For instance, the Network Appliance Filers use Fibre Channel connectivity in the form of optical and copper cabling to connect their storage shelves. While all this is integrated as a complete package, it is a "head" with attached storage. In fact, their ATA-based NAS systems use Fibre Channel cables to connect to ATA storage shelves. I don't know what you'd call it, but I call that a small Fibre Channel SAN with an ATA device interconnect.

Fibre Channel Disk Drives in JBOD and RAID Subsystems

Fibre Channel JBOD subsystems are fairly easy to understand. As with parallel SCSI, the host initiator communicates directly with a logical unit on a Fibre Channel drive inside the subsystem. However, unlike parallel SCSI, the protocol payload does not have to be converted from a serial to a parallel transmission. The only work the controller has to do is map external SAN addresses with internal interconnect addresses.

As with parallel SCSI, Fibre Channel RAID subsystems use virtualization to subdivide and aggregate storage on internal disk drives. Again, the SCSI addresses known to the internal controllers likely won't be the same as those used by host initiators. The host initiator establishes a connection with a logical unit in the subsystem controller, and an internal initiator in the subsystem controller finishes the work through multiple connections to Fibre Channel drives.

Figure 7-11 illustrates the basic traffic flows between a SAN host and a Fibre Channel RAID subsystem.

Figure 7-11 *A Fibre Channel RAID Subsystem*

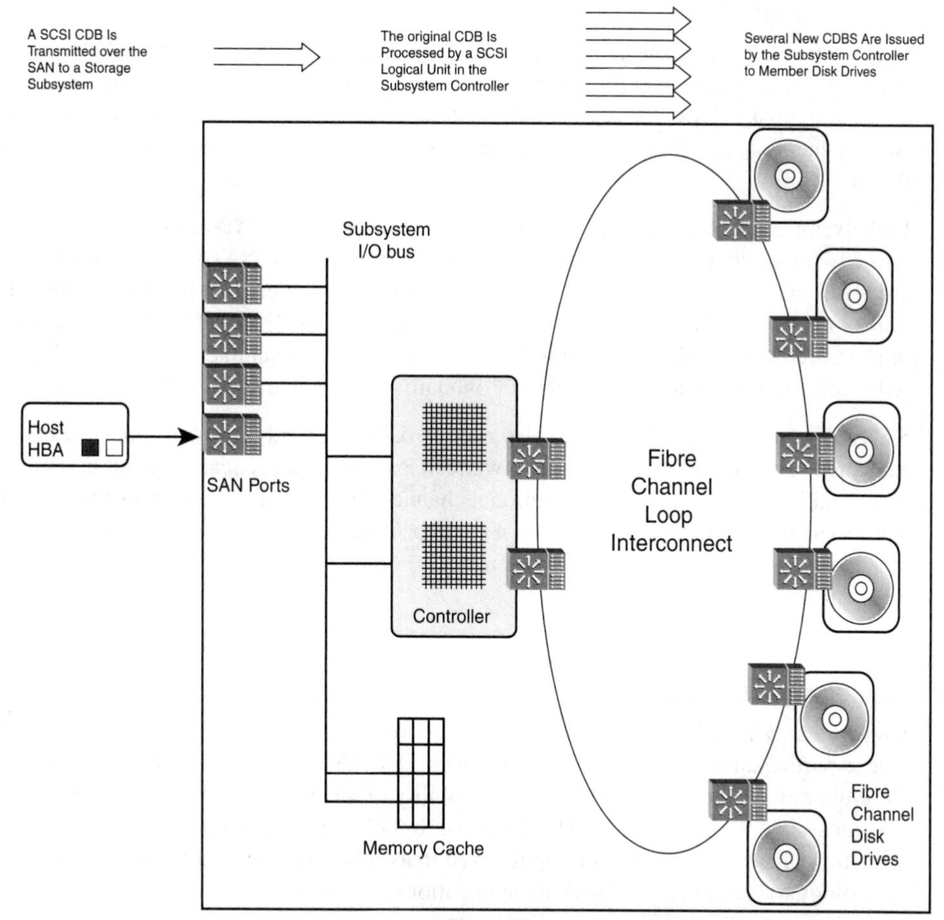

Retooling ATA Storage with Serial ATA

One of the most interesting developments in storage device interconnects is SATA. The basic concept of SATA is simple: it is a revision of ATA that retains the logical storing protocols and access methods of ATA but replaces the parallel bus with serial point-to-point connections. In a way it's like using SCSI-3 logic with Fibre Channel, except in this case the ATA logic is not abstracted from the connecting layer as a separate standard. SATA logic and connectivity are very much tied at the hip.

SATA is intended to be implemented as PC system storage that connects primarily to PC motherboards. In fact, the primary driver for the development of SATA is Intel, which would benefit from streamlined I/O processing, smaller motherboard connectors, and reduced power requirements for PC systems. SATA takes a major step in the continued miniaturization and efficiency of PC systems by significantly shrinking the connectors and cables used.

Point-to-Point Connections

SATA gets rid of the arcane addressing of ATA's master/slave designation by allowing only one device per channel in a point-to-point connection. While this simplifies the matter of configuring disk drives, it's not optimal for storage networking operations. With parallel ATA, two channels support four devices, whereas SATA requires four channels for the same four drives.

Initially, most SATA-equipped PC motherboards had only two SATA channels, which made it virtually impossible to expand SATA storage in a PC system. If SATA drives are being used strictly as boot drives, expandability is not necessarily a problem, but it could certainly be a problem if they are being used to store application data. The dearth of SATA channels on motherboards shouldn't last too long, because motherboard manufacturers, especially Intel, will likely start increasing the number of onboard SATA connections relatively soon.

SAN subsystems with SATA drives also need to design around the one-to-one channel limitation. The trick is understanding how much excess channel capacity to put in a subsystem if each additional drive needs an additional channel. This might not be a major problem for small to medium-sized subsystems, but it could be a serious obstacle for larger subsystems. All new storage technologies have problems initially before working out the details, and SATA will be no different.

The Short, Confusing History of SATA

Intel announced the formation of the Serial ATA Working Group early in 2000. Besides Intel, invited participants included APT Technologies, Dell, IBM, Maxtor, Quantum, and Seagate. In December of 2000 they announced the availability of what was referred to as Draft Specification 1.0, defining the SATA interface. In February of 2002, they announced the formation of another Working Group referred to as SATA II, intended to extend SATA 1.0 technology for server and networking applications.

Then in June 2002, Intel, HP, and Dell announced a plan to work together on compatible interfaces between Serial Attached SCSI (SAS) and SATA II. In January 2003, the SCSI trade association, a consortium of parallel SCSI vendors and the SATA II Working Group, announced a collaboration to enable compatible operations between SAS and SATA.

NOTE SAS is not discussed in this book other than its relationship to SATA in this chapter. I've made the mistake of writing about "the next great technology" before (InfiniBand or DAFS, anybody?). It's not clear whether the world needs and will buy products using an additional and redundant storage interconnect, although there do seem to be advantages to mixing SATA and SAS on the same interconnect.

In February 2003, a year after the 1.0 release, the Serial ATA 1.0a specification was released. Then, in November 2003, the work of the SATA II group released its Revision 1.1 of the Serial ATA 1.0a specification, which included such features as Native Command Queuing and the Port Multiplier.

Despite all these releases from the two SATA Working Groups, at the time this chapter was written, no SATA standards had been published by an accredited industry standards body. That said, it appears that significant work has been done by the T13 ATA standards committee to add Serial ATA to the anticipated ATA/ATAPI-7 standard as the third volume of three volumes in that publication.

NOTE It's only natural that companies involved in the development of new technology want to promote it and engage other industry members to participate. However, in this case it appears the promotional strategy was "Ready, fire, aim!" At least they don't try to hide it in their specification. When you download the 1.0a spec, the very first thing you read on page 1 is the following:

"This 1.0a revision of the *Serial ATA / High Speed Serialized AT Attachment* specification consists of the 1.0 revision of the specification with the following errata incorporated: 2, 3, 4, 5, 6, 7, 8, 9, 10, 11, 12, 13, 14, 15, 16, 17, 18, 19, 20, 21, 22, 23, 24, 25, 26, 29, 30, 31, 32, 33, 34, 35, 36, 38, 40"

It's amazing what a little time can do for the development of new technology! A risk for SATA moving forward through both the T10 SCSI committee (with SAS) and the T13 ATA committee is that there will be inconsistencies between two independent standards that are not easily resolved, forcing breakage in one place or another.

Performance Expectations for SATA

The first version of SATA has burst transfer rates of 150 MBps, which is not far off Fibre Channel's 200 MBps, or parallel SCSI's 160 MBps. Future versions are expected to have burst transfer rates of 300 MBps. While burst transfer rates are important, they are only part of the performance landscape. To have competitive performance with Fibre Channel and parallel SCSI, SATA needs to solve the problem of its ATA legacy not implementing command queuing and overlapped I/Os.

Fortunately, SATA developers seem to have solved some of these problems. For starters, when a drive has a dedicated channel, there is no possibility of not having overlapped I/O. If all storage access goes to independent channels, all I/Os are overlapped.

The SATA II 1.1 enhancements revision includes something called Native Command Queuing (NCQ), apparently named to distinguish it from ATA's mediocre command queuing capabilities. Similar to SCSI's command queuing mechanism (see Chapter 6, "SCSI Storage Fundamentals and SAN Adapters"), NCQ reorders commands for more efficient operations in addition to aggregating responses and reducing the number of interrupts on host systems.

Native command queuing will likely make a significant difference over time. The gating factor for now appears to be host software. Most existing Windows software does not take advantage of tagged I/O. Some Linux systems apparently do, however. Intel believes customers who purchase systems with its hyper-threading technology will be able to use command queuing to a limited degree.

SATA Port Multiplier

Another enhancement to SATA is a device called a port multiplier. The idea is fairly simple: the port multiplier provides connectivity to multiple devices over a single channel. The specification provides support for up to 15 devices to be connected to a single port multiplier. There is no provision in the specification for establishing priorities for drives connected through a port multiplier; those details are explicitly left as an implementation detail.

At first this sounds like it would solve most of the scalability problems SATA might have, but there are always a few pesky implementation details to work through. For instance, two modes of switching are defined for SATA host controllers working with port multipliers. One kind of switching is called command-based switching. It allows the host to have outstanding commands on only one device at a time. This is essentially a mode that restricts overlapped I/O and could have a detrimental impact on the system's I/O performance. NCQ would probably still work, but on only one drive at a time.

The other type of switching is called FIS-based switching. (FIS is the data payload in SATA communications and stands for *frame information structure*.) It is obvious from reading the specification that this is one of those things that can be described facetiously as "a simple matter of programming." In other words, there are no estimates when this can be implemented on a system in your business. Just as command queuing went unused in ATA since the ATA/ATAPI-4 specification, the use of FIS-based switching could have the same kind of response from the industry—especially if it involves getting the attention of large software developers that have other dragons to slay.

SATA Port Selector

The converse of supporting multiple devices with a port multiplier is allowing multiple controllers to access a single disk drive for redundancy purposes. An enhancement to SATA called the port selector provides a mechanism for doing that. The port selector is not the same as dual porting in Fibre Channel in that the drive itself does not have two ports, but the port selector acts as a miniature "front end" to provide that capability.

Its not clear yet whether this technology will be used or how much it would cost to implement, but it does show the depths to which the SATA Working Group has gone to make its technology applicable for applications outside the desktop PC. With the port selector in place, the SATA interconnect would be second only to the Fibre Channel interconnect for supporting fault-tolerant dual pathing inside the subsystem.

SATA Storage Network Applications and Configurations

SATA is a technology that will be much more capable than its predecessor, ATA, for many storage network applications. It is expected to cost less than either Fibre Channel or parallel SCSI. It also will deliver performance capable of handling moderately heavy I/O workloads such as web serving, non-transaction-processing databases, and streaming media. SATA is expected to be used effectively to support the I/O requirements of most Linux and Windows servers.

SATA Disk Drives Within Systems

Like parallel SCSI, SATA will be deployed both within systems as boot disks and NAS storage and in SAN disk subsystems. Figure 7-12 shows a NAS system with a four-port internal SATA RAID controller running RAID 5.

Figure 7-12 *A SATA-Based NAS System*

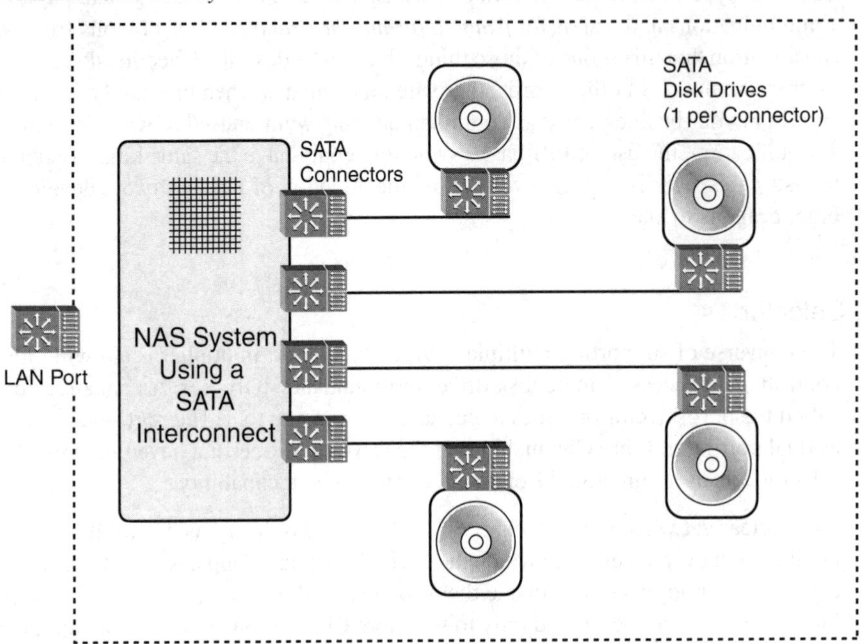

SATA in SAN Disk Subsystems

In addition to the port multiplier and port selector functions that are intended to give SATA more of an entry in storage networking applications, the SATA Working Groups have worked on defining backplane interfaces to work with SATA drives. There is little doubt that these drives will be better suited to adoption into disk subsystems than either parallel SCSI or ATA.

Because they are not SCSI drives, physically or logically, it is not possible to implement SATA in a way that allows SAN initiators to establish SCSI connections directly with SATA drives the way parallel SCSI and Fibre Channel can. SATA drives could still be used in a JBOD-like way where individual drives are exported for use by individual servers, but the disk subsystem controller would perform the entire target/logical units functions before reinitiating commands internally. There is no way the performance of such a system could rival either parallel SCSI or Fibre Channel.

The ability to use backplane connector technology with SATA makes hot swapping much easier than with either ATA or parallel SCSI drives. In addition, SATA port selector technology could potentially be integrated into the backplane circuitry to provide integrated multipath protection from controller failures.

Figure 7-13 shows a hypothetical SATA disk subsystem with port selector technology integrated into a five-disk RAID backplane.

Figure 7-13 *A SATA RAID Subsystem with Integrated Port Selector Technology for Dual Pathing*

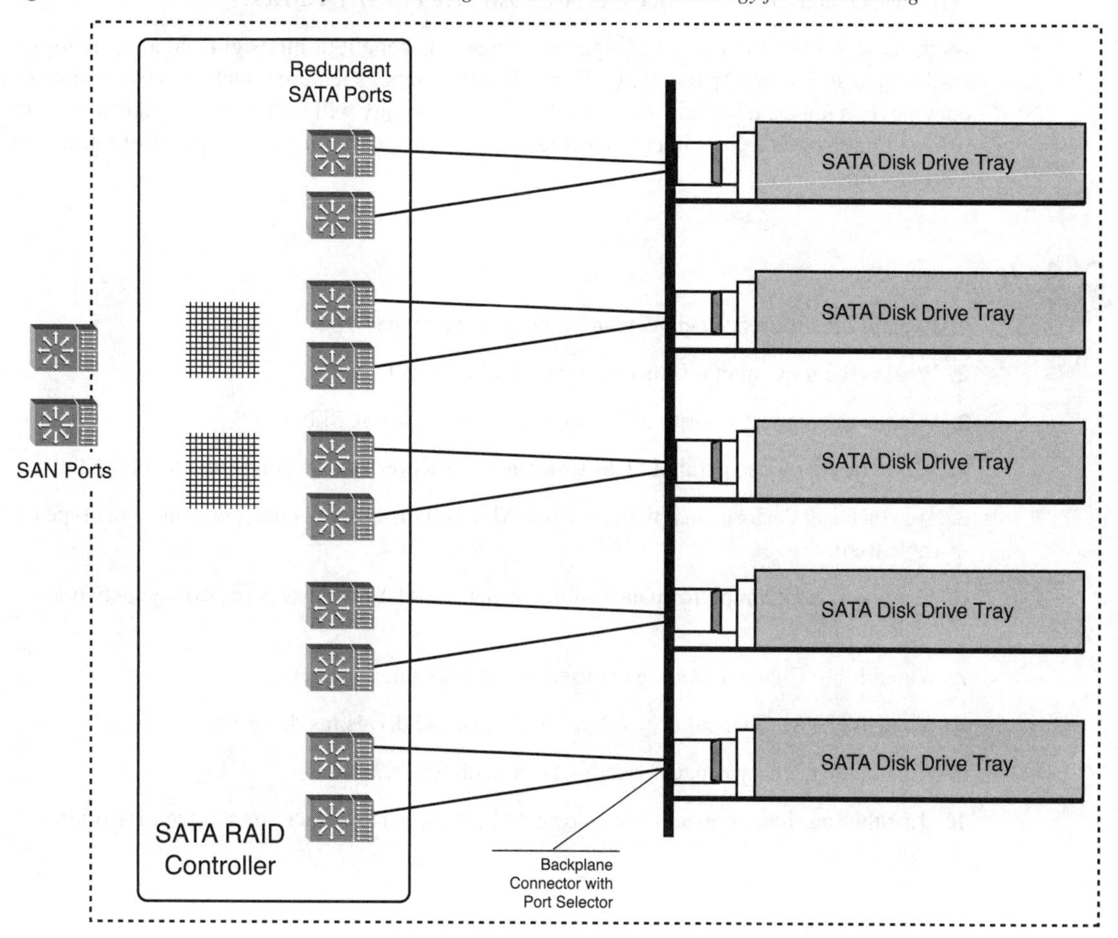

Summary

As disk drives are at the core of nearly all storage networking products, the interconnect technology that connects disk devices to their respective controllers can have a major influence on a product's capabilities. Traditionally, parallel SCSI and Fibre Channel disk drives have been the interconnects used in storage networking, although ATA and, more recently, SATA drives have been used successfully for certain applications.

The combination of tagged command queuing and overlapped I/Os with parallel SCSI and Fibre Channel interconnects makes them much more applicable for high-performance applications than ATA or SATA. However, many systems do not need this type of I/O performance and can run on much less expensive ATA or SATA drives.

As the newest interconnect, SATA appears to have the benefit of hindsight and a technology road map to add some of parallel SCSI's and Fibre Channel's features, such as native command queuing. It is not clear yet how successful SATA technology will be, but the cost advantages of using an improved desktop interconnect technology for low-throughput applications points to a bright future.

Q & A

1. Explain the difference between an interconnect and a SAN.
2. What is the maximum distance of a parallel SCSI LVD bus?
3. What is the highest-priority address on a 16-bit (wide) SCSI bus?
4. Why would you use parallel SCSI disks inside a server system connected to a SAN?
5. True or false: Performance with an Ultra ATA/100 disk drive is independent of the type of cable used.
6. Name the two main performance shortcomings of ATA disk drives for storage network applications.
7. Which Fibre Channel topology is used as a device interconnect?
8. Why isn't Fibre Channel used often for the internal drives inside system cabinets?
9. What is the primary capacity scaling issue with SATA?
10. List the four interconnects from slowest to fastest performance for storage networking applications.

Applications for Data Redundancy

Upon completing this chapter, you will be able to

- Participate in discussions with vendors and coworkers regarding data redundancy policies and methods in your organization
- Understand the difference between MTBF, MTDA, MTDL, and MTTR calculations in a storage network environment
- Identify locations in the I/O path in a SAN where mirroring can be implemented
- Explain the performance benefits of mirroring for read operations

CHAPTER 8

An Introduction to Data Redundancy and Mirroring

One of the most important and powerful concepts in storage networking is redundancy, which embodies the creation and management of spare copies of data, including encoded data and incremental changes to data; the use of multiple storage devices, subsystems, and media for storing these redundant data copies; and the ability to access data over multiple network paths. This chapter explores some of the different approaches used to create data redundancy and then takes an in-depth look at one of the most common forms of data redundancy—mirroring.

The Necessity of Redundancy in Storage Networks

Redundancy is the primary principle supporting data protection and high-availability computing. Without redundancy there would be no way to recover from even the smallest mistake or component failure, such as the failure of a disk drive. A data center that has tens of thousands of disk drives should expect to have regular drive failures in the course of normal operations. Without data redundancy, each of these disk drive failures could be catastrophic.

Of course, device failures represent only a part of the overall requirement for data redundancy. Large-scale disasters also occur and need to be protected against. The distance capabilities of storage networks mean it is possible to store redundant data at a secondary location that is far enough away to protect data from threats that could impact systems processors and primary storage.

Secondary storage locations for redundant data might be in an adjacent room, on another floor, across the street, across town, or even in another region, state, or country. The point is, if something happens to primary production data, it is necessary to ensure the business can continue operating through the application of redundant data and data-recovery techniques.

Threats to Data

There are basically three things that can go wrong and make data unavailable or unusable:

- **Loss of data**—Data is erased or overwritten, or the equipment it is stored on fails or is destroyed.
- **Blocked access**—The data itself might be unharmed, but the access to it may be blocked.
- **Loss of integrity**—The data might have errors introduced into it by bugs, accidents, or intent.

Business continuity experts try to evaluate the various threats to data that impact their data-processing capabilities. An abbreviated list of threats includes

- User and administrator accidents
- Component failures
- Intentional data destruction or corruption caused by authorized users or external intruders
- System and application bugs or malfunctions
- Major disasters such as earthquakes, floods, and fires
- Power outages
- Virus attacks

NOTE We like to think of the big events that cause data loss, such as floods, fires, earthquakes, hurricanes, tornados, and other types of storms. However, year in and year out the biggest threat to data continues to be the "protein robots"—users and administrators who fat-finger commands, respond to prompts like zombies while digesting lunches, and otherwise make the human screwups that we do in the course of doing something that might be insufferably mundane and repetitive. Operating a computer while half-asleep is not as dangerous as operating a motor vehicle while in the same condition—unless you happen to be the poor, unprotected data that at any time is just a few keystrokes from annihilation.

Redundancy Metrics: MTBF, MTDA, MTDL, and MTTR

Data redundancy in storage networks is measured by the reliability of storage and network products. As storage network vendors occasionally use reliability measurements in their marketing materials and presentations, it helps to understand what these measurements mean. This section discusses the terms used in accordance with definitions established by the Storage Network Industry Association (SNIA). The four metrics discussed in this section are

- Mean time between failure (MTBF)
- Mean time to loss of data availability (MTDA)
- Mean time to data loss (MTDL)
- Mean time to repair (MTTR)

MTBF

MTBF was introduced in Chapter 4, "Storage Devices," as a statistical method for predicting failure rates in a large number of disk drives. Similar methods are used to predict the reliability of all other components in a storage network, including storage controllers and switch-line cards.

MTDA

MTDA is a measurement that predicts loss of access to data in a storage network. This measurement includes MTBF calculations for all I/O path components between a host system initiator and a Small Computer Systems Interface (SCSI) logical unit, such as system interfaces, cables, network devices, subsystem controllers, and interconnect components. Individual storage devices contribute to MTDA if they are not participating in some sort of data redundancy scheme. Otherwise, storage (and data) availability is more effectively indicated by MTDL, discussed in the following paragraphs.

MTDL

MTDL measures the risk of losing data. Where data redundancy techniques are being used, data loss results from multiple component failures occurring within a relatively narrow span of time. The whole point of using redundancy techniques with storage is to increase MTDL to a number that is much, much greater than the MTBF of an individual disk drive. In most cases, MTDL is expressed as the probability of having two components that are part of the same SCSI logical unit failing before a replacement component can take the place of the first failed component.

Hot-spare technology (discussed in Chapter 5, "Storage Subsystems") can increase MTDL considerably by reducing the exposure to a second component failure that would cause permanent data loss.

MTTR

MTTR is a measurement of the time it takes to replace a failed component with another completely functioning component. Where disk subsystems are concerned, this means that the subsystem is operating normally and is not operating in reduced or degraded modes. In other words, MTTR includes the time needed to format and copy data to the replacement drives.

Forms of Data Redundancy

The countermeasure to losing data or data access is the application of redundancy techniques. If data is destroyed or made inaccessible, redundant copies of data can be used. There are three basic techniques or forms of redundancy applied in storage networks today that are discussed in this section:

- Duplication
- Parity
- Delta/difference

Duplication

The concept of duplication is simple: an additional copy of data is made on a different device, subsystem, or volume to protect the data from a failure to the underlying hardware or software. Duplication is used in several different storage and data management technologies, including backup, mirroring, and remote-copy (store and forward) products.

There are two primary ways duplication redundancy is accomplished. The first is to have a storage controller or a software program running in the I/O path generate two storage I/O commands for every I/O request/command it receives. In other words, instead of acting on data in a single device, subsystem, or volume, the data is acted on in two separate storage targets. This approach is the one used in mirroring and is shown in Figure 8-1.

Figure 8-1 *A Single Storage Command Is Duplicated by Mirroring*

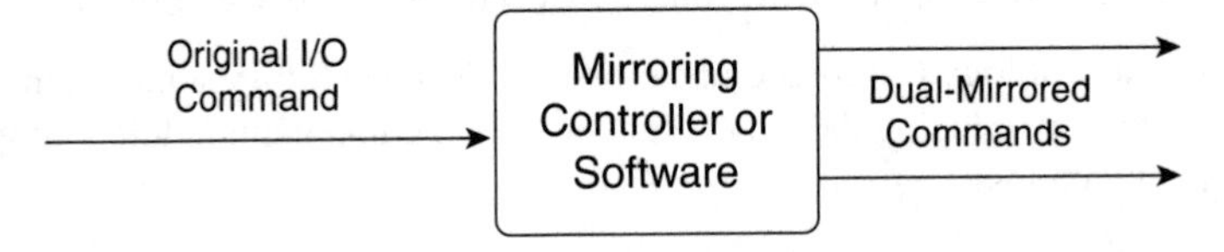

The second way to make duplicate copies of data is to have the first storage target copy the data to a second storage target. This approach, illustrated in Figure 8-2, is commonly used in products that provide remote-copy functionality. Remote-copy technology is discussed in more detail in Chapter 10, "Redundancy Over Distance with Remote Copy."

Figure 8-2 *A Remote-Copy Process with a Storage Target Sending a Copy of Data to Another Storage Target*

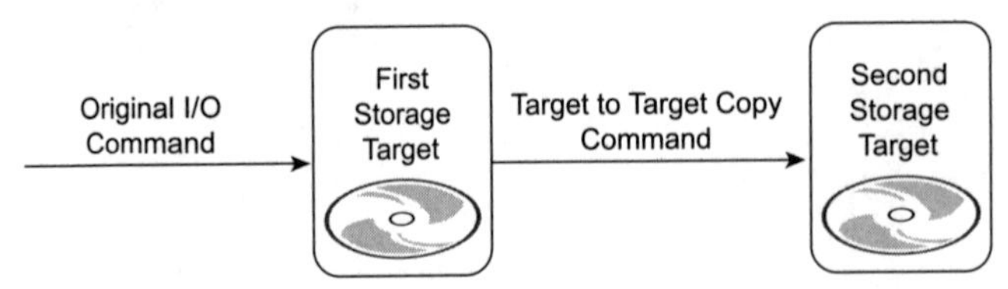

Parity

Parity uses an encoding scheme that provides a way to recover data without needing to keep a whole extra copy of the data. Parity is the technology used in redundant array of inexpensive disks (RAID), the topic of Chapter 9, "Bigger, Faster, More Reliable Storage with RAID." Using parity, a complete copy of the original data can be reconstructed using parity data and an incomplete set of the original data.

Delta or Difference Redundancy

Stored data changes over time as applications add, delete, and update data. *Delta redundancy,* also referred to sometimes as difference redundancy, takes advantage of the changes in data over time to achieve efficiencies in data redundancy.

The basic algorithm for delta redundancy is simple. At some time, t = 0, make a complete copy of the data, and then, at a regular interval—say, once a day—record the changes to the data, and store the change information as a separate data item. That way it is possible to reconstruct the data as it existed at each point in time that the change information was recorded.

For example, it would be possible to make a complete copy of data on the first day of a month and then make a delta record of daily changes every day at noon. At the end of the month, it would be possible to re-create the data as it existed at noon on any day of the month by applying all the daily changes, in sequence, from the first day until the day in question.

Delta redundancy is commonly used in backup and snapshot technology. One of the most common backup schedules employed is based on taking a full backup copy on the weekend and taking incremental backups of changed data on weekdays.

The process of creating an original duplicate copy and subsequent delta copies is shown in Figure 8-3.

Figure 8-3 *The Creation of an Original Copy and Subsequent Delta Copies of Data*

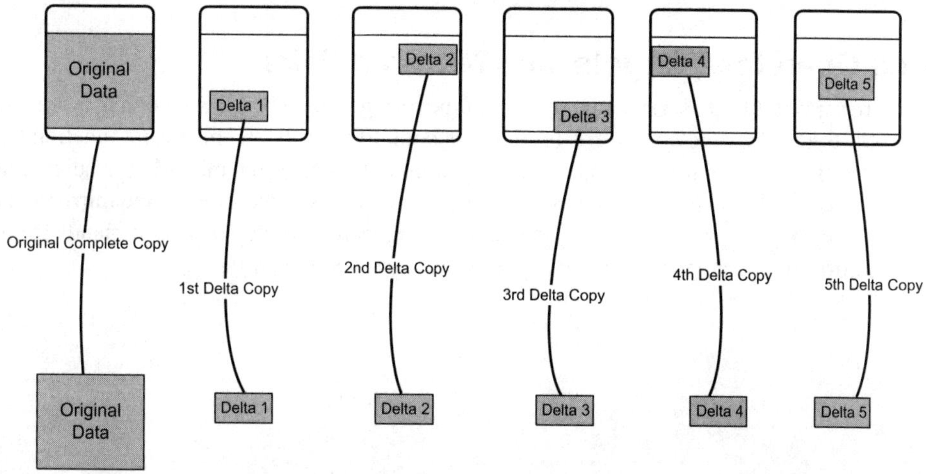

Mirroring

The most basic form of duplication redundancy is data mirroring, a concept that has been a staple of data center operations for decades. Mirroring is a storing-level function that is abstracted from higher-level functions, such as file systems and databases. Mirroring provides continuous storage I/O operations after a hardware, software, or communications failure keeps data from being accessed from a storage target.

The discussion of mirroring in this chapter does not include remote-copy technology, which is discussed in Chapter 10. While mirroring and remote copy are often discussed and described as being part of the same technology, they are actually quite a bit different. The two are used for different purposes and have significantly different costs.

Mirroring is primarily a real-time function that creates two I/Os that are processed in parallel. Both copies of data created by a mirror are available online to the system that uses the mirrored storage.

Remote copy, on the other hand, creates secondary, sequentially processed I/Os that are forwarded to remote storage by a storage subsystem. The remote copy of the data is not intended to be accessed online by the system that created the data. Other systems at the remote location access the remote copies.

The topics covered in this section are

- Mirroring operators, targets, and mirrored pairs
- Disk mirroring
- Location of mirroring operators
- The mirroring function
- Overlapped read operations for performance
- Assumptions about distance and mirroring

Mirroring Operators, Targets, and Mirrored Pairs

To simplify the discussion about whether mirroring is done in software or hardware controllers, the term *mirroring operator* is used in this book to describe the mirroring function that is performed. Similarly, to simplify the discussion of whether the mirroring is being done to devices, subsystems, LUNs, volumes, or partitions, this book refers to the mirrored storage as storage targets. With mirroring, two storage targets receive duplicate commands from a mirroring operator; these targets are referred to as a *mirrored pair*.

A mirroring operator and a mirrored pair are illustrated in Figure 8-4.

Figure 8-4 *A Mirroring Operator and a Mirrored Pair of Storage Targets*

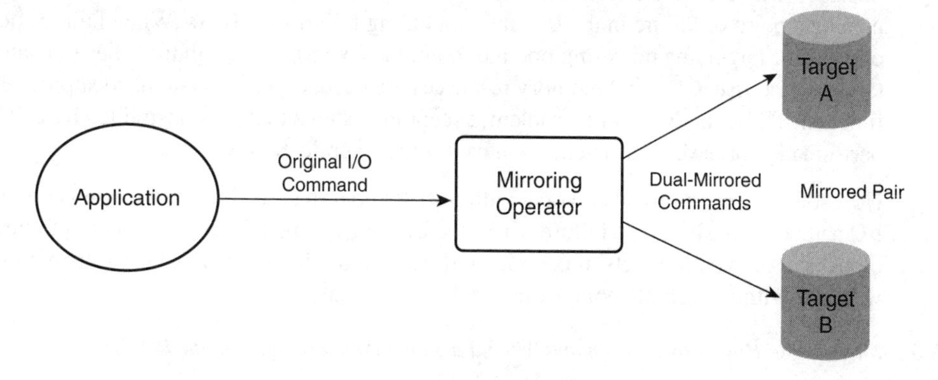

NOTE It's not really quite right to throw in the concept of volume or partition with device, subsystem, and LUN by calling them *targets*. A volume or partition is not a target in the SCSI sense of the word. However, where mirroring is concerned, these things do define the specific location where data gets stored. This is part of what makes talking about storage so much fun—there are different ways to skin or de-fur the same cat.

Disk Mirroring

Mirroring in storage networks today extends the original concept of *disk mirroring* that has been used for decades to provide online data redundancy. The idea of disk mirroring is very simple: if something goes wrong with a disk drive, the system continues working with the other drive.

The developers of RAID included disk mirroring in their work, calling it RAID level 1, as the most basic form of a redundant disk array. Mirroring is not only useful for data protection, but it also has some performance advantages that are discussed later in this chapter.

Location of Mirroring Operators

Mirroring operators can be positioned at almost any point along the I/O path between an application and storage targets. Operators can run in host-based volume-management software, device driver software, host bus adapter hardware, network devices, and switches and storage subsystems.

Mirroring in Host System Software

Data mirroring is often accomplished as a fundamental feature of an operating system, volume management, or device driver software. Mirroring in host software has the advantage of having no single point of failure in the I/O path, including failures to HBAs. When failures occur in one path or target, the mirroring operator continues working through the other I/O path and its target. Of course, CPU and memory resources are needed in host systems to support the function. This usually is not a problem, except in systems that are constrained by CPU performance or have insufficient memory for their application workload.

Host software mirroring also works with mirrored pair targets that are accessed on the same I/O path. Obviously, a path failure where the I/O path segment is a single point of failure would block access to both targets in the mirrored pair. Figure 8-5 compares host software mirroring with and without a single point of failure in the I/O path.

Figure 8-5 *Mirroring in Host Software with and Without a Single Point of Failure in the I/O Path*

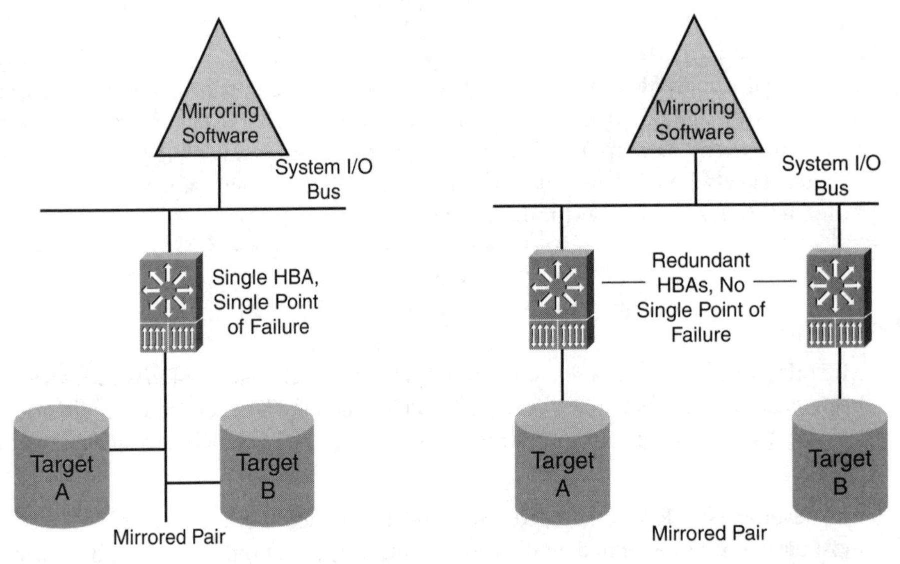

NOTE Not all operating systems support mirroring as a software function, although it is relatively easy to provide it. Windows 2000 and Windows XP Professional come to mind. While these products are sold as higher-level desktop environments, neither has an option to install this most basic data-protection functionality. You have to buy the server version of the product to get software mirroring.

Apparently, this was done to limit Microsoft's exposure to licensing violations where users take a disk mirror and install it in unlicensed systems. To further protect itself from "theft by mirror," Microsoft implemented mirroring in its server products in a way that prevented licensing information from being copied from the primary disk to the secondary disk. The result is that if the "wrong" drive fails, it's necessary to reload the license keys from the installation CDs before rebooting the server the next time. Just what you need—a disk mirror that makes you reinstall software.

Mirroring in Host Storage Controllers

Mirroring is sometimes provided in HBAs and integrated host system storage I/O controllers. While there is nothing necessarily wrong with mirroring in host hardware, it does establish the HBA or I/O controller as a single point of failure.

Multiported controllers allow the I/O path to be split so that both targets of a mirrored pair are connected to a different bus or network connection. Figure 8-6 shows mirroring in a dual-ported HBA, where both targets of a mirrored pair are connected to separate ports on the HBA.

Figure 8-6 *Mirroring in a Dual-Ported HBA*

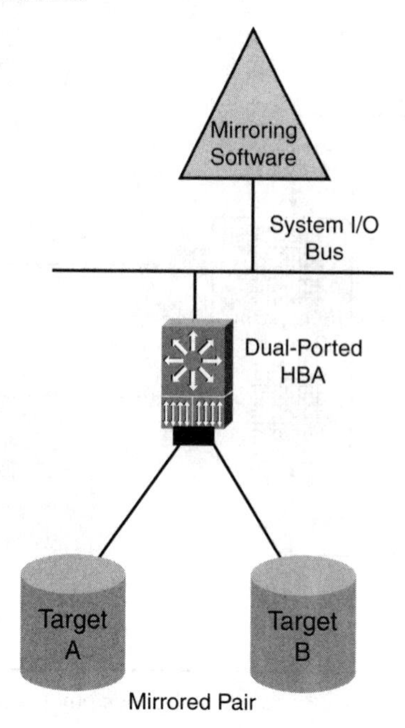

Mirroring in a Network Device or Switch

A new development in the evolution of storage networks puts the mirroring operator in the I/O path in a network device or switch. The mirroring function could be provided by software or hardware running as a storage application inside networking equipment. Many products in the market do this; they are referred to generically as SAN virtualization products. Chapter 12, "Storage Virtualization: The Power in Volume Management Software and SAN Virtualization Systems," discusses these products in more detail.

Mirroring in a Storage Subsystem

One of the most common locations for mirroring is within a disk subsystem. The mirrored pair in a subsystem is exported for use by host systems as a LUN address. Of course, this LUN address could be made available through dual ports for high-availability connections to host systems. In this case, there would be both mirroring in the subsystem for redundant data protection and multipathing between the subsystem and the host, providing redundant connectivity. Multipathing is discussed in more detail in Chapter 11, "Connection Redundancy in Storage Networks and Dynamic Multipathing."

Figure 8-7 shows a configuration where a mirrored pair inside a disk subsystem is exported as a LUN address by two different target addresses to a host with dual connections to the storage network.

Figure 8-7 *A Mirrored Pair in a Disk Subsystem Exported Over Two Different Target/LUN Addresses*

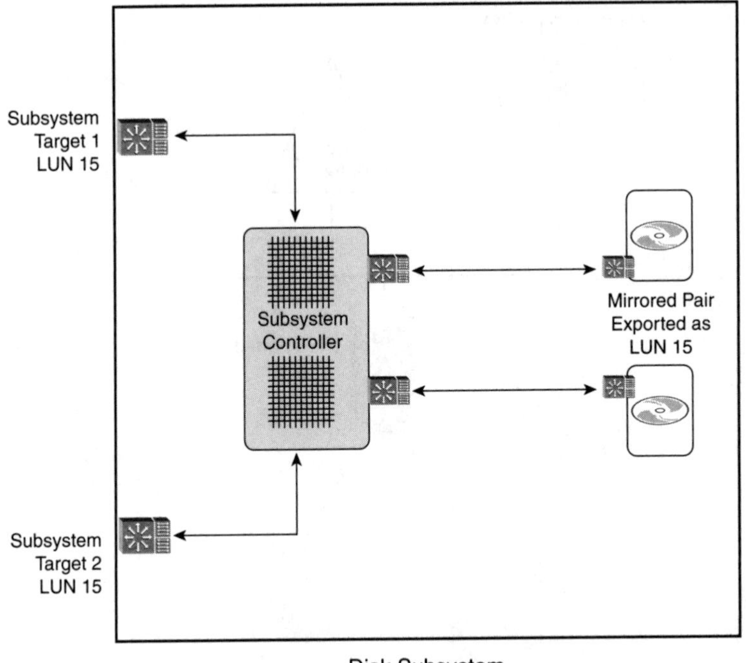

Mirroring can be used in other types of storage subsystems besides disk subsystems; for instance, it is possible to mirror backup operations to dual tape drives inside a tape library. However, the highly variable condition of tape media makes it more difficult to create an environment with dependable operations that meet performance expectations. While mirroring disks is a fundamental feature of most disk subsystems, it is not widely featured in tape subsystems.

NOTE Mirroring with host software to two different storage targets using two different I/O paths should not be confused with multipathing. With multipathing, two different I/O paths are established to access a single storage target in a disk subsystem. To put a fine point on it, you can *mirror* data over two different paths to *two different LUs* in a storage subsystem, or you can use multipathing to access *one LU* over one of the paths. The topic of multipathing is explored in more detail in Chapter 11.

Multiple Mirrors and Multilevel Data Redundancy

The mirroring function can be done many times, in sequence, along the I/O path. In other words, there can be mirroring operators in host software, HBAs, network switches, and disk subsystems all working with the same initial data. For example, two different disk subsystems could export a mirrored pair of internal disk drives as a LUN. An upstream mirroring operator, such as an HBA or volume management software, could then mirror these two LUNs and make them appear as a single target to the host system. So, instead of writing data to a single target, as the host software would assume, the data is actually being written to four different disk drives. Figure 8-8 demonstrates this scenario.

Figure 8-8 *Two Layers of Mirrors, Resulting in Four Copies of Data*

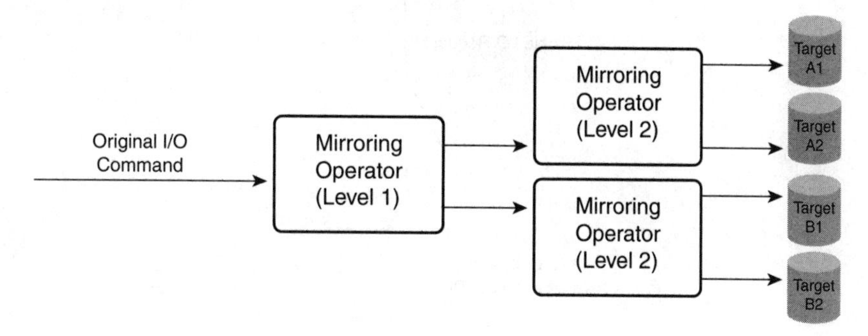

The Mirroring Function

Mirroring is a storing-level function; in other words, it works with blocks, block commands, such as SCSI command descriptor blocks (CDBs), and block storage address spaces. In essence, mirroring receives a storage command, copies it, sends it twice to two different storage targets, and then waits for acknowledgments from both targets.

I/O Termination and Reinitiation

Mirroring can be thought of as a real-time process where a single storage command arrives at the mirroring operator and is immediately forwarded to the mirrored pair targets. When the mirroring operator is running in the host system, the generation of the duplicate I/O commands can take place prior to being passed to the SCSI layer of the I/O stack. In other words, the mirroring operator does not have to interpret SCSI commands. Instead, it receives an I/O request from the file system through internal system interfaces, and then it formulates a pair of requests through the SCSI device driver's application program interface (API) layer. Figure 8-9 illustrates a single I/O request being exchanged twice between a host software mirroring operator and device driver software.

Figure 8-9 *Mirroring in Host System Software, Creating Duplicate Requests for the Device Driver's API*

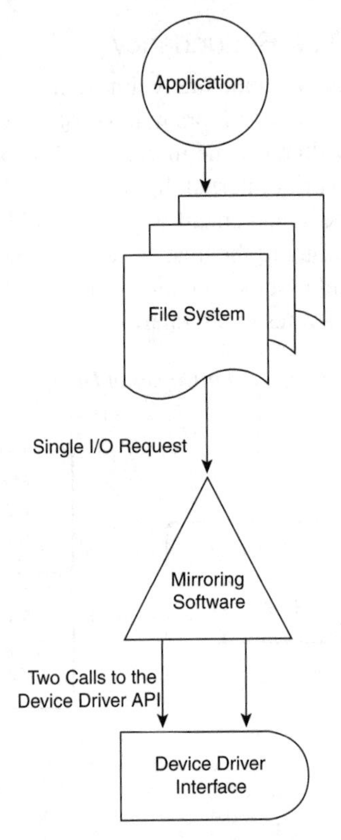

The situation is slightly different for mirroring operators in the network or in storage subsystems. In these cases, the original I/O command is received as a SCSI CDB that must be interpreted. Notice that the mirroring operator in this scenario is actually initiating a new set of commands to the mirrored pair targets. In other words, the mirroring operator functions as a target to the upstream controller-initiator and then changes roles to act as the initiator for mirrored I/Os sent to downstream targets.

This dual role is commonly talked about as the mirroring operator *terminating* the original SCSI CDB and *reinitiating* new SCSI CDBs for the mirrored pair. Figure 8-10 illustrates the termination of upstream CDBs (commands) and the reinitiation of two downstream CDBs.

Figure 8-10 *A Mirroring Operator Terminating an Upstream SCSI CDB and Reinitiating Two Downstream CDBs*

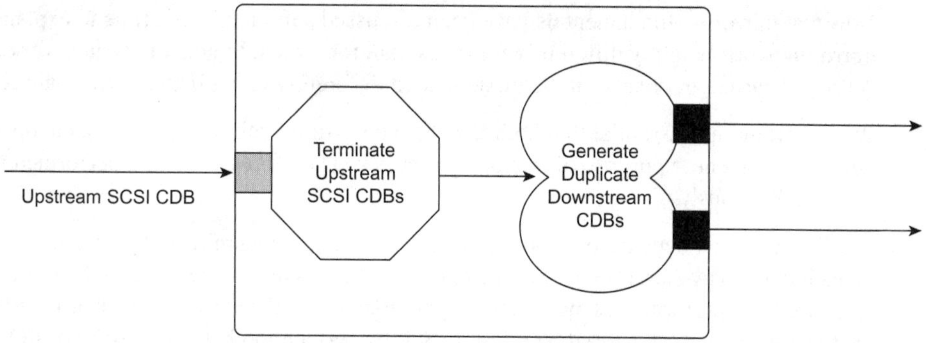

NOTE This issue of SCSI termination and reinitiation also applies to RAID and virtualization operators that are outside host systems in storage networks. In general, it's a good idea to know where all SCSI operations start and where they terminate.

When mirroring is understood this way, it's easier to see some of the challenges in mixing different kinds of disk drive technologies in the same mirrored pair, such as a SCSI drive and a SATA drive. In this case, the original command is not just duplicated, it is duplicated and converted to the other technology's protocol.

Host software might have an easier time working with different types of disk technology, because it does not have to issue two different types of commands and manage two different types of error conditions. However, it does have to issue two different requests and interactions with the system kernel and storage device drivers.

Identically Sized Storage Address Spaces

Mirroring is a basic form of storage virtualization that makes identically-sized storage targets appear as a single target to an upstream controller. It is important that both targets in a mirrored pair have the same storage address spaces (capacity). A file system or database system that writes to the mirrored pair is not aware of the mirroring and, therefore, creates only a single storage request when it reads or writes data. This includes a determination of the block address within the storage address space. In other words, the file system or database system has no way of differentiating between two different-sized storage address spaces in a mirror, and, therefore, it is essential that both targets in a mirrored pair be the same size. It simply cannot work any other way.

Overlapped Read Operations for Performance

Now that mirroring fundamentals have been discussed sufficiently, it's time to explain that mirroring works slightly differently for reads than for writes. In general, writes work as described earlier, but reads can be implemented differently to get better performance.

When writing, it is essential that both targets in a mirrored pair perform the same operation; otherwise, the entire purpose of mirroring is at risk. Therefore, writes are performed more or less simultaneously.

Reading data only depends on working with a single target in a mirrored pair. There is no point in reading from two targets if one of the read operations will only be discarded. For that reason, reads are often performed as overlapping operations where the work load is distributed between the two targets in the mirrored pair. Figure 8-11 shows a hypothetical division of I/O requests to different storage targets.

Figure 8-11 *Overlapped Reads from Targets in a Mirrored Pair*

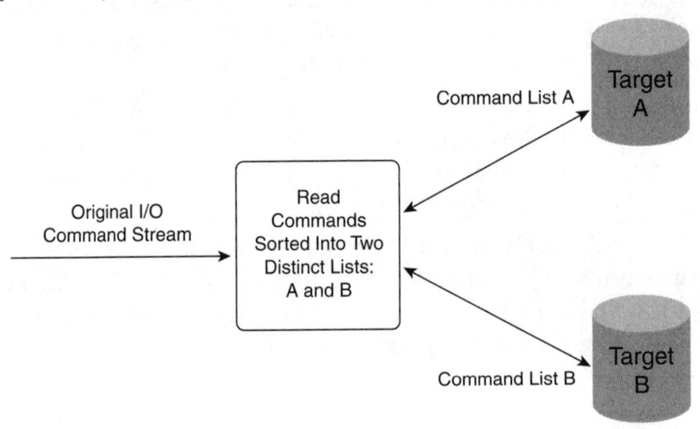

The result is that the compound effects of rotational latency and seek time can be reduced considerably in this process. Adding another disk arm and spindle to the I/O queue can make an enormous difference in system performance.

Assumptions About Distance and Mirroring

Many times people want to use mirroring over longer distances for disaster protection and business continuity purposes. The basic idea is to have one storage target running locally and the other one running some distance away.

This can work, but there are some important things to keep in mind. First, remember that mirroring operators duplicate all storage commands, which can take an enormous amount of LAN, MAN, or WAN bandwidth; this can be expensive. Second, mirroring is a real-time process that requires low latency and minimal transmission delays. High-throughput applications might not be able to perform as expected using extended-distance mirrors. That said, it's not uncommon to see IT organizations use mirroring to achieve data redundancy for distances ranging up to 10 miles.

Remote-copy or file-level replication technologies designed for long-distance data redundancy provide much better options for data redundancy over longer distances. Chapter 10 investigates this topic in much more detail.

NOTE The statement about mirroring operators duplicating all storage commands is not 100% correct. It is possible to implement mirroring so that only one target in a mirrored pair receives read requests. An example of a product that can do this is the Veritas Volume Manager. Changing the READ POLICY allows administrators to restrict reads to the local mirror target, which means the remote target would receive only writes and a few other commands, such as status requests. The end result would be a significant drop in bandwidth requirements for the remote link. Note that this would not reduce the latency of write operations over the remote mirror link, but the cost of that link could be considerably less.

Summary

Redundancy is one of the guiding principles for storage networks. Of the three forms of redundancy—duplication, parity, and delta—duplication as instantiated in mirroring and backup products has been the most heavily implemented over the course of several decades.

Mirroring is a simple concept developed for online, real-time duplication of storage I/O commands to two targets in a mirrored pair. The location of the mirroring operator can have a significant impact on the overall availability of a system and its data. It is often implemented at multiple levels to provide protection from different kinds of threats.

Often mirroring is confused with two other related and complementary redundancy applications: multipathing and remote copy. It's important to keep the differences between these technologies clear to be able to build and manage complete redundancy solutions.

The essence of mirroring is to access two storage targets, both of them online and operating in real-time to achieve high system availability. The essence of multipathing is to achieve system availability by providing different paths that access a single storage target. The essence of remote copy is to establish a remote storage target for high data availability and is intended to be accessed by another system in a remote location.

Q & A

1. Why is data redundancy important?
2. What are three different forms of redundancy?
3. What's the first step in using delta redundancy?
4. List four locations in the I/O path that could contain mirroring operators.
5. Why can't two targets in a mirrored pair have different sizes (capacities)?
6. How can mirroring improve system performance?
7. Explain how a mirrored pair in a subsystem can be accessed through two different target addresses in a SAN.
8. Mirroring is sometimes used for remote data protection up to what distance?
9. If there are three layers of mirrors working in an I/O path, how many copies of data will be created?

Upon completing this chapter, you will be able to

- Participate in discussions and planning sessions regarding the use of RAID technology in storage network designs
- Compare the advantages and disadvantages of parity RAID and mirroring
- Describe the exclusive OR (XOR) operation used in parity RAID, and describe the processes of degraded mode operations and parity rebuilds
- Discuss the difference between RAID 10 and RAID 5, including the RAID 5 write penalty

CHAPTER 9

Bigger, Faster, More Reliable Storage with RAID

RAID (redundant array of inexpensive disks) is one of the most important technologies in storage networking and is one of the main functions of storage virtualization. While many people associate RAID with hardware products, such as disk subsystems and RAID adapters, RAID is actually a set of software algorithms that aggregate storage input/output (I/O) operations across multiple storage address spaces. RAID is usually applied with disk drives in disk subsystems, but it can also be applied across multiple disk subsystems in a storage network. In fact, RAID algorithms can be applied across any combination of storage address spaces, whether they are storage devices, logical unit numbers (LUNs) exported by subsystems, or logical volumes created by host volume management software.

NOTE The "I" in RAID stands for inexpensive, although it is often referred to as "independent." Both work, but historically, inexpensive is correct. The "D" in RAID stands for disks, but that should not be taken too literally. The RAID algorithms are independent of the type of storing technology used, as long as they have the same storage capacity.

RAID History

RAID began as a research project at the University of California, Berkeley in the 1980s. At that time, the costs of disk drives were considerably higher than they are today. Mainframe and midrange disk subsystems were relatively expensive, but newer, smaller, and less expensive disk drives were starting to emerge for personal computers. The team at Berkeley perceived an opportunity to combine these newer, cheaper disk drives in ways that would allow them to be used to achieve the same reliability as mainframe and midrange disk products, but at a much lower cost. The goal of RAID has been to deliver similar or better reliability, performance, and capacity by aggregating several smaller disk drives.

Today, RAID is a staple in most storage products. It can be found in disk subsystems, host bus adapters, system motherboards, volume management software, device driver software, and virtually any processor along the I/O path. Because RAID works with storage address spaces and not necessarily storage devices, it can be used on multiple levels recursively.

RAID Fundamentals

RAID is a fairly simple concept with some surprisingly tricky implementation details. This chapter explores the basic ideas first and then moves into the more interesting and complex RAID techniques involving parity.

RAID Arrays and Members

The primary structural element of RAID is the *array*. (See Chapter 5, "Storage Subsystems," for a discussion of arrays.) RAID allows many individual storing entities to be combined in a single array that functions as a single virtual storage device.

The granular storing entities in an array are called array *members*. RAID arrays can have two or more. People often think that RAID arrays are constructed from member disk drives, but that is a bit misleading. It is more helpful to think about arrays as constructed from member disk partitions, as shown in Figure 9-1.

Figure 9-1 *A RAID Array and Its Disk Partition Members*

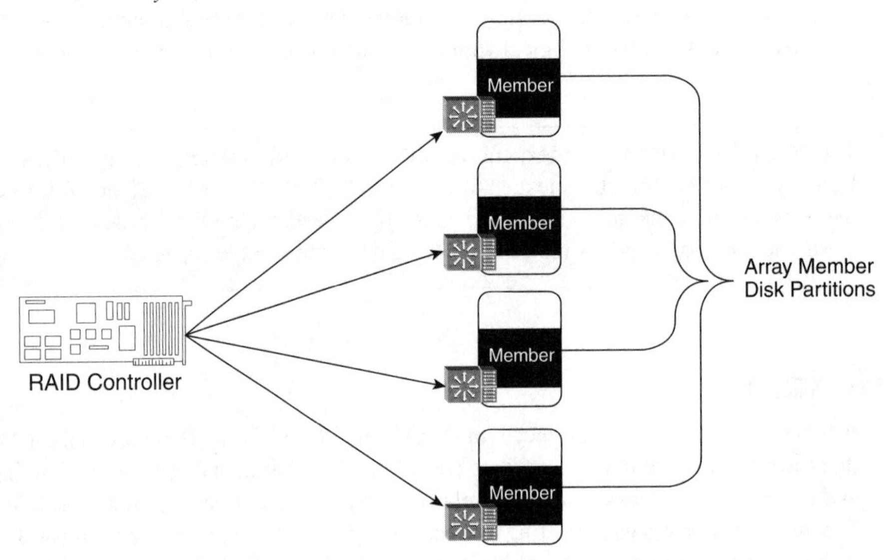

All members in an array must have the same capacity. RAID depends on having uniformly-sized capacity components called *stripes,* which are the granular storage elements where data is written. Each member of an array has equal-sized *strips* that form part of a stripe in an array.

RAID Controllers

RAID algorithms and processes are similar to the mirroring processes discussed in the previous chapter. They are often implemented in one or more storage controllers in the I/O path, such as host bus adapters (HBAs), subsystem controllers, or controllers embedded in networking devices. RAID is also commonly implemented in host volume management software.

RAID controllers usually receive a single I/O command from an upstream process or controller and create multiple downstream I/O commands for downstream storage targets. Like other storage operators in the I/O path, RAID controllers are responsible for detecting errors and performing error recovery. Fortunately, that's what they are designed to do.

Benefits of RAID

The power of RAID comes from four primary functions:

- Creation of data redundancy
- Creation of large-capacity storage
- Consolidation of management of devices and subsystems
- Use of parallelism for performance improvements

RAID Redundancy with Parity

The data redundancy in RAID is provided by a set of algorithms that add parity data values to the system or application data that is being written to storage. The extra parity data values can be thought of as "insurance data" that is used to reconstruct system and application data when a failure occurs to a storage device or interconnect component. Figure 9-2 illustrates the role of parity data in RAID.

Figure 9-2 shows five storage address spaces working together as a RAID array. In this illustration, four array members hold application data, and one array member holds parity data. The ratio of application members to parity in this figure is 4:1. In general, the ratio of data to parity members is *X*:1, where *X* can be any number. In practice, RAID arrays typically have ratios defined between 2:1 and 9:1, although RAID ratios can theoretically be as large as you want.

Figure 9-2 *Parity in RAID*

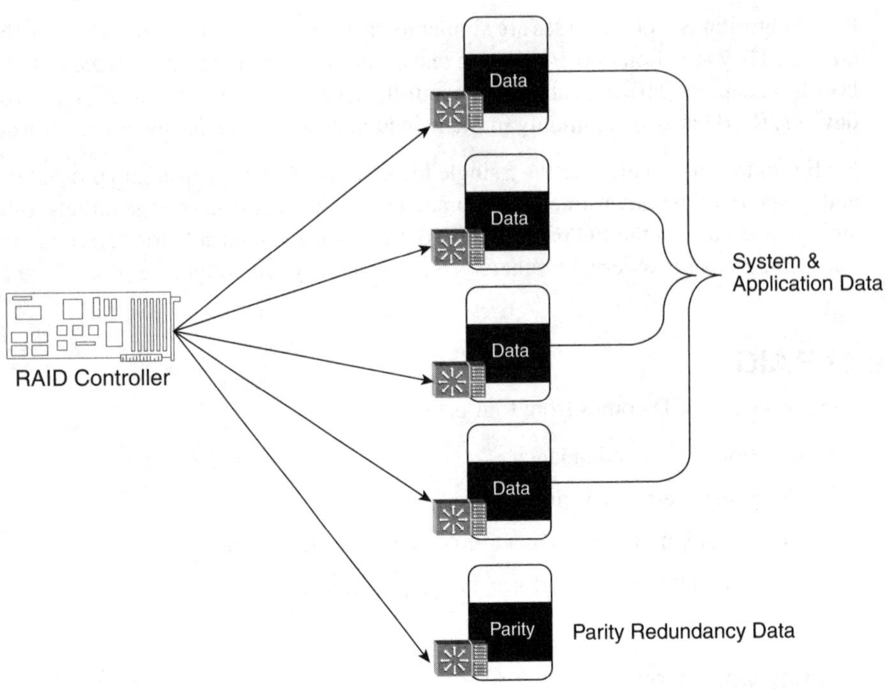

NOTE Mirroring, also known as RAID level 1, is implemented by RAID software and hardware and is the most commonly used RAID implementation. However, mirroring does not use most of the techniques commonly associated with RAID. For example, mirroring does not involve the calculation of parity data. More importantly, mirroring, by itself, does not provide scalability and/or consolidated management benefits.

Capacity Scaling Through Striping

A fundamental technique in RAID is *data striping*. In general, data striping aggregates the storage address spaces from multiple targets creating a single, larger and more scaleable storage address space. Using the SCSI architecture model, a host system initiator communicates with a single target logical unit, and the RAID controller manages multiple communications with all members of the array.

Simple data striping can be described as a round-robin process where each array member has data written to it in a cyclical fashion. In practice, parity RAID data access is more complicated than this, because parity data has to be calculated and written along with application data. In

RAID 5, the parity data is systematically scattered among all array members as data is being written. While parity RAID is often referred to as having "striped data," the access to the data is much more random than sequential and orderly. This random access is what inspired people to start thinking of RAID as a redundant array of *independent* (instead of inexpensive) disks.

One of the advantages of parity RAID is the efficiency that can be achieved in providing redundant data protection. Unlike mirroring, where the amount of storage required to protect data is doubled, with parity RAID, the amount of storage needed for redundancy is equal to the defined capacity of a single array member. The capacity overhead of parity RAID is inversely proportional to the number of members in the array. For example, if there are three members in an array, the redundancy overhead is 33%. If there are four members, the overhead is 25%. If there are ten members, the overhead is 10%, and so on. Compared to mirroring, with a 50% overhead, parity RAID is much more efficient.

Consolidated Management

As discussed in Chapter 5, the aggregation of multiple devices, LUNs, or volumes in a single RAID array provides management consolidation of storage resources. The consolidation of storage resources in RAID arrays makes it much easier to manage thousands of disk drives in a storage network.

Performance Through Striping

Striping data across members of a RAID array also increases performance, particularly when using SAN or interconnect technologies that allow overlapped I/O. By overlapping I/O operations across two or more members and executing them in parallel, it's possible to achieve significantly better performance than a system where only one I/O can be pending at a time.

Even though overlapped I/Os will increase performance, *hotspots* can occur where a small range of storage addresses are accessed in rapid succession by an application, creating resource contention bottlenecks on individual disk drives in an array. RAID arrays with a relatively large number of members are sometimes used to overcome database performance problems, where hotspots cause the application to be *I/O bound*. To illustrate, a database application could have its data spread over a four-disk array with a hotspot on two of the drives in the array. By spreading the array over six disks (50% more disk resources), it might be possible to alleviate the performance constraint by redistributing the hotspot data.

Figure 9-3 shows a before-and-after picture of database data spread over two different arrays. The first array has four members and two hotspots. The second array distributes the data over six members, alleviating the disk contentions that caused the hotspots.

Figure 9-3 *Spreading Hotspot Data Over Multiple Spindles*

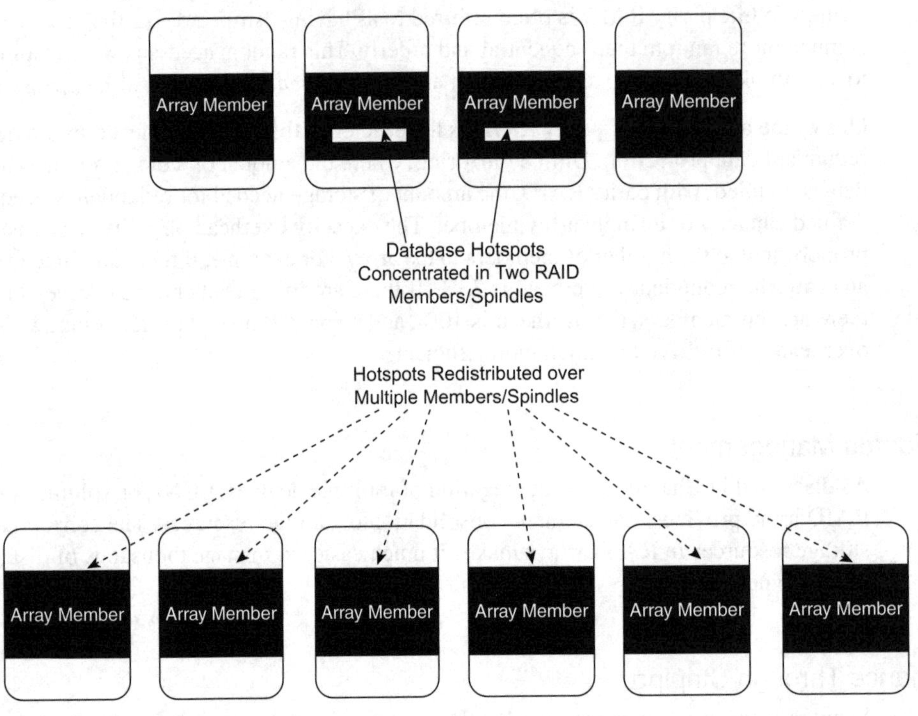

RAID Levels

The original RAID research defined five different levels of RAID with different performance, capacity, and redundancy characteristics. Of the original five RAID levels, only two are commonly used today: level 1 and level 5.

RAID Level 1

RAID level 1 is simple disk mirroring, which is discussed in Chapter 8, "An Introduction to Data Redundancy and Mirroring." Mirroring does not use parity or striping and, as a result, does not provide the performance and scalability benefits associated with other RAID levels.

RAID Level 5

When most people think of RAID, they typically think of RAID level 5. RAID level 5 is based on calculating parity values for stored data to achieve more efficient data redundancy than mirroring. Much of the discussion about parity RAID in this chapter focuses on RAID 5.

RAID Level 0

Since the original Berkeley research work, several additional RAID levels have been created that expand the capabilities of RAID. One such addition is RAID level 0, which is data striping across multiple members without using parity for data protection. The concept of striping without parity was rejected by the Berkeley team as having limited applicability because of an increased sensitivity to failures in disk drives. However, there are applications where performance is paramount and reliability is actually not a requirement; for these types of applications, RAID 0 provides the best combination of capacity and performance.

RAID 10 and Multilevel RAID

RAID 0, striping without parity, can be combined with RAID 1, mirroring, to form a new multilevel RAID called RAID 0+1, or RAID 10. As it turns out, this fairly simple concept of layering RAID levels is extremely effective in providing the combination of improved capacity, performance, and redundancy. RAID 0+1 is discussed in its own section later in this chapter.

The multilevel concept of RAID 10 has also been borrowed to create other new RAID levels, particularly RAID 15, which combines mirroring with RAID 5 striping with parity.

RAID 6

Another new level of RAID is RAID 6. RAID 6 uses two different parity calculations to create an additional safeguard to member failures. The original parity RAID definitions could withstand the loss of only a single array member. That works for arrays with a relatively small number of members, but it is not very effective for arrays with many members (say, 20 or 30) where another device failure could result in a loss of data. In other words, the reliable scalability of the original RAID definitions was pretty good, but they were certainly limited. RAID 6 is based on the idea that it would take failures in three members before data would be lost.

For the most part, RAID 6 has not been commonly applied in open-systems environments, although it has been used successfully in mainframe systems. In general, it is not clear that RAID 6 offers the kind of price/performance return needed to survive in open-systems markets and compete with lower-cost alternatives, such as RAID 10.

Parity Redundancy in RAID

The concept of parity and checksum data has been used for many years in computer science to verify that data that has been transmitted has been transmitted accurately, without corruption. The basic concept of the checksum involves a sending node calculating a checksum value based on the data values that it was transmitting. This checksum value would then be placed at the end of the transmission.

A receiving node receives the transmission and calculates its own checksum value for the data. If the receiver's checksum matched the transmitter's checksum, the data was considered to be accurate. If not, the receiver would discard the data and the transmitter would have to resend it.

RAID applies a similar concept, but instead of using the checksum value to verify whether or not data was transmitted correctly, RAID parity values are used to reconstruct data that might be unreadable on an array member due to device, subsystem, or some other I/O path failure.

Understood in the context of the original RAID research project, the basic idea of RAID was to create virtual storage and make multiple inexpensive disk drives act as if they were a single, larger, more expensive disk drive. One of the problems with that approach is that multiple inexpensive disk drives are much more likely to have failures than a single, large disk drive. In other words, the mean time between failure (MTBF) calculations for the multiple-drive RAID array were far less than a single drive.

So, the RAID research team employed the idea of parity to overcome the expected reliability deficiencies of disk arrays. In a RAID array, if a disk drive or I/O component fails, RAID parity algorithms are used to combine the remaining data values with the parity values to reconstruct the original data on the fly.

Table 9-1 shows data that the RAID controller writes as three data values and a single parity value. The top cell in each column indicates the status of the written data. In column 1 the data can be read without needing RAID to reconstruct data. Columns 2 to 4 show missing data that can be reconstructed using parity data. A RAID I/O operation can use any combination of two data values and the single parity values to reconstruct the original, missing data.

Table 9-1 *Reconstructing Data with Parity Data*

All Data Present	**Data 1 Missing**	**Data 2 Missing**	**Data 3 Missing**
Data 1	Reconstructed	Data 1	Data 1
Data 2	Data 2	Reconstructed	Data 2
Data 3	Data 3	Data 3	Reconstructed
Parity data	Parity data	Parity data	Parity data

Reliability of Parity RAID Arrays

As mentioned previously, one of the design problems with aggregating disk drives in RAID arrays is the associated decreased reliability. To illustrate, assume there are members on ten different disk drives in an array; the result is that the array is ten times more likely to have a disk drive failure than a single drive. In other words, the MTBF of an array without parity is 10% of the MTBF calculation for its member drives. Obviously, it was imperative for RAID technology to be more reliable than individual disk drives if they were to succeed.

With parity RAID, there must first be an initial failure before data is at risk due to another failure. The mean time to data loss (MTDL) after the first failure is 1/(N–1) the MTBF of the drives used in the array, where N is the number of drives in the array. In other words, the MTDL of a parity RAID array before experiencing any failures is

MTBF + MTBF/N

Obviously, the reliability is best when N (the number of members) is a relatively small number. The larger N is, the closer the array's reliability is to the MTBF of a single member. This shows a fundamental problem with parity RAID: it has limited scalability because of the diminishing redundancy protection as you increase the number of members in an array.

NOTE I'm often amazed when people ask me if it's possible to use two partitions on a single disk drive in the same array. This question is a real mind-blower. Not only would this put the data on the array at risk for a failure of a single disk drive, but it also creates a performance bottleneck where one would expect independent, overlapped I/Os.

XOR Parity

The parity logic used in RAID uses a basic Boolean exclusive OR (XOR) function. The XOR algorithm is shown in Table 9-2 using the binary Boolean values of TRUE and FALSE. The determination of the XOR result is simple: two similar values create a FALSE result, and two different values create a TRUE result.

Table 9-2 *XOR Boolean Results*

Value 1	Value 2	XOR Result
TRUE	TRUE	FALSE
TRUE	FALSE	TRUE
FALSE	TRUE	TRUE
FALSE	FALSE	FALSE

Properties of XOR

The XOR function is remarkable in many ways. First, it is commutative, which means the calculation can be done in reverse order and still achieve the same result. Second, it is associative, which means the data values can be grouped differently to achieve the same result. This means that the parity calculation can be done using any arbitrary grouping of data values in any order. As long as all the data values are included once in the process, you get the same result. Parity can be calculated any number of ways using a simple, fast algorithm in either hardware or software.

Table 9-3 shows all the possible combinations of four data values as well as the resulting parity value. Notice that you can arrange the data values in these rows any way you like, and you still get the same resulting parity value.

Table 9-3 *Parity Value Calculations for Four Data Values*

Value 1	Value 2	Value 3	Value 4	Parity Result
0	0	0	0	0
0	0	0	1	1
0	0	1	0	1
0	0	1	1	0
0	1	0	0	1
0	1	0	1	0
0	1	1	0	0
0	1	1	1	1
1	0	0	0	1
1	0	0	1	0
1	0	1	0	0
1	0	1	1	1
1	1	0	0	0
1	1	0	1	1
1	1	1	0	1
1	1	1	1	0

The other characteristic of XOR that makes it so useful for RAID is the fact that the XOR function is the inverse of itself. In other words, the exact same XOR function that creates parity from contributing members is also used to reconstruct missing data.

For example, given a string of five data values, the XOR function is used to create a sixth parity value. Assume that in reading the data at a later time, the fifth data value is unreadable for some reason and needs to be reconstructed. Logically, it makes sense to apply an inverse process to the parity values to regenerate the missing data value. As it turns out, the inverse process happens to be the XOR function applied to the other four data values and the parity value.

Referring to Table 9-3, you can try this out yourself and calculate any of the values in the rows by applying the XOR function to all the other values in the row.

Degraded Mode Operations

When a member is unavailable and the XOR function in a RAID controller is being used to reconstruct data as it is being read, the RAID array controller is said to be operating in *degraded mode*. The term *degraded* refers not only to the fact that an element of the array is missing from operations, but the performance of the array controller also suffers from the added I/O and processing overhead.

When the parity value is missing, as opposed to a data value, the array controller still operates in degraded mode, although the performance impact is minimal due to the fact that it is not necessary to reconstruct data. In RAID 5, which is by far the most common form of parity RAID, the parity data is spread across all members, which means a degraded mode operation always includes a minority of reads in which parity is the missing element.

Figure 9-4 shows the basic functions of degraded mode operations for a five-member RAID 5 array.

Figure 9-4 *RAID Array Controller Operating in Degraded Mode*

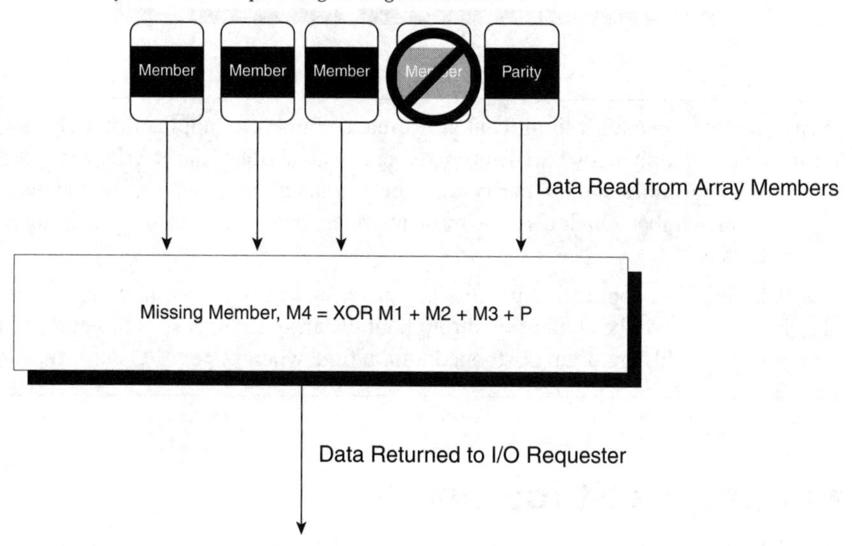

Parity Rebuild Operations

The basic principle of data reconstruction with parity allows array members to be removed and replaced in arrays and repopulated with data. When a member fails, the logic in the RAID controller removes the member from operations. Conversely, the controller can reinsert a new replacement member in the array.

After the replacement member has been reinserted, a parity rebuild process can be run, which reads the remaining data values as well as the parity value and reconstructs the data for the failed member on the new member. Figure 9-5 shows the process of a parity rebuild.

Figure 9-5 *A RAID Parity Rebuild on a Replacement Member*

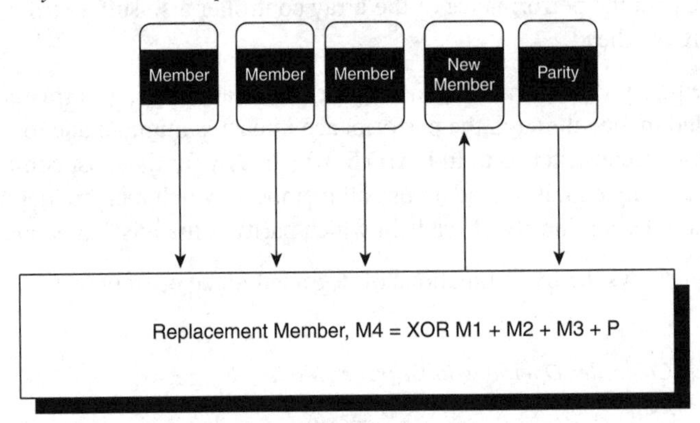

NOTE Parity rebuilds can have a significant performance impact on application I/O rates. Whereas mirroring can simply copy data from one member to another, the RAID parity rebuild has to read all data values and the parity value before calculating and writing the data to the replacement member. Obviously, the more members there are in an array, the more complicated this process is.

It is clear that if an application process is generating heavy I/O traffic while the parity rebuild is running, there will be contention throughout the array for disk spindles and actuators. That's why parity rebuilds are often postponed until a time when system I/O activity is minimal.

Strips and Stripes Stripe Depth

RAID arrays are organized in *strips* and *stripes*. The idea is that a certain amount of data, typically some multiple of the file system's or database's defined block size, is written in a single operation to a single member of the array. The data written to the individual array member is called the *data strip*. The amount of data (in bytes) written to a strip is referred to as the *stripe depth* (yes, stripe depth not strip depth). The number of data strips in a stripe is one less than the number of members in the array; one of the strips is used for parity data.

Another way to think about the relationship between strips and stripes is that a stripe is the combination of data strips and their corresponding parity strip. In other words, each stripe has a single corresponding parity strip (except for RAID 6, which has two parity strips).

By aligning the stripe depth with the block size of the host file system, data I/O operations can be performed consistently and quickly. In practice, this means that each I/O can be transferred between the host system and the RAID controller and then from the RAID controller into cache memory and/or through to the buffer memory of a disk drive member of the array.

RAID 5

RAID 5 is the only one of the original parity RAID definitions still in heavy use today. RAID 2 was defined for a specific type of disk technology that has become obsolete. RAID 3 synchronizes I/O operations over multiple members, but that approach has turned out to be useful only for single-application environments, not for multitasking, multiprocessing environments that characterize open-systems computing. RAID 4 writes strips of data independently to unsynchronized members and writes corresponding parity strips to a dedicated parity member. The dedicated parity member turns out to be a performance bottleneck in most cases.

NOTE Network Appliance Filer network attached storage (NAS) systems are an example of RAID 4 implementations that do not create I/O bottlenecks. Through clever use of nonvolatile RAM in the Filer subsystem architecture, the rotational latency and seek times that create bottlenecks are overcome.

RAID 5 also writes data in strips to independent array members, but it moves the parity and data strips around the various members of the array, alleviating the performance bottleneck of a dedicated parity member. Table 9-4 illustrates the interspersing of parity and data in array stripes.

Table 9-4 *Parity Distributed Through All Members of a RAID 5 Array*

Array Stripe	Member 1	Member 2	Member 3	Member 4
Stripe 1	Strip 1_a	Strip 1_b	Strip 1_c	Parity Strip 1
Stripe 2	Strip 2_a	Strip 2_b	Parity Strip 2	Strip 2_c
Stripe 3	Strip 3_a	Parity Strip 3	Strip 3_b	Strip 3_c
Stripe 4	Parity Strip 4	Strip 4_a	Strip 4_b	Strip 4_c

RAID 5 Write Penalty

When all the data strips in a stripe are written simultaneously, the parity can be calculated and written at the same time. However, in most instances data is being updated in a single strip, and the other strips in the stripe are left unchanged. Whenever data strips are changed in an array, it is necessary to also recalculate the parity strip and rewrite it to its corresponding array member. This process is at the core of what is known as the RAID 5 write penalty.

In a nutshell, when a strip is being changed, the old data and the parity data are read from the strip first and XORed to remove the contribution of the old strip to the parity value. For lack of a better term, this is referred to here as the temporary parity. Then the new strip data is XORed with the temporary parity to create the new parity strip. Finally, both the new data strip and the new parity strip are written to their respective members. Obviously, the process of reading old data and parity, making two parity calculations, and writing two strips is somewhat time-consuming. This is especially true when done in host system volume management software, where all the involved reads and writes occur over the complete host-to-storage I/O path.

NOTE

Seagate attempted to alleviate some of the pain of the RAID 5 write penalty by adding XOR functions and an initiator function to its disk drives. The idea was that a disk drive in an array could read and write the parity strip for a stripe and use this parity to make both required XOR calculations when new strips were written to the drive. It was a nice idea and has been used to some extent, but it has not caught on in a big way. This is an excellent example of how a disk drive manufacturer attempted to add real, useful value to its products but has not been able to turn the idea into a major business success.

Avoiding Parity Limitations of RAID with RAID 10

RAID 10, also called RAID 0+1, is not one of the original defined RAID levels, but it is extremely effective and in many ways is superior to RAID 5, except for the capacity required. RAID 10 combines the mirroring of RAID 1 with the striping of RAID 0.

In essence, RAID 10 mirrors every member in a RAID 0 array. Thus, RAID 10 removes the RAID 5 write penalty from the equation and also provides much more redundancy depth than RAID 5. A RAID 10 array can lose more than two members and still continue to operate, as long as it does not lose both pairs of a mirrored member. Figure 9-6 shows a RAID 10 array made up of four mirrored pairs.

There is also no loss of performance while operating in degraded mode, because there is no parity to calculate on the fly. Instead, the data is simply read from the remaining member in the pair. More importantly, parity rebuilds are avoided when repopulating a replacement member in an array—a relatively simple disk remirror operation is performed instead. The lack of parity also allows RAID 10 arrays to scale to include many more members than RAID 5. In fact, there are no immediate scalability limits with RAID 10. Reliability does not decrease as members are added. Parity data reconstruction processes that become more complicated as the number of members increases are avoided altogether.

The problem with RAID 10 is that it has a 50% redundancy overhead compared to RAID 5, which can be less than 10% in arrays with more than ten members.

Figure 9-6 *A RAID 10 Array with Four Mirrored Pairs*

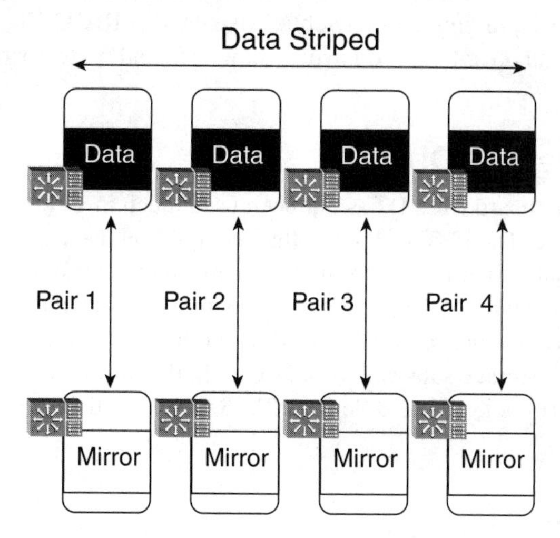

NOTE With disk drives being some of the least expensive elements in the data center, I'm not sure that the cost difference of capacity between RAID 10 and RAID 5 can seriously be justified as a reason for using RAID 5 instead of RAID 10. Some people have told me they still prefer RAID 5 because it can have a smaller footprint than RAID 10. Understanding that footprint actually is important to data center management, the question is one of priority: do you need to optimize the physical aspects of your data center at the expense of performance, flexibility, and redundancy?

RAID Product Options

The following sections briefly discuss several ways to implement RAID.

Host Volume Managers

Host volume management software typically has several RAID variations and, in some cases, offers many sophisticated configuration options. Running RAID in a volume manager opens the potential for integrating file system and volume management products for management and performance-tuning purposes. Another advantage of using host volume management is the ability to use less expensive just a bunch of disks (JBOD) disk subsystems, as opposed to expensive disk subsystems.

The performance impact of RAID on the host CPU is often overestimated, because the address space translation process for striping data is a relatively low overhead process. However, the element of RAID that is time-consuming is the reading and writing of data in RAID 5 operations. This highlights another subtle advantage of RAID 10 over RAID 5. RAID 10 only performs Boolean operations, and avoids slow read and write operations.

RAID on Motherboard (ROM)

RAID on motherboard (ROM) has not been used much in storage networks, but that could change over time. The idea of ROM is that a chipset on the system board provides the core RAID functionality that is used for motherboard-integrated storage I/O communications adapters. In general, ROM does not have nearly the flexibility and power of volume management software, but it can work reasonably well for limited environments, smaller storage networks, and inexpensive storage subsystems or JBOD. In the future, this will include combinations of Fibre Channel (FC), iSCSI, and Serial ATA (SATA)/Serial Attached SCSI (SAS).

Host Bus Adapters

RAID has been implemented in adapters/controllers for many years, starting with SCSI and including Advanced Technology Attachment (ATA) and serial ATA. RAID on FC HBAs has not been implemented yet, but there is no reason to believe it won't be in the years to come. The operating environment for HBA RAID is similar to ROM—smaller storage networks and inexpensive subsystems or JBOD.

Disk Subsystems

Disk subsystems have been the most popular product for RAID implementations and probably will continue to be for many years to come. There is an enormous range of capabilities offered in disk subsystems across a wide range of prices. Chapter 5 discusses these important products in much more detail.

Network Systems

Finally, RAID capabilities have been introduced in networking equipment, such as switches and specialized storage appliances. In general, most RAID applications in networking equipment are made for enterprise environments and involve technologies ported from volume management software or enterprise subsystem controllers.

Summary

Born from a research project at the University of California, RAID has become one of the mainstays in storage networking. While other storage technologies have become obsolete since RAID was invented, RAID has become increasingly useful through its ability to improve data availability, increase storage scalability, consolidate storage management, and boost I/O performance.

At the core of RAID is the Boolean XOR function, which has the unique property of being its own inverse operation. This allows RAID to be implemented very efficiently in either hardware or software. It also means the various failure modes and their remedies use the same function in performing their work.

Because RAID is defined primarily by algorithms, it can be implemented in many different ways and locations in the I/O path. Today, RAID levels 1, 5, and 10 are commonly found in a wide variety of products, including system motherboards, host bus adapters, storage subsystems, and SAN switches/systems.

Q & A

1. What does RAID stand for?
2. What kinds of storage entities can be members of a RAID array?
3. True or false: RAID members have to be the same size.
4. What is the Boolean function used in parity RAID?
5. What is the purpose of parity with RAID?
6. Describe the difference between strips and stripes.
7. What is the best possible MTDL in a RAID 5 array?
8. Briefly explain the RAID 5 write penalty.
9. What is the maximum number of member pairs in a RAID 10 array?
10. What is the most common type of parity RAID used today?

Upon completing this chapter, you will be able to

- Participate in planning meetings and discussions in your company related to disaster protection and remote copy solutions
- Describe and diagram remote copy designs, including bunker storage and remote tertiary storage
- Analyze the system performance impact of remote copy implementations, including distance
- Discuss designs of remote copy products with vendors and compare product feature capabilities

CHAPTER 10

Redundancy Over Distance with Remote Copy

Most redundancy technologies cover component failures such as disk drive, GBIC, cable, host bus adapter (HBA), or controller failures. But component failures are not the only threat to data access, of course. Storage subsystems can also fail or suffer disasters. And major, large-scale disasters such as floods, fires, earthquakes, industrial accidents, and terrorist acts can wipe out an entire computing facility in a single cataclysmic event. When catastrophes happen, businesses could lose all or most of their data as well as their data processing capabilities. In many cases, the ability of the company to continue serving its customers depends on having copies of data available on other storage subsystems and at other, remote locations.

Backup and recovery, the topic of Chapter 13, "Network Backup: The Foundation of Storage Management," has traditionally been the technology used to recover data. However, with data access becoming increasingly important to successful business operations, many organizations cannot afford the extended downtime that unavoidably accompanies a major recovery process using backup tapes. More importantly, the chances of achieving a full recovery become smaller and smaller as the amount of data gets larger and larger.

For that reason, many companies prefer to employ data redundancy technology that provides more immediate access to data on disk—on local storage as well as at remote sites. Not only is data on disk easier to access than tape, but it is also usually easier to verify that the data redundancy strategy is working as planned.

In response to these requirements, storage companies have developed remote copy technologies that make identical copies of data on secondary storage subsystems and at remote sites that are physically distanced from their primary data processing facilities. This chapter looks at this important storage application, discussing how it works and some of its implementation variables.

Fundamentals of Remote Copy

This section presents an overview of the common principles used in remote copy applications. Like many things in storage, the concept seems very simple, but the implementation is much more complicated and must be done with the highest attention to detail.

Basic Architecture of Remote Copy Applications

Remote copy applications store data temporarily from write I/O operations and forward it to another storage subsystem at the same or another site. Specialized storage controllers are used to forward and receive the remote copy data. We will use the terms *forwarding controller* and *receiving controller* in this chapter to indicate the roles these controllers assume in the remote copy system.

A network of some type is used to forward the data from one storage location to another. This *intermediary network* can be virtually any type of network, such as TCP/IP/Ethernet, SONET, DWDM, or ATM. The remote copy application running in the remote copy controllers is responsible for conducting the data transfers across this network. This basic architecture is shown in Figure 10-1.

Figure 10-1 *Basic Architecture of a Store-and-Forward Remote Copy Application*

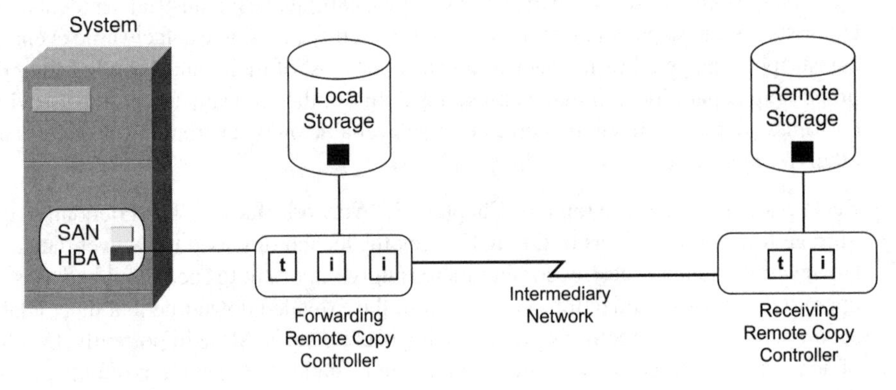

Remote Copy Sites and Storage Hierarchies

Remote copy implies a hierarchy among storage subsystems and sites. There are many ways businesses structure their remote copy storage hierarchies, made out of these four generic building blocks:

- Primary storage and sites
- Secondary storage and sites
- Tertiary storage and sites
- Bunker storage and sites

Primary Storage and Sites

In short, applications read and write data on *primary storage*. The role of primary storage is to support the data access needs of the company's production data center. It's also useful to talk about primary storage sites, where equipment, data, and staff are centralized. Primary storage can be implemented on many different types of storage products, including SAN storage subsystems and network attached storage (NAS) storage servers.

Small-to medium-sized companies tend to have a single primary site, while larger companies may have several primary sites. Primary in this case does not indicate a priority among data centers, but instead indicates that a significant number of applications are using primary storage.

Secondary Storage and Sites

Secondary storage is the first line of defense against a disaster or failure that strikes primary storage or storage sites. Remote copy applications copy data from primary storage to secondary storage. A secondary storage subsystem could be at the primary site or at a secondary site. The redundancy can be local or at some distance.

If a disaster occurs at a primary site, one or more secondary sites may be used to continue processing. Replacement servers are usually located or are quickly available at a secondary site in order to resume normal application processing as soon as possible.

Secondary sites may be geographically near or far from primary sites, depending on business variables and corporate risk/business continuity strategies. For instance, a secondary site may be across campus, across town, across the state, or located in another state hundreds of miles away. Companies with multiple data processing sites often use them as both primary and secondary sites, providing disaster protection within the broad corporate computing system. For instance, a company with two primary sites A and B could use each site as a secondary site for the other; A would be the secondary site for B, and vice versa.

Tertiary Storage and Sites

Tertiary sites and *tertiary storage* provide additional redundancy options for business continuity in case both the primary and secondary storage and/or sites experience a disaster. Tertiary storage could be located at a secondary site (if secondary storage is at the primary site) or at a separate tertiary site. Remote copy applications can copy data from either primary sites or secondary sites to tertiary sites.

Tertiary sites are usually not stocked with the same level of equipment as secondary sites. For instance, there might not be as much computing equipment available, and there are usually different assumptions about how quickly different applications can resume operating. Tertiary sites are almost always a meaningful distance from primary sites in order to be outside the geographic range of a single catastrophic event that could ruin a primary site. For instance, a tertiary site is usually not within the same flood plain or seismic fault line as the primary site it supports.

Bunker Sites

Bunker sites are located in the local vicinity of primary sites in facilities that are specifically established to support the remote copy mission. In other words, they do not typically have application or server systems and adequate facilities for people to work. Their sole mission is to function as a stepping-stone in the redundancy hierarchy.

Bunker sites typically house secondary storage subsystems that are accessible to primary storage over high-speed links spanning short distances. This provides the best opportunity to capture data off-site, on disk with optimal data integrity (consistency). Applications at the primary site can run with a minimum of delay imposed by the remote copy application.

NOTE There probably wouldn't be a need for tertiary sites and tertiary storage if there were not a need to put secondary sites—such as bunker sites—close to primary sites where they could be affected by the same disaster that wipes out the primary site. So we end up having these interesting discussions where secondary storage could be either local or remote and where remote storage could be either secondary or tertiary. At this point the rationale might not make much sense to you, so you'll need to read further, to the section "Performance Implications of Remote Copy."

Objectives of Remote Copy Applications

The objectives of remote copy applications are simple to state but considerably more difficult to meet. Remote site storage and data should be

- Immediately available for online use supporting ongoing business operations, including systems management functions like backup.
- Consistent. In other words, it should have complete data integrity without errors injected by the remote copy process.
- Capable of resuming normal operations at the primary site as quickly as possible.

Immediate Availability to Support Ongoing Operations

The word "immediate" has different meanings to different-sized businesses and organizations. Perhaps the words "practically immediate" would be more accurate. For many companies and transaction-processing applications, it may not be possible to have data copied to a geographically remote site in real time, meaning local and remote copies of data are not synchronized. The issue of data consistency is a primary element of how immediately available remote data may be. This topic is discussed later in this chapter in the section "Synchronous, Asynchronous, and Semisynchronous Operating Modes."

It is assumed that complete replacement data may need to be made operational following a disaster. This does not mean that the replacement data center will be a replica of the original data center and do all the data processing of the primary site. Instead, the remote data center will quickly be able to replace the functions of the highest-priority applications that were running at the primary site.

Remote storage equipment needs to have all the necessary connecting equipment readily available to establish connections to replacement systems. Servers that use secondary or tertiary storage might be at another nearby building location. If so, it is essential that connectivity between those servers and storage be available as quickly as possible.

Secondary sites and facilities also need to support the "normal" operations and systems management functions that are part of responsible systems management. There is very little that is "normal" about operations following a disaster, but it is important to maintain best practices for backup and recovery. Companies that have multiple levels in their remote copy hierarchies will probably want to continue running remote copy applications by copying data to another secondary or tertiary site.

Data Integrity, Consistency, and Atomicity

The term *data integrity* for storage means that stored data has not been altered in any way after it has been changed or created by the application that processes it. In other words, data in storage is what the application intended to write. As it turns out, this is more complicated than it appears at first.

One of the most intricate and challenging aspects of remote copy applications is their requirement to maintain write ordering, otherwise called *data consistency*. In short, data consistency refers to the relationship between related data values, whether they be data values from an application or are provided by the system. It is fairly common to have complex data structures that reference multiple data entries as part of a single high-level data object.

Applications and filing systems process their I/O operations in a precise, structured sequence that guarantees the order in which data is written. For instance, when an application updates data, it might store an internal reference to the data as located within a certain byte range—and shortly thereafter the file system may be requested to store the actual updated data. Both these actions are made on disk at different times. If something goes wrong with the process and one of them does not complete correctly, the two data values will not be synchronized—they will be *inconsistent* with each other. Not only will the data be wrong, but it is somewhat likely that other problems will arise, including abnormal application or system failure.

Where remote copy applications are concerned, it is necessary to preserve the *write ordering* that was executed on the primary storage subsystem on secondary and tertiary storage. In other words, any secondary or tertiary storage must have data written to it in exactly the same order that it was written on primary storage.

Local storage interconnects and SAN technologies have no problem with write ordering because SCSI protocol processes dictate the sequence of I/Os in these environments. With direct attached storage (DAS) or SAN storage, SCSI WRITE CDBs sent by initiators to logical units (LUs) are acknowledged by the LU after successful completion of the command. Applications wait to transmit subsequent I/O commands until their pending commands are acknowledged.

However, with remote copy applications, data is sent over an intermediary network that has its own set of protocols. It's important to realize that remote copy data transfers and communications are distinct from local storage transfers. Even though remote copy data might be forwarded in the same order as local writes, there is no guarantee that it will be *received* in the same order due to network congestion and error conditions.

Another example illustrates the nature of the errors that can occur. Assume a database system writes an update using the following hypothetical sequence:

Step 1 Write a journal entry describing the update to be performed.

Step 2 Perform the update.

Step 3 Make a journal entry confirming the update occurred.

If Steps 1 and 3 are committed to disk in secondary or tertiary storage, and Step 2 is skipped due to a transmission error or delay of some sort, the actual data on disk is inconsistent with the database journal entries that indicate everything worked as planned. Besides databases, many other applications could have their data and metadata stored out of sync if write ordering is not followed properly by a remote copy application.

Write atomicity is another aspect of remote copy applications that can result in the loss of data integrity. Multiple I/O WRITE commands are often needed to complete a single application data writing process. If they do not all complete, the stored data does not have integrity. Therefore, all writes need to be made in order, and all need to be made completely in order to have data integrity and consistency.

NOTE Many years ago I developed a mnemonic for remembering the relative importance of different storage assumptions—along the lines of a hierarchy of needs. My mnemonic, *IRSAM,* stands for

- Integrity
- Recoverability
- Security
- Availability
- Manageability

Data integrity is like breathing. If data does not have integrity, systems will fail miserably. Storage that does not maintain integrity may as well just be a bit bucket in outer space. This applies to all forms of storage, including backup systems and remote copy applications.

Recoverability is more like drinking water. Its not quite as important as having good data, but if data is not recoverable, it may become lost in the great void of lost data.

Security is akin to food and is close in importance to recoverability—but not quite. If weak security allows threats that change or destroy data, the data is worthless. Then you have to be able to recover other copies of good, unharmed data.

Availability is like coffee. Availability is considered the top priority by many, but it applies only if the data exists. Data can be preserved while availability is reestablished. You want to be wired for availability, but there are much more severe conditions than a temporary loss of availability.

Manageability is the lowest priority in terms of fundamental needs and is analogous to painkillers. It is extremely important, but a lack of manageability does not guarantee failure. It simply suggests we may have a miserable existence without it.

The challenge in maintaining write ordering with remote copy operations is the fact that the intermediate networks used to transport remote copy data may not be able to guarantee delivery—much less in-order delivery. Therefore, it is up to the remote copy application to maintain write order at secondary and tertiary storage.

Resuming Normal Primary Site Operations

In addition to making data accessible to replacement systems following a disaster, remote copy systems can also be used to recover data to the primary site to resume normal data center operations. In general, this involves forwarding new data created at the remote site back to the (original) local site.

Assuming the disaster is short-lived and does not result in loss of data or equipment, as during a major blackout, the remote site assumes data processing operations on an interim basis. All subsequent data updates that occur at the remote site are stored locally and logged so they can be copied back to the primary site later when power is restored and equipment is made operational again. Then the remote copy function is reversed and the primary site is brought back in sync with the remote site. At some point, operations at the remote site are temporarily suspended and resumed again at the primary site with remote copy operations reestablished as they were originally. Some companies with redundant data centers regularly switch their primary and remote sites to make sure everything is working as planned if an actual disaster should occur.

Major, high-impact disasters with data and equipment loss that take days to recover from have much more complicated recovery scenarios and operations. Chapter 13 discusses some of the aspects of major disaster recovery.

Remote Copy Application Processing

Remote copy applications use storing level functions that work with SCSI processes, commands, and data. This means that primary, secondary, and tertiary storage will have identical storage address spaces, because the commands forwarded by remote copy specify the block address where the update is to be made.

If the remote site storage needs to be used to access data after a disaster, a system will need to connect to the storage and mount it as local storage. This system will need to be able to access and use the same filing system as the one that is used by the application system at the primary site.

The Remote Copy System

It helps to think of the workings of a remote copy application as being a distributed system where two nodes work together to complete a single process but are separated by an intermediary network.

The same command/response protocols and operations that are used for local SCSI storage are also used for remote copy operations. Both forwarding and receiving controllers assume both initiator and target roles. The sections that follow explain the various SCSI roles assumed by forwarding and receiving controllers in a remote copy system.

Forwarding Controller as SCSI Target

All actions of the remote copy system begin with a forwarding controller receiving an incoming SCSI command from a host initiator. Obviously, this means the forwarding controller has to function as a SCSI target. If the incoming command is a WRITE command, the remote copy system is invoked, and the process of forwarding the command starts.

This forwarding controller traditionally resides in a disk subsystem, but it can also be located in a network device such as a switch, router, virtualization engine, or specialized remote copy appliance.

In its role as a SCSI target, the forwarding controller has to interact with the host initiator as a good citizen of the SAN, providing all necessary SCSI command responses, which are often referred to as acknowledgments in the context of remote copy systems.

Forwarding Controller as SCSI Initiator

Regardless of the type of SCSI command (READ, WRITE, or STATUS) sent by the host initiator, it is passed to its intended local LU for processing. If it is a WRITE command, the forwarding controller makes a copy of the command and then prepares to forward it to a receiving controller on the other side of the intermediary network.

The forwarding controller assumes the role of a SCSI initiator when forwarding commands to the receiving controller. It changes the target/LUN address of the original SCSI CDB and assigns the appropriate target LUN address that has been configured for secondary or tertiary storage in the remote copy system. It then reissues the command to the receiving controller.

Figure 10-2 shows how the forwarding controller processes WRITE I/O commands.

Figure 10-2 *A Forwarding Controller Processes WRITE Commands*

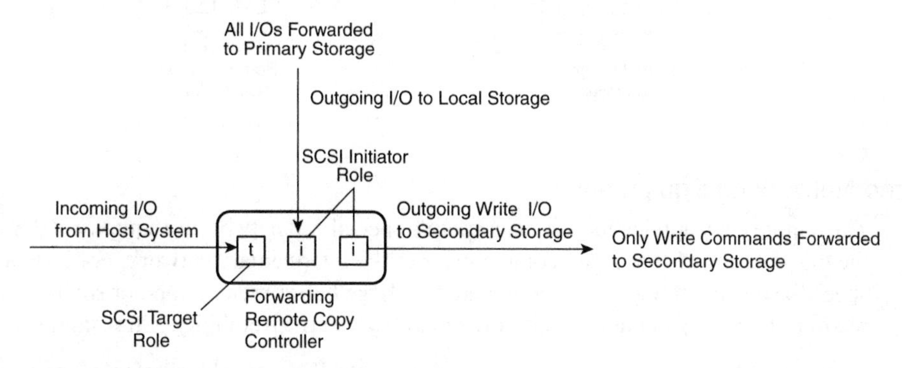

Receiving Controller in Dual Modes: SCSI Target and Initiator

The receiving controller assumes the role of a target in relation to the forwarding controller. It is assigned a target/LUN ID that is used by the forwarding controller initiator.

Upon receiving the forwarded command, the receiving controller is responsible for delivering the command to storage at the secondary site. That means it switches roles to act as an initiator. If the receiving controller is embedded in a disk subsystem, it only has to write data to memory cache or to disk storage. If the remote copy controller is external to a storage subsystem, it assumes the role of an initiator in the SANs and generates an I/O command for storage in a SAN.

In general, the receiving controller "owns" the storage address space on secondary or tertiary storage until the data needs to be used for running actual applications. At that time, a local system takes over operations and ownership of the storage.

When the command has been executed to completion (successfully or not) with secondary or tertiary storage, a SCSI command response (acknowledgment) is sent to the forwarding controller.

Figure 10-3 shows the various SCSI roles assumed by both forwarding and receiving controllers in a remote copy system.

Figure 10-3 *SCSI Roles of Both Forwarding and Receiving Controllers in a Remote Copy System*

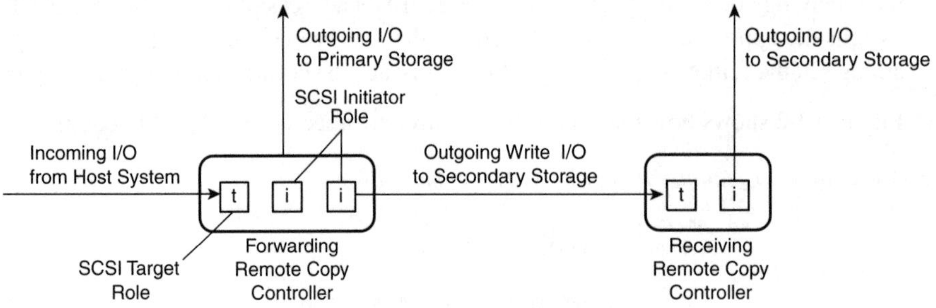

Specialized Networking Equipment

The remote copy application may incorporate specialized networking equipment that improves the transmission of forwarded commands over the intermediary network. For instance, a specialized networking system equipped with large buffer memory and/or sophisticated error recovery technology could improve the reliability and recoverability of transmitted commands.

Such networking equipment or the forwarding controller may add transfer information such as parity calculations, sequence numbers, time stamps, or some other type of data to the forwarded command so that the receiving controller can correct transmission errors and avoid write-order violations.

Performance Implications of Remote Copy

The forwarding controller is responsible for acknowledging I/Os from host system initiators. This little detail of SCSI processing turns out to have an enormous impact on application performance and the budget allocated for business continuity operations.

Application performance can be constrained by the performance of the system's I/O channel. This is particularly noticeable with transaction processing applications that are sensitive to I/O latency. If acknowledgments are not returned quickly enough from storage, the application must constantly wait before sending the next I/O. As a result, the I/O channel becomes a bottleneck for application performance.

The challenge where remote copy is concerned is balancing the desire to maintain exact, synchronous mirror images of data on remotely located secondary or tertiary storage with the need to keep high-throughout applications running at an acceptable speed.

Of course, if money were not an issue, this challenge would not be so terrible. A company would simply use an intermediary network with sufficient bandwidth to support the amount of

I/O write traffic generated by the application. But money usually is an issue. Despite the advancements made in recent years in reducing the costs of bandwidth, it still costs a great deal of money to support the number of write I/Os from a high-throughput application.

Latency of Light Propagation

Sometimes people mention the speed of light as a limiting factor for remote copy performance. While it certainly sounds great to say the words "speed of light," the speed isn't the problem. The latency related to the propagation of light signals through fiber-optic cables is the issue.

Light signals propagate in fiber cables at a rate of 5 microseconds per kilometer, or 8 microseconds per mile. You can use these numbers to calculate the latency of remote copy transmissions over fiber-optic links. For instance, the latency of sending a signal over a 20-mile piece of fiber is 160 microseconds.

This latency takes only the physics of light propagation into account. When you look at the complete picture, there are several other latency contributions to consider. These include the conversion of light to electrons on both ends of the connection, the interpretation and execution of the SCSI commands at the remote location, and any error corrections/retransmission processing that takes place, especially the impact of suspending command execution while waiting for late or missing transmissions in order to avoid violating data consistency requirements.

The Four-Stroke SCSI Write Process

Another issue to consider when analyzing remote copy performance is the need to transmit four signals across network cabling for SCSI WRITE processing. SCSI initiators send an initial command to an LU that indicates the intent of the write. The LU then responds that it can accept the transfer with a transfer-ready response. Then the initiator sends the data to the LU, which is written to cache or disk media, before acknowledging the second SCSI command.

Altogether that means four signals for each command need to be sent over the intermediary network. Using the 20-mile distance suggested earlier, we see that a single forwarded command has an associated remote copy command transmission overhead of 80 miles, or 640 microseconds. This is not insignificant compared to the I/O rates of high-throughput transaction processing systems. Figure 10-4 illustrates the four-stroke SCSI write process.

Figure 10-4 *Four SCSI Signals for Each Write Operation*

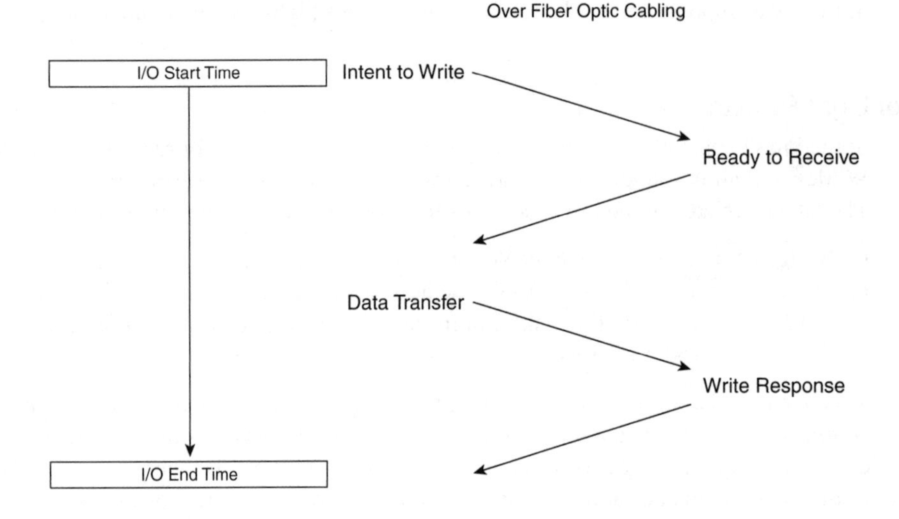

Synchronous, Asynchronous, and Semisynchronous Operating Modes

As it turns out, it is not always practical to maintain synchronization between primary and secondary or tertiary storage. For that reason, remote copy applications provide three different modes of operation:

- Synchronous
- Asynchronous
- Semisynchronous

Organizations must find a balance between the requirements of data consistency, distance between storage sites, and cost. It's not easy. Most companies find themselves wishing they could have synchronization of data for guaranteed data consistency, but they are unable to afford the cost.

Synchronous Mode

Synchronous mode works as outlined in the preceding descriptions of remote copy functions. The forwarding controller does not respond to the initial SCSI WRITE command from the host until it receives a response from the receiving controller that the write has been executed successfully. This is obviously the slowest, most conservative process.

Storage companies like to split hairs about whether the data is written to cache memory or to disk storage in synchronous mode operations. Obviously there is some associated risk that data written to cache memory might not ever make it to disk. For most companies it is a moot point because the cost of bandwidth for synchronous operations is too high.

Figure 10-5 illustrates the sequence of steps used with synchronous remote copy operations.

Figure 10-5 *Sequence of I/Os and Responses in Synchronous Mode*

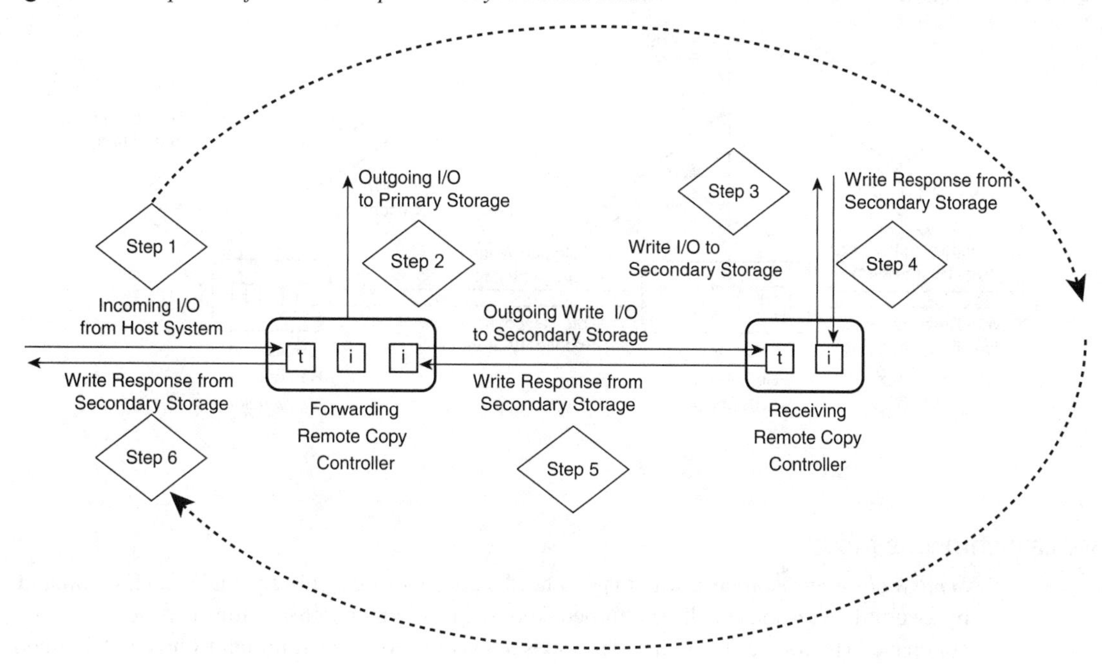

Asynchronous Mode

Asynchronous mode allows the forwarding controller to acknowledge the completion of the WRITE command, after it is acknowledged by primary, local storage and without having to receive an acknowledgment from the receiving controller.

High-throughput applications are virtually unaffected by asynchronous mode operations. The downside, of course, is that there is no way of knowing what data transmissions have succeeded at the remote site at any given time. This makes recovering from remote communication failures slightly more complicated because more pending remote commands need to be tracked.

The forwarding and receiving controllers exchange all the normal SCSI commands and responses, even though the forwarding controller "spoofs" the host initiator with an early response for its original WRITE command. The forwarding controller retains forwarded commands until a response is received for them in order to recover from possible communication failures. Some remote copy products have a limit to the number of unacknowledged commands that can be pending. They will slow or stop responses from the forwarding controller to the host initiator in order to avoid getting too far behind in the process. The section "Link Failure Mode" discusses this further.

Figure 10-6 shows the sequence of steps used in asynchronous remote copy operations.

Figure 10-6 *Sequence of I/Os and Responses in Asynchronous Mode*

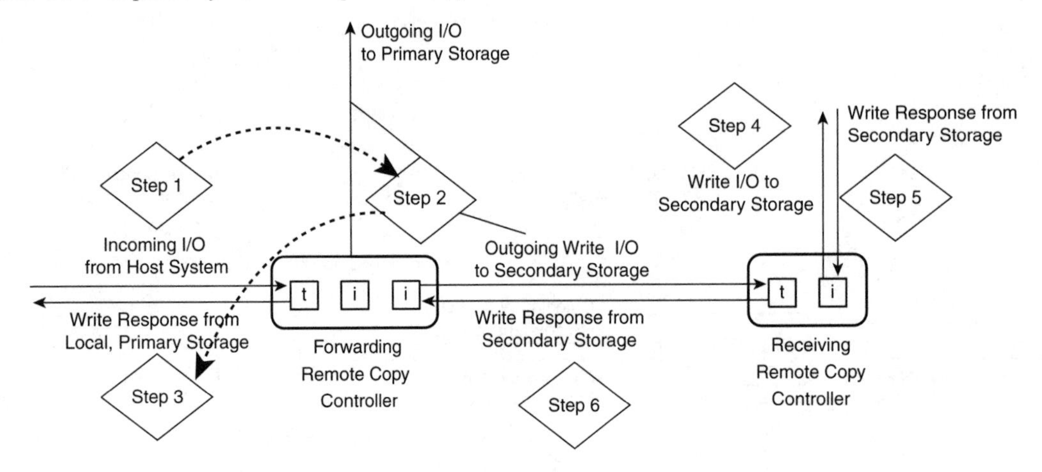

Semisynchronous Mode

Semisynchronous mode is a way to get a head start on a single subsequent WRITE command by assuming a response will be returned from the receiving controller for the pending command. The forwarding controller issues a response to the host initiator immediately upon receiving a response from the primary storage LU, as long as there are no pending I/Os in the remote copy system.

Link Failure Mode

When the forwarding controller loses communications with the receiving controller, the entire remote copy application is at risk. Different vendors have different ways of dealing with this problem. One way is to stop writes altogether. Another approach is to use local disk storage and create a remote copy cache that functions as a proxy remote site. The remote copy application tracks the data updated in the cache, and when the remote link is reestablished, the application sends the cached data to the remote site.

Cache data is marked using a storage block space bitmap. In other words, an index address space is created that has a single bit representing each block of storage. As the data is written to the cache, its corresponding index bit is turned on, indicating this block needs to be written to remote storage later. Bitmaps are used by other storage applications as well, including copy-on-write processes for backup, which are discussed in Chapter 13.

One of the interesting aspects of using a bitmap remote copy cache involves newer writes to cache that supersede previous writes on the same block. As it turns out, there is no need to send both writes, only the most recent one, saving time and bandwidth. Hotspot writes can be coalesced this way to reduce the amount of traffic sent over the intermediary network. In fact, this concept has been applied in some remote copy products that temporarily store writes in a cache and then send them as a group, as opposed to sending each write at a time. This technique would be effective in reducing remote copy bandwidth for applications like databases that have "hot spots" with repeated updates to the same blocks in rapid succession.

Remote Copy Implementation Options

With an understanding of how remote copy processes work, it's possible to explore different points along the I/O path at which remote copy applications can be implemented, including host software, networking equipment, and disk subsystem controllers.

We'll now explore these options and attempt to highlight their relative advantages and disadvantages. One of the issues with all remote copy implementations is they are proprietary products that do not interoperate. When you choose a remote copy solution, you need to have matching forwarding and receiving controllers from the same vendor. However, it is possible to have multiple remote copy applications running in the same environment, even using the same intermediary network, but the two systems cannot be used as spares for each other.

Remote Copy in Disk Subsystems

Most remote copy implementations today run as software in disk subsystems. Examples of disk subsystems remote copy products are the EMC SRDF (Symmetrix Remote Data Facility), IBM PPRC (Peer-to-Peer Remote Copy), Hitachi Truecopy, HP Storageworks DRM (Data Replication Manager), and Storageworks Continuous Access EVA products.

There are different variations of how these products work and which operating modes they support, but all are designed to provide data integrity at remote storage sites.

The main advantage of these products is that they have been in the market the longest and have the longest successful track records. And it needs to be stated that these products have been proven in some of the most difficult environments and have come through with flying colors.

Another advantage of the subsystem approach is that it does not depend on external storage to get the job done. All remote copy operations are done in a "closed" environment where all variables are known, with relatively few surprises. Internal engineering with known configurations and disk drives is less likely to experience unexpected SCSI command responses.

The main weakness of these products is that their scope is limited to a single subsystem and they do not coordinate writes written to multiple subsystems. It is certainly possible that an application could be using storage on different storage subsystems. Certainly both subsystems could have remote copy applications running, but there is no way to coordinate their functions. Write ordering and write atomicity may not be able to be maintained if remote communications problems occur.

NOTE There are business advantages and disadvantages to be weighed in using subsystem remote copy solutions. To start with, the same vendor's subsystem products typically need to be used at both ends, which means seldom-used remote storage might cost a lot more than you want to pay (this would be a disadvantage). However, it may be easier to get the support you need when you need it if you've already spent all that money with a vendor that, by now, ought to like you for sending all that money their way.

Remote Copy in the SAN with SAN Virtualization Systems, SAN Appliances, and Switch Application Blades

Chapter 12, "Storage Virtualization: The Power in Volume Management Software and SAN Virtualization Systems," discusses SAN virtualization in detail. For now, it's worth knowing that systems between servers and storage have the ability to merge storage address spaces for use by host filing systems. This is an area that has seen a great deal of innovation and development in recent years as existing vendors and startups have created a wide variety of products. Remote copy is often integrated with virtualization products that run in SAN switches, routers, and appliances.

One of the more interesting opportunities for providing remote copy functions in a SAN is to put the function in an application blade running in a SAN switch or routing device. Integrating remote copy functionality in a SAN switch consolidates more functions where they can be centrally managed. Examples of this approach include Cisco's MDS9000 product line with its Advanced Services and Caching Services modules. Other SAN switch vendors also offer remote copy application solutions.

Some of the products that fall into this category that could provide remote copy functions are the IBM SVC (SAN Volume Controller), Dell Powervault 530F, Kashya KBX4000, StoreAge SAN Volume Manager, StorageTek Mirrorstore Replication Appliance, Data Core SAN Symphony, HP CASA (Continuous Access Storage Appliance), Falconstor IPStor, Revivio CPS (Continuous Protection System), and VERITAS Storage Foundation for Networks.

Obviously, there are many options in this category, none of them having the stellar track records of the subsystem products. With so many entrants it is difficult to predict at this point what the future holds for these products.

One of the main advantages of the in-SAN approach is the main weakness of the subsystem approach: applications that write data to multiple subsystems can do so through a centralized in-SAN virtualization system, which can theoretically coordinate the writes from multiple servers, solving the write ordering and atomicity problems of an application using more than one subsystem.

In addition, the independence of in-SAN remote copy means companies may be able to use storage products from different vendors in their remote copy solutions. That way, secondary and tertiary storage tiers can be implemented with different and less expensive storage products than those used for primary storage. This has the potential of saving IT organizations significant amounts of money in their remote copy budgets.

The disadvantage of the in-SAN approach is that storage is not integrated within the same system that the remote copy controllers are, opening the possibility for unexpected behavior related to SCSI command execution and responses. For that reason, the certification of downstream storage subsystems by in-SAN remote copy application vendors is the key to creating a reliable and stable remote copy system.

Remote Copy in Host Software

Remote copy can also be implemented in host software, where it is often referred to as *replication*. Host replication applications include the Veritas Volume Replicator, the Fujitsu Softek Replicator, and the Topio SANSafe.

These products do not necessarily work with SCSI commands, but they do work with I/O operations targeted for specific block storage address space. In other words, they operate "above" the SCSI device driver layer. For that reason the data that is forwarded does not necessarily need to use SCSI protocols and SAN products. It can use many different networks, including IP networks.

Like in-SAN remote copy, host-based replication can use different storage subsystems at both local and remote sites. In addition, all I/Os from the system can be forwarded to the remote site, maintaining consistency and atomicity independent of the mix of primary storage subsystems used by the application.

The drawback of host-based replication is the CPU load that can be placed on the system. The faster the I/O rates are for an application, the more work that is required of the replication application. At some point this could potentially become a problem.

NOTE Another class of host software, also referred to as replication, works on file system objects, as opposed to I/O operations. The subject of file replication is covered in more detail in Chapter 17, "Data Management."

Examples of Remote Copy Architectures

The rest of the chapter looks at a couple of different remote copy designs.

"Ping Pong" Remote Copy Between Two Sites

In this example a company has two data centers in the same region or city. Each of them has primary storage and uses the other for secondary storage in a remote copy system.

Figure 10-7 shows two sites named East and West. Both sites have storage and remote copy controllers providing forwarding and receiving roles. If one site experiences a problem, the work resumes at the other site. Companies with multiple data centers sometimes use this type of arrangement because they have full-time staff available in both locations.

Figure 10-7 *Two Sites Providing Secondary Storage for the Other*

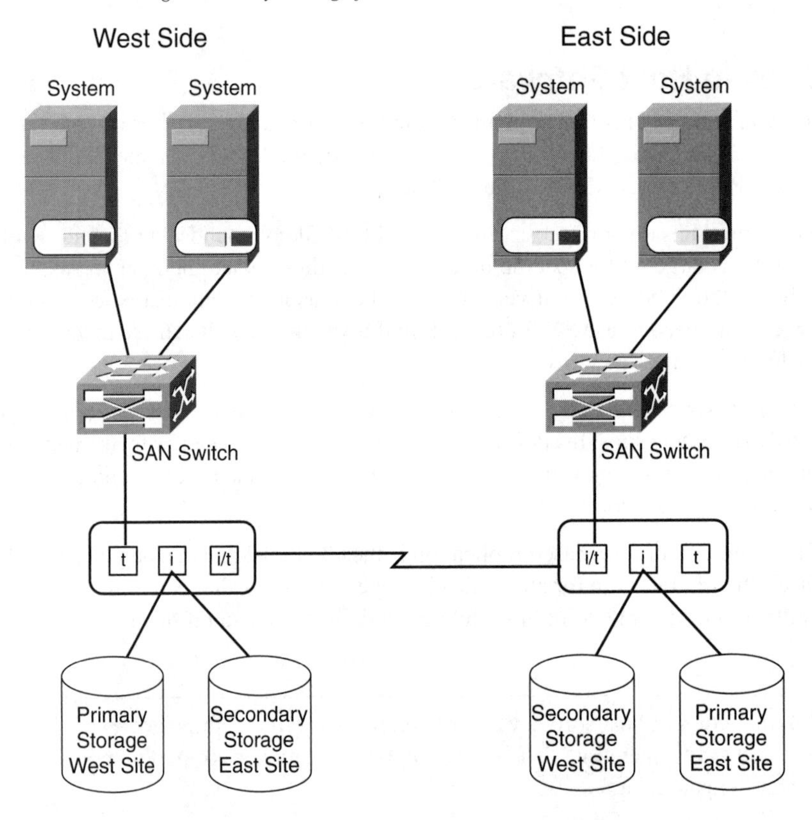

While it is not often done, this type of arrangement could also be used by two different organizations with compatible systems and storage products. Sharing the cost of remote copy could make the technology affordable for companies that cannot afford to implement it alone.

Bunker Secondary Storage and Remote Tertiary Storage

The bunker approach is shown in Figure 10-8. Writes are sent from a forwarding remote copy controller to secondary storage in a bunker site connected by a high-speed MAN network using synchronous remote copy mode. From there writes are sent to tertiary storage in a distant remote site over a slower WAN network using asynchronous mode.

Figure 10-8 *Remote Copy Using Bunker Storage on a High-Speed Network and Tertiary Storage Over a WAN*

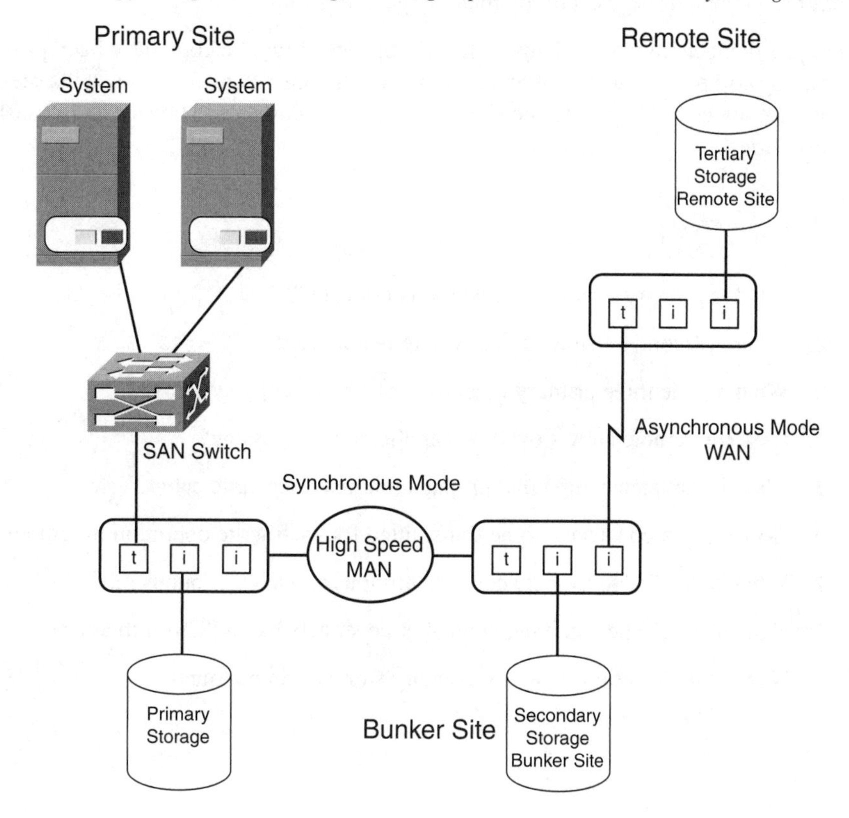

Summary

This chapter examined the technology and methods of remote copy storage management applications. Remote copy is used to create data redundancy for disaster recovery purposes. With remote copy, writes are forwarded from a primary storage controller to a secondary and/or tertiary storage controller. Controllers in a remote copy system can be located locally within the same building or campus as well as remotely, hundreds of miles apart.

The requirements for remote copy systems can be extremely challenging. The performance of the remote copy system must be fast enough to not hinder a system's application performance, and write ordering of transmitted data must be guaranteed to ensure data consistency.

One of the constraints is the speed at which signals propagate in fiber-optic cabling, which means that distance is also a limiting factor. The technique of using nearby bunker storage for high-speed transmissions and then forwarding data from the bunker site to a distant tertiary site has been adopted successfully by many large companies.

Despite the technology challenges, the capabilities of remote copy have been proven many times by companies that relied on them to maintain operations following a disaster. The use of remote copy technology is expected to grow as more companies bolster their disaster recovery capabilities.

Q & A

1. What is primary storage, and where is it located?
2. What is secondary storage, and where is it located?
3. What are the three primary objectives of remote copy systems?
4. How can remote copy slow down application processing?
5. What is the latency of signal propagation in a fiber-optic cable?
6. How many signals have to be transmitted for each write operation in remote copy?
7. What is the difference between synchronous and asynchronous mode?
8. True or false: The receiving controller never acts like a SCSI initiator.
9. Name three locations where secondary storage can be found.

Upon completing this chapter, you will be able to

- Participate in planning or analysis meetings discussing redundancy methods used in your organization
- Analyze dynamic multipathing solutions and products that you are using or considering
- Participate in planning sessions for provisioning LUNs within storage subsystems
- Diagram multipathing designs, including all hosts, initiators, and subsystem ports

CHAPTER 11

Connection Redundancy in Storage Networks and Dynamic Multipathing

The construction of a storage network infrastructure needs to balance the competing goals of flexibility and stability. A storage network infrastructure should be flexible enough to allow a large number of systems to use it, but it also needs to provide stable data services that can be depended on to work on-demand. In a world driven by the demands of wireless Internet access, IT organizations must develop methods to make data access as stable and reliable as possible.

Redundancy techniques that remove single points of failure are used to make data access reliable. Storage redundancy techniques such as mirroring, redundant array of inexpensive disk (RAID), and remote copy, which are used to provide redundancy for data, were discussed in the previous three chapters. This chapter looks at the architectures and techniques used to create redundant communications between systems and storage. Redundant communications allow systems to continue operating normally if a failure of some type occurs that blocks communications. Most system designs assume that primary disk storage is available and can fail or shut down if communication with primary storage is lost. Therefore, it is important to provide redundant access paths to storage for high-availability systems.

The first part of the chapter examines the physical machinery of the I/O path and briefly discusses how redundancy can be provided by duplicate components. The second part of the chapter is devoted to the highly specialized techniques of dynamic multipathing, which provide the logic for taking action when I/O communications fail.

Redundant I/O Path Elements

The concept of the I/O path was introduced in Chapter 3, "Getting Down with Storage I/O," as a way to understand the complete picture of how data is transferred between systems and storage. Redundancy can be applied to all the physical components of the path, including

- Host server systems
- HBAs and cables
- Network equipment and routes
- Subsystem ports
- Subsystem interconnects

We'll look at each of these in the following sections.

Redundant Server Systems

Infrastructures for data access necessarily include options for redundant server systems. While server systems might not necessarily be thought of as storage elements, they are clearly key pieces of data access infrastructures. From a storage I/O perspective, servers are the starting point for most data access. Server filing systems are clearly in the domain of storage. To a large degree, network attached storage (NAS) systems are primarily designed around the filing functionality they provide. Chapter 15, "Network File Systems and Network Attached Storage," discusses NAS technology in more detail.

Redundant server systems and filing systems are created through one of two approaches: clustered systems or server farms. Farms are loosely coupled individual systems that have common access to shared data, and clusters are tightly coupled systems that function as a single, fault-tolerant system. If a server fails in a farm, the application job has to be restarted on another server. If a server fails in a cluster, the application job can continue to run with minimal interruptions on another system in the cluster. The topic of clustered and distributed filing systems is explored further in Chapter 16, "New Directions in Network Filing: Clustered File Systems, Distributed File Systems, and Network Storage for Databases."

NOTE It is certainly possible that redundant servers in server farms can eliminate the need for redundant I/O paths in those servers. If a client/server application is stateless and the client can reconnect with any available server in the farm and access data, there is no need to provide redundant I/O paths on every server. Redundant data access is simply provided by the farm itself.

Redundant HBAs, HBA Ports, and Cables

Multipathing software depends on having redundant I/O paths between systems and storage. In general, changing an I/O path involves changing the initiator used for I/O transmissions and, by extension, all downstream connections. This includes switches and network cables that are being used to transfer I/O data between a computer and its storage.

A single multiported HBA can have two or more ports connecting to the SAN that can be used by multipathing software. However, while multiported HBAs provide path redundancy, most current multipathing implementations use dual HBAs to provide redundancy for the HBA adapter.

Passive and active cabling components can fail or be damaged, effectively shutting down communications. Cables and connectors don't fail often, but they can be cut or physically damaged, resulting in the loss of communications. Electro-optical transceivers are less likely to suffer damage, but they have been known to fail and block communications. Redundant cabling is a natural result of using redundant ports on network nodes and switches.

Network Switching Equipment

Switches (including storage directors) can fail also. Most SANs have been designed with redundant switches to keep a switch failure from occurring and stopping SAN communications. Many possible switch topologies can provide high availability, but that discussion is beyond the scope of this book.

Switches are typically made with redundant, hot-swappable power supplies that allow the switch to continue running after a power supply fails and continue running while a replacement is installed and made active.

SAN Directors are high-availability SAN switches with 64 or more ports and redundant supervisor modules that control the operations of the director. If one supervisor fails, the other assumes control of all director operations until the failed unit is removed and replaced.

In addition to the hardware in a switch, there are also software modules in a switch that manage its operations. The switch control software in a director with dual supervisors can typically be upgraded, one supervisor at a time, without impacting the director's availability.

An important function of SAN switches is building routing tables that determine the path traffic takes through a multiswitch SAN. There can be multiple routes through a network of more than one switch. Network routing and storage multipathing should not be confused—they are completely different functions. Routing determines which switches traffic is forwarded through, and multipathing determines which initiators and logical unit numbers (LUNs) are to be used.

Subsystem Ports

Storage subsystems, the topic of Chapter 5, "Storage Subsystems," can have multiple network ports connecting to switches in the SAN. The ability to direct storage traffic through different subsystem ports is a critical component of multipathing. Typically one host system HBA is configured to communicate with one subsystem port while the other subsystem HBA is configured to use the other subsystem port. A considerable part of this chapter discusses the subsystem connections and LUN assignments needed to make multipathing work.

Subsystem Interconnects

Although it is not necessarily visible to host system initiators, the storage interconnect used inside a subsystem can have an important impact on the subsystem's ability to provide multipathing support. For instance, a subsystem with a single interconnect has some level of risk for that interconnect failing and making data unavailable. This is one of the reasons storage subsystems tend to use backplanes for connecting devices—to eliminate most of the physical exposures that could stop internal communications.

More important than the physical interconnect technology is the design of the controllers and cache in the subsystem. Subsystem controllers may have two or more multiple interconnect controllers to provide redundancy should one of them fail.

Dynamic Multipathing

The rest of the chapter discusses the logical operations of path redundancy, which is commonly called dynamic multipathing (DMP). In this chapter, the shortened term *multipathing* means the same thing as dynamic multipathing.

The Big Picture of Dynamic Multipathing

Multipathing is concerned with a very small subset of the overall I/O path: the Small Computer Systems Interface (SCSI) architectural elements responsible for SCSI layer transmissions between host systems and storage. In a nutshell, multipathing establishes two or more SCSI communication connections between a host system and the storage it uses. If one of these communication connections fails, another SCSI communication connection is used in its place. Figure 11-1 illustrates.

Figure 11-1 *A High-Level View of Multipathing*

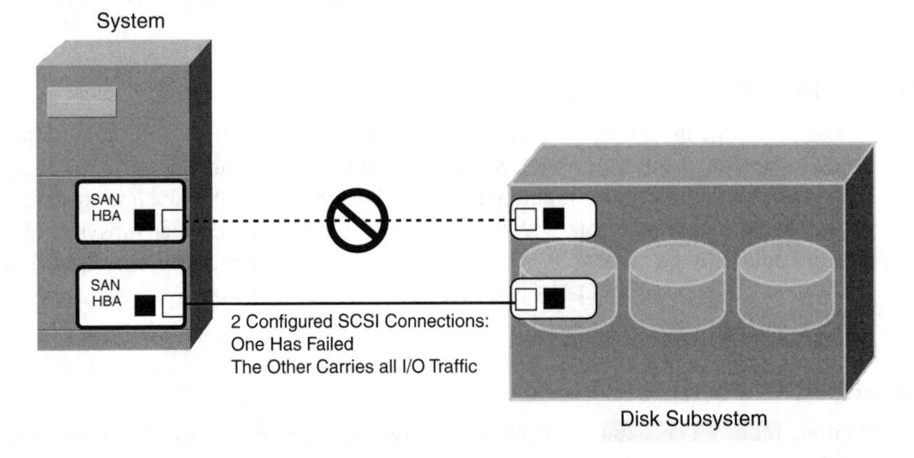

NOTE Notice the lack of a network or bus in Figure 11-1. While the word "path" might be assumed to refer to a network path or route, it doesn't. The path in this case is actually better thought of as a SCSI nexus. (See the section "SCSI Nexus and Connection Relationships" in Chapter 6, "SCSI Storage Fundamentals and SAN Adapters.") Of course, nobody in their right mind refers to this topic as multinexusing, or nexi-ing, or whatever it would be, because nobody understands how to modify the word nexus, much less use it.

Differentiating Between Mirroring, Routing, and Multipathing

Multipathing is sometimes confused with other redundancy functions, including storage mirroring and network routing. Often all three are combined to support high-availability data access to mission-critical applications. Table 11-1 summarizes the different roles and relationships these technologies have in providing redundancy for SAN communications.

Table 11-1 *Differentiating Different Redundancy Functions*

Redundancy Function	Relationship	Role
Mirroring	Generates two I/Os to two storage targets	Creates two copies of data
Routing (convergence)	Determined by switches independent of SCSI	Recreates network routes after a failure
Multipathing	Two initiators to one target	Selects the initiator-LUN pair to use

Subsystem Multipathing Structures

Among the more challenging aspects of SCSI communications are the various relationships between SCSI initiators and targets, LUNs, and logical units. Multipathing provides a context that helps clarify how these elements are related, but it is practically impossible to understand multipathing without understanding these fundamental relationships.

A Review of SCSI Logical Units and LUNs

As discussed in Chapter 6, a SCSI logical unit (LU) is the command process running in a storage subsystem controller that manages I/O operations for a particular storage address space. Most storage address spaces in storage network subsystems are composed of redundant storage from multiple disk partitions configured using mirroring, RAID, or other virtualization techniques.

Logical units in SAN storage subsystems are accessed through the combination of the subsystem SAN port and a particular LUN that is associated with the LU. A single subsystem port can have multiple LUNs, each of them associated with a single LU. Figure 11-2 shows a subsystem where I/O commands enter through SAN Port P and are directed to LU abc through LUN X. The storage address space is formed by two mirrored disk drives forming a single storage address space.

Figure 11-2 *I/O Traffic Enters a Subsystem Through SAN Port P and Is Directed to LU abc Via LUN X. A Pair of Mirrored Disks Forms a Single Storage Address Space.*

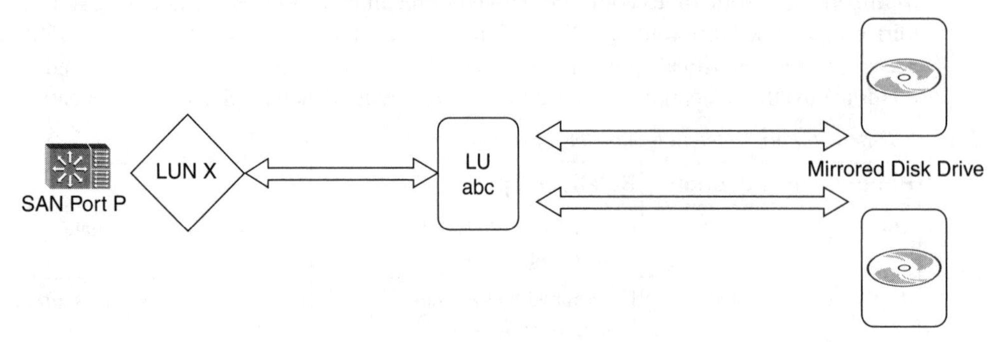

It is important to understand that the LUN is not an identifier for the LU, but simply provides an access role. If you consider the entire subsystem and all its exported storage, LUNs provide a mapping method that allows storage I/O traffic to be directed through subsystem SAN ports to the proper LUs. Each subsystem SAN port has one or more LUNs that are available for directing I/Os to specific LUs.

The LU has its own unique identifier within the subsystem. A serial number or a universal unique identifier (UUID) is created in the subsystem. Multiple LUNs associated with different SAN ports in a subsystem can all index the same LU by its unique UUID.

The way LUNs are assigned to SAN ports is an administrative decision. While LUs are unique in a subsystem, the LUNs that index them do not have to be. For instance, it is possible to have the same LUN ID defined on multiple ports that map I/Os to different LUs. For instance, LUN 3 could be defined on Ports 1 and 2, with LUN 3 on Port 1 mapping I/Os to LU aaa and LUN 3 on Port 2 mapping I/Os to LU bbb. In general, it is a good practice to associate all occurrences of the same LUN ID with the same LU within a subsystem. In other words, all occurrences of a particular LUN ID would map to the same LU, regardless of the subsystem port.

NOTE For what it's worth, no architectural limit is placed on the number of host system initiators that can communicate with each port/LUN in a subsystem. Limits on host/LUN communications are accomplished through LUN masking, a process discussed in Chapter 5.

Figure 11-3 expands Figure 11-2 by showing two identical LUNs in two different SAN ports mapping to LU abc.

Figure 11-3 *Two Identical LUNs Accessed Through Different SAN Ports Mapping I/Os to a Single Logical Unit*

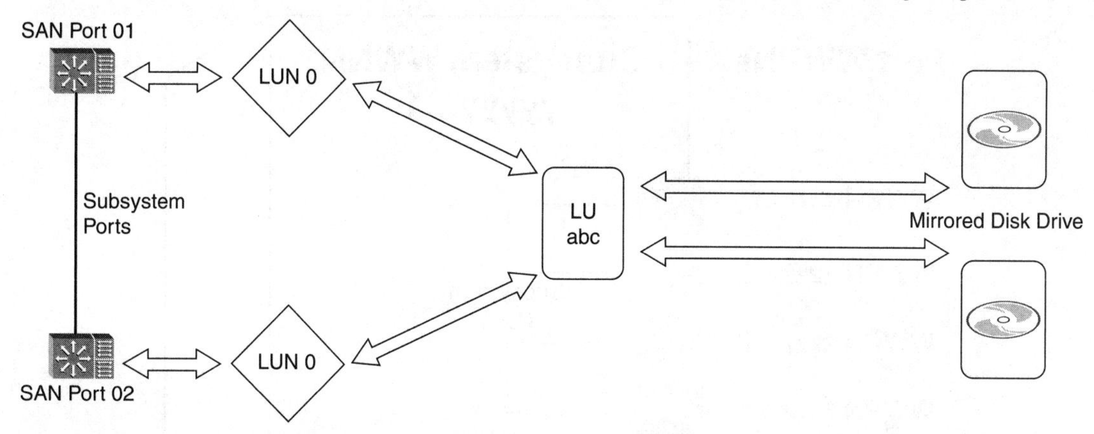

World Wide Node Names and World Wide Port Names

Fibre Channel uses the notion of global, unique identifiers to locate resources in the network. All port hardware in a Fibre Channel network has a 64-bit identifier assigned at the factory called a world wide port name (WWPN). It is used to uniquely identify the port, even after the network is powered down or rebuilt. The idea of the WWPN is to provide *persistence* in the SAN, to facilitate fast recovery of functions following some sort of failure or other disaster. For instance, an initiator that retrieves configuration information about the storage it was using should be able to find it in the network again, following a complete network power cycle.

The term world wide name (WWN) usually refers to the WWPN, but where multipathing is concerned, the world wide node name (WWNN) is also needed to uniquely identify the subsystem. The WWNN is the ID of a system or subsystem that has multiple ports. Now there are some interesting problems trying to figure out how to create a unique WWNN with a system that may be sold without any SAN HBAs whatsoever, but you can assume that for multipathing, the subsystem can identify itself as an entity containing multiple WWPNs.

Figure 11-4 illustrates a subsystem with four SAN ports, each with its own WWPN.

WWPNs, LUNs, and LUs

The whole picture of the subsystem can now be made. Each port has a unique WWPN. Associated with those ports are one or more LUNs, which map storage I/O traffic to specific LUs, each having its own specific UUID. The LU is the command processor for I/O commands operating on the disk drive partitions that form the storage address space. All these entities are pictured in Figure 11-5.

Figure 11-4 *Multiple Ports with Unique WWPNs in a Storage Subsystem with a Unique WWNN*

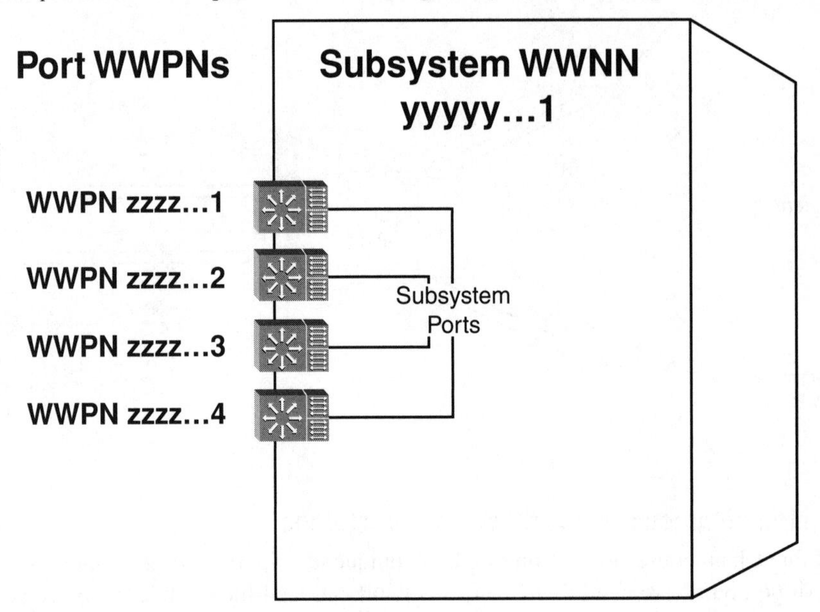

Figure 11-5 *Subsystem SAN Ports with WWPNs and Associated LUNs Mapping I/O Traffic to a Specific LU*

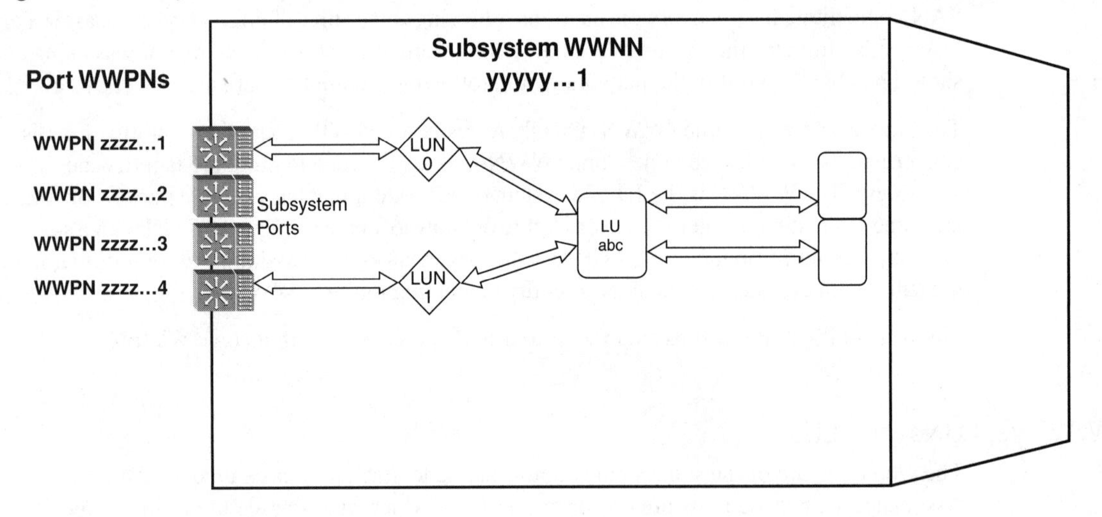

Host System Multipathing Functions

Subsystem architectures for multipathing are half the story; the other half of the multipathing equation occurs in host systems.

Host Storage Initiators in Multipathing

Multipathing software monitors host storage initiator functions where storage I/Os originate and where communications failures are identified. If a failure is identified, multipathing software changes the initiator port being used.

In many multipathing implementations, the HBA has a single port and therefore a single instance of an initiator process. This has created the perception that multipathing software requires multiple HBAs. However, it is certainly possible to use multiported HBAs, with each port's operations being controlled by its own discrete initiator process. When multiported HBAs are used, multipathing software can switch to a different path by using a different initiator process associated with a different port on the same HBA where the failure occurred.

Nonetheless, multiple HBAs will continue to be commonly used in SAN multipathing solutions in order to protect against HBA failures.

Implementing Multipathing Software

Multipathing software typically runs in kernel space in host systems, which means it has to run quickly without errors. It does not create or alter storage transfers. Instead, it determines the storage path that is used, which in turn determines the network connections that are used and all other parts of the I/O path all the way to the LUN in a subsystem.

There are many different ways to implement multipathing software, depending on the operating system. Some operating systems, like Microsoft Windows Server operating systems, have application programming interfaces (APIs) for integrating third-party multipathing software. Other operating systems do not have APIs, which gives multipathing software vendors much more leeway in implementing their solutions but also creates significant challenges for testing and debugging.

Using a stack analysis, the multipathing software is typically placed between the SCSI command driver and the low-level connecting HBA device driver, as shown in Figure 11-6.

Figure 11-6 *Multipathing Software in the Storage Software Stack*

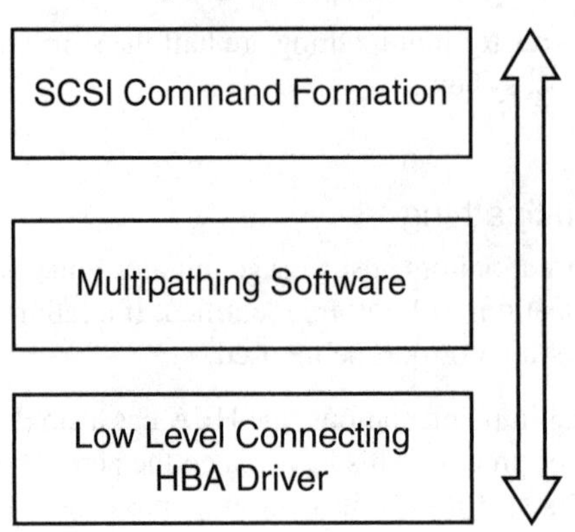

Determining Paths

Paths in multipathing solutions have three elements:

- The initiator, which originates commands
- The subsystem SAN port and LUN (WWPN+LUN) where commands are sent
- The LU that processes commands for a given storage address space

In the remaining sections, these three elements of the path are sometimes indicated using the construct "initiator/WWPN+LUN/LU."

One of the most interesting aspects of multipathing is how the software determines which initiator/WWPN+LUN/LU paths can be used for I/O transmissions. Multipathing software can be thought of as a SCSI investigator that gathers information about a subsystem's storage resources and uses deductive reasoning to determine all the paths that reach a specific logical unit.

There are several ways multipathing software could be designed to discover multiple storage paths between systems and an LU in a subsystem. One possible discovery process is outlined in the following steps:

1. For each initiator in the system, get a list of all storage target WWPNs (subsystem ports) from the name service of a SAN switch.
2. Query all WWPNs to report all associated LUNs. (LUN masking would prevent "masked" LUNs from being reported to certain HBAs.)
3. For each reported LUN, acquire the UUID for the LU it references.
4. Create a list of all initiator/WWPN+LUN/LU paths that can be used to transmit I/Os between a system and a particular LU.

For full redundancy in the storage path, there need to be at least two paths with different pairs of initiators and WWPN+LUNs. Obviously the LU UUIDs have to be the same. The LUNs could be the same or different, as long as they both refer to the same LU.

Figure 11-7 shows a hypothetical list of storage paths discovered by multipathing software in a system. Redundant storage paths are indicated by dotted lines.

Figure 11-7 *A Hypothetical List of Storage Paths Maintained by Multipathing Software*

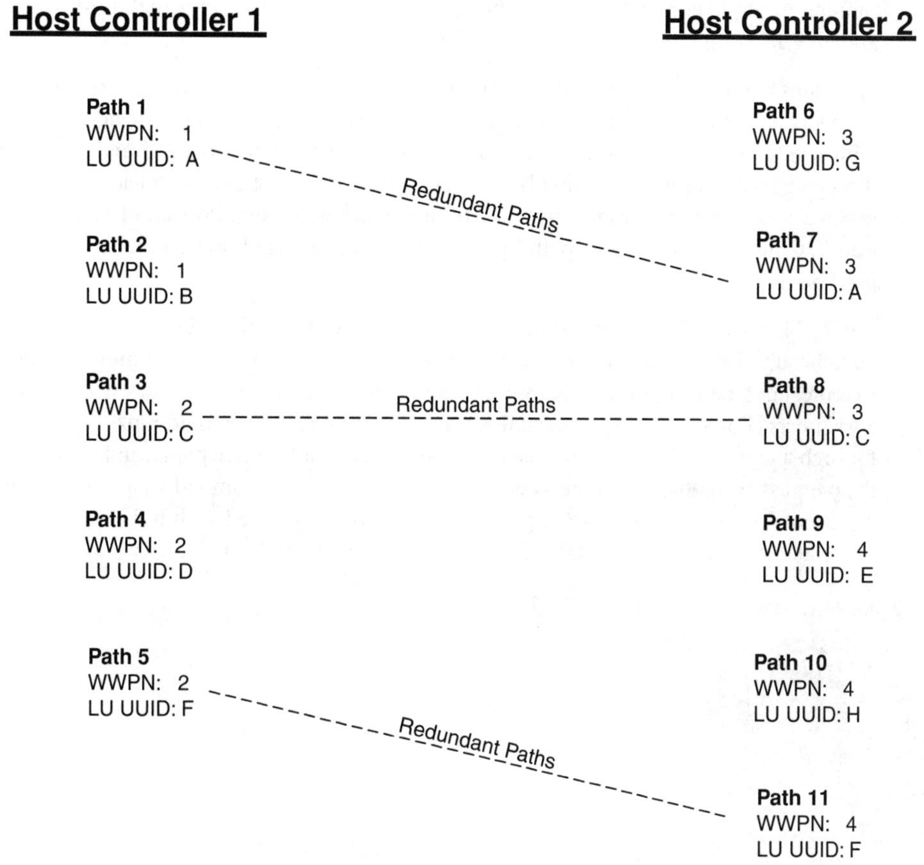

Host Controller 1

Path 1
WWPN: 1
LU UUID: A

Path 2
WWPN: 1
LU UUID: B

Path 3
WWPN: 2
LU UUID: C

Path 4
WWPN: 2
LU UUID: D

Path 5
WWPN: 2
LU UUID: F

Host Controller 2

Path 6
WWPN: 3
LU UUID: G

Path 7
WWPN: 3
LU UUID: A

Path 8
WWPN: 3
LU UUID: C

Path 9
WWPN: 4
LU UUID: E

Path 10
WWPN: 4
LU UUID: H

Path 11
WWPN: 4
LU UUID: F

Redundant Paths (Path 1 – Path 7)
Redundant Paths (Path 3 – Path 8)
Redundant Paths (Path 5 – Path 11)

Active/Passive Configurations and Static Load Balancing

A common configuration for multipathing follows an active/passive model where the active storage path carries all I/O traffic while the passive storage path is idle. Active/passive configurations such as these require an administrator to select which storage path will be active and which path will be passive.

Active storage paths are used for all I/O until something occurs that keeps I/O transmissions from reaching their destination. When a path failure is recognized, the passive path automatically is elevated to become the active path, and the formerly active path is made inactive to prevent it from inadvertently restarting and creating problems.

It is important to differentiate between physical SAN links and the initiator/WWPN+LUN/LU paths used by multipathing software. A single physical link can be used by multiple paths concurrently. For instance, a single host system with two HBAs (or a single multiported HBA) running multiple applications can define active and passive paths for both host controllers, allowing I/O traffic to be divided between them.

Assigning the I/O traffic from different applications to active paths defined on different host initiators is a practice referred to as *static load balancing*. For instance, consider a server system with two HBAs (Initiator 1 and Initiator 2) running two applications, #1 and #2, storing data through two different LUs, A and B, respectively. Assume both ports can access both LUs. It is relatively simple to define an active path for application #1 using Port 1 and a passive path using Port 2. Conversely, the active path for application #2 can use Port 2, and the passive path can use Port 1.

Figure 11-8 shows this simple static load balancing configuration, where Application #1 stores data through LU A and Application #2 stores data through LU B. This figure uses dotted lines to represent a pair of point-to-point links connecting the system initiators with the subsystem SAN ports (Ports A and B). In actual SANs, these connections would most likely be made through a pair of SAN switches. The bold solid lines denote active paths, and the thin solid lines denote passive paths within the system and subsystem. The diamond shapes in the subsystem represent LUNs; each subsystem port has two LUNs associated with it. LUNs 1 and 3 are associated with LU A, and LUNs 2 and 4 are associated with LU B.

Figure 11-8 *An Active/Passive Multipathing Configuration*

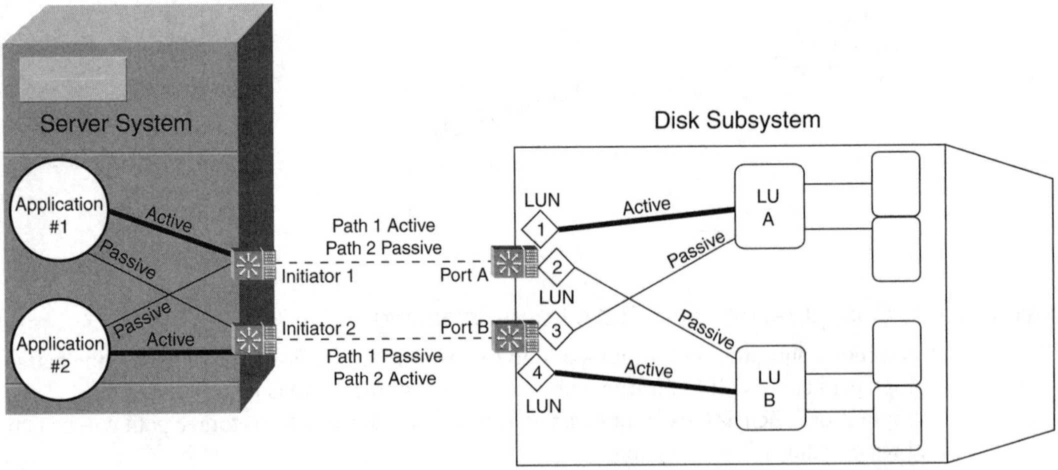

NOTE Some readers might wonder why Figure 11-8 does not include SAN switches. While the addition of switches would have been more representative of actual SANs, Figure 11-8 is already busy enough without the presence of switches and switch connections. It would have been possible to use the familiar network cloud to indicate network connections, but it probably would have required two clouds (for redundancy) and a lengthy discussion of single SANs versus dual SANs. So let's just say you could use one or two SANs and that multipathing software doesn't care what you do because the switches and switch ports are not defined as part of the initiator/WWPN+LUN/LU path.

Active/Active Configurations with Dynamic Load Balancing

More advanced multipathing solutions allow active/active connections, where multiple storage paths provide redundancy as well as *dynamic load balancing*. In a nutshell, active/active configurations use one or more storage paths as part of normal operations. If one of the paths should experience a failure, the remaining path carries all I/O traffic.

Dynamic load balancing distributes I/O transmissions over the available paths. Three basic algorithms are used to distribute storage traffic in dynamic load balancing:

- **Round robin**—Each I/O command is sent to the next path available for an initiator/LU connection. When two paths are available, the I/O commands alternate between both paths.
- **Least blocks**—The next I/O command is sent over the path that has the fewest blocks in transit. This method is most useful for streaming applications.
- **Least I/O**—The next I/O command is sent over the path with the lightest measured I/O load. This method is most useful for transaction processing applications.

Failover Processing

The process of changing paths with multipathing technology is called *failing over*. Failing over involves recognizing that a storage path has failed, preparing to restart operations on a redundant path, and then reinitiating operations on the redundant path.

Recognizing Path Failures

Path failure recognition is the responsibility of the host-based multipathing software. Failures are detected when I/O operations are not acknowledged after a defined period of time, or timeout value. Usually the operation is retried to allow for an intermittent problem of some sort, but subsequent timeout failures are determined to be a path failure. Timeout values are not specified by any standard and are determined by the design of the multipathing software. Some vendors allow users to select the timeout values they want to use. Common timeout values range from 30 seconds to up to several minutes.

Preparing to Fail Over

There may be several "housekeeping" actions that need to be done prior to commencing operations on the passive path. This can involve changing the state of system variables and flushing "dirty" data stored in write-back cache to disk drives.

Initiating Operations on the New Active Path

It might not be possible to detect what the status was of a pending I/O that was unacknowledged. Assumptions should be made that the I/O failed prior to reaching the subsystem and that the I/O operation needs to be retried on the newly active path. From that point on, all I/O operations use the newly activated path.

Failing Back

In an active/passive configuration, after all problems with the former active path have been resolved, it may be desirable to "fail back" to the original configuration in order to restore the balance of I/O processes in the SAN. The failback process is identical to the failover process except that it is not precipitated by a path failover. Failing back stops I/O operations on the active path, prepares the repaired path for operations, and then starts processing I/O commands again through the original active path.

Multipathing and Network Route Convergence

Multipathing is not the only automated way to recover from a network problem in a SAN. SAN switches use the FSPF routing protocol to converge new routes through the network following a change to the network configuration, including link or switch failures.

Multipathing software in a host system can use new network routes that have been created in the SAN by switch routing algorithms. This depends on switches in the network recognizing a change to the network and completing their route convergence process prior to the I/O operation timing out in the multipathing software. As long as the new network route allows the storage path's initiator and LU to communicate, the storage process uses the route. Considering this, it could be advantageous to implement multipathing so that the timeout values for storage paths exceed the times needed to converge new network routes.

Summary

Systems depend heavily on access to storage and data. When data access is stopped, systems stop working. Therefore, it's important to maintain data access. Connection redundancy improves data availability in SANs by creating multiple options for server-to-storage connections.

Hardware components such as HBAs, cables, and switches are often duplicated to allow uninterrupted operations following a component failure. SAN storage subsystems typically have multiple ports that can be used for redundant connections.

Dynamic multipathing software manages the processes of recognizing I/O transmission failures and failing over to a redundant path. The paths used by multipathing software are defined by the host initiator, the subsystem port/LUN combination, and the LU that processes storage commands for subsystem storage. As long as a host initiator can access the LU where data is stored, multipathing software should be able to maintain I/O operations.

Because multipathing is based on SCSI architectural elements, it is a very good idea to plan and use SCSI resources carefully, particularly watching the way LUNs are assigned to subsystem ports and LUs.

Q & A

1. Is multipathing more of a connecting (network) technology or a storing (SCSI) technology?
2. What is the minimum number of HBAs needed for multipathing?
3. How many LUs can a single LUN be associated with?
4. What is the difference between a WWNN and a WWPN?
5. What three pieces of information define a path?
6. True or false: Multipathing always uses active/passive configurations with static load balancing.
7. How long are typical timeout values for failing over?
8. Describe the difference between mirroring, multipathing, and SAN routing.
9. What identifies the LU uniquely?

The Foundations of Storage and Data Management

Upon completing this chapter, you will be able to

- Participate in meetings and planning sessions about storage virtualization strategies and products
- Participate in evaluations of virtualization products
- Discuss the benefits and risks of virtualization products with coworkers and vendors
- Describe the differences between volume management and SAN virtualization systems

CHAPTER 12

Storage Virtualization: The Power in Volume Management Software and SAN Virtualization Systems

The manipulation of storage address spaces through storage virtualization technology is certainly one of the most important enabling technologies in storage area networking. In fact, it can be argued that all working SANs make use of some form of virtualization and that the value of the storage area network (SAN) is related to the extent to which it is applied to manage SAN resources. However, what this means in terms of products and architectures is a matter of opinion for the time being, depending on one's involvement with specific products and strategies.

A few years ago it was difficult to find SAN products that were not marketed on the strength of their storage virtualization capabilities, even if the application of virtualization was somewhat trivial and the benefits existed only in sales presentations. Unfortunately, all the noise over storage virtualization made it difficult to understand what it was or how it could be most effectively used.

This chapter explores the mechanisms of storage virtualization and its implementations in two different types of products: volume management software and SAN virtualization systems. The use of Redundant Array of Inexpensive Disks (RAID) technology, the topic of Chapter 9, "Bigger, Faster, More Reliable Storage with RAID," is assumed with any storage virtualization product, as are the concepts of subsystems (see Chapter 5, "Storage Subsystems") and Small Computer Systems Interface (SCSI) (see Chapter 6, "SCSI Storage Fundamentals and SAN Adapters").

The Concept of Storage Virtualization

Storage virtualization is the storing-level process for forming "upstream" storage address spaces (block storage) from downstream storage address spaces (typically logical units [LUs] exported by storage subsystems). Figure 12-1 shows a virtual storage address space on the left being formed from a virtualization process acting on two other storage address spaces on the right.

Figure 12-1 *The Creation of Upstream Virtualized Storage Structures*

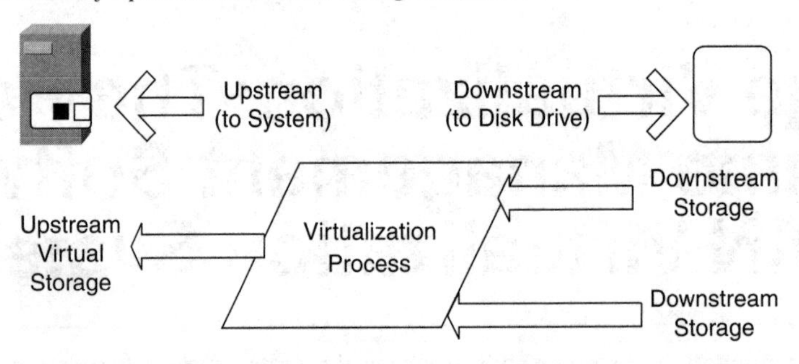

The terms *downstream* and *upstream* define I/O path directions. Something that is downstream is in the direction going away from the host. It's no surprise, then, that something that is upstream is in the direction going to the host.

A Review of Technologies Used in Storage Virtualization

As a fundamental technique in storage networking, there have been numerous other discussions pertinent to the understanding of storage virtualization in this book. Readers who want a review of this material may want to look at the following sections:

- Chapter 2
  - "Block I/O"
  - "The Storage Address Space"
  - "Storage Address Space Manipulation"
- Chapter 3
  - "Volume Managers"
- Chapter 4
  - "Logical Block Addressing"
- Chapter 5
- "Storage Address Space Management"
- Chapter 6
- "SCSI Logical Units"
- Chapter 8
  - "Identically Sized Storage Address Spaces"
- Chapter 9
  - "Capacity Scaling Through Striping"
  - "RAID Product Options"

Virtualization Products: Volume Managers and SAN Virtualization Systems

Two basic types of virtualization products are analyzed in this chapter—volume management software and SAN virtualization systems. SAN virtualization systems can be further classified as using either an *in-band* approach or an *out-of-band* approach.

NOTE Storage virtualization technology is the heart and soul of storage subsystem controllers. However, while storage subsystem controllers tend to have extremely powerful virtualization capabilities, they are not often referred to as being "virtualization" products, per se.

Yes, this is another one of those confounding areas where the language of storage makes things more difficult and convoluted than they need to be. The term *storage virtualization* is used in this chapter to identify the fundamental storing-level functions provided in volume managers, subsystem controllers, and SAN virtualization systems. The term *SAN virtualization system* refers to the implementation of virtualization in a system that resides in the SAN.

Volume Management

Volume management is a generic name for host system software that manages storage address spaces for systems. It is sometimes referred to as *disk management software* or *software RAID*. Disk partitioning software can be thought of as a very simple form of volume management.

Volume management implements storage virtualization functions that interact with the system kernel as a low-level I/O process. It runs between the storing level host bus adapter (HBA) device drivers and filing systems in the I/O stack, which is why volume management is sometimes referred to as a *shim layer*. When the volume manager receives a request from a filing system for an I/O operation on certain blocks in a storage address space, it translates that request into the multiple address spaces that it is managing. For example, if the volume manager is providing mirroring on two storage address spaces, a single I/O request is processed by the volume manager, which passes two requests to lower-level storage device drivers. If the volume manager is striping data with RAID, the volume manager determines how to segment the original request into multiple requests that are turned into storage commands by lower-level storage device drivers. Figure 12-2 shows where volume manager processes run in relation to the filing system storage device drivers.

Volume management software became popular as open-systems computers started to scale in size and need larger capacities and higher data availability. Veritas Corporation developed a volume management product for Sun systems that was widely deployed by Sun customers. Volume management was originally developed for parallel SCSI storage devices and subsystems, many of which were relatively inexpensive JBOD subsystems.

Figure 12-2 *Volume Management Runs Between the Filing System and Storage Device Drivers*

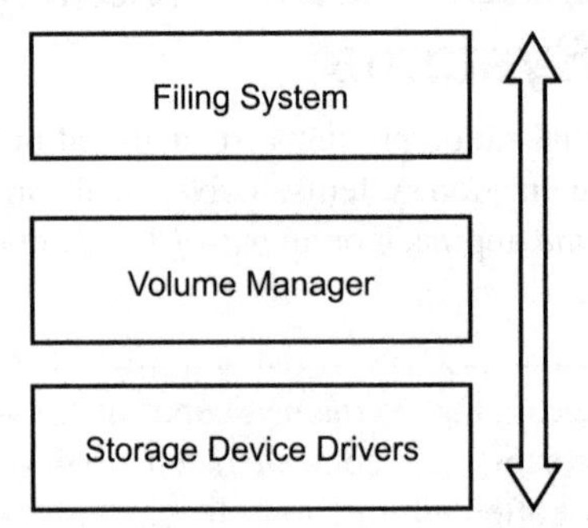

Volume managers have adapted well to SAN environments by being able to incorporate a wide variety of storage products as resources for host systems. However, as products that were traditionally licensed and installed on individual systems, traditional volume manager designs do not inherently provide centralized control of storage in a SAN. While multiple volume managers may be able to be managed centrally, that does not mean that all their combined storage resources can be managed centrally as a shared resource.

SAN Virtualization Systems

By contrast, SAN virtualization systems are separate, external implementations of storage virtualization that run in the I/O path between host systems and storage subsystems. They can be thought of as processors of SCSI storage transmissions. They have SAN ports with LUNs that direct storage I/Os to LU processes that manage communications with host initiators. In addition, SAN virtualization systems also act as SCSI initiators for commands that are transmitted to downstream storage subsystems.

The I/O process through a SAN virtualization system begins with an incoming SCSI command from a host initiator that is transmitted to a target controller/LUN and processed by the associated LU in the virtualization system. Each SCSI command is interpreted by controller logic running in the virtualization system in the order it is received and is sent back out over the SAN through the appropriate initiator/port to the downstream storage subsystem.

One way to think about SAN virtualization is that it moves the storage controller function out of a subsystem and locates it in a network. A key architectural difference is that SCSI communications with host systems are managed by LUs in the virtualization system and not by LUs in the storage subsystem. This LU can be thought of as a *proxy LU* because it does not act directly with devices and media. Similarly, communications with downstream storage subsystem LUs are started by initiators in the virtualization system that can be thought of as proxy initiators. The initiator/LU connections then assume the following form:

host system initiator to proxy LU + proxy initiator to storage LU

Proxy LUs in virtualization systems that manage host SCSI communications are sometimes said to be *terminating* the I/O. In the same vein, proxy initiators *reinitiate* the I/O and send it to downstream storage. Transmission to downstream storage often involves several separate I/Os to separate storage subsystems or LUs, depending on the type of address space manipulation being performed by the virtualization system. For instance, a virtualization system that implements mirroring would forward two separate downstream I/Os for every I/O it receives.

Figure 12-3 shows a SAN virtualization system in the I/O path. In this figure, the host initiator sends an original I/O to the proxy LU in the virtualization system, and a proxy initiator in the virtualization system sends a downstream I/O to a real LU in the storage subsystem. This virtualization system is not performing any storage address space translations but is serving a simple proxy role.

Figure 12-3 *I/O Communications Through a SAN Virtualization System in the I/O Path*

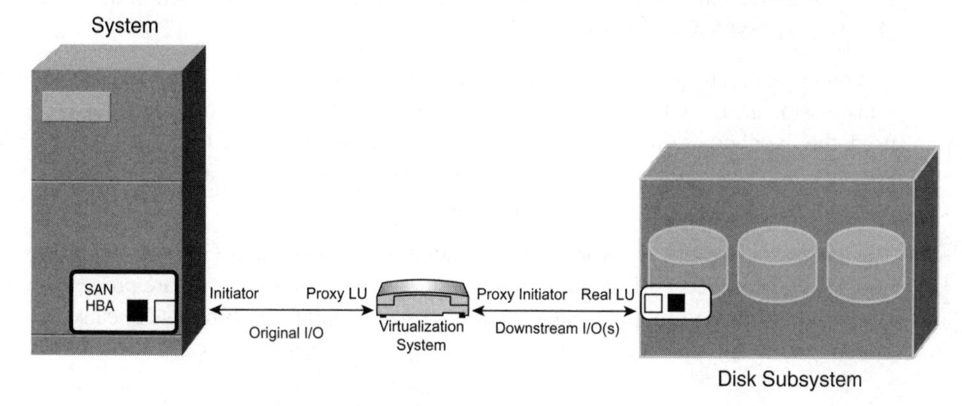

Whereas volume management software typically runs in a single system, SAN virtualization systems are designed to support communications with several host systems simultaneously. They can have multiple ports and fan-in communications sessions from multiple host HBAs over a single switch link.

A SAN virtualization system can be a dedicated computer system with specialized software for providing virtualization functions, or it can be a networking product that has integrated virtualization capabilities. For instance, a SAN switch or router product can provide virtualization functionality integrated along with its networking services. A dedicated virtualization system can be implemented as an add-in application on a line card and installed in SAN switches.

In-Band Virtualization

Virtualization was initially developed by SAN vendors using two competing architectures—*in-band* and *out-of-band virtualization*. *In-band virtualization*, described in the preceding section, is the most widely implemented architecture and appears to be on its way to being the de facto standard in the industry. In-band virtualization solutions are also referred to as in-path because they operate in the I/O path between systems and storage. As described, they interpret SCSI I/O commands from host initiators and then reformulate them for transmission to downstream storage.

One potential shortcoming of in-band virtualization is the potential for increased I/O latency in SAN operations. It only makes sense that adding multiple initiator/LU sessions would result in transmission delays of some sort. As it turns out, the performance impact might not be an issue in many cases. In fact, I/O performance can even be improved through the use of cache memory in the virtualization system. Performance with virtualization is discussed in the section titled "Performance of SAN Virtualization."

The other potential shortcoming of in-band virtualization is the increased likelihood that transmission errors will occur. Again, it only makes sense that if more connections are being used, the likelihood of having a problem with one of them is greater. For that reason, SAN virtualization systems are sometimes designed with error recovery and redundancy technologies such as hot spare and clustering.

The primary advantage of in-band virtualization over out-of-band virtualization is the lack of host software needed for in-band virtualization. As virtualization software processes run in kernel space, the possibility exists for out-of-band virtualization products to cause severe system problems.

Out-of-Band Virtualization

The *out-of-band virtualization* architecture is more like a distributed volume management system than the in-band virtualization systems just described. The idea is to control the operations of virtualization software agents running on multiple systems from a centralized management console. Each virtualization agent acts like a volume manager for the system it runs on, but all of them can be working with common, shared storage resources.

The architectural advantage of out-of-band virtualization is the lack of additional latency and complexity in the I/O path. However, its primary disadvantage is the presence of virtualization agents running in the system kernel space. Problems with kernel space software can cause system failures and can be very difficult to troubleshoot.

Performance of SAN Virtualization

There are two primary performance topics to discuss with SAN virtualization systems:

- Latency
- Caching

Latency

As mentioned previously, one of the disadvantages of virtualization is the possibility of introducing latency into I/O operations and slowing down application performance. This certainly is a possibility. Companies purchasing SAN virtualization products should test and verify what the performance impact may be of the systems they are considering.

The issue is that the virtualization system must first read the entire incoming I/O and interpret it and then create one or more I/Os that are retransmitted to downstream storage. Obviously this is not an architecture for SAN networks that may be stretching supported distance limits or where errors are higher for some reason.

SAN virtualization products can be designed to minimize latency through designs that minimize the processing time involved. It may be that the latency injected by a virtualization product is inconsequential compared to other latencies that occur in normal I/O processing. For example, a delay of a few hundred microseconds is relatively small—less than 5% of the total latency incurred in a normal I/O transmission. If application performance does not need every possible microsecond, I/O latency is not a problem.

Caching

For those cases where latency is a problem, performance can be significantly improved through the use of caching in SAN virtualization systems. Memory caches in SAN virtualization systems are designed to significantly improve I/O performance rates of high-throughput applications like transaction processing.

One of the advantages of caching in SAN virtualization systems is the flexibility in assigning the cache to different LUs and block ranges within those LUs. For instance, it may be possible to assign cache memory to a small area of block addresses in order to eliminate an important application's hot spots. Testing with actual applications and data is the best way to determine if caching in a SAN virtualization system will deliver the desired performance benefits.

Scaling Storage with Virtualization

Virtualization is a powerful storage tool that encompasses many other technologies and techniques, including RAID. The power of virtualization comes from its ability to create scalable storage by utilizing the flexibility of SAN connections. This section examines the fundamental ways virtualization applies simple geometric connection flexibility to build scalable storage.

The Virtualization "Lens"

To make it easier to discuss storage virtualization processes, we will use the word "lens" to pinpoint functions at a certain point in the I/O path. Just like an optical lens is used to define the scope and range of a visual image, the storage virtualization lens narrows or widens the "view" of block addresses in a storage address space.

To clarify, the virtualization lens does not perform any magnification, and of course it does not (or shouldn't!) distort the data in any way. Another major difference is that virtualization can seamlessly assemble address spaces from many different sources simultaneously so they can be "viewed" as a single, composite structure.

Figure 12-4 shows a virtualization lens in the I/O path between a host system and a pair of storage LUNs.

Figure 12-4 *A Virtualization Lens in the I/O Path*

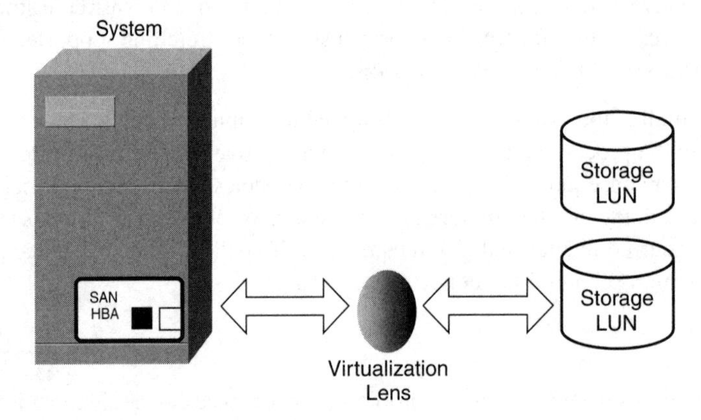

Fan-Out of a Virtualization Lens

Fan-in was discussed in Chapter 5 as a way for a single subsystem port to export multiple storage address spaces, where they can be accessed by multiple host systems. Fan-*out* is the inverse process and refers to the number of downstream targets that can be accessed by a single virtualization lens. Figure 12-5 shows a virtualization lens with a fan-out ratio of 1:5.

Multiple hosts can connect through a single link between a switch and a SAN virtualization system. Each of these host sessions can then connect to multiple downstream LUNs after passing through the virtualization lens.

Figure 12-5 *Fan-Out of a Virtualization Lens*

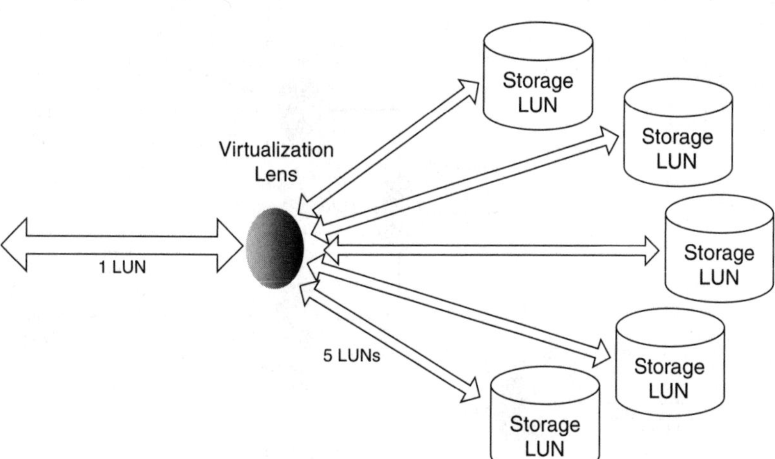

Recursivity of Virtualization

Virtualization lenses can be used sequentially. For example, a geometric "virtualization tree" can be formed to aggregate storage from several downstream LUNs, which, in turn, are formed by LUNs that are downstream from them. Figure 12-6 shows recursive virtualization in a tree topology with three layers of lenses.

NOTE Multilevel tree topologies are not necessarily recommended. They are shown merely to illustrate a simple idea. There is always some latency incurred with moving I/Os through a SAN virtualization system. This could cause problems, depending on the product implementation and the I/O requirements of the application (read transaction processing.) Don't assume all SAN virtualization products are the same in this regard. They aren't.

Figure 12-6 *Recursive Virtualization Lenses Forming a Tree of LUNs*

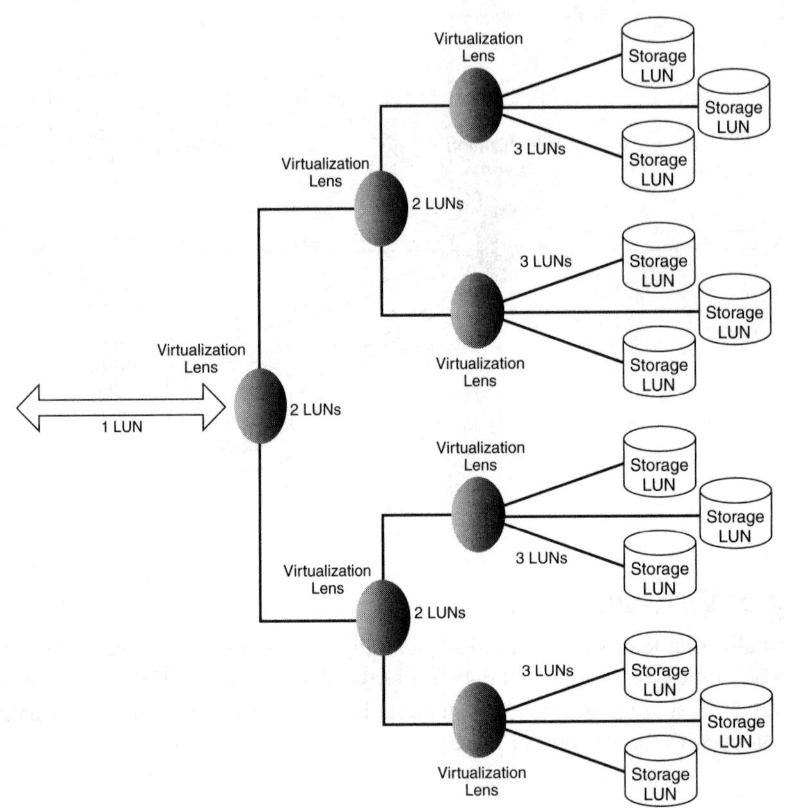

Comparing the "Views" of Volume Managers, SAN Virtualization Systems, and Storage Subsystems

Scalability and flexibility in storage networking depend on the ability to locate and use downstream storage resources. By virtue of being connected to storage over a *network,* as opposed to a device interconnect, volume managers and SAN virtualization systems have much better "views" of storage resources in the SAN than disk subsystems do. Figure 12-7 compares the view of a storage virtualization product with disk subsystems.

Figure 12-7 *Comparing the Downstream Storage "Views" of Storage Virtualization Products with Disk Subsystems*

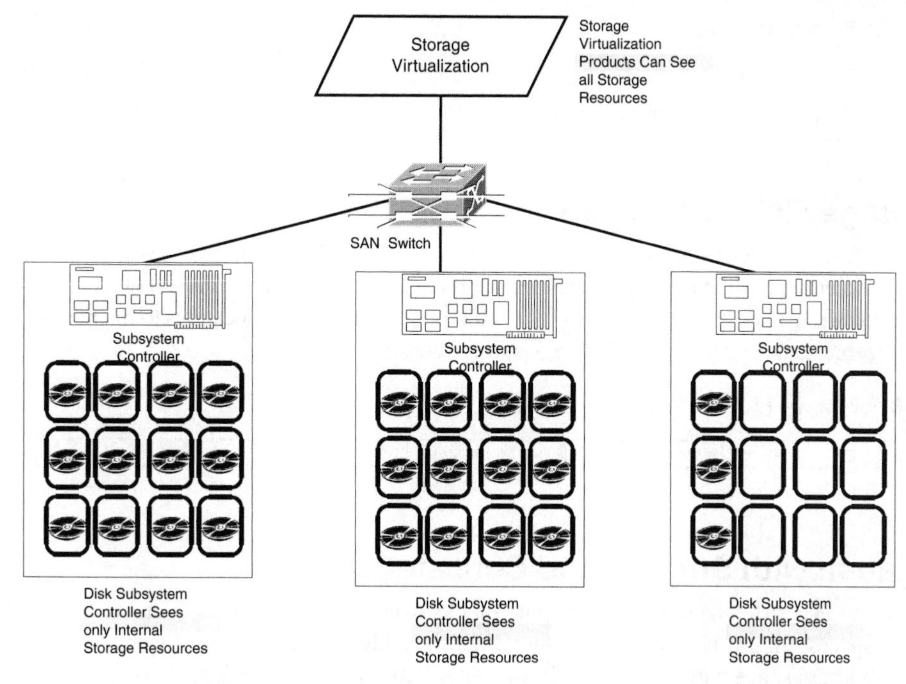

Volume managers and SAN virtualization systems have essentially the same downstream views of the network, because both of them connect to SAN switches. Any resource "seen" by one can be seen by the other. In most SANs, the views of storage are managed by fencing technology that blocks access to SAN resources. Examples of fencing technology include LUN masking (see Chapter 5) and switch-based technology such as virtual SANs (VSANs) and zoning, which are not discussed in this book.

There is a big difference between the upstream views that volume managers and SAN virtualization systems have. The volume manager is limited to presenting I/O responses upstream to a single system. The SAN virtualization system, on the other hand, often works with many upstream host HBA initiators. This gives the virtualization system much stronger capabilities for centralizing management of the storage.

Address Space Manipulation Techniques

This section explores the address space manipulation techniques used in SAN virtualization and volume management. Among the topics covered are

- The storage flat address space
- Aggregation

- Subdivision
- Substitution
- Mirroring
- Private data areas and metadata

The Storage Flat Address Space

Storage (block) address spaces are referred to as "flat." This means they have a simple one-dimensional structure with a beginning address, an ending address, and all other addresses in between, in order. There are no rows or columns or tuple address locations to figure out. Figure 12-8 represents a very simple 20-block storage address space.

Figure 12-8 *A Simple, Flat, 20-Block Address Space*

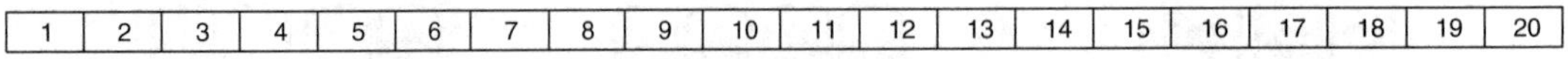

1	2	3	4	5	6	7	8	9	10	11	12	13	14	15	16	17	18	19	20

Aggregation with Striping and Concatenation

Storage virtualization can aggregate blocks from different sources to create larger address spaces. Figure 12-9 shows a 25-block virtual address space created by combining a 20-block address space with five blocks from another 20-block address space.

Figure 12-9 *Concatenation of Storage Address Spaces*

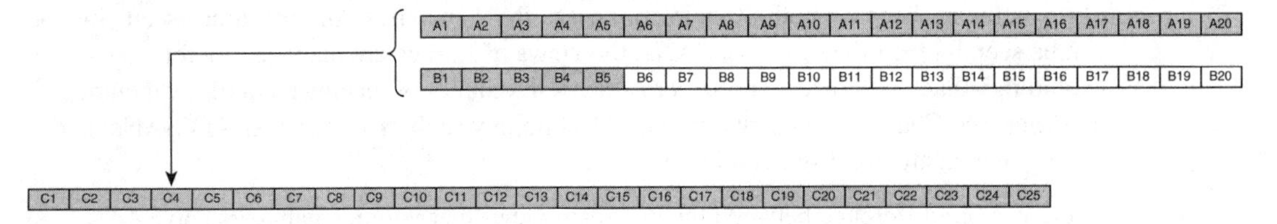

The process used to aggregate blocks in Figure 12-9 is an example of concatenation. Concatenation does not intertwine the downstream address spaces; it appends one address space to another.

RAID striping, described in detail in Chapter 9, is a special case of block aggregation where all array members contribute the same number of blocks to the upstream address space. RAID intertwines the downstream storage address spaces by associating *strips* from the various member drives to form a segment of the upstream address space.

Subdivision

Subdivision allows an address space to be segmented into smaller units. Figure 12-10 shows an eight-block address space and a 12-block address space created from a single physical 20-block address space.

Figure 12-10 *Subdivision of Storage Address Spaces*

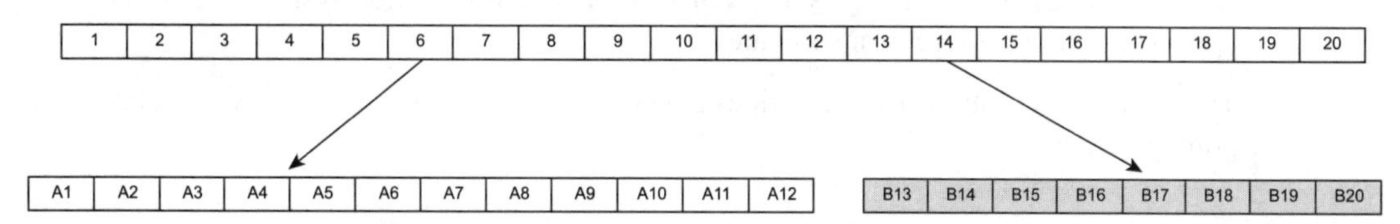

Subdivision allows storage to be purchased in volume to reduce costs and then be parceled out as needed to applications. If the need for storage capacity is known in advance, it may be simpler and less expensive to purchase a large amount of storage all at once. Storage virtualization enables both approaches: buying in bulk or paying as you go.

Substitution

Storage virtualization can substitute one storage resource for another, transparently to the host systems using it. This substitution can be done with different devices/subsystems or address spaces. One common example of virtual storage substitution is using disk storage as a substitute for tape storage in backup, a topic that is explored more in Chapter 13, "Network Backup: The Foundation of Storage Management."

Mirroring

Mirroring, described in Chapter 8, "An Introduction to Data Redundancy and Mirroring," is a special case of storage substitution that takes two identically sized storage address spaces and presents a single, identically sized upstream storage address space. When a failure occurs that keeps one of the mirrored pairs from working, the other continues to fulfill the storage function.

Private Data Areas and Metadata

Virtualization products often have private data areas or metadata that are not part of the exported address space that is used by file systems and databases. Private areas or metadata are for the exclusive use of the volume manager or SAN virtualization systems and are used to store historical information about product operations and configurations.

Storage Pooling

There are many significant advantages to centralizing the management of storage in an organization. Centralized storage management gives administrators the best control over and information about how storage is being used. One of the most powerful concepts in storage networking is a storage management approach called *storage pooling*. Storage pooling is usually associated with storage subsystems and SAN virtualization systems, but it can also apply to volume management software.

The sections that follow discuss various benefits of storage pooling with SAN virtualization point products.

Storage Utilization with Pooled Storage

Storage utilization is expressed as a percentage of storage that is populated with data as a part of the total storage capacity available. Storage utilization measures the capacities of storage assigned to file systems and databases as well as unassigned storage that has not been allocated to any systems yet.

It is generally very difficult to accurately predict what the storage capacity requirements will be for a given system and what the growth rate will be. Typically, storage is purchased in bulk amounts, anticipating an initial need for capacity with a projected growth rate for several years. The problem is that some systems grow as projected, but often they grow faster or slower than expected. Data that grows faster than expected will require administrative action sooner than planned for. A system with lower-than-expected growth rates may wind up having lots of unused storage capacity. It's not unusual for a business with a lot of systems to have both higher-than-necessary storage administration costs and underutilized storage.

Obviously, it would be best if storage space could be flexibly assigned to different systems as it is needed; that way, companies would not have to over-purchase storage that may go unused. In other words, the storage capacity could be available on demand. Storage pooling is one of the key SAN applications because it provides a solution to these utilization problems.

Utilization problems are easiest to identify using direct attached storage (DAS) technology like parallel SCSI. With DAS, the storage attached to a system can be accessed only through that system. Data availability is at significantly higher risk due to the unexpected, premature filling of storage and the need to shut down the system to fix the problem. If one system's storage is full and another system's storage is mostly empty, it only makes sense to try to reassign that storage. However, if you want to assign disk storage from one system to another, you must first physically move it from the subsystem it is in and place it in another subsystem. This requires shutting down *both* systems and involves a fair amount of administrative work at odd hours of the day or on weekends.

Storage utilization can also impact I/O performance. Storage that is overutilized may cause applications to run much more slowly, causing a variety of problems for the IT organization. As it is with processors and systems, you want to operate with optimal price/performance ratios. Disk capacity is too expensive to be insufficiently populated, and applications should be able to run without I/O performance bottlenecks.

NOTE There are no solid rules of thumb for optimal disk utilization levels, because it depends on the application. Some applications can perform well at high utilization levels—say, between 80 percent and 90 percent—while others need to be in the 60 percent to 70 percent range.

To best understand, we'll examine an IT environment with three servers, each with its own DAS storage. When the servers were installed, the IT staff projected growth rates based on expected application usage. Referring to Figure 12-11, Server A has a data growth rate that matches the company's projections. Server B has been a surprising success, and its data growth has been much faster than expected. Soon it will need to add more storage. Server C has an application that has had problems, and its storage is mostly unused. It was expected to need a lot of storage, but instead it needs very little. The unused DAS storage attached to Server C will be wasted.

Figure 12-11 *Storage Utilization Without Pooling*

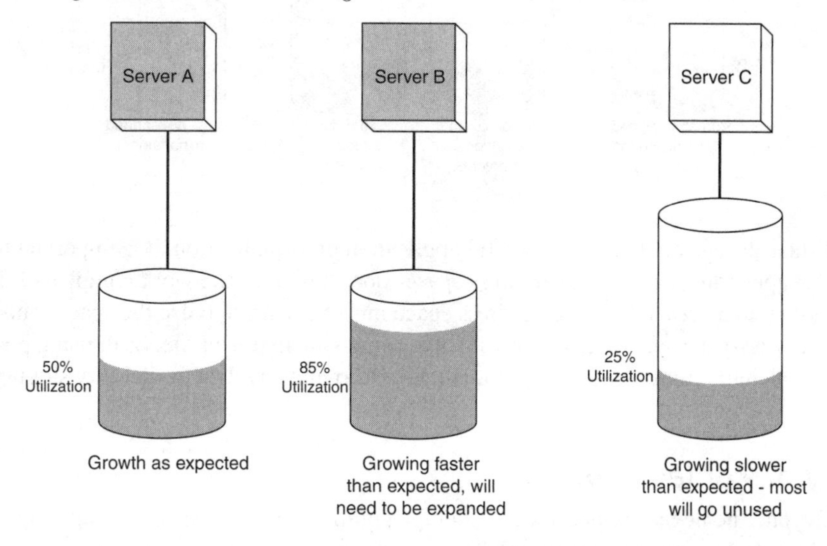

Using storage pooling in a SAN, it is possible to assign smaller amounts of storage initially and add more when it is needed. In other words, smaller virtual address spaces can be used as opposed to assigning the whole storage subsystem's capacity. Figure 12-12 shows the servers pictured in Figure 12-11, but with smaller initial storage configurations. Server A is growing as planned and will probably need to have more storage allocated from the pool at some future time. Server B has already outgrown its initial allocation of storage but had more storage added from the pool. Server C has not used as much storage as expected, but there is far less wasted storage than in Figure 12-11.

Figure 12-12 *Storage Utilization with Pooling*

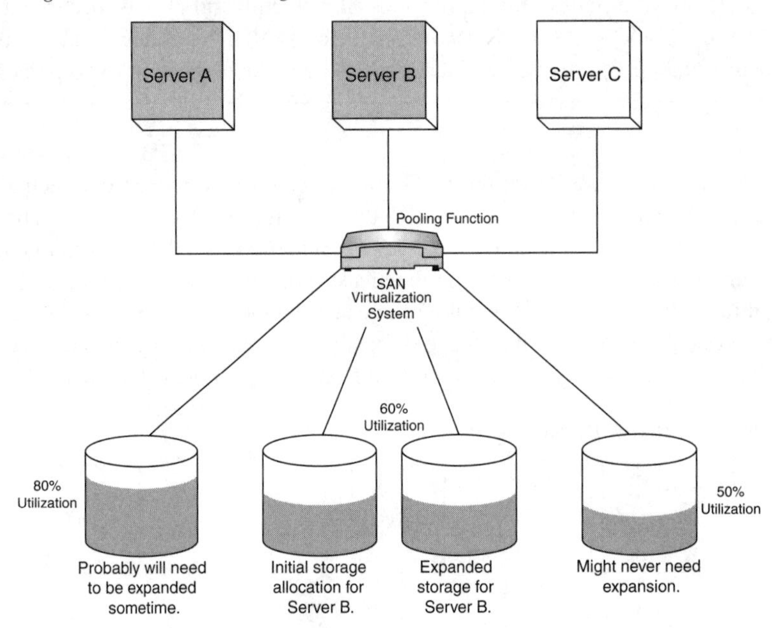

While storage pooling is a powerful application of virtualization, it is important to understand that appending new storage address spaces does not finish the work completely. The filing system that uses that storage address space must be resized to use the space. This is not necessarily a trivial task and may involve some system downtime. Still, using pooling significantly minimizes both administrator effort and any data availability shortages.

Scalability of Pooled Storage

Beyond the flexibility provided by storage pooling to easily expand storage capacity, it also supports the creation of extremely large storage address spaces. Unlike storage subsystems that are constrained physically by the cabinet size, the number of disk drive connectors, and power capabilities, storage pooling in a volume manager or SAN virtualization engine scales with the network. In most cases the size limitation of the virtual storage address space is more a function of the scalability limitations of backup and recovery for protecting a very large address space.

NOTE So what about subsystems? you ask. Can't they provide storage pooling too for this kind of seamless storage address space expansion? The answer is yes, they can—up to the capacity and internal connectivity limits of the subsystem. In fact, many companies have successfully used their subsystems this way.

A SAN virtualization system can be described as a subsystem controller pulled out of a subsystem and stuck in the SAN. The major difference is the total amount of storage that can be addressed. SAN virtualization products can connect to almost any available storage in the network. Most storage subsystems can't. That might change someday, but that's the way it is today.

Target Mix and Breadth in Pooled Storage

Storage pooling accommodates a wide range of dissimilar types of storage targets and allows them to be used together. For instance, data stored on a large enterprise storage subsystem with high-performance Fibre Channel or SCSI disk drives could be backed up to a much less expensive ATA or SATA storage subsystem.

Remote copy applications could also use different classes of storage for local online and remote offline data access. Figure 12-13 shows a SAN virtualization system with an integrated remote copy application that connects to a local enterprise disk subsystem and copies data to an inexpensive remote subsystem.

Figure 12-13 *Remote Copy Through a SAN Virtualization System to an Inexpensive Remote Subsystem*

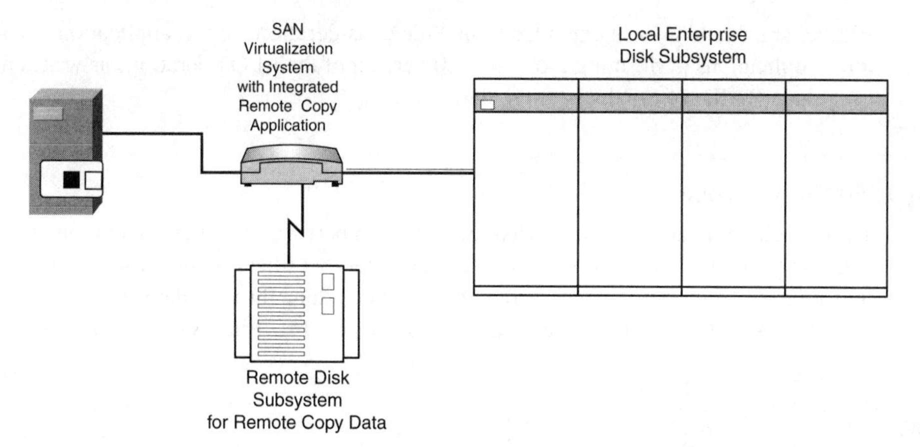

The example shown in Figure 12-13 expresses the desire of many companies that would like to use less expensive storage for remote data and business continuity purposes. They cannot do so because the remote copy application on their primary storage subsystem does not support lower-cost subsystems on the remote end.

Tiered Storage Pools

The concepts of primary and secondary storage were used in the preceding section to describe an application-driven distinction between two different classes of storage. One of the seminal concepts in storage pooling is the definition and creation of different storage tiers to respond to different application needs. In most cases this amounts to finding optimal cost levels for certain performance goals—in other words, getting the most bang for your buck.

Performance Classifications for Tiered Storage

The following sections describe some of the primary performance characteristics that could be associated with tiered storage.

Device Performance

Disk drive performance topics were discussed in Chapter 4, "Storage Devices." A storage tier definition should include metrics for disk rotation speed and seek time. Seek time can be further reduced by short-stroking the drive for the highest-performance applications.

Parallelism in Storage

A useful storage tier definition includes the number of member drives in RAID arrays. For instance, an array with ten drives is much more likely to provide better transaction processing performance than an array with five drives.

Parallelism should also be extended to include considerations for an application's read/write mix. Applications performing more than 20 percent of their I/O operations as writes may want to exclude RAID 5 from that storage tier.

Capacity Utilization Levels

The capacity utilization of storage has an impact on performance. Fragmentation of disk drives and hot spots tends to be more problematic as capacity utilization increases. A policy for maximum utilization of a given storage tier could be done through the use of storage resource management (SRM) software, as discussed in Chapter 14, "File System Fundamentals."

Block Size

The size of the disk blocks defined by the filing system can have a significant performance impact on an application. For instance, large block definitions improve streaming applications by reducing the number of seeks disk drives need to make. Conversely, small block definitions may be useful for transaction processing applications by limiting the amount of data transferred in each I/O.

NOTE Some of the performance parameters that could be used to classify storage, such as block size and capacity utilization, are not determined or managed by either volume management software or SAN virtualization systems. In order to add them to a performance classification, there needs to be some way to integrate this information from file systems or storage management products.

Application Types for Storage Pooling

As discussed in the preceding section, storage pooling can include different types of storage products and implementations to get the best mix of price, performance, and capacity for different types of applications. Some of the different types of applications that could be optimized with specialized storage pools are

- Database (transaction processing)
- Streaming: scientific and engineering
- Graphics
- Office automation

Some hypothetical storage pools are defined in Table 12-1.

Table 12-1 *Hypothetical Storage Pool Definitions for Common Applications*

Application Type	Device Performance	Parallelism	Cache	Utilization	Block Size
Database	High-speed	High	Yes	60–70%	Small
Streaming	High-speed	Medium	No	70–80%	Large
Graphics	Medium	Medium	Yes	70–80%	Large
Office	Low	Low	No	80–90%	Medium

Tiered Storage Pools for Data and Storage Management

Data and storage management applications such as point-in-time snapshot, remote copy, backup, archiving and hierarchical storage management (HSM), are excellent candidates for the application of lower-cost tiered storage. In general, the performance of these applications does not have to be exceptional, but they may need to scale to very large sizes.

Extending Management Functions in Volume Management and SAN Virtualization Systems

Once virtualization lenses and storage pools have been implemented, they tend to remain in place for a long time. It's not surprising that volume management and SAN virtualization system vendors have integrated other management functions into their products, including hot sparing and automated storage migration.

Hot Sparing with Volume Managers and SAN Virtualization Systems

The basic idea of hot sparing is to have storage resources in reserve that can be used to take the place of a failed member in a mirror or RAID array.

Whereas storage subsystems work with internal disk drives in the subsystem, volume managers and SAN virtualization systems work with downstream subsystems in the SAN. This means that many types of storage could be used as hot-spare storage to cover a wide range of address spaces. The flexibility of SAN access with volume managers and SAN virtualization systems results in the widest range of options for hot sparing.

Automated Data Migration Using Volume Managers and SAN Virtualization Systems

Sometimes it is preferable to replace existing storage instead of adding storage. Some of the reasons for replacing existing storage are as follows:

- It eliminates maintenance charges on existing storage products.
- Faster performance is needed that cannot be achieved with the existing storage product.
- Existing storage is nearing end of life.
- You can install storage with new management features.

Data migration can be done at the storing or filing level, but where storage virtualization is concerned, it is a storing-level function. Virtualization-driven migration is a process that transfers data from one or more LUs to one or more other LUs. Although the new storage will likely be larger in capacity than existing storage, the migration process needs to use the same-sized address space so that the filing system that uses it can access data with the current set of addresses.

Traditionally, data migration was done while the system is unavailable to users and applications to avoid potential data integrity problems. However, it is also possible for a volume manager or SAN virtualization system to migrate data on a running system without having to stop any application processes.

To accomplish this, the virtualization product starts copying block data from the first address space on the old LU(s) to the new one(s), keeping a record of all block addresses that have been copied. When a request is made to read data that has already been copied, the request is serviced from new storage. When a read request is made to access an address that has not been moved yet, it is serviced from old storage. When an update is made to data that has not been moved yet, it can be written to both new and old storage, eliminating the need to copy those blocks from old to new storage.

After all the data is copied, the volume manager or SAN virtualization system applies substitution to transparently switch over to the new system. While the new storage presents a new network address and identity to the virtualization product, the host filing system is "spoofed" into believing the old storage is still being used. At some point the system may be stopped and the actual addresses and identities may be configured. A good time for this would be when expanding the capacity of the filing system.

Reliability and Risk Considerations

Some of the biggest challenges in owning and developing a SAN are identifying potential problems and planning to minimize their impact. This section discusses a few topics that should be considered when implementing volume management and SAN virtualization systems.

The SAN Network Environment

Although storage subsystems are not the subject of this chapter, comparing their connection architectures with volume managers and SAN virtualization systems can be useful. The connection environment inside a storage subsystem is very well known and predictable. There are few surprises, if any, involving downstream communications within the subsystem. More importantly, the risk of the interconnect failing inside a disk subsystem is minimal due to designs with passive backplanes and protected connectors.

As is often true, the greatest strength of a technology is also its main weakness. In this case, the flexibility of volume managers and SAN virtualization systems creates greater ambiguity about the connecting environment.

Volume managers and SAN virtualization systems have more networking and storage variables to work with than storage subsystems. Whereas the reliability of a disk subsystem is essentially a function of disk drive failure modes, the reliability of SAN virtualization systems includes such additional networking variables as GBICs and HBAs in the virtualization system or line cards in switches. Not only that, but potential congestion problems in the SAN can also become a reliability issue if they become serious enough. SAN virtualization systems may be more sensitive to network congestion problems due to the actions required of proxy LUs and initiators to manage I/O communications.

Unlike SAN virtualization systems, volume management software does not depend on any additional hardware in the system. However, the more connections that exist between systems and storage, the more likely it is that problems will occur. Insofar as volume management software may use more SAN connections (fan-out), there is a corresponding increased probability that a connection failure will affect a system running volume management software.

Multipathing with Volume Managers and SAN Virtualization Systems

Volume managers and SAN virtualization products are often implemented along with multipathing technology in order to overcome connection failures that might occur.

For SAN virtualization systems this means redundant SAN virtualization systems may be used in different paths. Host systems with two initiators could connect to two different SAN virtualization systems, both providing the same virtualization services with access to the same downstream storage resources. To do this the virtualization systems need to agree on the LU UUID or serial number for the proxy LUs that communicate with host systems. The best way to implement SAN virtualization systems with multipathing is probably in cluster configurations, which are discussed in the next section.

The situation with volume managers is much easier to understand because volume managers typically operate between file system and multipathing software in the I/O stack in host systems. Multipathing software running beneath the volume manager defines the connections between multiple initiators and a single logical unit in a disk subsystem. A volume manager might "see" a single storage resource, while multipathing software "sees" two or more ways to access that resource.

Figure 12-14 is the same drawing of the I/O stack as in Figure 12-2, except for the presence of multipathing software.

Figure 12-14 *Storage I/O Software Stack, Including File Systems, Volume Manager, Multipathing, and Storage Device Drivers*

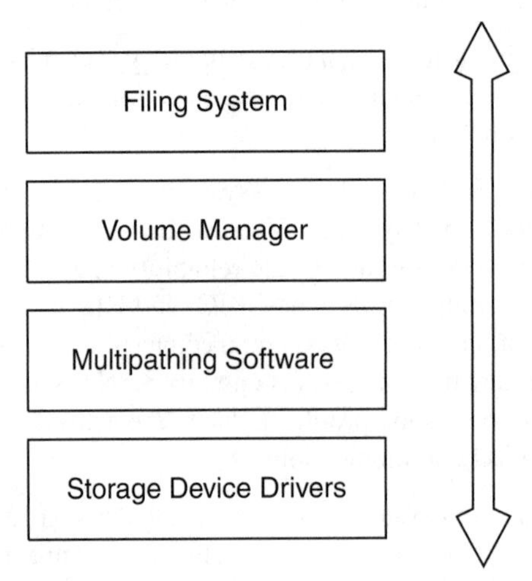

SAN Virtualization System Clusters

A single SAN virtualization system carries the risk of being a single point of failure. To alleviate this risk, multiple SAN virtualization systems can be used in a clustered configuration. Host systems using the virtualization cluster need multipathing software that allows them to access other cluster members to continue working.

The subject of system clustering is complex, especially when you consider the cluster may be supporting high-performance I/O between servers and storage. To keep the discussion simple, this analysis focuses primarily on two-node clusters.

All nodes in the SAN virtualization cluster must be able to access all storage used by the cluster. Furthermore, they must share the same configuration information that defines the various virtualization lenses for all hosts using the cluster. As long as any cluster member can present a host system with the correct virtualization lens, a host system can access its storage through any of the cluster members.

One of the main challenges of operating a SAN virtualization cluster is dealing with any and all I/O actions that may be pending when a failure occurs on a cluster member. There is a chance that newly updated data may have been written to write-back cache memory on the failed system with stale data still on disk storage. It is essential that subsequent reads access the most recent copy of data, whether it is in cache or on disk.

A simple solution to this problem is to turn off caching in the cluster. That way, there is no risk of data consistency problems. However, this might not be acceptable if the SAN virtualization cluster is being used for high-throughput I/O applications.

A better way to work is to ensure that cache contents are shared between cluster members. One of the ways to do this is to mirror cache contents between nodes in the cluster. With mirrored cache, a write I/O is written to cache in both cluster members before it is acknowledged to the host initiator. This architecture is similar to that used for synchronous remote copy operations, as discussed in Chapter 10, "Redundancy Over Distance with Remote Copy," except the connection speeds between the cluster members is much faster.

Summary

Storage virtualization is one of the most important technologies in all of storage networking. This chapter examined the fundamental architectures, benefits, features, and risks involved with using storage virtualization.

Storage virtualization is a tool for manipulating storage address spaces and is implemented in two different types of products: volume management software and SAN virtualization systems. Volume managers work above the storage device driver layer, manipulating storage address spaces as they are presented to the host system. SAN virtualization systems are in the SAN between systems and storage. They perform their functions using proxy LUs and initiators to receive, interpret, and reinitiate I/Os that are received from host systems.

The main advantage of volume managers and SAN virtualization systems in SANs is the connection flexibility available in SANs. Many different types of storage can be combined in a number of ways to create reliable, redundant, super-scalable, cost-effective storage.

Q & A

1. What is the primary function of storage virtualization?
2. What is the similarity between a SAN virtualization system and a storage subsystem?
3. How do volume managers and SAN virtualization systems differ in their "view" of the network?
4. Describe the difference between concatenation and striping.
5. What is the difference between fan-in and fan-out of a SAN virtualization system?
6. How can high utilization of storage lead to poorer I/O performance?
7. True or false: Storage subsystems have more predictable connection environments than volume managers or SAN virtualization controllers.
8. Starting with the filing system and looking downstream, name the elements of the I/O software stack in a host system.
9. If a SAN virtualization system is a single point of failure, what can be done to improve availability?

Upon completing this chapter, you will be able to

- Participate in discussions and meetings regarding backup strategies and operations in your organization
- Discuss the designs of backup solutions with coworkers and vendors
- Explain the strengths and weaknesses of different backup approaches, including legacy LAN-based backup, LAN-free backup, serverless backup, and disk-based backup

CHAPTER 13

Network Backup: The Foundation of Storage Management

There is little doubt that responsible storage management begins with the discipline of backup and recovery. In the unlikely and unfortunate event of a loss of systems or storage equipment, the nearly miraculous process of restoring data is used to re-create the data that we depend on so heavily.

This chapter analyzes the fundamental processes and technologies of backup and recovery and outlines the difficulties that companies commonly have with them. A variety of approaches are discussed, starting with legacy LAN-based backup before moving to SAN-based backup methods. At the end of the chapter we discuss the growing use of disk subsystems as storage for backup data.

Fundamentals of Backup and Recovery

The concept of backup and recovery is very simple. Data is copied to offline or secondary storage during backup operations and is kept there in case it needs to be restored following some type of disaster that causes the loss of data. Backup traditionally uses both duplication redundancy and delta redundancy with file granularity. In other words, legacy backup can copy all the files in a storage address space, or it can copy only those that have changed.

Historically, backup copies have been made to tape storage devices and tape media. In recent years, this scenario has changed somewhat with the introduction of less-expensive ATA disk drives. The use of disk for backup is discussed toward the end of this chapter in the section "Disk-Based Backup." Although disk storage is used, many of the logical operations are based on operations developed for tape devices and media. For that reason, most of this chapter is devoted to the analysis of tape backup because an understanding of tape backup is essential to understanding most disk backup schemes.

Backup Versus Recovery

The execution of backup and recovery processes is complex and involves a surprising number of variables. Backup and recovery processes are also considerably different. Backup is usually implemented with the goal of minimizing the impact on production systems. Restore, on the other hand, has to provide the mechanism for a complete restore of a system. Backup simply copies data to secondary storage of some sort, where it can be restored by backup software at a later time. Restore, on the other hand, has to make sure that restored data can be used correctly by system and application software. Restoring data also involves the possibility of over-restoring data and creating a number of problems associated with a disk-full condition.

NOTE It is truly amazing how the added complexity of recovery is often either ignored or underestimated. Beyond the scary problems of backup data being incomplete or missing from backup media, there can be a lot of file system cleanup following the restore to get rid of unwanted garbage that was restored by mistake.

As the amount of stored online data increases (online data is data that is readily available to applications on disk storage), the problems of backup compound. While backup technology has made great strides in the last ten years, it never seems to be able to catch up with the expanding requirements for storage capacity and data availability.

Backup Applications

The four primary uses for backup are

- Business continuity protection
- Historical archiving
- System and application migration
- Data sharing

Business Continuity Protection

Backups are part of most disaster recovery operations. If systems or data are destroyed for any reason, the organization must be able to re-create its systems and data in order to resume normal operations. For organization that are not using any remote copy data protection technologies, backup data on magnetic tape is usually the only automated way of recreating data.

Historical Archiving

Companies use backup systems to archive data for historical purposes. Copies of data can be made to easily restore historically important versions of software and data. For example, software development companies typically make archival copies of projects when they reach certain milestones. Archiving to tape is also used to satisfy audit requirements by taking backup "snapshots" of monthly or quarterly financial data. Of course, today there are new regulations such as the Sarbonnes Oxley Act that mandate the storage and archiving of nearly all management communications.

System and Application Migration

One way to transfer data from one system to another is to back it up on the first system and restore it on the other. In general, it is preferable to migrate data over a network, but that is not always practical.

Data Sharing

Similarly, data sharing in the form of the "sneaker net" can be accomplished with tape copies made by a backup system. This method is still used (amazing, but true!) in situations where data sharing involves a large number of extremely large files. However, as storage capacities increase, storage networks are replacing these "socially friendly" data sharing methods.

Backup as a Filing Application

Most backup systems are designed as a filing process to allow individual files to be identified and restored easily. End users who want data restored ask for a particular file or group of files. Database backup can be done by naming files or tablespaces. Both of these are filing-level functions because they specify data as a data object as opposed to by its storage block address.

File systems and database systems usually have programming interfaces that allow backup systems to copy data as files or database objects. Backup software designers usually integrate these interfaces in their backup products to provide the most complete, consistent, and orderly copies of data. In addition to copying data, most backup systems also keep their own log files or metadata database that stores additional information about the files and objects that have been backed up. For instance, the backup metadata may contain an entry for the date and time that the data object was backed up.

Backup can also be done as a storing (block-level) process to back up entire storage volumes en masse. Like many other storage management techniques, as the amount of stored data grows, this approach becomes less realistic. There have also been some backup products that had the ability to copy storage blocks for particular files, an idea that is being retried as serverless backup (discussed later in this chapter).

Offline, Online, and Near-Line Storage

The location where backup data (data that is being backed up or that has been backed up) is stored is an important element in all backup systems. Some terms used to delineate different types of storage by the location and access to data are

- Offline
- Online
- Near-line

Offline Storage

Offline storage is storage or media that cannot be accessed without an administrator's making it available. The most common example of offline storage is tape, which must be loaded into a tape drive before its data can be accessed. CDs and DVDs are also offline when they are not loaded into a device. In general, optical disks lack the required write I/O performance and capacity to be broadly useful in network storage environments.

In some cases offline storage can also refer to disk storage that needs to be connected to a system in order to access it. Portable devices such as USB/FireWire external disk drives are often used this way. However, like optical storage, it is much more practical for personal storage than it is for network storage.

The major advantage of offline storage is that it can be transported easily to other locations for business continuity purposes and for data exchanges where network connections are not practical or affordable or do not exist.

Online Storage

Conversely, *online storage* is storage or media that can be used to access data directly, without administrator intervention. Most disk storage is designed as online storage. Backup can use online storage successfully as long as administrators understand its limitations and how it differs from the offline media methods designed into backup software.

NOTE While most backup software supports the use of online storage, most of these products were designed primarily to use offline tape storage. The difference is enormous: online storage is managed by a file system, which imposes limitations on how it can be used.

For instance, most file systems do not allow two files with the same name in the same directory. This makes storing multiple versions of a file (a common backup requirement) difficult, because these different versions must be given different names or be placed in different directories. Both of these scenarios make restoring data much more difficult and error-prone than it normally is—a scenario most sane people would try to avoid like the plague.

Near-Line Storage

Near-line storage uses automation techniques to quickly make data available that is not online. For example, files stored in a tape library that can automatically load tapes on demand, without administrator intervention, are said to be on near-line storage.

The software that uses near-line storage is usually not backup software per se, but something related, called hierarchical storage management (HSM), which is discussed in the next chapter. However, as HSM and backup usually need to be integrated to avoid operational conflicts, the discussion of near-line storage sometimes enters into discussions of backup systems.

The Backup System

The equipment and software used for backup and recovery are usually referred to simply as the *backup system*. Backup systems can be relatively small, including a tape drive with single-system backup software, or they can be large, involving a SAN with automated tape libraries and distributed, multiplatform backup software. The backup system is also used for restoring data, of course, but it is rarely referred to as the *backup and recovery system*.

The generic parts of a network backup system are

- Backup engine
- Backup agents
- Operations scheduler
- Backup transfer network
- Media management
- Devices and subsystems
- SAN or device interconnect
- Backup metadata

The sections that follow describe these various components of backup systems.

Backup Engine

The *backup engine* is software that controls and processes backup and restore operations, including device control, media management, and metadata management. The backup engine can be installed on a dedicated system or on one that also processes other applications.

Multiple backup engines are often used in a company to divide the work or to optimize platform coverage. Just as other applications may run better on some platforms than others, backup engines typically work better on certain, targeted platforms. For instance, a company might use one type of backup software for Windows systems and another type of software for UNIX systems.

Backup Agents

The backup engine communicates with *backup agent* software to determine what data to back up and to manage the data transfer process. On a detailed level, the backup agent uses the programming interfaces of the file or database system to access data and to ensure data consistency. Backup agents typically run on the systems where the data is stored.

Backup agents are also used during restore processes to facilitate complete restore operations. Different file and database systems have their own unique set of programming interfaces, which means that backup systems must have multiple backup agents available to cover all the various platforms businesses use. In addition, backup agents are usually made to work with only specific backup engines. The backup engines and agents tend to be proprietary, even if the network protocols might be standard.

NOTE The lack of standardization in engine/agent communications is a prime example of how a great deal of energy and money can be wasted by an industry and its market when standardization is not pursued as a priority. Without standards, every backup software company has been forced to develop, test, implement, debug, and support its own application interfaces and communications. Conversely, companies that purchase and use backup systems have to learn the unique installation and operations tools provided by each backup vendor. This is not nearly as simple as it might appear. A great deal of time is spent learning how to make backup software work. The cross-training that comes with standardized interfaces would save a great deal of money every year.

Backup agents are responsible for handling the unique requirements of various operating systems, file systems, and databases. Not all agents are equal, and there can be important differences in their results. This is one of the reasons companies sometimes use different backup systems for different platforms in their environments.

Operations Scheduler

Backup operations are typically scheduled to run periodically at certain times of the day. While the backup scheduler is considered part of the backup engine, it often has its own interface and tools for managing backup operations. The operations scheduler decides what data to back up and when to copy data. Its work is usually integrated with media and device management that determines which media and devices to use.

Backup Transfer Network

Legacy network backup uses LANs for transferring data from a backup agent to a backup engine. In most cases, the backup transfer network is the same as the LAN used for normal day-to-day operations and applications. However, in some cases, companies install dedicated LANs for carrying backup traffic.

NOTE Bypassing the LAN and backing up to devices directly over the SAN is a much better solution, if possible. Why use a backup transfer network if you don't need to?

Removable Backup Media and Media Management

The term *removable media* is used generically to encompass a variety of products used for storing backup data. It includes magnetic tapes, optical disks, and removable disk cartridges. By far the most common form of removable media for backup in storage network environments is tape.

Tapes are used for a certain period of time, as determined by the tape rotation schedule, and then are stored locally or remotely in accordance with corporate business continuity policies. Tapes are often copied so that one copy can be kept locally for fast restores and another copy can be stored remotely for restoration following a major disaster.

Backup tapes store corporate data assets and should be taken care of deliberately. For that reason, media management is one of the key disciplines in all of storage networking. Backup operations can easily involve thousands of backup tapes used for a variety of different data restoration goals.

Tape rotation algorithms define when and how tapes are used. For example, the popular grandfather, father, son (GFS) algorithm generates a sequence of tapes that is aligned with the calendar. Full backups are written to weekly tapes on the weekends, incremental backups are written to daily tapes on Monday through Thursday, and a monthly tape is written at or near the end of the month. Table 13-1 is an example of the sequence of tapes from a GFS algorithm.

Table 13-1 *GFS Tape Rotation Scheme*

Friday Through Sunday	Monday	Tuesday	Wednesday	Thursday
Weekly Tape 1	Daily Tape 1	Daily Tape 2	Daily Tape 3	Daily Tape 4
Weekly Tape 2	Daily Tape 1	Daily Tape 2	Daily Tape 3	Daily Tape 4
Weekly Tape 3	Daily Tape 1	Daily Tape 2	Daily Tape 3	Daily Tape 4
Weekly Tape 4	Daily Tape 1	Daily Tape 2	Daily Tape 3	Daily Tape 4
End of Month Tape 1				

Media management is a central part of backup software and includes not only the tape rotation algorithm, but also information about tape usage and any special-purpose tapes, such as historical archiving. Media management in a storage network environment usually keeps track of the number of times a tape has been used (sometimes referred to as tape passes) and the number of errors that occur on each tape. Old or failing tapes should be removed from regular tape rotations before they fail. Media management can also recommend the movement of tapes between local and remote locations for disaster recovery protection.

Whatever tape rotation algorithm is used, it is highly recommended that you follow it closely to avoid unexpected coverage "holes" in the backup data. Using tapes out of sequence can result in the loss of data on backup tapes that might be needed during a disaster recovery operation. Unfortunately, with so many tapes in an organization, it's not hard to understand how mistakes are made in the execution of tape rotation. Paying close attention to media management reduces backup errors. Using automated tape equipment such as autoloaders or libraries also helps reduce administrator errors.

Tape Devices and Subsystems

Tape devices and subsystems were discussed in Chapters 4 and 5. Tape equipment has been practically synonymous with network backup for many years. However, as remote storage network transmissions become more affordable and as the need for faster backup processing continues to increase, disk-based backup techniques will take a larger share of the load. Disk backup is discussed toward the end of this chapter.

Device Interconnect or SAN Connection

Tape devices and subsystems have to connect to either a device interconnect technology or a SAN. In legacy network backup, the backup server usually connects to tape equipment over the SCSI bus. In most SANs, tape devices attach to a device interconnect within a tape subsystem, which connects to systems over a SAN.

Backup Metadata

The core of most network backup systems is the internal database or catalog system that contains information about the data that has been backed up. This backup information base is also called the backup *metadata* (data about the data). Information kept in backup metadata could include things like the full extended name (which includes the directory path), the date/time stamp of file creation and access, the date/time of backup copy, file size, file owner, access rights, tape name, tape location data, and the operation used for that backup task. Backup metadata can also include a field identifying if the file had been deleted. It can be a great benefit to *not* restore files if they had previously been deleted.

In some backup systems, the metadata functions like a real-time transaction processing system that records information about data as it is being backed up. In other systems, the backup metadata is processed as a batch job from a log file after all the data copies have been made.

Backup metadata provides the underpinnings for most restore functions of the system by allowing administrators to easily determine which files and versions to restore. Metadata significantly speeds up restore processing compared to manual methods.

Backup metadata can become very large, requiring administrative oversight in order to maintain an efficiently running backup system. For example, a server with 250,000 files must have a minimum of 250,000 records in its metadata if each file in the system has been backed up only once. But, in fact, most files are backed up multiple times by different backup operations. Assuming each file is backed up ten times, creating ten records, the total number of records would be 2.5 million. At some point in all backup systems, the metadata reaches a size that starts impacting backup performance. The key issue is the number of files and objects being backed up and tracked individually.

The Big Picture of Backup

Figure 13-1 shows the location of the backup functions just discussed in a legacy LAN-based backup system. The arrows indicate the direction in which data is copied by the backup process.

Figure 13-1 *Legacy Network Backups*

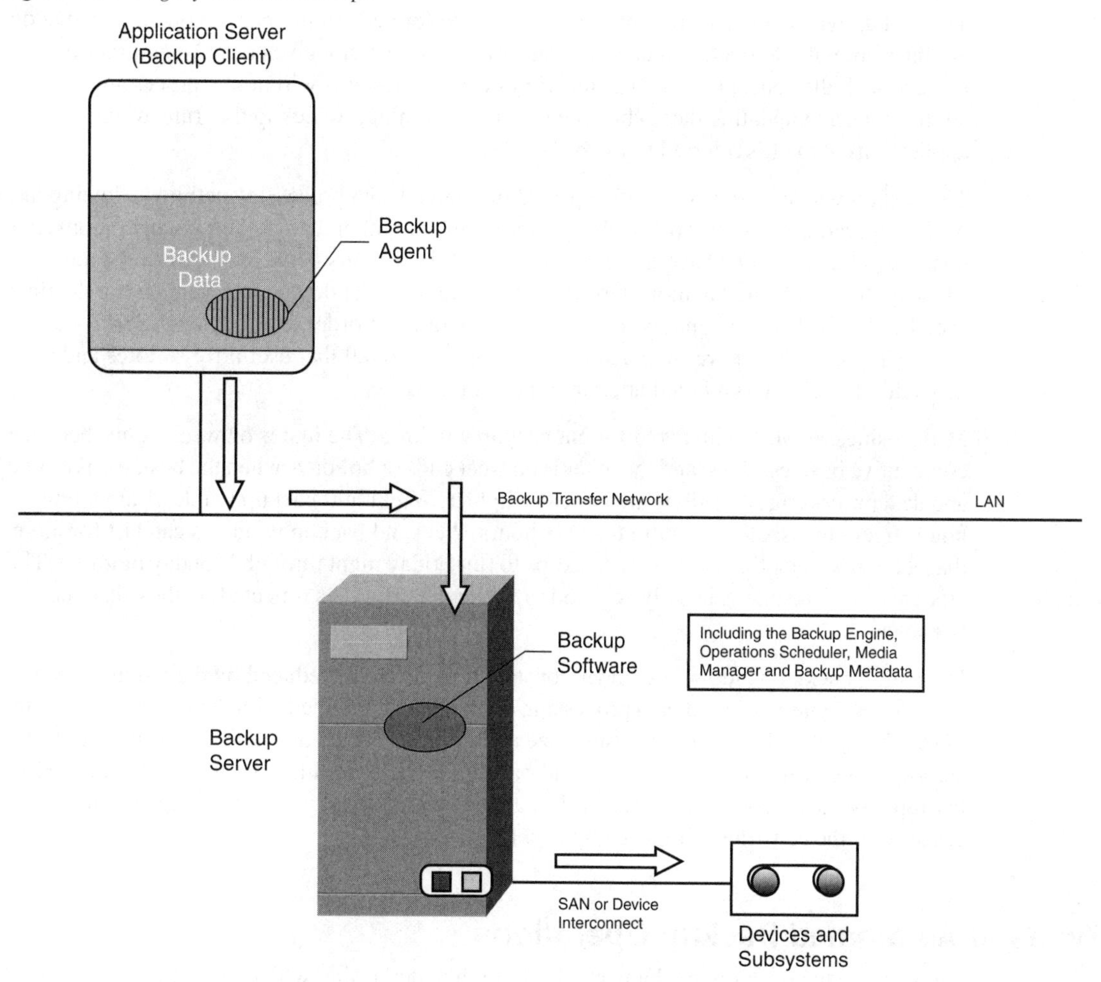

Backup Operations

While backups tend to run in an automated fashion, a surprising amount of detail is involved in day-to-day backup operations. This section discusses three related topics: the concept of the backup window, commonly used automated backup operations, and hot backups, including copy-on-write technology.

The Backup Window

The backup window is the amount of time available for performing backup operations that do not interfere with production data processing operations on any given day. An assumption that is made with the concept of the backup window is that systems will not be processing applications and updating data while the backup is running. A backup that runs when applications are not is referred to as *cold backup*.

The backup window coincides with a period of reduced data processing activity, allowing the backup operation to do its work without interfering with other data processing operations. For instance, a business may have a backup window of three hours between 1 a.m. and 4 a.m. Monday through Thursday mornings. Backup operations that do not complete within the time specified by the backup window may have to be aborted in order to allow normal data processing operations to resume. Aborted backups are not all that useful for restores and are generally thought of as a failed attempt to back up data.

Most businesses work with two different backup windows. The first is on weeknights, between consecutive business days, and the other is on weekends or holidays when the business is closed and data processing operations are typically lighter. Weeknight backup windows are a few hours in length, usually not more than six hours. Weekend backup windows can last for more than 24 hours, sometimes allowing backups to run Friday night through Monday morning. The tape rotation schedule is usually selected to fit the opportunities reflected by these backup windows.

In general, backup windows are under constant pressure to be reduced by the requirement to move to 24/7 Internet-based data processing operations. Combined with the increasing amount of data being stored and the increasing size and number of media-rich files, it is becoming steadily more difficult to finish successful backup operations within the backup window. Hot backup, discussed later in this chapter, is a generic technology that some companies use to circumvent the constraints imposed by backup windows.

Types of Automated Backup Operations

Automated tape rotation mechanisms do more than determine which tapes to use on any given day; they also automate the selection of the backup operation to perform. The type of backup operation determines generically how much data is backed up in any scheduled backup operation.

There are three basic automated backup operations:

- Full backups
- Incremental backups
- Differential backups

Full Backup

Full backup operations copy all the files or objects of a storage volume to tape. Using the terminology of redundancy as used in this book, the goal of full backups is to create duplicate redundancy. A full backup on a server system copies all the files on all the storage volumes belonging to the server. A complete system can be restored from the tape or tapes that contain the contents of a full backup operation. However, a full backup that does not have all the data for whatever reason obviously cannot generate a complete restore.

Full backups can take many hours to perform and usually exceed the weeknight backup window. Therefore, they typically can be performed only during the weekend backup window or on holidays when the business is closed.

Incremental Backup

Incremental backups copy only files that are newly created or that were updated since the last backup operation ran. Obviously, they provide a level of delta redundancy. Whereas full backups are intended to create full redundancy at the time they are run, incremental backups create delta redundancy, which allows a new composite full redundancy image to be restored. Incremental backups are used for their efficiency of backup and the fact they back up less data and take less time to complete than either full or differential backups.

Files copied during incremental backup operations are typically selected for backup either using the archive bit or from file system date attributes. Incremental backups can be appended to an existing full backup tape, can be written to a single incremental backup tape that is used several consecutive days, or can be written to a separate tape. Appending incremental backups to the last full backup tape makes restore processes easier because they involve fewer tapes, but it also results in greater risk that data may be lost if something occurs that destroys the tape containing several days of backup data.

Differential Backup

Differential backup operations copy files that are newly created or that were updated since the last full backup operation. They are another example of delta redundancy, which attempts to make restore operations more efficient by reducing the number of tapes needed for a full restore. Another way to think of differential backups is that they aggregate all changed data onto a single tape. There is no need to keep a differential backup tape in a tape drive for the next day's backup operation, so they are removed daily, reducing the risk that data could be lost in a disaster or accident of some type.

For example, assuming a full backup was done on the weekend, a differential backup on Monday night would copy the same files that an incremental backup would. However, on Tuesday night the differential backup would combine the data from a Tuesday incremental backup with Monday's data. Of course, if a file changed on both Monday and Tuesday, only the version changed on Tuesday would be backed up on Tuesday. On Thursday night the differential backup would include all the latest changes to files that occurred from Monday through Thursday. Table 13-2 compares incremental and differential operations used in the GFS rotation scheme.

Table 13-2 *Incremental and Differential Operations in a GFS Tape Rotation Scheme*

Scheme	Weekend	Mon	Tues	Wed	Thurs
Incremental	Full	Monday only	Tuesday only	Wednesday only	Thursday only
Differential	Full	Monday only	Monday + Tuesday newest changes	Monday → Wednesday newest changes	Monday → Thursday newest changes

Special-Purpose Backup Operations

Administrators sometimes need to run special-purpose backup jobs for historical archiving, system or application migration, and data sharing. Usually these operations are done manually, where the administrator selects the specific files to back up and creates a tape name for the operation. In general, mixing special-purpose backup data on backup data on the same tapes used for regular backup operations is a bad idea.

Hot Backup and Copy-on-Write

To get around some of the problems with shrinking backup windows and growing data, a technology called *hot backup* was developed to allow backup operations to run outside the backup window during "normal" production data processing hours. In many cases today, especially in Internet server environments, hot backup is the only option for backup and recovery.

Cold Backup Operations

To start understanding hot backup, we'll first look at normal legacy backup operations, referred to as cold backup, which were introduced previously in this chapter in the section "The Backup Window." Cold backup does its work copying files when the system is not accepting any updates to files or the creation of new files. In other words, the system is operating in a read-only state. With cold backups there is virtually no chance that an update will occur to a file while backup is trying to copy it.

The assumption with cold backups is that the system will be unavailable for any applications that need to write data while backup is running. For backup operations taking many hours, this is a serious productivity problem.

Hot Backup Operations

Hot backups allow files to be backed up while applications are creating or updating data. The potential for problems with hot backup revolves around two basic areas:

- Each file or group of files being backed up needs to have guaranteed integrity.
- The load of running hot backups along with applications can strain processing resources in a system.

The concern over data integrity with hot backups is based on the probability that an update can occur to a file while it is being copied for backup. Chapter 2, "Establishing a Context for Understanding Storage Networks," discusses byte range file I/O, where it is possible to access data by its byte range location within the file. Often, updates occur in rapid succession to different byte ranges in the file. If the backup process has already copied one of those byte ranges and not the other, the file stored by backup will be *inconsistent* with itself. This inconsistency is similar to the inconsistency that can occur with remote copy applications, as discussed in Chapter 10, "Redundancy Over Distance with Remote Copy."

Figure 13-2 shows the multiple byte ranges of a file. The shaded byte ranges indicate which ones have already been copied by a backup program that is in process. An update to the file occurs, which updates two different byte ranges—one that has already been copied by the backup program and one that has not been copied yet. The backup copy of this file will be inconsistent with any version of the file that existed on disk. Data integrity in the backup version is lost.

Figure 13-2 *The Creation of an Inconsistent Backup Copy*

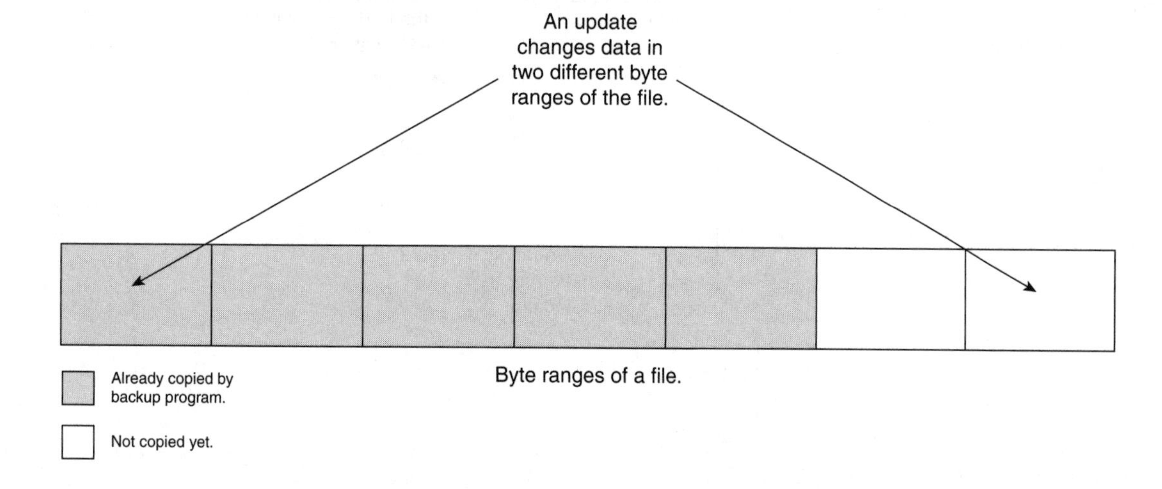
An update changes data in two different byte ranges of the file.
Already copied by backup program.
Not copied yet.
Byte ranges of a file.

Copy-on-Write

The key technology providing data consistency for hot backups is *copy-on-write* (COW). COW is a generic concept that was originally developed as a memory management technique to reduce the amount of system memory needed for multiprocessing environments. It has since been adapted to work with file system technologies as a way to facilitate reliable hot backup and other data management processes.

The basic idea of COW is to place new data updates in a temporary storage location until another process that is running can finish its task. Subsequent accesses to the same data use the temporary data location until backup finishes running and the updated data is copied to its permanent location.

COW is typically implemented in conjunction with backup agent software. A COW-enabled backup agent monitors file accesses on each file as it is being backed up. If updates occur to the file, they are temporarily redirected to a temporary storage location until the backup system finishes copying the file. Then the COW process writes the new data to its intended location.

Figure 13-3 illustrates the fundamental process of COW for backup. A backup process is copying a file with seven storage locations. During the backup process, an update is made to location 5 and is written by COW to temporary location 5'. After backup finishes, the updated data is copied from temporary location 5' to permanent location 5.

Figure 13-3 *Copy-on-Write Process for Backup*

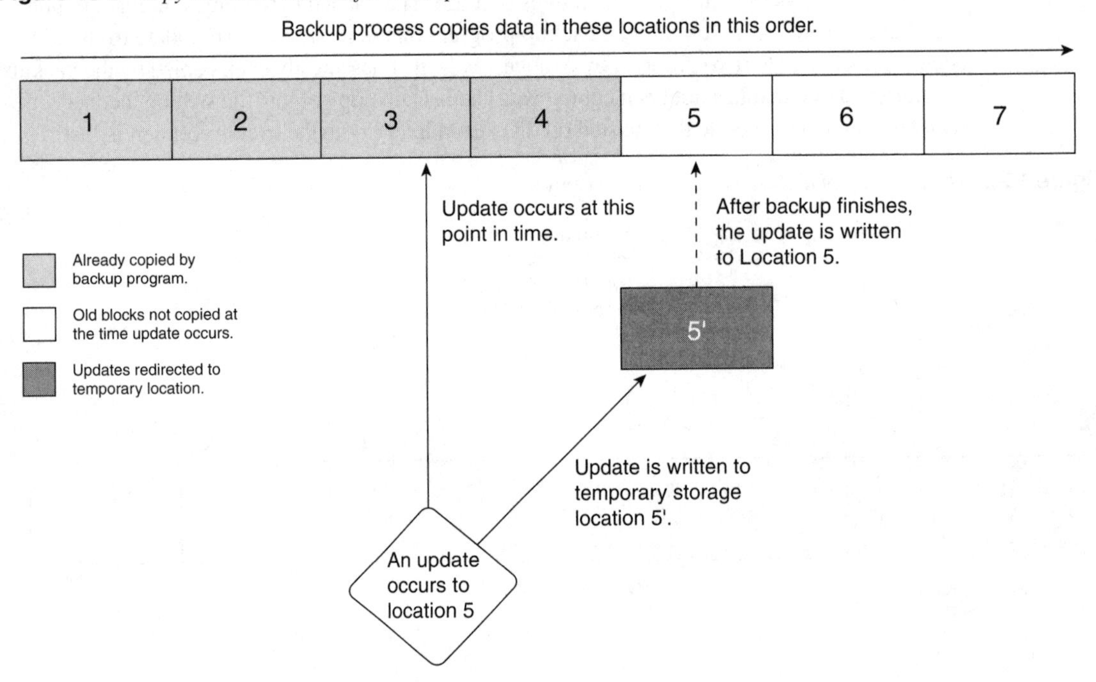

NOTE COW can also be done where the updated data is written to the permanent storage location and the older, obsolete data is written to a temporary location. However, this method has possible disadvantages for serverless backups, as discussed in the section "Serverless Backup Agent Software."

Continuous Backup

Copy on write allows IT organizations to run backup as often as they like. Some companies have used this to implement continuous backup, where as soon as one backup operation stops, another one begins. Obviously, this would use more tapes, but it also gives these companies more complete backup protection. If the goal of the company is to not lose more than a few hours of data for mission-critical systems, continuous backup may be able to meet the requirement.

Other technologies such as remote copy (see Chapter 10) and point-in-time copy (see Chapter 17, "Data Management") can be used to achieve the same recovery goals.

Limitations of Hot Backup

On the surface it appears that hot backup would be the answer to everybody's problems. Unfortunately, it is not. The heavy processor and I/O loads that backup places on server systems can cause severe problems. Servers that are already heavily utilized can sink to unacceptable performance levels when attempting to perform backups along with their normal application load. Not only that, but backup processing can completely foul up normal caching patterns in storage subsystems that are needed for acceptable performance.

Backup Applications in Storage Networks

Backup has been a problematic systems management application for many years as the amount of data needing backup has consistently outpaced the capabilities of the networks and equipment to do the job. SANs provide several architectural advantages for backup processing and promise to provide solutions that keep pace into the future. The following section explores some of the new SAN backup technologies that are likely to change the nature of data management for years to come.

Problems with Legacy Network Backup

Legacy network backup has several architectural limitations that are making it less plausible over time. Two fundamental areas are creating most of the problems:

- LAN performance and congestion
- Distributed management of backup systems

LAN Limitations

Legacy network backup depends on a LAN to function as the backup transfer network to copy data over. Unfortunately, most LANs, not even many Gigabit Ethernet LANs, have the bandwidth capabilities to handle the massive data transfer requirements of backup. This is not only unacceptable for backup performance, but it also wreaks havoc with the other applications running on the LAN by creating long periods of network congestion.

When backup performance is too slow for the backup job to finish in the allotted backup window, nothing earth-shattering happens, and business processing goes on as normal. Most administrators simply stop the backup operation prematurely, which means the data on tape is inconsistent and untrustworthy for restores. The only time backup failures ever have a real impact is during restores—and by then it is clearly too late to do anything about it.

It is possible to use a dedicated LAN for backup, but realistically, there are many environments where LANS are simply inadequate and impractical to get the job done. Part of the problem lies in the multiple transfers and processes involved in LAN-based backup.

A backup agent initially reads the data from a storage device or subsystem and writes it into system memory, where it is temporarily held until it is transferred over the LAN. The data is then processed by the system's network protocol stack and transmitted by the network interface over the network. In the network, the transmission may encounter congestion in switches en route, which slows performance and often results in dropped frames and retransmissions. When the transmission is received by the backup server system, it is processed in inverse fashion through the network interface and protocol stacks, buffered in memory, and then written to a tape device of some sort.

NOTE The problem of clobbering LAN traffic with backup traffic in the wee hours of the night has given many administrators troubles for many years. There is nothing quite like coming to work in the morning and finding out that the network didn't do half as much as it was supposed to. If you are reading this and nodding in agreement, and you are not using a SAN for backups, you need to get out of your seat and do something about it!

Distributed Backup Systems and Management

To circumvent the performance problems of LAN-based backup, backup devices and subsystems can be dedicated to individual application servers running backup software. In this case, backup traffic travels from disk storage through the system and out to tape storage. This approach is often used on large systems that cannot be backed up over a LAN.

While the performance is optimal, these multiple backup systems create administrative problems and overhead. One of the best things about LAN-based backup is that the management of backup can be centralized and leverage tape automation equipment. The implementation of multiple, dedicated backup systems results in high management costs; instead of leveraging management across multiple servers, the cost of management is multiplied by the number of independent backup systems. When individual servers have their own tape equipment, administrators have to manage multiple rotation schemes and tape collections. This not only takes a great deal of time, but it also contributes to confusion and errors in media management.

Optimal Performance and Management with SANs

LAN-based backup forces administrators to choose between inadequate performance and distributed management. In contrast, SANs allow administrators to have the best of both worlds: fast performance and centralized management. That's not asking too much, is it?

Whereas LAN-based backup performance is limited by LAN performance, SAN-based backup is limited by the performance of server systems, backup devices, and subsystems. In other words, backup performance could not be any faster.

Centralization can be achieved by virtue of the longer distances supported by SANs. Servers do not have to be in the data center, but can be spread throughout the organization and still have their data backed up to centralized tape equipment.

Separating the Control and Data Paths

One of the interesting architectural notions with SAN-based backup is that the control of backup operations and execution of data copying during the backup operation can occur over different networks. This is sometimes called separating the control and data path. SANs are used as the data path, and the LAN is used as the control path. Figure 13-4 illustrates.

Figure 13-4 *Data Path in a SAN and Control Path in a LAN*

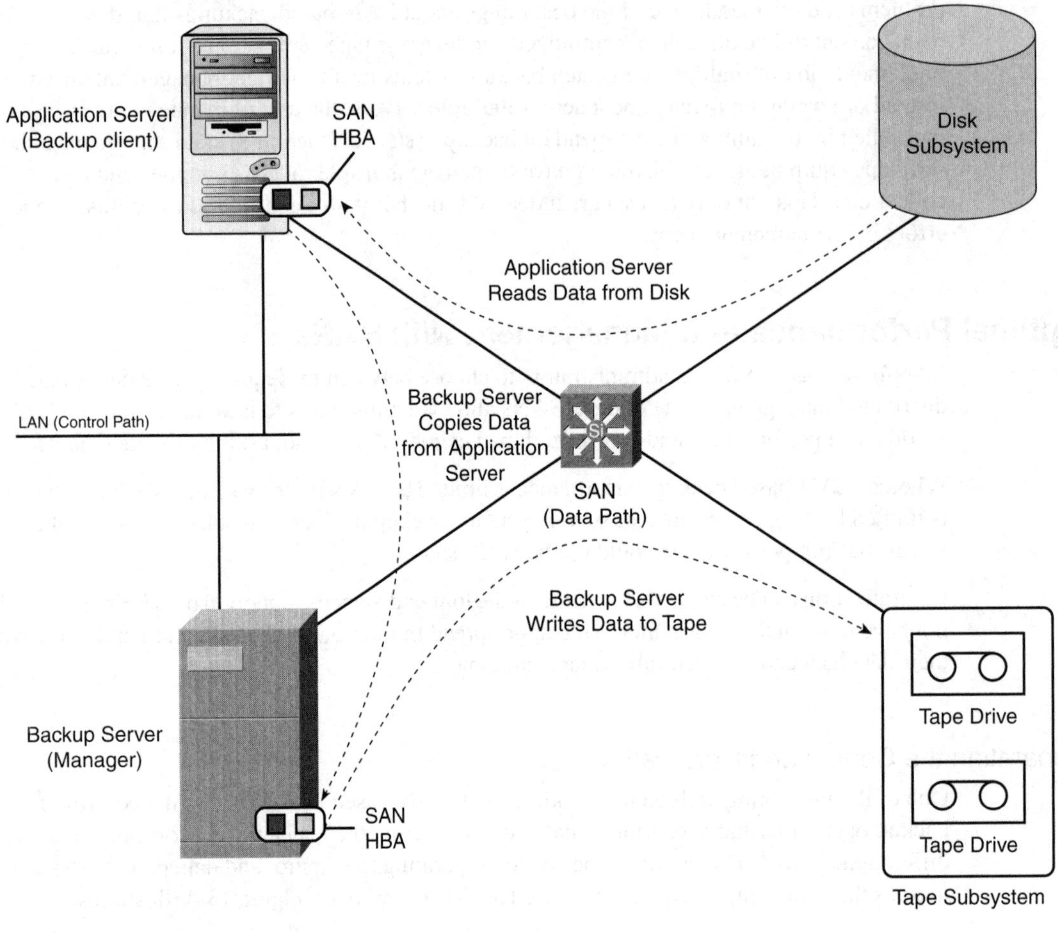

LAN-Free Backup

LAN-free backup is a simple concept where applications servers copy their data to centralized backup storage over a SAN, as opposed to transmitting data over a LAN. It was one of the first applications identified to justify SANs when the technology was originally introduced, and it continues to be a strong reason to implement SANs.

Figure 13-5 shows a simple design for a LAN-free backup system in a SAN.

Figure 13-5 *LAN-Free Backup*

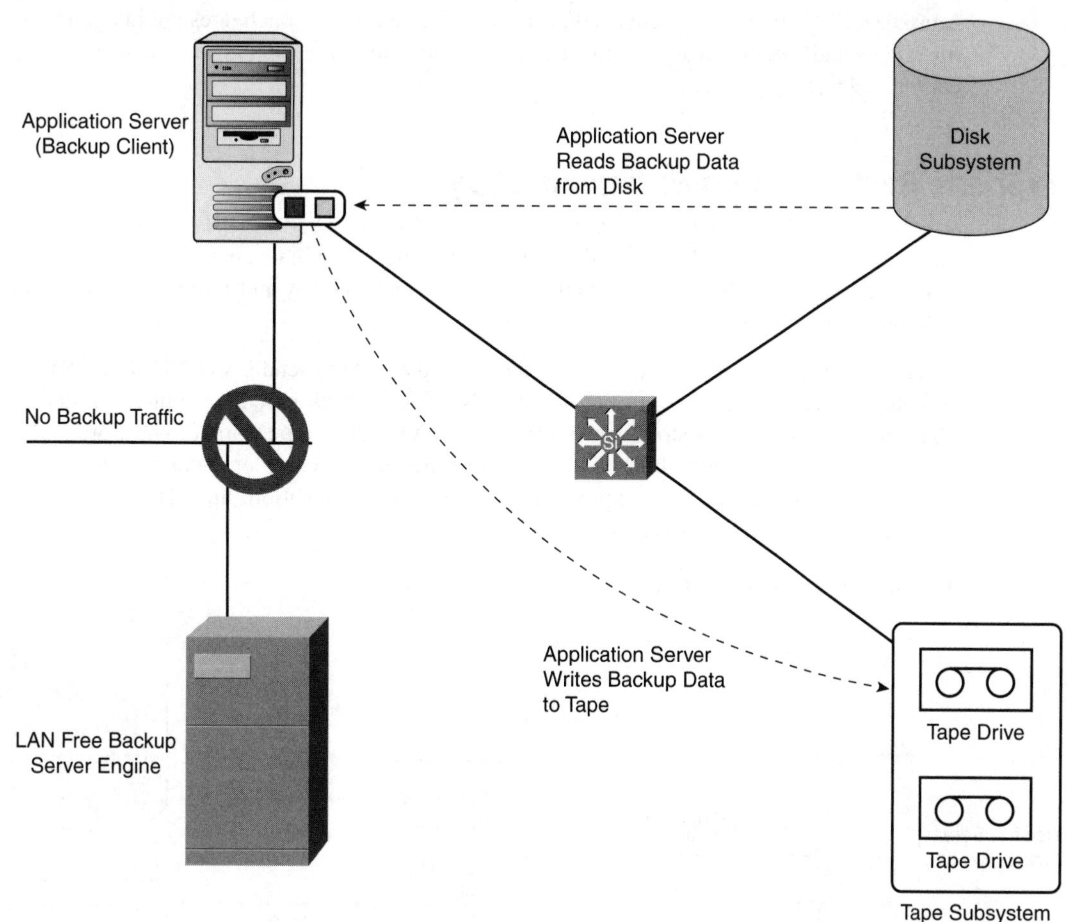

Backup operations in LAN-free backup are basically the same as with legacy network backup. The scheduling of backup operations and tape rotations is similar to those used for standalone backup, although more systems, tape subsystems, and tapes are integrated under a common management system.

The main feature of LAN-free backup is that the I/O path avoids the LAN altogether. LAN-free backup agents residing in application servers transfer data directly to tape subsystems in the SAN. This is similar to using dedicated direct-attached backup devices, except that the tape equipment is located in a SAN, and the management of the process, including backup metadata operations, is performed by a centralized backup management engine.

While many LAN-free backup systems today are designed as a single-distributed, heterogeneous system with a single point of control, it is also possible to set up a "poor man's" LAN-free backup system simply by running multiple single-system backup systems connecting to centralized SAN tape subsystems and/or devices. Using this approach does not integrate the operations and media management in a single system, but it at least allows high-speed, centralized backup processing.

Serverless Backup Using Extended Copy

Another new and potentially powerful backup technology is called *serverless backup,* which is based on the concept of SCSI extended copy. This is discussed in Chapter 6, "SCSI Storage Fundamentals and SAN Adapters," in the section "Extended Copy and Third-Party Copy" and is pictured in Figure 6-7.

The basic idea of serverless backup is for the backup engine to send EXTENDED COPY commands to a dual-mode controller in the SAN, which acts as a "remote control" initiator to read data from server disk storage and write it again to backup tape storage. The word "serverless" is used because backup data transfers are not processed or conducted through the application server that creates and processes data. The communications model used by a simple serverless backup system is shown in Figure 13-6.

Figure 13-6 *A Simple, Serverless Backup Design*

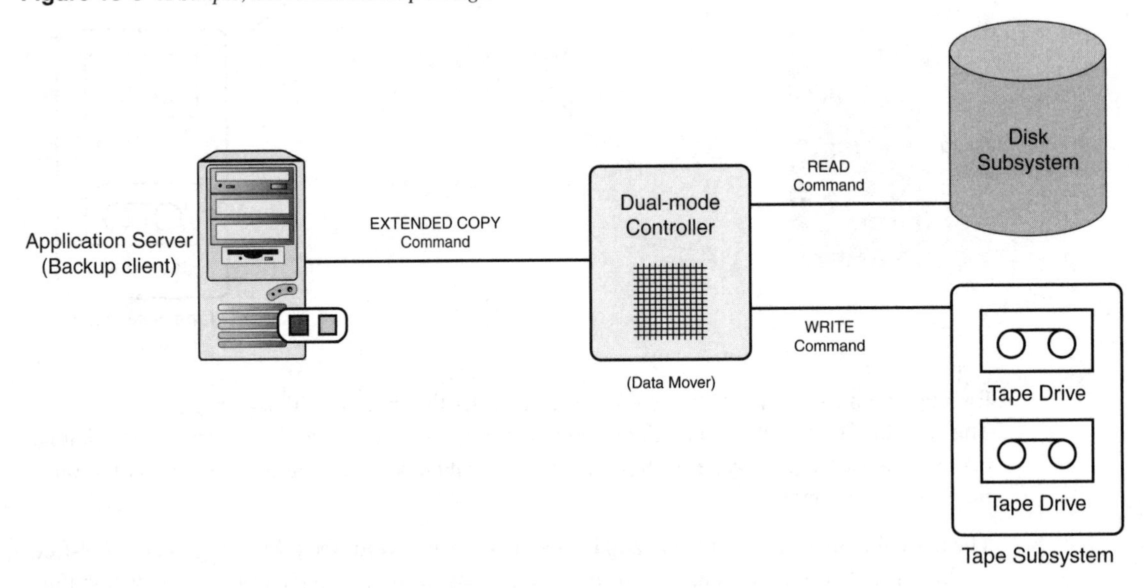

Serverless Backup Data Movers

The key architectural element in serverless backup is the dual-mode controller, which is more commonly referred to as a *data mover.* The data mover receives EXTENDED COPY commands as well as generating READ and WRITE commands to storage subsystems in the

SAN. Theoretically, the data mover in a serverless backup system can be located in any system, subsystem, or device connected to a SAN, including computer systems, disk subsystems, tape subsystems, and networking equipment. There are many possible designs and architectures.

The EXTENDED COPY command contains information about the target/LUN address, the block locations where the data is located, and the command to perform. For instance, when reading data in a serverless backup process, the backup engine's initiator sends an EXTENDED COPY command that tells the data mover to read a certain group of blocks from a certain subsystem port and LUN address. When the data mover completes the READ command, it sends a response for the EXTENDED COPY command confirming a successful READ to the backup engine. Then another EXTENDED COPY command is generated by the backup engine for the data mover to WRITE data to a tape subsystem at a given target/LUN address in the SAN.

Serverless Backup Engines

Like other backup systems, serverless backup systems need to maintain backup metadata and recover from processing and transmission errors that sometimes occur. In other backup system designs, there is a direct SCSI connection between the initiator directing backup transmissions and the target receiving them. Acknowledging the completion of a file copy or recognizing problems with a transfer are relatively straightforward processes. However, in serverless backup, the data mover is a second, proxy initiator that executes SCSI commands on behalf of the backup engine. This means that all commands, responses, and status/error messages need to be conducted through the EXTENDED COPY mechanism. Obviously, the engine software in a serverless backup system needs to be designed for a completely different processing model.

Serverless Backup Agent Software

Backup agent software used in serverless backup systems also requires different designs. Instead of transferring data over a LAN or a SAN, the backup agent is responsible for identifying the block storage locations that are to be transferred during EXTENDED COPY operations. This means that the agent needs to get block address locations from the file system instead of data. While this might seem like a small detail, it is not, because file systems are typically designed to deliver bytes of data to applications—not the block locations for data.

It is essential that other system processes that run during serverless backup do not change the block locations of data after the agent has transmitted them to the backup engine. This includes the COW process described earlier. For instance, an alternative COW method that copies old data to temporary storage for backup processing and writes new updates over old data locations could result in inconsistent backup.

NOTE No insult is intended toward any type of COW. As with nearly all storage processes, there can be many workable designs. COW is one example. Either old or new data could be placed in temporary storage and processes developed to make things work correctly. It is also possible to make adjustments to serverless backup EXTENDED COPY commands and processes to accommodate such changes. It is important not to take your COW for granted. Love and know your COW.

Virtualization and Serverless Backup

Serverless backup depends on sharing precise block storage information between the application server's file system and the data mover in the SAN. For that reason, the data mover and the application server must use the exact same virtualization "lens" to access the blocks of data. If the virtualized view of data is different, serverless backup will be inconsistent and worthless.

Disk-Based Backup

The remainder of this chapter looks at ways disk device and subsystem technology are being used to augment tape technology in SAN backup and recovery systems. The last couple years have seen a renewed interest in this type of solution, but like so many other storage techniques, it is considerably trickier than it first appears. Disk technology in the form of virtual tape has been attempted several times but has rarely worked as well as hoped, except in mainframe environments.

NOTE Some old pros I know who worked on computer storage technology half a century ago tell me they were predicting the death of tape in the early 1960s. Ever since, there has been something supposedly far better than tape, and every time the new technology couldn't be developed or had some sort of pathological problem.

Millennia from now, when there is nothing left of our civilization, cockroaches will probably still be using tape.

Advantages and Disadvantages of Disk Technology for Backup

There are a number of reasons people want to replace tape with something better:

- Tape is perceived to be too fragile and failure-prone.
- Tape capacity is too small for server disk capacities.
- Tape is not fast enough or flexible enough for both backups and restores.

Here are some reasons why people seem to think disk can finally work for backup:

- ATA disks are finally cheaper than tape on a cost-per-GB basis.
- New applications and techniques are being developed for disk.
- Network communications methods like remote copy are replacing backup in some instances.

Here are some reasons why tapes will still be needed:

- Tapes are better for maintaining historical versions of data.
- Tapes are still the most convenient and least expensive way to get off-site disaster protection.
- Virtual tape on disk creates difficult media management problems.

Now, we'll examine some facts, perceptions, and opinions.

Problems with Tape

The physical structure of magnetic tape is truly amazing. The number of layers, the chemistry involved, and the magnetic and protective coatings are all the result of advanced materials research. However, that does not mean that tape is always as reliable as we would like it to be. Oxidation is a constant threat, and we live with many environmental hazards, such as heat and humidity, that are very hard on tapes.

In addition to environmental variables, the process of using tape is hard on tape. Tapes are stretched under tension in order to track correctly past the tape heads. Unlike disk technology, where the media is never touched, the tape surface is usually in contact with something else—usually the back of another section of tape. The capstans and rollers in tape drives all collect particles of various sorts, which are constantly rubbing on the tape surface.

While individual tape cartridges for newer technologies such as Super DLT and LTO Ultrium can exceed 200 GB of uncompressed data, most tape equipment has capacities that are much smaller. The main issue is the size of tape compared to the amount of stored data a server has. The more tapes that are needed for a restore, the more likely it is that one of them will be bad—this is simple statistics. Tape storage does not scale incrementally; when you exceed the capacity of a cartridge, you have to use an additional cartridge. In some respects that's an easy solution for storage capacity, but it is a definite negative for reliability.

The trend is for server storage to increase faster than tape storage capacity. As servers store more data, tape has an increasingly difficult time keeping up with the growth. Even when new tape technology is introduced, if it is necessary to replace old tape technology every three years or so, an alternative to tape may be a better option.

Another big problem for tape is its performance. While new tape drives can move at streaming speeds of 70 MBps (estimated with compressible data), that is still less than a high-speed disk subsystem that does not depend on whether data is compressible. With backup continuing to be a problem for some time to come, administrators will choose brute-force solutions to get the job done faster. Disk subsystems are the fastest storage options now and will likely continue to be.

Advantages of Disk Subsystems for Backup

In general, the main advantage of using disk for backup is that it is the same technology used for primary storage. Where capacity is concerned, disk subsystems for backup can scale as large as primary disk storage.

As for reliability, disk is far superior to tape. Disks have fewer media errors, and for all practical purposes, disks do not wear out like tape does. Furthermore, disk technology uses RAID, which accommodates disk failures automatically without stopping the works. There is no such thing as a graceful failure with tape.

As mentioned, disk can be faster than tape through the use of striping techniques; however, avoiding the RAID 5 write penalty by using RAID 10 is probably a good practice. It's also worth pointing out that without striping, a streaming tape drive is likely to be faster than a single disk drive. It is also important to understand that caching is virtually worthless for backup processing due to the large amounts of data being transferred—after the cache fills, it provides no benefits. Disk subsystems used for backup processes are better off turning off their caching functions. In general, a disk subsystem is faster than writing to tapes, but the configuration of disk is an important variable.

Despite the functional advantages of disk subsystems, a big reason disk is suddenly getting so much attention is its cost. ATA disk drives are now cheaper than tape storage for equivalent capacity. That's why many of the discussions about disk for backup center on ATA and SATA disk technologies.

Another interesting aspect of disk is that random access to disk is much better than sequential access to tape for working with backup metadata, which could be used to great efficiency. For example, virtual views of backup data on disk are easier to create than they are with tape. Although not technically backup, software snapshot technology built into file systems on disk storage provide instantaneous access to historical versions of files. The same kind of access with tape could take hours.

Finally, the removable aspects of tape that allow data to be kept outside a local geography for disaster recovery protection are being diminished by high-speed networking and store-and-forward remote copy technologies. Again, the retrieval of data using electronic methods is much faster than a delivery van in most cases.

Reasons for Tape's Continued Use

Despite its shortcomings, tape has been used a long time for disaster protection. Companies have significant operations and plans that revolve around tape. These infrastructures and methods will continue to be used for a long time.

Although snapshot technology is excellent for restoring recently changed data, tape is still very good for storing and recovering historically important data. As it happens, old data almost never needs to be restored, but when it is needed, the reasons and motivations to do it are usually cogent.

It is true that MANs and WANs are making it easier to transfer backup data over a network, but the cost of the network is still higher than the cost of transporting tapes. Most companies using remote copy software are also using physical movement of tapes to off-site storage of tape for their less-critical systems.

But the main reason tape will continue to be used is because backup software packages were written to use it and the entire operation of backup has been developed around the use of tape.

For example, consider the following scenario: Assume you back up to disk with a tape backup program. The tape operation calls for a specific tape—let's say "Charlie-8." The backup operation writes to disk and updates its metadata to reflect that the data is on tape Charlie-8. You then start a process to make a copy to a real physical tape named Charlie-8, but the tape drive ejects the tape, telling you it has tape errors and cannot write to the tape. At this point there is a real problem: the data you just wrote may need to be restored from Charlie-8, but you can't throw the old one away and create a new Charlie-8 because it might still have data on it that you might need to restore. (Just because you can't write to a tape does not mean you can't read from it.) You could create a second Charlie-8, but that is precisely the sort of thing that makes media management difficult in addition to leading to lost data during restores. As it turns out, this is not an admin-friendly situation. Unfortunately, it is not necessarily a corner case either. Unfortunately, it is not necessarily a corner case either because tape problems are a way of life.

One way to make disks work with backup is to use two different backup systems: one to go from primary disk to backup disk and the other to go from backup disk to tape. Obviously this is far from optimal, because it requires two separate backup-and-restore operations. A better solution allows data to be restored in the most direct or fastest way possible and skip the disk as a middleman.

The best solution is using software developed to use both disk and tape and can that accommodate both of them flexibly.

Disk Backup Architecture

Three common architectures are used with disk-based backup, reflecting the way disk is integrated into backup operations:

- Disk to disk
- Disk to disk to tape
- Integrated disk and tape

Each of these will be discussed briefly in the sections that follow. One thing to keep in mind with all disk-based backup solutions is the level of backup software integration that has been done—there are many possible designs within each generic architectural category. Just because a hardware solution provides data copy capabilities, do not assume that software understands what the hardware has done. Each solution needs to be evaluated for the consistency of information between backup software and all media used.

Disk to Disk

Disk to disk, otherwise referred to as D2D, was discussed briefly in the preceding sections as an architecture that backs up data to a disk subsystem. This architecture works well for full backups but does not work well if the goal is keeping historically important versions of files.

D2D backup can be coupled with tape-based backup so that the backup data on disk can be backed up to tape using separate operations, metadata, and media management. The idea is that disk backup is used for restoring recently backed-up files and for disaster recovery, and that the tape backup would be used for locating historically interesting files. However, restore processes necessarily take two steps: from tape to backup disk and from backup disk to system disk. This means there are twice as many restore processes to go wrong.

Disk to Disk to Tape

Disk to disk to tape (D2D2T) is an expansion of the scenario just described for D2D, but with an integrated second-stage backup operation for copying backup data from disk to tape. This approach overcomes the historical shortcomings of the D2D architecture and includes a single integrated metadata and media management system for locating data that has been backed up. Copying data from backup disk to tape is typically part of the same extended backup operation, as opposed to being two completely independent administrative operations. Restores are typically two-stage restore with D2D2T, although it is certainly possible to restore from tape to server storage using this architecture.

Integrated Disk and Tape

Another approach to using disk for backup is to create a single-level store for backup that integrates both disk and tape as common backup storage resources. The idea of a single-level store incorporates all backup storage, both disk and tape, as an abstract, virtual storage layer that can be used during backup. Policy-based management determines how the disk and tape storage resources are used.

In general, recent, high-priority backup data is stored on disk, and historical versions of data are stored on tape. The integrated disk and tape backup system automatically transfers data between disk and tape resources. Media is managed as a single integrated set of resources. Restores can be made from either disk or tape resources. Integrated solutions are more advanced and require a higher level of integration with backup software to be able to use and manage the virtualized resources provided by hardware.

Are Snapshots Backup?

Chapter 17 discusses a technology called point-in-time copy, also called data snapshots. Point-in-time copies of data provide both duplicate and delta redundancy and are used to restore individual files as well as for disaster recovery.

So the question is this: Should point-in-time copies be considered backup technologies since they can provide many of the same functions? In this book they are not, although in time they may be thought of as different variations of the same larger storage technology.

The processes and methods used by a technology *do* matter in differentiating between them. Considerably different processes and methods are used in legacy backup technologies and point-in-time snapshots. Backup is a process that runs over an extended period of time to make copies of data. Point-in-time snapshots are processed instantaneously to create redundancy.

The results also matter a great deal. Backup is very well suited to making historical copies of files, whereas point-in-time snapshot technology is really mostly good for disaster recovery. The two are often used together by IT organizations using a modified disk-to-disk-to-tape approach. First, point-in-time snapshots are used to make disk-to-disk copies, and then these snapshot images are backed up with a backup system.

It's clear that these two different functions can be integrated into a single data management solution that provides both instantaneous images of data as well as historical copies. These larger integrated solutions probably merit a new name or classification. The moniker ILM (Information Life Cycle Management) looks like it is the front-runner, although the ambiguity of this term could force the creation of a new term and classification.

Summary

This chapter discussed the wide variety of technologies and approaches used in backup technology. For many years, backup to tape has been the basis of data management and disaster recovery operations and will continue to be an important storage management application for many years to come. Backup technology has a long history of adapting to new technologies and requirements.

With the advent of SAN technology, backup has changed to take advantage of the new architecture possibilities. LAN-free backup and serverless backup are two examples of new backup architectures that leapfrog the capabilities of legacy backup systems. While some believe tape will be replaced by disk storage soon, tape will likely continue to be used for many years due to its portability and ability to store historically relevant data for many years. Combinations of disk and tape will evolve to significantly change the capabilities, but not the goals, of backup.

Q & A

1. Name four uses for backup technology.
2. What is offline storage?
3. What does backup metadata do?
4. What does tape rotation do?
5. Explain the difference between incremental and differential backups.
6. What is hot backup?
7. Name two advantages of backing up over the SAN.
8. True or false: LAN-free backup requires backup data to move through the application servers being backed up.
9. A data mover is used in what kind of SAN-based backup?
10. Why does disk capacity for backup scale and tape capacity not scale?

PART V

Filing Systems and Data Management in Networks

Upon completing this chapter, you will be able to

- Understand the fundamental role file systems play in storage I/O processes
- Explain the differences between file systems and operating systems in storage I/O processes
- Describe the structural elements of file systems, including the directory system and layout reference system for locating data
- Identify different file systems' components and features

CHAPTER 14

File System Fundamentals

This final part of the book discusses the different forms of filing software. In general, filing is responsible for placing and locating data within storage address spaces. The most common types of filing products are file systems and databases, but certain data management applications like backup and Information Life Cycle Management are also applications of filing.

If you analyze storage as a hierarchy or stack of functions, filing is always the topmost level inside a system initiating an I/O request. The relationship between systems and storage is not necessarily symmetrical because SAN storage, or block storage, does not provide any filing functions. NAS storage, however, by definition, does. NAS is discussed in the following chapter.

Regardless of whether SAN or NAS storage products are used, filing functions are seminal to all storage processes as the starting point for I/O operations. While it is true that applications read, create, and update data, filing systems initiate the storage I/O process in the system on behalf of the application that requests services from it.

This chapter introduces the fundamentals of file systems and is the basis for more advanced topics in the chapters that follow.

The Strange and Wonderful Relationship Between File Systems and Operating Systems

Operating systems and file systems are often confused as the same technology because operating systems have traditionally promoted the features of a matching (or "native") file system as highlights of the operating system. In fact, file systems and operating systems are almost always different entities in order to facilitate the development and maintenance of both. The development of a system and the subsequent patches and upgrades that are bound to occur are much easier to work with if the operating and file systems can be treated as independent software entities.

NOTE Microsoft's decision to delay the introduction of the WINFS file system in their Longhorn operating system emphasizes the fact that file systems and operating systems are, indeed, different things.

File systems determine many of the usage characteristics of a system. End users typically develop their attitudes, likes, and dislikes about a system based on how easy, difficult, or powerful the file system is. One could argue that the file system is almost as important to the usability of a system as the system's user interface. Clearly, the representation of the file system is of the most important aspects of any operating system.

The Separation of Time and Space in Systems

Operating systems are complex software products that provide access to all systems resources. However, when considering storage processes, it can help to narrow the scope of the operating system to its storage role. Within the context of storage operations, the main difference between operating systems and file systems is that operating systems manage CPU resources by scheduling the relative *time* a process runs, and file systems manage storage resources by placing data within a storage address *space*. This difference is illustrated in Figure 14-1.

Figure 14-1 *Operating Systems Manage CPU Time Resources, and File Systems Manage Storage Address Space Resources*

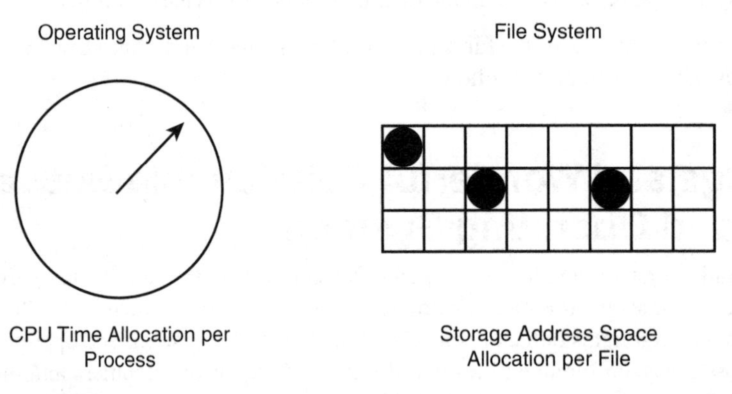

It is worth pointing out that operating systems control access to storage host bus adapters (HBAs) through their device driver interfaces. In other words, the operating system, not the file system, is the system software that engages storing-level processes.

File systems depend on operating systems to supply the fundamental parameters for the storage address spaces they manage. For instance, the operating system supplies information about the number of blocks that are in a certain storage address space when the file system is initially created. Beyond that, the job of managing how storage space is used belongs to the file system.

NOTE Most descriptions of file system designs assume a disk drive is being used to provide the storage address space. Of course, in a network storage environment, the actual disk drives are abstracted from the file system by layers of RAID controllers, virtualization systems, or volume management software. So don't be fooled if you read something else about how a file system works with disk drives: substitute "storage address space" for "disk drive," and you'll be better off.

File Systems as High-Priority Applications

It can be helpful to think of a file system as another application running in a system with special requirements and access capabilities. File systems have their work scheduled by the operating system like any other application, although the file system is often called on to do work that interrupts some other application process that may be running. For that reason, file systems have to run very efficiently. A simple end-user operation such as saving or renaming a file might involve many small and intricate steps by the file system to make sure the file is created or updated correctly and that it can be accessed without problems in the future.

File systems run in both kernel space and user space, depending on the function they are performing and the design of the particular file system. For instance, an operation that searches for a file named "my dog has fleas" is likely to run in user space, while an operation that reads data from the same file on behalf on an application is likely to run in kernel space.

NOTE The sequence of steps involved and the number of operating system-file interactions that occur are somewhat of a mystery, even to people who have intimate knowledge of both products. There are no clear, crisp exchanges like one expects from studying OSI reference models in networking. It's more like watching two people standing in a phone booth playing a game of tag.

Compared with most other applications, file systems have to be extremely robust and avoid failures or errors that could cause a system failure. You simply cannot afford to have unrecoverable application errors in file systems, because they would result in lost or inconsistent data.

Public and Private Interfaces

The development process for a commercial operating system often corresponds with a parallel effort to develop a native file system that will be distributed with the operating system. At this time there may be a substantial amount of interaction between the two development teams. However, after the operating system is released, there is an established method of interaction that could be used by other file systems.

Whether that interaction method is published as an open interface or unpublished as a closed interface depends on the technology and marketing strategies of the operating system developer. Of course, it is possible for an operating system vendor to use unpublished interfaces for its native file system while still allowing nonnative, third-party file systems to work through published interfaces.

File System Structures

There are two fundamental structural elements to understand in most file systems:

- The logical directory structure
- The layout of data within a storage address space

Logical Directory Structures

The most obvious and intuitive structure in a file system is the logical structure of directories, also referred to as folders. This structure is usually represented as a tree hierarchy that starts with a single root directory. Each directory in the hierarchy can contain a number of files and subdirectories, which in turn can have additional files and directories. It's assumed that readers of this book are familiar with file system directory structures as users of computer systems. A hierarchical directory tree is shown in Figure 14-2.

Directory hierarchies allow users as well as system and application developers to organize their stored data. Without this hierarchical structure, finding data would be difficult, at best, and naming would become much more difficult to manage than it is.

Directory hierarchies allow users as well as system and application developers to organize their stored data. Without this hierarchical structure, finding data would be difficult, at best, and naming would become much more difficult to manage than it is.

Figure 14-2 *The Structure of a Directory Hierarchy*

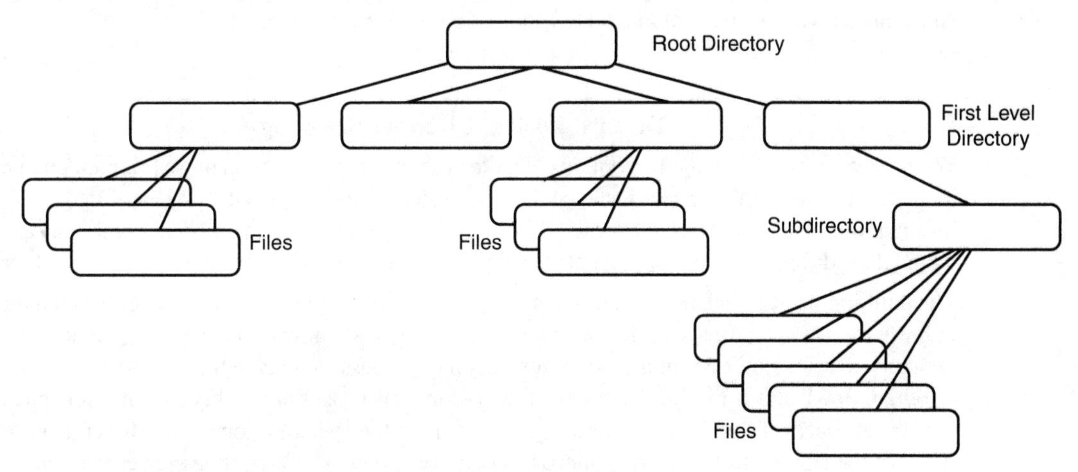

Access to files in directories can be made through the graphical user interface of some operating systems as well as through a command-line interface (CLI). Most file system interfaces have a concept for a "current" directory that is being viewed by the user. Clicking the file or entering its name and pressing the Enter key normally results in the file system opening the file.

Files

Files are granular containers of data, created by the system or an application. Applications and system processes often include formatting and interpretation data along with raw application data composed of such things as numerical values and text strings. For instance, a word processing document may have information about the margins, fonts, and styles used in addition to the alphanumeric text that communicates the message of the document.

Files can be unstructured, meaning the data does not have an externally understood, regular logical structure. They also can be structured, which means the file has prescribed, regular boundaries for placing data values that are associated with each other. In general, file systems store unstructured data, and databases store structured data.

Directories

Directories are special-purpose container files that list all the files and subdirectories that are in them. In addition to files and subdirectories, directories also contain references to their parent directory as well as a reference to itself.

The listings of files and subdirectories also contain data from the file system's internal reference system that indicates the addresses where the file or directory is stored within the storage address space. For instance, when you click an icon for a directory in the file system's user interface, the file system "jumps" to the referenced storing location, opens that directory file, and creates a view of its contents that is shown in the user interface.

A Detailed Look at Directory Scanning

The process behind viewing the contents of a file system is actually much more fragmented than it appears to a system user. For instance, the file system does not provide a view of its information—the user interface does. While each file system/operating system combination would do it differently, here is a hypothetical process that approximates how it might be done:

The pointing device click action causes the GUI to determine the object that is being acted on; in this case, it's a subdirectory. Assuming the operating system recognizes the object is a directory file, it creates an internal directory-display process to receive the directory information when it is available from the file system (this process probably runs in user space, not kernel space). Then the OS communicates with the file system to open the (directory) file. Because the storage I/O process is approximately five orders of magnitude slower than the processor cycle speed, the operating system continues managing all other system processes, including the execution of other file system processes.

The file system determines the location of the (directory) file in storage and notifies the operating system when it is ready to open its contents. The file system and the operating system kernel exchange a reference handle to identify the directory scan uniquely amid all the other file I/O processes that are occurring. Optionally, the OS kernel and the directory display process also exchange a separate handle.

The operating system then requests that the contents of the directory be read by the file system. When the data starts arriving from storage, the file system notifies the kernel and transfers data to internal buffer memory. The OS notifies the directory display process and points to the buffer location where the directory information was stored. The directory display process reads this data and formats it for display through the GUI, sending the data to it through the system's display interface. When the subdirectory is displayed, the whole process can begin all over again when the user clicks another file or directory.

The point of this discussion is to show that the file system acts like a logical go-fer on behalf of other processes and applications. It does not have its own user interface that allows it to interact directly with users or applications. Instead, it takes its orders from the operating system kernel. Furthermore, the file system does not interpret the data it is working with—that is the responsibility of the application. It looks like you think you are interacting directly with the file system, but you are actually interacting with the GUI.

Full and Relative Path Names

The sequence of directories, beginning with the root directory and including all the directories used to access a particular file, form the *full* or *absolute path* to the file. The full path filename includes this full path and appends the filename at the end. A full path filename must be unique.

In other words, a file system can have files with the same name in different directories (such as setup.exe), but two files are not allowed to have the same name and be located in the same directory.

A relative path is the sequence of directories taken from a given directory to access a file. Usually, this refers to a directory that is currently being viewed through a user interface. For instance, if a user is viewing the C:\black directory and wants to access a file named beige.txt in the C:\black\brown directory, the relative path would be \brown.

Layout of Data Within a Storage Address Space

The logical directory structure of a file system is completely independent of the way data is located in a storage address space.

Storage address spaces are flat, which means they are a sequence of contiguous addresses stretched between a beginning and an ending address. File systems provide the method that determines where files are placed within a storage address space and how they are accessed later. The complete collection of file placements on block addresses can be thought of as the *layout* of data in the block address space. Figure 14-3 shows a storage address space and the location of three different files within that block address space.

Figure 14-3 *The Layout of Three Files Within a Storage Address Space*

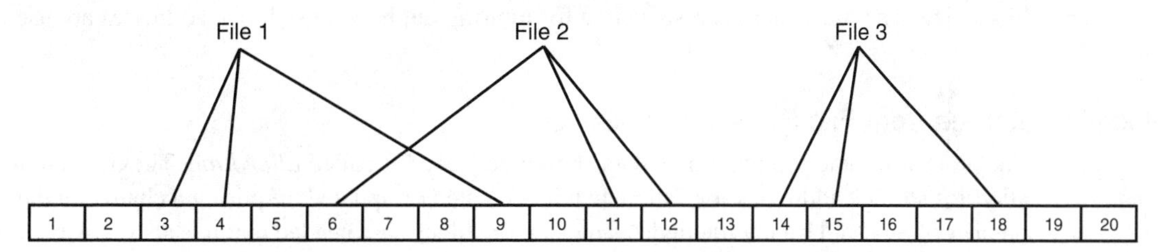

Sometimes the layout of data in a storage address space is referred to as the "physical layout" or the "on-disk" layout of data. Unfortunately, those intuitive terms are not necessarily very accurate when virtualization and volume management are involved. More often than not, the file system is presented with a virtual storage address space rather than an actual physical storage address space.

Several different file system technologies have been developed over the decades that lay out files in a number of different ways. The discussions that follow are intended to describe generalized layout processes and are not intended to reflect any particular file system.

NOTE File system design discussions tend to use specific terminology from specific file systems. This makes it difficult to analyze in general, abstract terms. These terms work if you are trying to develop a file system, but they don't necessarily help communicate concepts. So, the discussions here depart from some of the language that may be more familiar but obscures the bigger picture.

Block Size Definition

File systems store files in block address locations, which are defined by the file system as the granular capacity of storage used by the system. The file system's block size definition determines how large or small most storage I/O operations are. File systems used in open-systems computers typically have fixed block sizes that are consistent across the entire storage address space. These block sizes can be set to many different values by most file systems, and multiples of 4 KB are common.

As discussed in previous chapters, storage address spaces are made from one or more discrete block storage locations and formed into a logical sequence of incremental addresses. Downstream storing-level processes such as volume management software, RAID, and virtualization processes are responsible for creating the collection of block address locations. All contributing storage resources that are managed by the same file system have the same block size. The file system is responsible for figuring out how those block addresses are used.

Allocating Storage from File System Free Space

The process of determining where data should be placed is called *allocation*. The file system allocates storage addresses for a file when it is created or updated, requiring a change in the number of blocks. Usually file updates mean more blocks are needed, but it is also possible for file updates to decrease the size of a file.

Allocation depends on the file system's method for determining which addresses are available for storing data. This is often done through a bitmap table that the file system maintains. The *free block map* has a single bit for each block that indicates which blocks are not storing data.

When a file system is first installed, most of the storage address space is available as free blocks. When files are written to an empty file system, a relatively high percentage of data can be stored in contiguous blocks to provide excellent performance.

File system designers take into account the mechanical limitations of disk drive performance. As a result, one of the design goals of most file systems is to provide fair (as in equal) performance to all files, regardless of when they are written. Allocating storage by scattering data throughout the complete address range ensures that I/O performance levels will degrade slowly as the storage address space is filled.

In general, I/O performance is best if file blocks are contiguous. For this reason the allocation method employed by most file systems typically attempts to place file data in "clumps" of contiguous blocks in the various block ranges where the file is stored.

NOTE Although it could be an advantage, file systems typically do not differentiate between different classes of files, such as system files, application files, or data files. Therefore, there is no QoS element in file systems today. That could certainly change in the future.

Fragmentation

Fragmentation is a natural process that occurs in file systems. It refers to the gradual reduction in the number of contiguous address spaces that can be allocated to a file. As a file system ages, its free space is consumed, and data is stored in fewer contiguous blocks that are scattered over more locations that are farther apart. This results in more actuator movements to read files and a corresponding decrease in I/O performance.

Administrative actions and file system utilities that "clean up" disk space return blocks to the free block map so they can be re-allocated. However, to improve performance, a defragmentation tool is needed to restructure the disk layout and place fragmented data back together in longer contiguous block sections.

The Layout Reference System

One of the most important parts of any file system is the reference system it uses to record where files are written. In UNIX file systems this is commonly referred to as the inodes.

The *layout reference system* is used to locate all file data created in the system and stored by the file system. Each file in the system is stored in one or more blocks. The reference system provides the method that identifies all the blocks used to store a file. The layout reference system must correctly identify all blocks as well as their relative order within the file. Figure 14-4 shows the layout reference system data that exists for files and subdirectories located in a directory called Forrest.

NOTE The term *layout reference system* may strike some readers as odd or unnecessary, considering that there is already a reasonable term, *inode,* from UNIX systems that can be used. The problem with using terms like inode is that it specifically reflects UNIX system implementations. There is no reason to believe that a layout reference system for a non-UNIX file system would resemble inodes or be called inodes.

Figure 14-4 *Layout Reference Data for Files and Directories in a Directory Named Forrest*

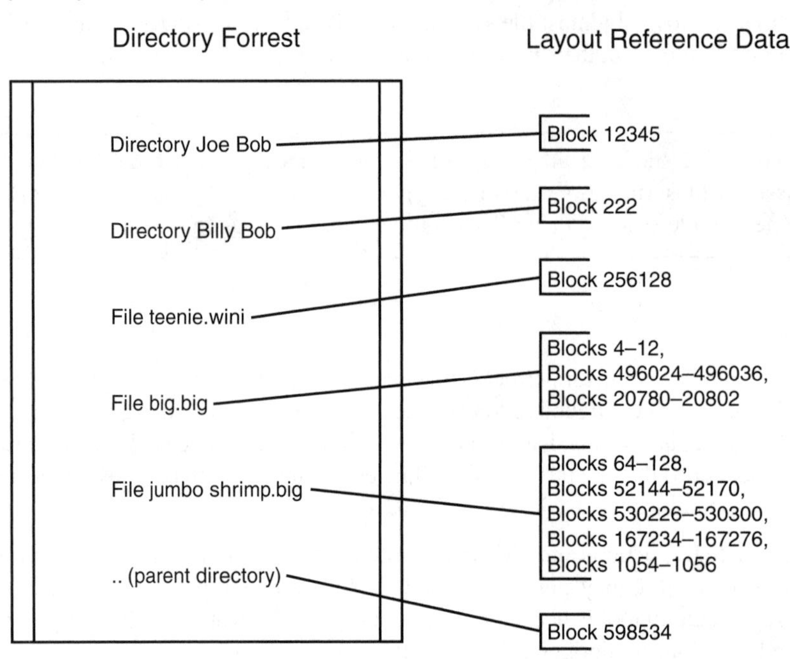

When a user or an application makes a request for a file, the request is converted to a full path name by the operating system and passed to the file system. The file system finds the filename in the appropriate directory and then looks up the requested block location(s) using the file system's reference data.

Byte-range file I/O requests are accommodated by locating data at byte offsets from block locations that correspond to the file system's block size. For instance, if an application is seeking data beginning at the tenth KB of a file in a file system with 4-KB blocks, the file system can locate the data requested by moving to the file's third block, starting at 8 KB and reading ahead an additional 2 KB within that block.

It is obviously essential that all files written by the file system have data and layout reference data that match each other. This is referred to as file system consistency. A loss of file system consistency is equivalent to losing data.

The layout reference system used by a file system can have a profound effect on the scalability of the system and its performance. Historically, these reference systems were structured as indexes, and the file system had a limited number of them, limiting its size. Over time, these evolved to include multiple levels of indexes to increase the scalability of the file system.

However, the more indexes there are, the slower the file system performance. Not only that, but recovering from errors and unexpected system shutdowns becomes a much bigger problem.

Most newer file systems use a reference system based on B-tree algorithms. B-trees have the advantage of being relatively compact and fast and are generally viewed as superior technology for creating scalable storage.

Traversing the File System

User searches for files and system management utilities such as backup and virus scanners traverse (scan) the entire reference system and all the files in a file system. Typically this involves moving from directory to directory, looking for a particular name, reading attributes, or scanning the data within a file. Backup and virus scanning create an enormous amount of work for a file system.

The efficiency of the file system's reference system is paramount to the performance of these utilities and applications. As file systems increase in size, automated utilities that traverse the file system will become needed to help administrators handle the workload.

File System Constructs and Functions

In addition to the basic structures of file systems just discussed, several different constructs and functions are common in file systems today:

- Superblock
- Name space
- Metadata
- Access permissions
- Interface semantics
- Locking
- Buffers
- Journaling

These primary file system functions are discussed in the following sections.

Superblock

File systems usually have a reserved location in a storage address space to keep internal information about their operation, configuration, and status. This reserved location is called the *superblock* in UNIX file systems and the master file table in Windows server file systems.

The Name Space

The file system's name space provides a method for interpreting and displaying file and directory information to end users and applications. Some of the major usability differences between different file systems result from having different name space implementations. For instance, different name spaces might treat uppercase and lowercase characters differently, have different reserved characters, and allow different numbers of characters.

NOTE For you networking people who want a networking analogy, the name space is the presentation layer of the storage stack. I used to talk about name spaces as the data representation function, but I've stopped doing that because people seem to prefer using the term *name space*. I still think that "data representation" is the correct abstract notion. After all, you can have operating systems with GUIs and sound capabilities (really!) where visual icons and audio leitmotivs can be associated with data files in an abstract way that could hardly be thought of as a "name" made out of letters. The file "°," formerly known as "prints.dat," immediately comes to mind. However, for this book, I'm going with the traditional and conceptually limited term *name space*.

Metadata and Attributes

As file systems hold increasing amounts of data, it is essential that mechanisms be found that help manage data in meaningful ways. The main file system facility for supporting data management is metadata. Metadata is descriptive information retained by the file system that describes inherent characteristics, control information, or usage history of a file. In other words, it's data about data.

Traditionally metadata has been implemented as file system attributes that indicate such things as the size of a file; various date and time stamps for when files were created, opened, and modified; and whether the file needs backing up. Metadata normally is used by system or data management functions like backup processes.

Metadata can be stored many different ways. It can be stored with the file or it can be stored in a separate and independent storage area. Chapter 16, "New Directions in Network Filing: Clustered File Systems, Distributed File Systems, and Network Storage for Databases," shows how some distributed file system products are structuring metadata differently.

NOTE Some discussions of file systems and metadata include the layout reference system as part of the file system's metadata. That's fine, but I prefer to think of the reference system as a different entity that is often stored and used independently of qualitative descriptions of the data.

Access Permissions

File systems usually have some form of access permission scheme that determines what data different users and applications can access. As users attempt to open files, their IDs are checked against the security data associated with the file. If the user is authorized to work with the file, he or she gains the appropriate level of access. It is possible to keep files from being updated or viewed that way.

This is the most common method of providing security in storage networks. SCSI storing processes do not have any security whatsoever. SAN networking technology can provide network access security, although this is not commonly done currently.

Interface Semantics

Access control can also be provided through the file system application interface using *file system semantics*. The semantics of a file system describe the methods by which data is exchanged between applications and a file system and can include control over which users or applications get to work with data.

For example, a file system may have several options for opening files that can be used by application vendors for a number of reasons. The semantics *open with deny-write* or *open with deny-open* can be used when first opening a file to ensure that other workers or application processes cannot interfere with the work being done by the person or application that opened it initially. This is why you may have seen a message telling you that you cannot access a certain file because another user is working on it.

Locking

As illustrated in the preceding section, locking is a mechanism that allows file systems to support exclusive or prioritized access to a file. Locking allows the first user to finish working on a file without risking interference from other users or applications.

Locking is not necessarily done the same on every file system, and there are significant differences in the locking mechanisms used on UNIX and Windows systems. Chapter 16, which covers network attached storage, discusses some of these differences in greater detail.

File System Buffers and Cache

Memory I/O operations are approximately five to six orders of magnitude faster than disk I/O. Considering that file system performance has a major impact on overall system performance, it is not surprising that file systems load parts of their data in memory to improve performance.

File systems also keep application data in memory buffers to improve performance. In essence this is equivalent to caching, but it is done by the file system, which has detailed information about all the storage addresses where a file is stored. Unlike block-based caching, which has no file or directory context to work from, file system caching has 100 percent accuracy.

Operating systems can provide a significant amount of available system memory to be used as file system cache buffer memory. The way this memory is allocated depends on operating differences between operating systems, the amount of memory in the system, and the number of applications running.

File system buffering and caching create some consistency difficulties for storage management applications such as block-based backup and point-in-time copy. If there is data stored in host memory that has not been written to disk and there is associated data (data linked by the file system's reference system) that has already been written to disk, there is a chance that the system could suddenly fail unexpectedly, resulting in inconsistent data. Different operating systems provide various levels of support that allow storage management functions to synchronize inconsistent data. The main methods are discussed in the following section.

File System Checking and Journaling

The requirement to maintain file system consistency between stored file data and the file system's reference system is normally dealt with in one of two ways:

- File system consistency checking
- Journaling

In general, file system consistency is a problem only when an abnormal system stop occurs due to such unexpected occurrences as a sudden loss of power, a natural disaster, or an operating system bug. Most file systems have information in the superblock that indicates if the file system followed an orderly shutdown, maintaining file system consistency. When a file system starts, it reads the superblock to determine if an orderly shutdown process occurred. If it didn't, data consistency is at risk.

The file system's reference system contains information that is duplicated for redundancy. Using these redundant reference system structures, a process called a file system check (FS check) can determine whether the file system is consistent. If not, the FS check process can correct the problem to restore the file system to a usable state.

The FS check process has to verify and correlate all stored data with its internal information and reference system. The FS check process takes a long time to run for very large file systems. (A file system is large if it has a lot of files in it, and file system size is independent of the size of the storage address space it manages.) FS check operations can take hours, or even days for very large file system.

The time needed to run FS check is obviously a problem for IT organizations trying to run 24/7 operations. As systems and file systems increase in size, the time needed to check file system consistency becomes a larger liability. For that reason, file systems have adopted journaling techniques that simplify consistency detection.

File system journaling is based on database journaling concepts that maintain the referential integrity of data. Before data is written to disk, a journal entry is written, indicating the nature of the write operation. After the data is written, another journal entry is made that indicates the write completed correctly. If a journaled file system starts and discovers from its superblock that data might be inconsistent, it can look at the journal for any incomplete writes and roll back its reference system to a state that can be guaranteed to have consistency.

Obviously the overhead of journaling slows performance. However, most would agree that it is well worth it in order to allow fast recoveries from system failures.

Scaling File Systems

One of the main problems administrators face is storage scalability. When file systems reach a certain threshold of filled capacity, they tend to become fragmented and perform poorly. Those thresholds depend on a number of variables, including the application, the particular file system used, and the configuration of underlying storage.

Virtualization and volume management technologies are used to increase the size of storage address spaces, but unless the file system adjusts to use the increased storage capacity, there is no benefit to be had from scalable storage. Therefore, it is essential to have a way to increase the boundaries of the file system that manages the underlying storage address space.

Copying Files into a New File System on New Storage

One way to increase the size of a file system is to copy its contents to a new, larger storage address space. This is a fairly straightforward approach that has the side benefit of defragmenting file data as it is being written to its new location. Although it might not seem obvious, this process actually creates a new file system that manages the allocation of the new, larger storage address spaces for existing files.

The problem of using this approach is maintaining consistency with updates that occur in the original file system as data is being copied to the new file system. This is done by either quiescing the system so that it does not receive updates or through the use of a data migration facility that includes copy-on-write capabilities. Eventually, all the data is copied to the new file system, and the system can cut over to start using it for all functions.

The cut-over process can be performed manually or be accomplished by products that automate the process. Because manual processes disrupt system and application processes, automated data migration products may be well worth their cost.

File System Expansion

When a file system is created, it establishes an internal structure and reference system to fit the size of the storage address space. Unless special processes are run, there is no way for the file system to know that the storage address space it manages may have been increased. Some file systems include these processes and can expand their boundaries to accommodate increases in the storage address space they currently manage.

There are two methods: static expansion and dynamic expansion. Static expansion is done when the system is quiesced. The file system is given the new dimensions and may redistribute data over the new, larger storage address space. This redistribution process is a bit like defragmentation, but it is easier to accomplish because there is more free space to work with.

Dynamic expansion is done while the file system is running (it's always a good idea to stop application processing anyway). It appends the new storage address space to the end of the previous address space. File system expansion is a fairly complicated task given the complexity of the reference systems used in file systems and the absolute requirement to maintain data consistency.

The ability to dynamically expand a file system depends on the capabilities of the operating system, the file system, and a volume manager that can clearly identify all the various components that need to be integrated in the process.

Summary

It is virtually impossible to understand how storage networks work without understanding filing functions. As the top functional layer in any storage process, filing is responsible for determining where data objects are located within the available storage address spaces.

This chapter introduced the fundamental concepts of file system operations. It began with a discussion contrasting file systems and operating systems and then moved into a discussion of the two primary structures in file systems: the directory system and the layout reference system. The directory system allows users and applications to logically group and locate data. The layout reference system is used to locate data precisely within a storage address space.

The end of the chapter explored other common aspects of file systems, such as the superblock, name space, metadata and attributes, locking, and journaling.

With this basic knowledge of file system operations, it is possible to look at the more advanced filing concepts that are employed in storage networks and that are discussed in the remaining chapters.

Q & A

1. What is the file system's primary responsibility?
2. True or false: The operating system/file system interface is a clearly delineated abstract boundary.
3. The layout reference system in most UNIX file systems is called what?
4. True or false: The directory structure and layout of data in the storage address space are closely related.
5. What is the importance of the file system's layout reference system?
6. What is metadata?
7. True or false: Storage expansion by virtualization methods or volume managers is automatically detected by the file system.
8. What is the reason for using a journaled file system?
9. Why is file system caching more accurate than storing-level block caching?

Upon completing this chapter, you will be able to

- Participate in discussions and meetings regarding implementations of network attached storage products and file server software
- Discuss the primary differences between NFS and CIFS, including their applicability for different types of client applications
- Participate in the evaluation of file server software and NAS systems for your environment

CHAPTER 15

Network File Systems and Network Attached Storage

Storing data files on server systems is one of the most common functions in local area networks (LANs). The software products that provide these filing functions are known by several different names, but in this chapter they are referred to generically as *Network File Systems*. Network file systems are generally considered to be the simplest and most direct way to implement storage networking, especially if network attached storage (NAS) products are used.

Network file systems extend traditional file system functions into client/server network environments. From their inception, network file systems have been implemented aggressively. In fact, one can argue that network file storage has been the most influential application spurring the growth of LAN technology in the last three decades. The widespread use of network file servers inspired the creation of the sizeable NAS storage industry.

This chapter examines the basic structures, operations, and applications of network file systems. The first part of the chapter is spent discussing network file system technology, and the second part analyzes its close cousin, NAS.

Fundamentals of Network File Systems

Network file systems were introduced in 1985 by Sun Microsystems with Network File Systems (NFSs). NFS allowed teams of users working on Sun UNIX workstations to exchange data files over a LAN without having to use removable storage diskettes or tapes. In fact, NFS allowed systems to be made that had no local storage whatsoever (diskless workstations) by allowing systems to load the operating system over a network. NFS was an immediate success and was quickly adopted throughout the UNIX industry as a standard for storing and sharing files. Today NFS is one of the oldest and most widely used standards in network storage.

Soon afterward many similar and competing network file storage products were introduced by companies in the PC LAN industry, such as Novell, Banyan, 3-Com, IBM, and Microsoft. A class of software products known as network operating systems (NOSs) emerged that allowed groups of users to share storage resources and printers connected to server systems. Today, network file systems are primarily sold as optional features for commercial UNIX, Linux, and Windows operating systems.

NOTE The term *network file system* is used generically in this chapter to refer to all software products that provide network filing services. References to the NFS standard simply use the acronym NFS. Hopefully the context will be clear enough to avoid confusion.

Network file systems use a simple *client/server* relationship model between client systems running applications that create and manipulate data and the server systems that store it and manage the access to it. This relationship is shown in Figure 15-1.

Figure 15-1 *Client/Server Network Storage Model*

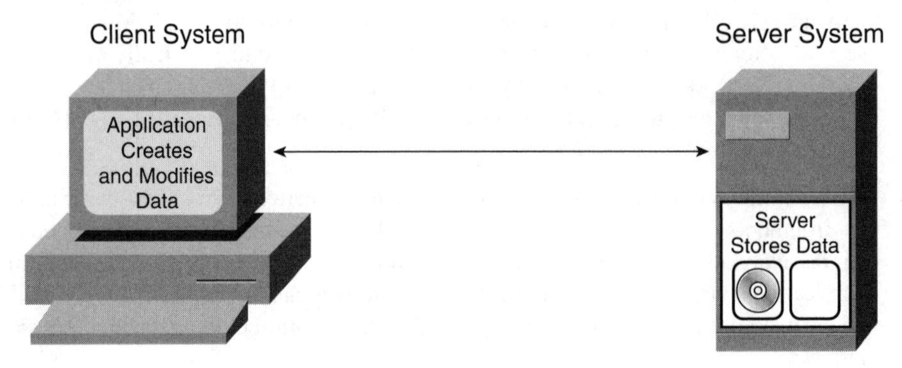

A Review of Block I/O and File I/O

Chapter 2, "Establishing a Context for Understanding Storage Networks," discusses both block and file I/O briefly. Up to this point in the book, most of the I/O descriptions and technologies have involved block (storing-level) I/O. In the remaining chapters, many of the I/O concepts involve file I/O. Clients exchanging data with network file servers use the extensions to basic file I/O operations that are discussed in this chapter.

File I/O processes involve the way applications interact with file systems to create and access data. While the file system maintains all information about where files are stored in a block address space, applications have only names to identify their data. Applications locate files by their full or relative path names and access the data within files using the file system semantics and application programming interfaces (APIs). Before an application accesses data within a file, it first opens it for access, and then it performs file I/O operations on the contents of the file. File I/O operations can be performed on the entire contents of a file or on certain byte ranges within the file. The file system is responsible for converting byte ranges within files to the blocks where the data is stored in a storage address space.

In contrast, block I/O involves system architectures with initiators, targets, and logical units that have nothing to do with most applications. Unlike file I/O, where the application and file system provide a context that identifies the data, block I/O processes have no context for the data that is being transmitted.

Network File System Clients

The role and functions of the client in network file systems should not be underestimated. While most of the storage functions are determined by file server software, the functions of servers need to match the capabilities and usage methods of client systems. Economic pressures to reduce costs on client machines and use client software that ships with the operating system have significantly influenced the client/server relationship.

File I/O Redirection

Client systems access files in the network through a file system facility called *I/O redirection*. I/O redirection is responsible for two primary functions: it presents files that can be accessed over the network in the client's interface, and it establishes communications with network file servers for transparently accessing data. I/O redirection interacts with the system kernel to assume responsibility for file I/O operations performed over the network. Essentially, file redirection performs the same type of functions that the local file system does, but it does so remotely with a file system service located in a server.

Network file systems normally appear as a logical drive letter in the client system, such as H: or I:. Network file systems can also be represented with server and directory names—for instance, as a directory called Jay on a server named Kramer.

Remote-Mounting the Network File System

The process of a client I/O redirector establishing communications with a network file system is called a *remote mount*. The remote mount process usually includes some type of network login process to ensure the client is authenticated to access the network file system.

The term originates from the mount process that is used by file systems and operating systems to ensure the two are ready to work together within an individual system.

File Server Systems

Network file systems are practically synonymous with file server system hardware. File serving can place a considerable load on a system—particularly the I/O and storage components and subsystems within a server system. Therefore, network file system software is typically installed on heavy-duty systems designed for extended reliability, much larger storage capacities, and better I/O performance.

File servers can use Small Computer Systems Interface (SCSI), Advanced Technology Attachment (ATA), Serial ATA (SATA), or Fibre Channel as their storage interconnect. There is nothing particularly unusual or difficult about a file server using a SAN to communicate with storage on the storing (block) level. The filing-level function between a client and a server is fundamentally different from the storing-level function between a server and its storage. The physical network can be the same, but the protocol interaction is completely different.

File Server Software and the Network Filing Service

File server software typically runs on server systems as a tightly integrated application on a common operating system. Windows, UNIX, and Linux desktop systems can be converted into file servers with the addition of file server software. UNIX and Linux operating systems typically come with optional NFS software, while Microsoft Windows Server software is an additional software package that upgrades a desktop system to become a server.

File server software provides a service that manages client access to files. A file system on the server controls how storage blocks are allocated and how the storage address space is used. This approach allows many clients to share the same storage address space but maintains control of detailed file system operations such as space allocation on the server.

In fact, it is a bit paradoxical that the thing we refer to as a network file system often does not include a file system, but instead includes a *file service* that provides access to another existing file system. For example, even though the acronym NFS stands for network *file system,* NFS does not create a new or different file system on the server when it is installed. Instead, its file service prescribes the manner in which clients access files in an existing file system.

The file service runs as a high-priority application that requests files using an operating system interface, just the same as any other application. The operating system passes requests to the file system, and the file system retrieves the data as requested. More than most other kinds of applications, these file services have many more file operations to track, requiring more system memory to store file handles and other I/O processing data.

NOTE File servers need lots of memory for running the file service and for caching data for clients. Just say "Fill 'er up" when buying memory for file server systems.

Of course, there are variations to the scenario just described. Network file systems can also be designed with a unique integrated file system and operating system combination that are more or less inseparable because you would never use one without the other.

The Server File System

As discussed in the preceding section, the file system used by a network file system can be an existing standard file system or an integrated, specialized file system. It's important to understand that the characteristics of the server's file system apply to the data that is stored in it. The file system naming conventions, attributes, locking methods, access permissions, and interface semantics are all part of the data that is stored on behalf of client systems.

Client file systems and server file systems may differ, which can create problems. Applications written for a particular operating system platform assume the native file system will be used to store the application's data and metadata according to specified formats. However, if the server file system does not support the same metadata formats, some of the assumptions made by the client application could be incorrect. For instance, it is possible for a file's name to be altered or to have its access permissions changed by the server system. Most file server file systems have evolved to allow data to be stored on them from a variety of clients, but problems still occur.

On a different matter, it is highly recommended that server file systems use journaling for recovery purposes as well as to decrease the time needed to reboot the server following an unexpected shutdown.

The Complete I/O Process for File I/O in a Network

Readers sometimes find it helpful to think about the complete storage process used for file I/O operations. The steps taken to read data using a network file system are shown in Figure 15-2 and are discussed in the following list. Each letter in the list corresponds to a location in the I/O path where there is some interaction involving network filing data access. Notice that most letters show up twice in the list. That's because commands and responses travel the same path, but in opposite directions.

1. The client application asks the client operating system for a file. The application and the client operating system establish handles to exchange file contents.

2. The client operating system engages the file I/O redirector and establishes the necessary handles to transfer file contents.

3. The file I/O redirector in the client communicates over the network with the file service application in the server, requesting the file.

4. The file service application asks the server operating system for the file and establishes handles for exchanging file contents.

5. The server operating system engages the server file system and establishes handles for transferring file contents. The server file system locates the file using its internal reference system and submits read I/O commands through the server's operating system kernel.

6. Read I/O commands are processed by I/O drivers, including any multipathing, volume management, and SCSI-layer device drivers. One or more commands are transmitted over the I/O networks or interconnect buses to storage. All involved storage LUs execute the commands they receive and read data from storage media before making a response and transferring data to the server's operating system.
7. The operating system passes the aggregated block I/O information to the server file system, which converts the block data to byte streams. The server file system exchanges the file data with the server operating system, which stores the data.
8. The server operating system exchanges the file data with the file service application.
9. The file service application in the server communicates with the file I/O redirector in the client and transfers the file data to the client over the network.
10. The file I/O redirector exchanges the data with the client operating system, which stores the data in memory buffers.
11. The client operating system exchanges data with the client application.

Figure 15-2 *The Process of Reading a File Using a Network File System*

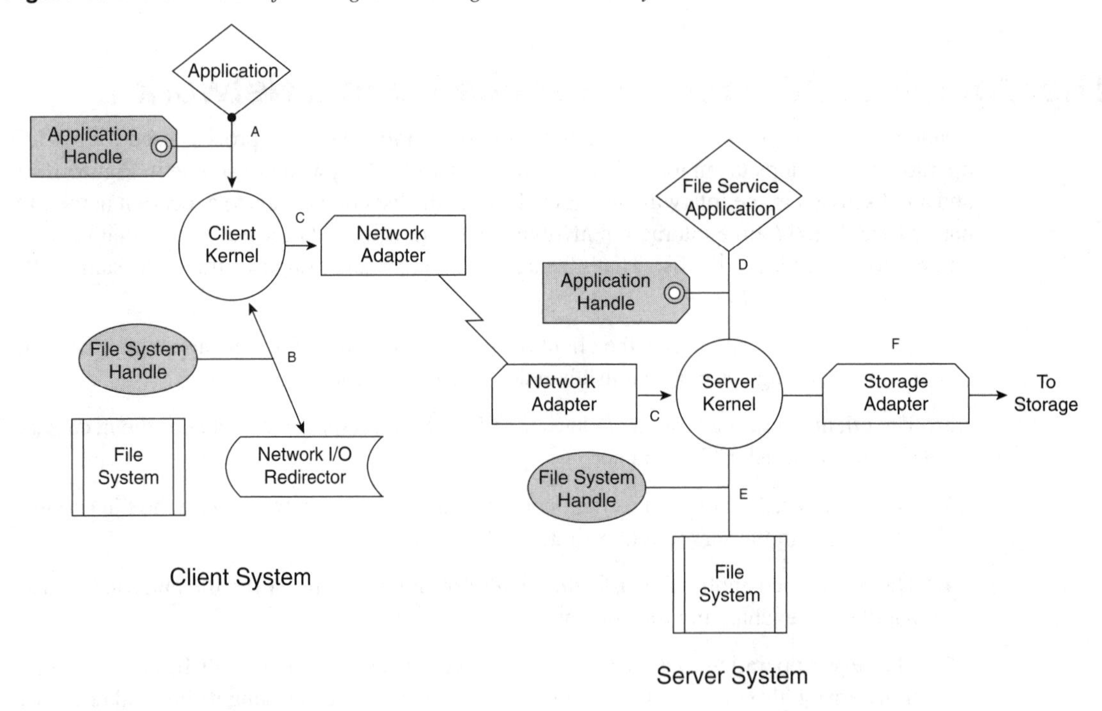

Despite the number of steps and the complexity involved, accessing files on file servers can be faster than accessing files locally on disk drives in client systems. This assumes that client systems have relatively slow I/O hardware compared to server I/O hardware. Also, the large amounts of cache memory that can be implemented in servers can make significant performance differences by reading from memory instead of disk.

NFS and CIFS Protocols for Network File Systems

The differences between UNIX and Windows clients and file systems resulted in different protocols being developed for network file systems. This is not so hard to understand. If the end node processes differ, the protocols to exchange data between those end processes could also be different—and they are.

The protocol developed for UNIX environments is NFS, and the protocol developed for Windows is now called Common Internet File System (CIFS).

NFS

NFS is an approved industry standard, with many companies contributing to its development in the last 20 years. That said, NFS is mostly a UNIX standard that has not been strongly supported and implemented by Microsoft in its products due to the lack of support for Windows file semantics in NFS. The lack of Windows support in legacy NFS is not surprising when you consider that it was being developed at the same time as the original IBM PC and DOS (disk operating system).

The historical context for technology development is always influential. When NFS was initially developed, LAN technology was in its relative infancy, and errors were much more common. Therefore, NFS was initially designed as a stateless protocol for reliable and fast service in early LAN environments where clients and servers could lose network connections. If a client became disconnected from a server (and the file it was working on), it could simply try to access it again later after the connection was reestablished. In the meantime, other systems were allowed to access the file and work on it.

The transport protocol selected for NFS was the User Datagram Protocol (UDP), a fast, connectionless, lightweight protocol restricted for use to a single Ethernet network. The third generation of NFS added support for TCP, allowing NFS traffic to be integrated more closely with TCP/IP networks.

NFSV4

NFS is now in its fourth iteration, not surprisingly called NFSV4. There are many changes in NFSV4, mostly related to becoming more compatible with Windows client systems. Among the advancements in NFSV4 are

- Support for Windows metadata and access permissions that allow Windows clients to store data without losing metadata

- Stateful processes, based on the assumption that networks are reliable and to be compatible with Windows client processes
- Byte-range locking within files—again consistent with Windows client processes
- Lock leases to eliminate locks being held for extended periods of time after a client or connection failure
- Integrated locking within NFS to eliminate the need for NFS's network lock manager (NLM)
- Compound remote procedure calls to aggregate commands and achieve more efficient network operations
- Improved security mechanisms in response to general network security threats

While NFSV4 makes NFS mostly compatible with Windows, it is not clear how widely the NFSV4 software will be implemented in Windows client systems. Microsoft could choose to include it at some point, but Microsoft has different network file system technologies it is trying to develop and promote.

CIFS

In contrast to NFS, Microsoft's CIFS protocol is not an industry standard, and Microsoft has rejected attempts by the industry to create a standards organization around it. CIFS and its future derivations are core technologies for future operating file system developments at Microsoft, and Microsoft doesn't want to compromise its product developments through a standards committee process.

The origin of CIFS can be tied to the IBM PC LAN program, which was introduced in 1985 for peer-to-peer file sharing in Token Ring networks. The protocols used in this product were adopted by Microsoft and introduced in the early 1990s as the Server Message Block (SMB) protocol of its LAN Manager product. SMB included printing and other network services in addition to its network file system technology. SMB was repeatedly reworked by Microsoft for its server products and became known as CIFS in the late 1990s.

Windows desktop operating systems since Windows 95 all support some version of SMB or CIFS. That means the majority of desktop systems in use today have a free client for Windows network file systems.

CIFS is a stateful protocol that assumes client/server connections are reliable. If a client/server connection is broken, the processing context using that connection is saved in both the client and the server. Microsoft's vision for CIFS is broader than network file system functionality and includes distributed client/server applications where processes are split between clients and servers. A stateful protocol allows clients and servers to resynchronize their work after a temporary network error.

SMB initially was designed to run on top of the NetBIOS protocol, mostly as a way to identify network resources. Today CIFS runs directly on TCP/IP without NetBIOS and uses network domain services to locate and identify resources. CIFS is routable, allowing servers and clients to be in different IP networks. The concept of domain services for locating network file system resources is tightly coupled with CIFS networks.

Locking Differences Between NFS and CIFS

While locking is primarily a file system function, the semantics of locking need to be implemented in some sort of protocol to extend that function to clients of network file systems. The protocol could be the same as the one used to access files, or it could be independent. The NFS and CIFS protocols have taken distinctly different approaches to locking, which has caused considerable heartburn in the network storage industry for several years.

NFS's implementation of *advisory locking* does nothing to prevent multiple clients from accessing and updating a particular file. Advisory locking depends on client applications that have the ability to recognize when locks exist and inform their users that there could be a conflict. In other words, the user is advised that a lock condition is intended. Users can update the file as they wish, because advisory locking does nothing to prevent updates in the server file system.

For reasons related to file system internals, the separate locking protocol NLM was developed to implement locking with NFS. The necessity and complexity of using two protocols to provide locking resulted in many application developers ignoring it altogether.

NFSV4 has overhauled the locking mechanism of NFS with the implementation of a lease mechanism that depends on client systems renewing their lease at regular intervals. If the lease between a client and server is broken, the server removes the lock.

In contrast, CIFS extends the *strong locking* semantics of Windows file systems to clients. Strong locking refers to the ability of a file system to restrict the read and update access granted to clients. You might have had firsthand experience with strong locking if you have ever attempted to open a file in a Windows network file system that was locked by another user. A message indicating the file cannot be opened or can be opened only as a read-only version is generated by the Windows file system and communicated by the CIFS protocol.

Windows systems have an access priority that is determined by the order in which clients access a file. The first client that accesses a file gets to determine the access rights of other clients that attempt to access the file later. Locking is secondary to access permissions in Windows systems. Clients that do not have the proper credentials to access a certain file cannot gain access to it through a separate lock resolution process.

Applications for Network File Storage

Network file storage has two basic applications: centralized storage management and data sharing.

Centralized Storage Management

Network file systems provide centralized storage for large numbers of users and applications, significantly easing storage administration tasks. Instead of managing storage for hundreds or thousands of individual systems, administrators can concentrate on a much smaller number of servers.

Centralizing storage on servers also enables a systematic approach to fundamental storage management tasks like backup. In general, the end user community cannot be trusted to do this work, and workstation backup is impractical. Putting data on file servers provides the best opportunity to care for important and valuable corporate resources.

Data Sharing

Some applications and business processes are performed by multiple workers using the same data files. Data sharing with a network file system provides excellent support for this type of work. Data sharing also provides a way to distribute data to a large group of users. For example, sales and marketing materials can be placed in a network file system to ensure employees can get access to the latest news and competitive information.

Data sharing works by granting access to multiple users or applications to the same directories and files. The file service application is responsible for managing this access. Most of the time different users and applications access data files at different times, but sometimes access is made concurrently. When that happens, locking mechanisms in the file system resolve conflicts over which users and applications can perform reading and writing to files.

Some business processes involve multiple steps that occur in sequence. Network file systems provide an easy way for all users and applications to locate and use this data, regardless of the stage of the process. Engineering applications such as electronic design automation (EDA) and software development are both good examples of applications that involve a sequence of steps carried out by multiple users and applications.

Another application of data sharing is farm computing, where multiple systems perform the same or similar functions and need access to the same data. Internet server farms are an excellent example of a server farm environment. Compute-farms for solving large computations are also becoming popular for their efficiency and relative low cost. A network file system is a practical prerequisite for farm computing.

Extended Features of Network File Systems

Several key features of network file systems differentiate them from single-system file systems, as discussed in the following sections.

Disk Quotas

Considering that network file systems are a shared resource, it makes sense to control how it is used. Disk quotas set capacity limits for the total amount of storage individual users can consume. This can be done by associating a directory in the file system with a particular user and then limiting the size of that directory, including subdirectories.

Name Space Virtualization

The name space (directory and file organization) viewed through a client's I/O redirector can appear to be much different from the actual name space of the file server's file systems. For example, a client user could see several different files from multiple file systems as existing within the same virtual directory.

For the purposes of this book, we'll refer to the transposition of name space elements as name space virtualization. This technique is sometimes referred to as file-level virtualization, but it is probably best to specify that it is a name space manipulation and does not impact any of the underlying file system operations.

Name space virtualization can be accomplished at either the client side, the server side, or both. For instance, a server system could present the contents of several different directories as a single directory for clients, and each of those clients could aggregate files from several different server virtual directories. There are many ways file system views can be assembled.

Large Block Size Definitions

The file systems used for network file systems can be designed with large block sizes to fit certain applications. For instance, a network file system could have a block size definition of 2 MB for working with large engineering or multimedia data files. Large block sizes like this provide optimal throughput for streaming I/O applications.

Volume Management

Volume management software is an excellent technology match for network file systems. The redundancy, scalability, and performance benefits of volume management can be used very effectively in support of many client systems.

Basic volume management software is sometimes sold as part of an operating system, as it is with many Linux distributions. On Windows systems, however, volume management functionality is sold as part of Windows network file server products.

Storage Resource Management

File server software products usually include advanced management, diagnostics, and reporting capabilities to help administrators identify trends and problems. Storage resource management (SRM) is a set of functions that help administrators manage usage-related elements of storage.

For instance, SRM analyzes a file system's contents to determine the trends and dynamics of how its capacity is being consumed. For instance, an SRM report could identify files that are both greater than 5 MB and have not been accessed within the last 180 days. Obviously, this kind of analysis would be very helpful for administrators who need to identify ways to reclaim disk space when they are running low.

NOTE There is no way to know how full a storage address space (volume) is without querying the file system. The file system is the only logical entity with information about how the file system has been used and how much free space there is.

Domain Services

File server systems often provide network *domain services* that help administrators structure network access and help clients locate and identify network resources, including network file system files and directories.

SAMBA

In 1992, a computer scientist named Andrew Tridgell at Australia National University in Canberra, Australia reverse-engineered the protocol used by Digital Equipment Corporation (DEC) for its Pathworks network file system product. In the years since then, Tridgell's software creation has evolved, expanded, and become an open-source software initiative called SAMBA (a filling out of the acronym SMB) for turning Linux systems into CIFS servers for Windows clients.

SAMBA is a CIFS file service running on Linux systems that allows Windows clients to store data on Linux-based file systems. It is possible to use any number of file systems available for Linux, but implementers need to pay attention to Linux system details (as is true for any open-source system software) to ensure implementations will work as planned.

As Microsoft continues to modify CIFS, the open-source developers working on SAMBA continue to reverse-engineer it and implement it in SAMBA. In addition to providing file services, SAMBA also provides Windows Server domain controller functionality. Readers interested in reading about SAMBA can go the organization's website at http://www.samba.org.

Network Attached Storage (NAS)

NAS is a product concept that packages file system hardware and software with a complete storage I/O subsystem as an integrated file server solution. All of the technologies that have already been discussed in this book, plus additional management features, can be rolled into a single NAS product offering.

NAS systems are often referred to as *storage appliances* because, like kitchen appliances, they are designed for ease of use and convenience. They save significant administration effort compared to traditional file server systems. NAS bypasses the selection and installation of system, CPU, memory, network cards, storage HBAs, storage devices and subsystems, network file system software, and specialized device drivers. The typical installation of a NAS server appliance can be accomplished in a matter of minutes, as opposed to hours or days.

NOTE The concept of NAS was developed by Auspex, a company founded by Larry Boucher, one of the most influential and visionary engineers in the history of storage networking. Larry was at Shugart and Associates as one of the inventors of SCSI, and he left there to start Adaptec, a very successful developer of SCSI controller technology, before starting Auspex. His current company, Alacritech, is a developer of TCP offload technology for iSCSI. Few people have contributed more to the storage industry and, more admirably, to their community. All props to Larry.

NAS Designs

NAS appliances come in a wide variety of packages and prices. Enterprise-level NAS systems can cost more than $100,000, and entry-level NAS systems with a single disk drive may cost less than $300. Some of the design options that go into NAS products are discussed in the following sections.

Physical Dimensions

NAS systems come in a wide variety of shapes and sizes, from small desktop packages barely larger than a disk drive to modules that fill complete 19-inch vertical rack spaces.

Storage Capacity

NAS systems are sold with a few hundred gigabytes of usable storage capacity and extend up to tens of terabytes. Capacity is one of the primary design decisions of any storage product, NAS included. The number of disk drives, the selection of RAID technology used, and the number of I/O channels are some of the primary storage elements that make up a NAS design. Equally important are the power subsystem and the physical cabinet dimensions.

Interconnect and Disk Technology Selection

NAS products are typically designed with a particular kind of interconnect and disk technology, including ATA, SATA, parallel SCSI, and Fibre Channel. This selection has a significant impact on the capacity, scalability, and performance of a NAS system.

Operating System

NAS products have historically been implemented using a commercially available or specialized operating system. The primary commercial operating systems include Linux, FreeBSD, and Windows. Often some type of customization is done to the operating systems to minimize nonstorage functions and optimize storage functions.

Specialized operating systems have been used to excellent effect by some NAS vendors. Instead of trying to reengineer an existing commercial operating system, with all its underlying complexity, NAS developers can build their own special-purpose operating systems optimized for NAS functions. Sometimes these operating systems are referred to as micro-kernel operating systems because their kernels are much smaller than the kernels of commercial desktop operating systems.

File System

The selection of the file system to use in the NAS server obviously determines many of its characteristics and capabilities. The file system selection can be made independently of the operating system, but the two are often implemented as a pair. If Windows is chosen as the operating system, it is highly likely that a Windows file system will also be used. However, if Linux or FreeBSD is used, the NAS vendor may be inclined to use an open-source file system such as SGI's XFS or Red Hat's GFS. There are more file system options for open-source operating systems than there are for Windows.

Just as special-purpose micro-kernel operating systems have been implemented in NAS systems, special-purpose file systems have also been used very successfully. An independent file system has the advantage of being neutral to Windows and UNIX and therefore can potentially accommodate both types of clients and protocols (NFS and CIFS) more easily. As with the micro-kernel operating system, it may be easier to build and maintain an independent file system than to continue to alter and maintain a “foreign” file system generated externally by another company or as the result of an open-source software initiative.

A file system may be chosen for its affinity for certain applications. For example, a NAS design could include a large block-file system to optimize performance for streaming I/O applications. Another NAS system could incorporate a file system with name space virtualization features that could be used in collaborative computing environments or for data management functions.

Journaling (or Not)

Most NAS systems have journaled file systems to aid in the recoverability of the file system following an unexpected shutdown. However, it is also possible that a file system, such as the Linux file system, could be used, because it does not provide journaling. Journaling takes time, and there are applications, such as real-time data acquisition applications, where recovery is secondary to fast operations.

Data Management

Data management refers to the functionality of storing and encoding data files in a way that helps administrators locate and perform operations on files quickly as well as responsibly protect the business from a variety of errors, accidents, and disasters. Data management is distinct from storage management techniques like RAID, mirroring, and remote copy, because data management works on files or other objects, as opposed to operating on blocks of data.

One form of data management that has been used successfully with NAS is a file-level snapshot. This allows administrators to keep several aging versions of files available for users if they need them. The topic of snapshots is discussed further in Chapter 17, "Data Management."

NOTE Network Appliance has been the industry leader in NAS for many years, based in large part on the integration of data management with its proprietary write anywhere file layout (WAFL) file system. Surprisingly, many would-be competitors have fallen on their swords, not understanding the importance of data management in a product whose reason for existence is storing files. What's with that?

Performance and Throughput

NAS systems can be designed for high performance. The speed of the processor used, the number of processors in a system, and the speed and number of network interfaces can all contribute to performance gains in a NAS system.

The file system access can also be accelerated. While this is easier said than done, there are companies that have developed hardware and software technology designed to achieve better performance for certain applications, such as genetic sequencing, film/video rendering, and seismic analysis.

Availability and Reliability

NAS systems have a variety of options for data availability. Starting with disk mirroring and RAID, NAS systems can also implement things like hot sparing and remote replication of files to other NAS systems. Some NAS systems can be implemented as clusters so that if one NAS system fails the other can continue supplying applications with file data.

Dual-Function Storage: NAS and SAN

It is possible to integrate the functionality of both NAS and SAN storage within a single product. After all, if disk drives will be spinning inside a cabinet, why not allow them to be used as either block or file storage?

This type of dual-function subsystem depends on having an integrated network file system (file service and file system) running in the subsystem in addition to a storage controller that creates storage address spaces. The software for the network file system could run on processors and memory in the subsystem controller circuit board, but it could also run on a separate processor circuit board. Figure 15-3 shows a dual-purpose storage subsystem. Half of it is used for storing-level block I/O, and the other half is used for NAS file serving.

Figure 15-3 *A Dual-Purpose NAS + SAN Storage Subsystem*

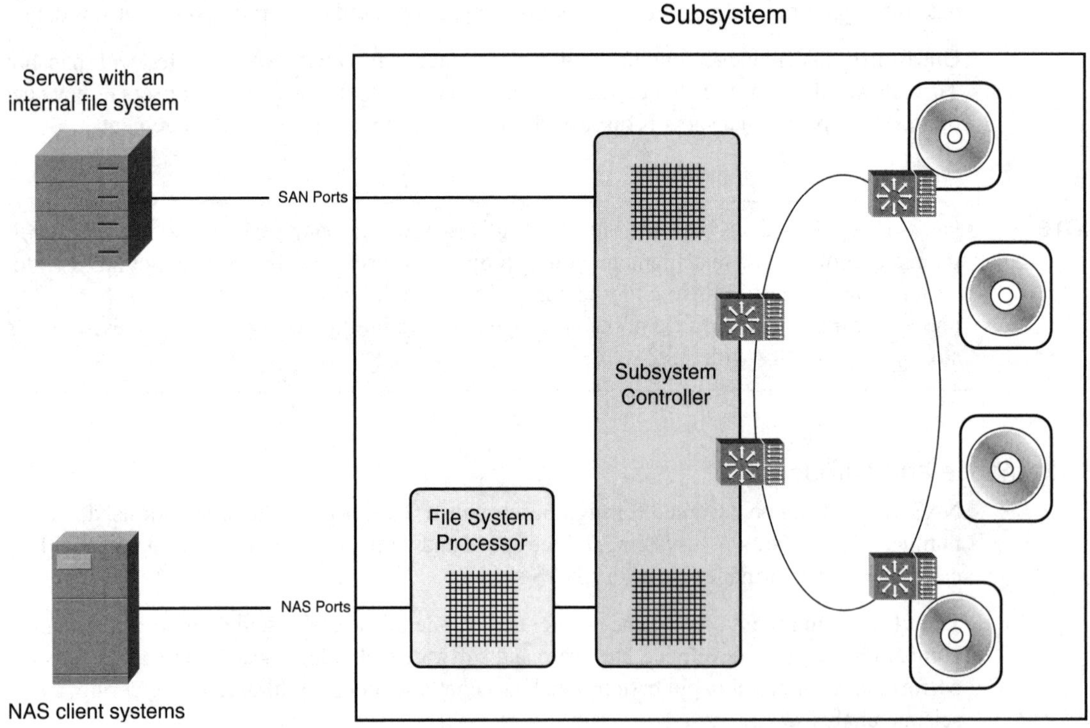

Network Domain Services

NAS systems can participate in Windows networks as domain controllers, much the same as file servers running Windows file serving software. This is usually accomplished in NAS systems through the use of licensed Windows software or SAMBA.

Backup and Recovery of NAS Systems with NDMP

NAS systems built with reduced-functionality or micro-kernel operating systems have scant, if any, support for tape backup hardware and also usually lack backup agent software that works with network backup software. These systems have basically two options for backup: back up over the LAN or use Network Data Management Protocol (NDMP).

To back up over the LAN, a backup system mounts the network file system and then copies files from it as if it were a local disk volume. This approach works well for small NAS systems but is not necessarily realistic for larger NAS systems due to the amount of data that regularly needs to be backed up. Instead, they are usually backed up with NDMP.

NDMP is a protocol for remotely controlling SCSI tape equipment connected to a NAS system. It can be thought of as a TCP/IP tunneling protocol for SCSI data between a backup server and a NAS system. The backup server issues SCSI commands that are sent via NDMP to the NAS system. The NAS system extracts the commands and sends them to tape equipment. Similarly, SCSI command responses from tape equipment are received and processed by the proxy driver before they are transmitted to the backup server over the NDMP connection.

Figure 15-4 shows the basic NDMP backup model.

Figure 15-4 *The NDMP Backup Model*

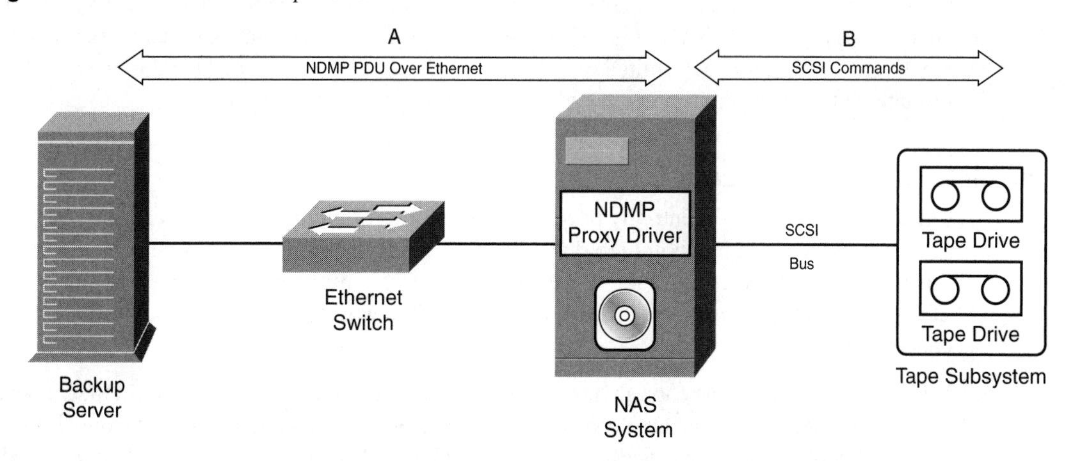

NAS Scalability

Beyond the techniques of using RAID or disk striping, NAS systems are often designed for expandable storage capacity. Most have a way to increase the number of additional disk drives or disk drive expansion cabinets that can be connected. Other capacity technologies relevant to NAS are discussed in the following sections.

Dynamic File System Expansion

Some NAS systems have dynamically expandable file systems that can take advantage of new capacity as it is added. While this might seem like an obvious feature to include, the storage devices of many NAS systems with ATA or SCSI disk drives do not allow new storage to be added without shutting down the system. Beyond that there needs to be some way to initiate a process that recognizes changes to the storage address space.

NAS Head

Related to the discussion of dynamic file system expansion are NAS products designed to be attached to independent block I/O storage subsystems. *NAS heads* are basically NAS systems with the operating system and network file system running, but without the bulk storage that would be used to store files. Users or systems integrators are expected to connect the NAS head existing storage and use the storage address space(s) available there.

While this might seem counterintuitive for a product class that is commonly thought of as being complete storage appliances, the advantage of the NAS head approach is extended scalability for the NAS file system. If the storage address space of a NAS system is constrained by its physical configuration, there is a point where no more disk storage can be added, which creates problems for administrators (see the next section). If storage can be added to a NAS system by attaching to it through a SAN, it is possible to create NAS systems that are much more scalable. However, scalability is not limited only by physical constraints. Other I/O and logical limitations for file systems prevent endless scaling through a NAS head.

Adding More NAS Systems: Less Than Wonderful

The simplicity of NAS eventually becomes problematic when the maximum capacity of the system is reached. At that point the only option is to install another NAS system. Sometimes, this is done as a forklift upgrade, where a new, larger system replaces an older one that is out of capacity. Other times, a system is introduced and the workload is divided between the old and new systems.

While these sound simple enough, neither process is as straightforward as it would first appear. In the first case, the data on the old system is copied from the old system to the new one. If there is a lot of data to copy, the process can take many hours. When the data is completely copied, the old server needs to be removed from the network. If it is being used as a domain controller, that function also must be accounted for. Obviously it is important that the transfer of data be 100 percent complete. Administrators may run complete system backups for insurance in case something goes wrong with the copy process.

The scenario where an additional NAS system is added to the network is more difficult. Some users and applications will continue to use the old system, while others will switch to the new one. Still others may use both new and old NAS systems. Administrators have to determine which clients can access which directories and files on both NAS systems.

After the planning is done, the process of changing mount point definitions in client I/O redirectors starts. With potentially hundreds of clients to adjust, this process can take a great deal of administrative effort and can result in a few inevitable oversights and errors that reduce both IT and user productivity.

Summary

Network file systems are the oldest and most commonly used storage network technology in open-systems computing. In general, network file systems are implemented either with file server software on file server systems or as NAS products.

Client system file systems have strongly influenced the development of this technology. NFS was developed by Sun Microsystems for networking UNIX systems, and CIFS (SMB at the time) was developed by Microsoft for networking Windows systems. As a result, network file system software products are biased toward either UNIX or Windows. While NAS products can also have a bias, they can also be designed to be neutral. The most successful NAS products have been designed for client neutrality.

One of the more interesting observations to make about network file systems is that in many cases they do not actually include a special file system. Instead, network file systems incorporate client-side I/O redirection technology and a server-side application for managing client network file I/O requests.

Q & A

1. What are the two major transport protocols used in network file systems?
2. True or false: NFS was originally designed to run over UDP.
3. What kind of locking does NFS provide?
4. True or false: CIFS is a published industry standard.
5. What is the benefit of a stateful protocol?
6. Name one of the two primary applications for network file systems.
7. True or false: Name space virtualization resolves naming conflicts from different clients.
8. What is SAMBA used for?
9. What protocol was developed for backing up NAS?
10. How does data management differ from storage management?

Upon completing this chapter, you will be able to

- Describe the architectures of data access in clustered systems
- Participate in product evaluations for distributed file system products
- Discuss the implementation of storage used with database systems

CHAPTER 16

New Directions in Network Filing: Clustered File Systems, Distributed File Systems, and Network Storage for Databases

Traditional file systems are a single point of failure for data access. If a system becomes unavailable, access to the data managed by file systems that were running in it is blocked. Although systems can be built with redundant components and high-availability architectures, they can still fail—and their file systems along with them.

Obviously, there is a need to create redundancy for the file system itself. One way to do that is through the use of clustering technology. While clustering is often thought of as an advanced topic in systems, one can make a convincing argument that the primary purpose of clustering is to provide redundant file system access. A cluster cannot work properly if the systems in it do not have access to all the data.

Another shortcoming of traditional file system implementations is scalability. Modern file systems running on single systems can be very large, but past a certain point, their performance suffers. Spreading the file system work over multiple systems gives file systems the parallelism needed to grow in size without losing performance.

Because farm and grid computing are more commonly deployed, it only makes sense to think about the server architectures that provide the best match for them. If tens or hundreds or even thousands of distributed systems are working together in a single application environment, what is the optimal file system architecture? Not a single point of failure with capacity/performance limitations. It's clear that a different type of network filing system is the answer.

This chapter looks at ways to distribute the file system function in system clusters and distributed file system technologies. The chapter closes with a discussion of storage for database systems, first looking at traditional database storage architectures and then looking at storage designs for clustered and grid database architectures.

Cluster File Systems

System clusters are high-availability designs where two or more systems provide mission-critical application support. If a system in the cluster stops working, another system assumes the work without having to stop and restart any applications.

Systems in clusters often have the exact same configurations, including the same type of processors, memory, network adapters, and host bus adapters (HBAs). They also usually have the same software environment, including the operating system level, file system, and application versions.

File systems for clustered systems, referred to as *cluster file systems* (*CFSs*), have special requirements. Traditional file systems typically assume that only one instance of the file system is running on a single machine. Detailed information about the data being accessed and its storage status (in system memory, pending completion to disk media, or on disk) is contained within a single system. In contrast, cluster file systems have to assume that multiple systems are accessing data, each one having a detailed storage status about the data it is working on. If any of them fail, the detailed storage status has to be retrieved by another system so it can finish the task and continue operating. This may involve rolling back interrupted transactions so they can be executed again by another system.

Clustered file systems are designed for distributed operations. File system internal operations such as cache control, locking, and updates to the layout reference system become much more challenging when multiple systems are concurrently working on the same storage address space. For instance, if two systems attempt to access the same data at the same time, how are locks granted and released? If two systems simultaneously access the same data, how do you know where the most recent version of the data is? Is it on disk, or is it in one of the system's memory caches?

Things that seemingly would not interfere with data access must also be considered. For instance, installation and license information written in the superblocks of a clustered file system must be usable by all the systems in the cluster. Likewise, private areas written by volume managers also need to work correctly in clusters.

Basic Cluster Designs

Three basic cluster designs determine cluster file system operations:

- Two-node active/passive clusters
- Multinode active/passive clusters
- Active/active clusters

Two-Node Active/Passive Clusters

The simplest clustering design is a two-node *active/passive cluster* where one of the systems is actively processing the application while the other system is operating in *standby mode*. By isolating the processing and data access to a single system, most of the complexities of cache control, locking, and metadata updates can be avoided. This simple active/passive cluster design is shown in Figure 16-1.

Figure 16-1 *A Two-Node Cluster with Active and Standby Systems*

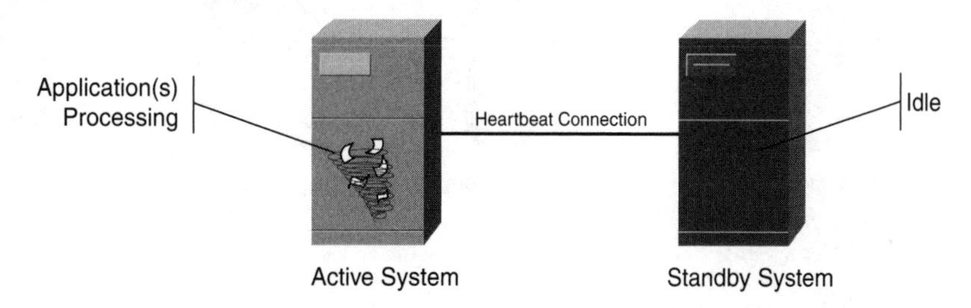

In the design shown in Figure 16-1, the systems are connected by a heartbeat connection. Heartbeats are single-frame, low-latency messages exchanged by systems in a cluster that are used to determine if other systems in the cluster are functioning normally. In the two-node active/passive cluster, if the standby system determines that the active system has failed, it initiates a failover process so it can take over processing operations.

NOTE Some would argue that the two-node active/passive cluster is a just a simple example of the general active/passive clustering approach. I agree, but I believe it's worth singling out because it operates more like a single system than a cluster. The two-node active/passive cluster provides system-level redundancy, but its operating environment is contained in a single system as opposed to being distributed, as it is with other cluster architectures.

Multinode Active/Passive Clusters

An expansion of the two-node active/passive cluster is a multinode (more than two) *n+1 cluster,* where one or more systems are running in standby mode, waiting to take over for other systems that fail. Cache management and locking are necessarily more complicated, because the active systems must have a way of coordinating these functions.

Failover operations involve multiple systems agreeing that another system has failed. The complexity of the failover operation is simplified somewhat by the fact that the standby system can assume the workload of the failed system without having any impact on other application processes it is running.

The multinode active/passive cluster design is shown in Figure 16-2.

Figure 16-2 *An n+1 Active/Passive Cluster*

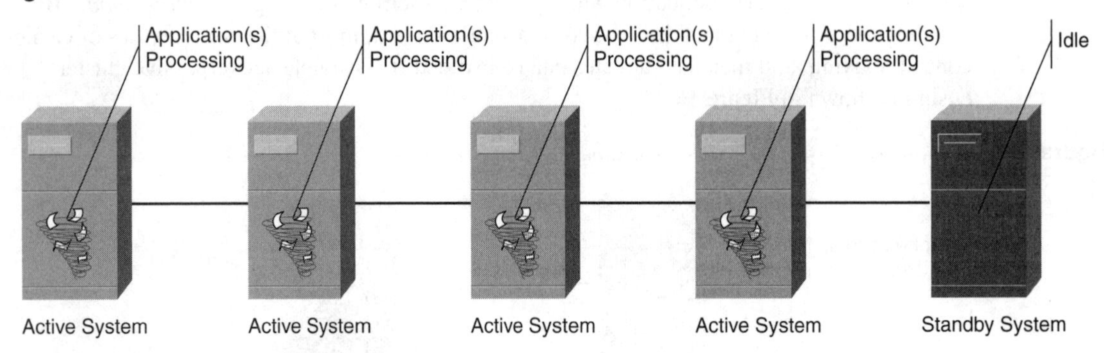

Active/Active Clusters

An *active/active cluster* has two or more systems sharing all responsibilities, including failover operations, without a standby system. All nodes in the cluster determine if another system has failed and distribute the work of the failed system to other nodes. In general, it is the most intricate and scalable cluster design.

An active/active cluster design is shown in Figure 16-3.

Figure 16-3 *An Active/Active Cluster*

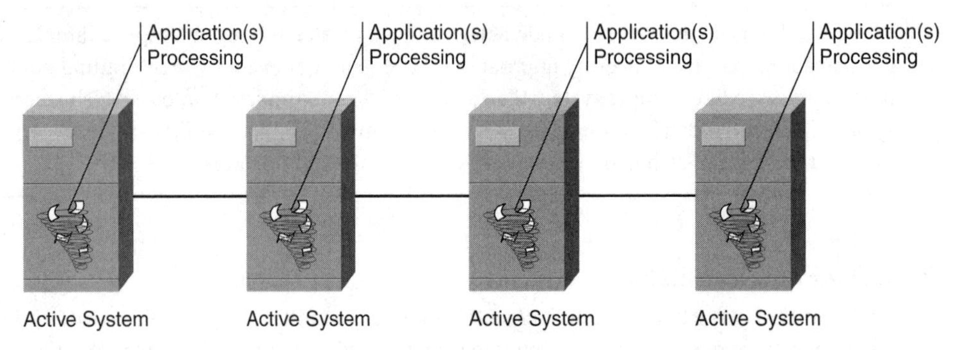

NOTE Database clusters can be done with rip-roaring success using active/active clusters. Some of the fastest database systems on the planet are implemented this way. The Transaction Processing Performance Council (TPC) is an organization that produces benchmark results for database configurations. Active/active clusters are often at the top of the list. The TPC's website has a lot of interesting information about the configurations used, including storage configurations. Interested readers might check them out at http://www.tpc.org.

Two File System Approaches for Clusters: Share Everything or Share Nothing

In addition to the three basic cluster designs, two basic cluster file system designs provide access to data:

- Shared everything
- Shared nothing

These approaches differ significantly in how the layout reference system and locking are handled.

Shared Everything Cluster

Shared everything cluster file systems are designed to give equal access to all storage. Each system in the cluster mounts all storage resources and accesses data as requested by applications. The relationships between servers and storage in a shared everything cluster are depicted in Figure 16-4.

Figure 16-4 *Relationships of Systems and Storage in a Shared Everything Cluster*

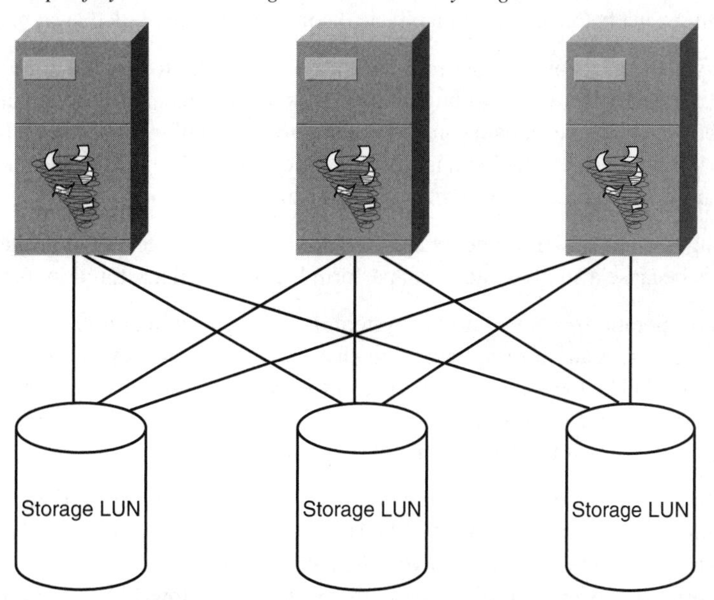

The shared everything approach depends on having a single layout reference system used by all cluster systems to locate file data within the storage address space. As updates occur, layout references are also updated and made available to all cluster systems.

Locking is an intricate process in shared everything clusters. The locking mechanism needs to be able to resolve "ties" where two systems access data simultaneously. It's not as easy as it may seem because there has to be a way to recognize that concurrent access is being made.

Shared Nothing Cluster

Shared nothing cluster file systems combine a traditional file system architecture with a peer-to-peer network communications architecture. Systems in shared nothing cluster file systems have their own "semiprivate" storage, which they access directly like a traditional file system. However, data that is stored on a peer system's storage is accessed using a high-speed peer-to-peer communications facility. A requesting system sends a message to its peer, which accesses the data and transmits it to the requesting system. In clustering terminology, this is sometimes called *cross-shipping* data. Using the shared nothing approach, cluster systems mount only their semiprivate storage, as opposed to mounting all storage like shared everything cluster systems do.

While the storage mountings may be different between shared everything and shared nothing clusters, the physical connections might be exactly the same. Failover processes require the system that assumes the processing load to be able to mount the failed system's storage. This mounting can't be done without a physical connection to the failed system's storage.

Each system has its own layout reference for semiprivate storage but does not have detailed layout references for data residing on peer systems' storage. Nonetheless, all cluster systems must be able to locate all data somehow, using some sort of modified layout references that can locate the server where the data is stored. A two-system design is easiest; if the data is not in the local layout reference system, it is in the other one.

Locking is much easier to understand in shared nothing clusters than in shared everything clusters because a single system can perform locking for data stored in its semiprivate storage.

Failover operations require another system in the cluster to mount the failed system's storage and ensure it is ready for use, including ensuring the consistency of data. Considering that a system has failed, there is a reasonable chance that data consistency errors may have occurred. Therefore, journaled file systems are required to quickly identify incomplete I/O operations and minimize the time it takes to resume cluster operations.

The obvious downside of the shared nothing approach is the overhead needed for peer-to-peer communications to cross-ship data. The latency added by cross-shipping data can be minimized through the use of high-speed networking technologies and I/O processes. Even if the intercluster link is not optimized for performance, many low-I/O-rate applications like e-mail can be implemented successfully on shared nothing designs.

Any type of network can be used for cross-shipping data, as long as the performance meets the requirements of the application. For example, a storage area network (SAN) or Gigabit Ethernet local area network (LAN) would likely meet the requirements of many applications.

The relationships between servers and storage for a shared nothing cluster are shown in Figure 16-5.

Figure 16-5 *Relationships of Systems and Storage in a Shared Nothing Cluster*

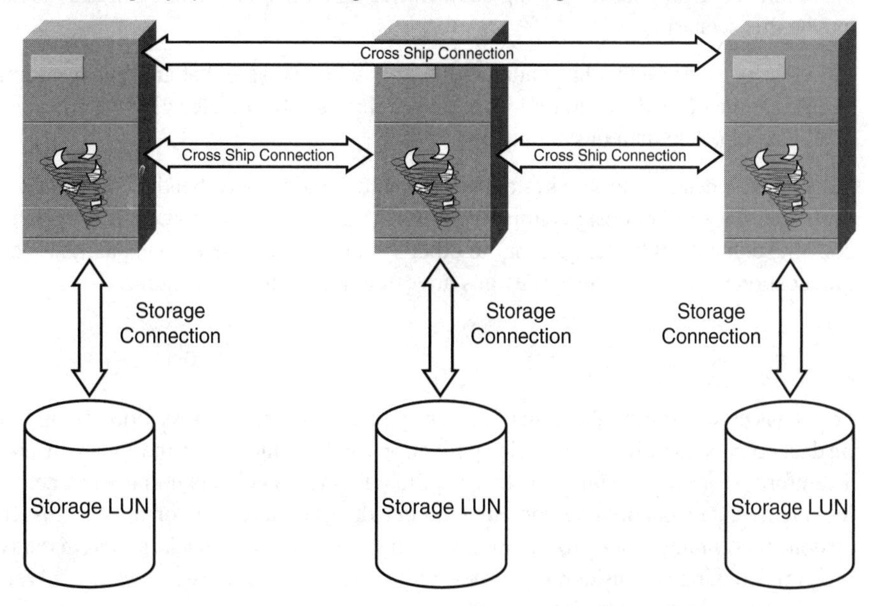

Structural Considerations for Cluster File Systems

Cluster file systems have the same type of structural elements as traditional file systems, but the cluster versions are often altered to fit the requirements of multisystem clusters. Some of the more interesting modifications are discussed in the following sections.

Layout Reference System

All file systems map files and data objects to block address locations through their layout reference system. Clusters add a level of complexity by requiring all changes to the layout reference system to be immediately recognized by all systems in the cluster. If the layout references for a data file are inconsistent among systems in the cluster, the data accessed by an application could also be inconsistent.

Buffer Memory

Traditional file systems place data in buffer (cache) memory. In addition to application data, systems also place system information such as layout reference data in system buffer memory to accelerate storage performance. While this practice works well for file systems in single systems, it creates data consistency quandaries for cluster file system designers.

Data updates written to one system's buffers may be requested shortly thereafter by a second system. If the data is not flushed to disk from the first system before the second system reads it, the second system reads the wrong data. Buffering data in clusters requires a mechanism to handle this scenario.

Conversely, a system that has data in buffers may be unaware that another system may have updated some of its data "behind its back." In this case the cluster file system needs a way to invalidate obsolete data in system buffers.

Some cluster designs disable system buffering to avoid the overhead of constantly "snooping" buffer memory. Other designs implement mirrored cache, or mirrored memory, where systems copy the contents of buffer memory to other systems in the cluster using a high-speed link. For practical reasons, these cluster designs are often limited to two systems.

Locking

Locking is used to reserve the right of certain applications or users to perform certain I/O operations on data objects. In a cluster, a single application can have modules running on different systems. Therefore, shared everything clusters require a locking mechanism that all systems use. This locking mechanism could be implemented in a distributed fashion on all systems. It also could be done by running a lock process on one of the systems (with a backup system ready to assume the job). Locking is considerably easier with shared nothing clusters, where only a single system manages the locks for any particular data object.

Journaling

The *journaling* function in a cluster file system records the sequence of all I/O operations for all systems in the cluster. If something occurs that stops the entire cluster, the journal is used to reestablish its last valid data state. Similar to locking, journaling is easier to understand with shared nothing designs than it is with shared everything designs. With shared nothing designs, journaling can be done by a single system to its semiprivate storage. With shared everything designs, there could be many possible ways to implement journaling. A single journal (with backup) could be used, or each system could maintain its own journal record that could be reconciled with other journals through the use of time stamps.

Global Name Space

A file system's name space represents its file and directory contents to applications and users. Just as the layout reference system has to be the same for all systems, the name space must also be uniform across all systems in the cluster so that all systems can locate data accurately. The term used to describe this is *global name space*.

Implementing Storage for Clustered File Systems

Storage implementations should match the requirements of the applications they support. Clusters add their own storage requirements to those imposed by the applications running on them. Some of these are discussed in the following sections.

Multipathing and Clustering

Clustering is similar to I/O multipathing, as discussed in Chapter 11, "Connection Redundancy in Storage Networks and Dynamic Multipathing." The difference is that multipathing provides dual connections from a single system to storage in case one of them should fail, whereas clustering provides access to storage from two different systems. Multipathing is usually used in clustering designs, but it is not an architectural necessity.

Importance of SANs in Clusters

Clustered storage depends on having a connecting technology that allows all systems to access all storage. SANs are by far the easiest way to connect clustered systems and storage, especially for clusters with more than two systems.

Clusters require multiple storage initiators due to the presence of multiple systems, most of them using two initiators in multipathing configurations. Whereas parallel Small Computer Systems Interface (SCSI) was designed primarily for single-initiator connectivity, SANs were designed for multi-initiator environments.

NOTE Although SCSI was designed for single-initiator connectivity, it was—and is—used for multi-initiator schemes also. Multi-initiator SCSI implementations are usually proprietary and expensive, but they do work and provide excellent availability. The point is that SANs make this a whole lot easier.

SAN flexibility is also an important advantage with clusters. Systems and storage can be connected to the cluster SAN without having to stop the operation of the cluster. It may be necessary to stop cluster operations in order to incorporate new elements into the cluster configuration, but it is not necessary to stop operations just to connect the cables.

Uniformity of Storage Address Spaces in Clusters

As described in previous chapters, storage address spaces can be formed by many different techniques. These techniques can also be used with clusters as long as the unique requirements of clusters are considered. For starters, it's essential that all systems in a cluster work with the exact same storage address spaces, however they are generated. If SAN-based virtualization is used, all systems need to use the same virtualization "translation lenses." Similarly, if volume managers are used, all systems must have the same volume definitions. All maintenance operations that impact storage address spaces must be carefully considered to avoid problems.

All systems in the cluster need to use the same type of file system software. While there may be more than one storage address space used by a cluster, and therefore more than one file system, they all need to have the same logical structure, including the location of superblocks, internal reference system data, name spaces, and attributes.

Data Caching in Clusters

Buffer (cache) memory in host systems needs to be distinguished from cache memory implemented in storage subsystems or SAN virtualization systems. In general, I/O latencies should be kept to a minimum in clusters to avoid complicating intricate functions like locking. Subsystem cache can significantly reduce I/O latencies.

Using caching to minimize the mechanical latencies of disk drives is generally a good idea, but the variables of multisystem operations and the possibility of creating inconsistent data must be accounted for. While caching lowers latency, it also increases the possibility of creating inconsistent data.

All possible paths from all servers to storage logical units must be identified and understood for both normal and post-failover operations. *Mirrored* or *shared cache* between two different subsystem controllers can be used to ensure that two distinct I/O paths have access to the same cache contents. With mirrored cache, all logical unit numbers (LUNs) used to access a specific logical unit in a subsystem are given access to the same cache data. Cache in storage should be implemented with battery backup, both for the entire system or subsystem where the cache is located and for the cache memory itself.

The most conservative approach to caching in clusters is to avoid write caching altogether. While caching is likely to be the most effective way to reduce write latencies, several other techniques and technologies can be applied, such as broad spreading of data across a relatively high number of smaller-capacity disk drives and avoiding the RAID 5 write penalty by using mirroring or RAID 10.

Disk Drive Considerations for Clusters

With availability and performance driving the selection of disk technologies for clusters, Fibre Channel and parallel SCSI drives are obvious choices. However, SCSI drives should be used only when they are implemented inside a Fibre Channel storage subsystem.

The command queuing capabilities of both SCSI and Fibre Channel drives increase performance significantly over drives that do not implement command queuing. Serial ATA (SATA) drive manufacturers have developed a similar technology called native queuing, but it is unclear how well SATA native queuing will compare with the stellar results of command queuing in SCSI and Fibre Channel disk drives.

The mean time between failure (MTBF) numbers for clusters should be at least 1 million hours, which also includes server-class SATA drives. ATA drives are relatively poor choices for high-availability, high-performance cluster environments.

A technique to reduce latency in disk drives is short-stroking, as discussed briefly in Chapter 4, "Storage Devices." By limiting the physical distance that the disk arms must move, the average access time of disk drives can be shortened considerably. The capacity lost by short-stroking may be able to be compensated for by using RAID 10.

NOTE Short-stroking is not necessarily a feature of all disk subsystems, even though it would be relatively simple to add in a disk partitioning utility. Reducing the usable capacity of disk drives in a storage subsystem might seem stupid, but it's not—especially when performance is the ultimate goal. For the fastest storage, minimize mechanical latencies and get as many disk actuators as possible involved in doing the work in parallel.

RAID Levels for High Availability and Performance in Clusters

Emphasizing performance over capacity, the best RAID levels for cluster storage are RAID 1 and RAID 10. There is no reason to slow the processing of write I/Os due to the write penalty of RAID 5. RAID 10 provides the best performance by allowing data to be striped across many sets of mirrored pairs. Not only that, but RAID 10 can survive the loss of more than one disk drive in the array. As the size of arrays increases, this becomes much more significant.

If higher levels of data availability are needed to guarantee data availability after the loss of two disk drives, it is possible to use double parity protection. For instance, the concept of RAID 6 uses an additional parity calculation besides XOR and writes parity information to two separate disks.

NAS Clusters

Traditional network attached storage (NAS) systems are single points of failure for the clients that access files through them. A web server farm that depends on a single NAS system has a realistic risk of having its entire website risk go down due to a problem with the NAS system. To address this, some NAS vendors have implemented clustering technology in their products.

Beyond the obvious availability benefits of clustered NAS, clustering can also be used to increase the capacity of a NAS system. For instance, if a single NAS system has a maximum capacity of 10 terabytes, a two-system cluster could have a maximum capacity of 20 terabytes. Clusters also can be used to improve performance by doubling the number of network file services and I/O channels. Even shared nothing designs that cross-ship data can improve performance if the intercluster connections and processes are fast enough.

NAS clusters can use any combination of cluster designs, including active/active or active/passive failover and shared nothing or shared everything storage designs. All systems in a NAS cluster export the same name space for clients to access data in the cluster. Any data caching done by NAS cluster systems needs to have a mechanism to prevent the loss of data consistency.

NOTE An example of NAS clustering can be found in Network Appliance Filer products. Netapp implements NAS clustering with two-node, active/active, shared nothing clusters. Data consistency is assured through mirrored memory that is carried over a high-speed link between the two systems.

Super-Scaling Network File Systems with SAN-Based Distributed File Systems

The concepts used in cluster file systems and NAS clusters can be extended to larger network file system implementations. A distributed file system (DFS) is another variation on the traditional file system design. A DFS runs the various functions of a file system on multiple systems that communicate over one or more networks.

Distributed file systems address several fundamental storage requirements and storage management needs. First and foremost, they provide excellent file system scalability without risking data loss due to system failures. Second, they provide excellent throughput for distributed applications such as cluster or grid-based databases. More importantly, the performance can scale independently of capacity for some applications, allowing administrators to build customized file system environments tuned to the needs of their applications.

Many different DFS designs have been made over the years that include different types of networks, including LANs, WANs, and SANs. One of the difficulties with understanding DFS technologies is the number of possible relationships that can be established between the various distributed file system functions, the systems they run on, the storage address spaces they work with, and the storage where data is located. To simplify matters in this book, the focus is limited to DFS designs that integrate SAN networks as the storage interconnect.

DFS Designs

DFS designs include the following elements:

- Farm-style redundancy
- Global name space
- Application integration or separation
- Layout reference system location
- Integrated volume manager
- Distributed or centralized lock manager
- Expanded metadata (optional)

Farm-Style Redundancy

Distributed file systems differ from cluster file systems by using a server farm approach to achieve high availability. DFS designs assume off-the-shelf, low-cost servers that may have completely different hardware and software configurations running common file system software and communication functions. High availability is achieved through multiple, redundant DFS servers; if one server or connection fails, another server provides access to files. File system journaling can be used to determine the status of I/O processes that were in progress when a failure or error occurred.

Unlike cluster file systems, the internal memory states of servers in a DFS are not replicated between each other. There are no assumptions about the reliability and speed of the connections between servers in most DFS farms. In fact, it is not necessary for all servers in a DFS farm to be able to communicate with each other, as long as there is a way for all of them to share information. For that reason, SAN-oriented distributed file systems are more likely to use shared everything designs, because shared nothing cross-shipping between servers cannot be assumed.

There are many ways to design a distributed file system. Options include the location of the various file system functions, their relationships, and how they are managed.

Global Name Space

Similar to cluster file systems, distributed file systems have a global name space that clients and applications use to identify files and data objects. Any client should be able to access any DFS server and be presented with the same view of the file system.

The global name space for an average DFS is much larger than an average traditional file system, resulting in longer searches for data objects and long data management processes, such as backup and virus scanning. To address the potential management problems resulting from very large name spaces, a DFS can be designed with name space filters that subdivide the work of management applications that traditionally "walk" the entire file system.

Application Integration or Separation

DFSs can run alongside applications in systems or be accessed over the network like network file systems. Figures 16-6 and 16-7 illustrate the differences in the two approaches. Figure 16-6 shows a web server farm with a DFS running in each of the web servers. Each web server has direct access to storage.

Figure 16-6 *A DFS Running in Web Server Systems*

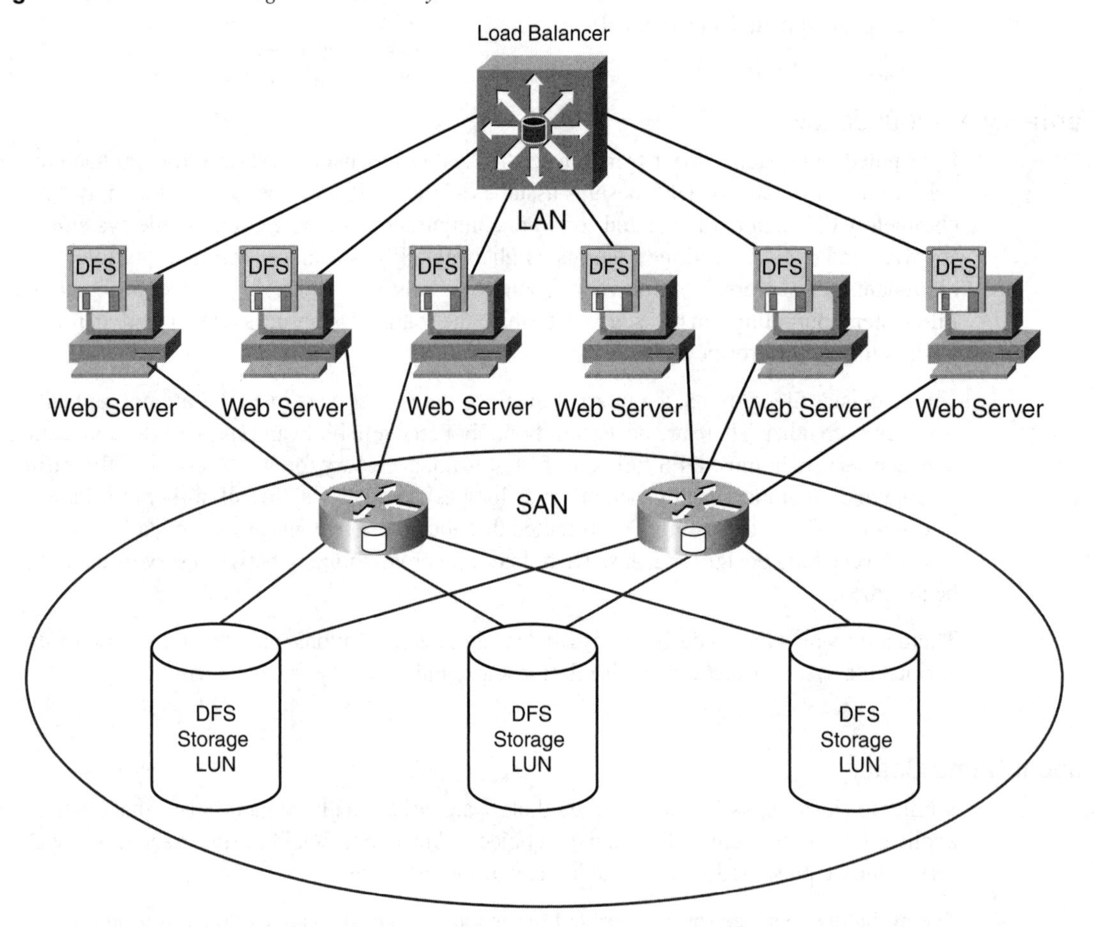

The size of the name space and the resources needed to process it can influence the decision on integrating the name space with an application system.

Figure 16-7 shows a web server farm that accesses a DFS using NFS, where the DFS software runs on dedicated DFS servers, each having direct access to storage. This diagram also shows a load-balancing switch between the web servers and the DFS servers that spreads the work among different DFS servers.

Figure 16-7 *Web Servers Accessing Data Through DFS Systems Using NFS*

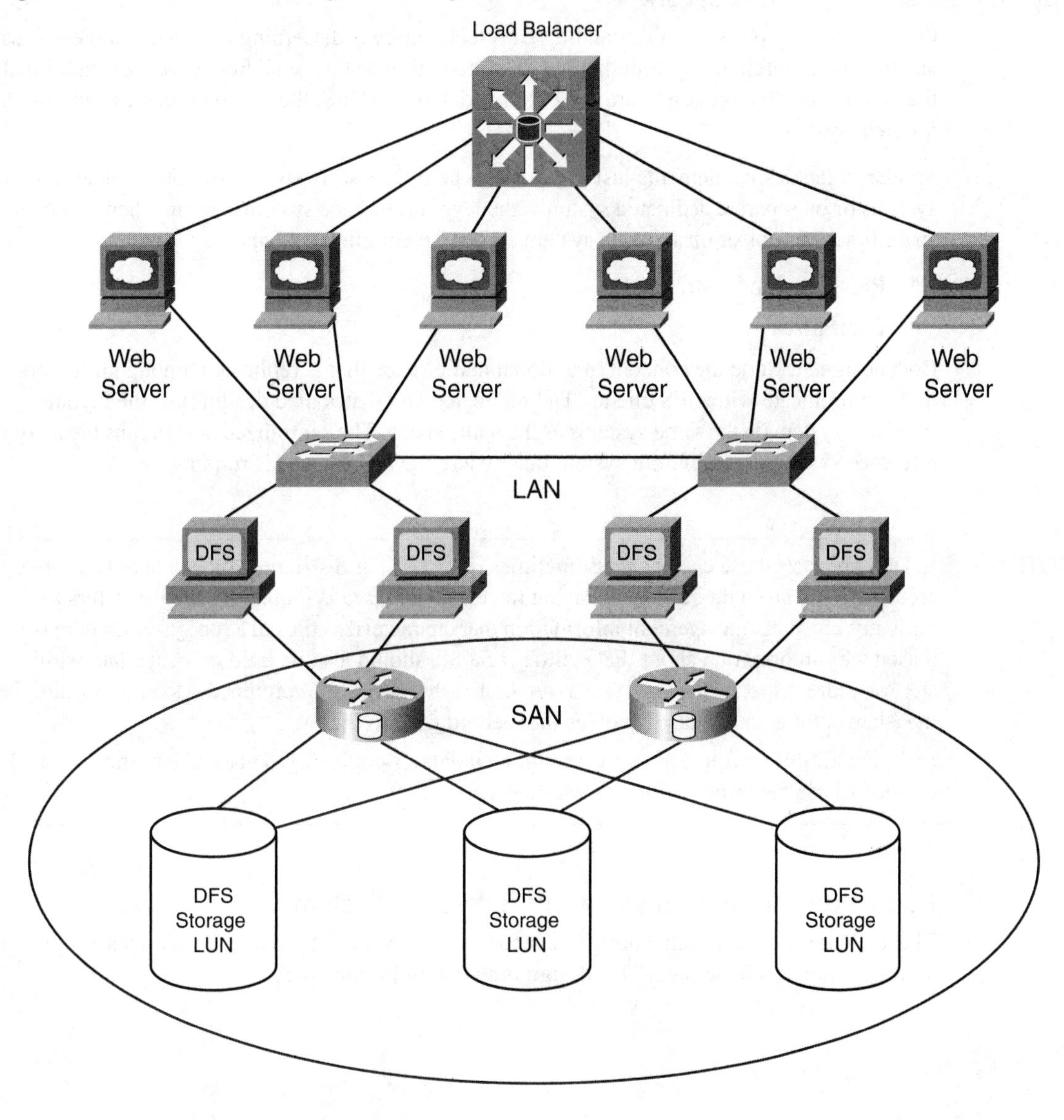

A DFS implementation can also mix the two approaches. Some servers could run on application systems, while others could service different applications over a network connection. All DFS server nodes would still access the same storage.

Layout Reference System Location

One of the tricky parts of understanding DFS technology is discerning between storage access and the layout reference system that locates data within a storage address space. In traditional file systems the two processes are closely linked, but in a DFS, these two processes can run on different systems.

Similar to the design elements just discussed, where DFS software can run on applications systems or on separate dedicated systems, the layout reference system can run where the name space function runs or on separate systems. The two common designs are

- Replicated and distributed
- Centralized

Both designs include the concept of a global name space that is replicated among all servers that communicate with DFS clients. The replicated and distributed design runs the layout reference system on the same systems as the name space. The centralized design runs the layout reference system on a different system than where the name space is running.

NOTE In DFS products these designs are sometimes referred to as distributed metadata or centralized metadata. The problem I have with using the term *metadata* is that metadata also refers to attributes and data management information that characterizes files in a file system. There is no reason why information about the qualities of a file should also be used to locate data within a storage address space. It's important to remember that the layout reference system is not simply the address for data, but also involves the method used to find it.

Lumping all this stuff under a single term, metadata, is confusing. That's one of the reasons I decided to use the term *layout reference system*.

Replicated and Distributed Layout Reference System

The replicated and distributed design depends on all servers that provide file services also being able to locate data in storage. This design is shown in Figure 16-8.

Figure 16-8 *A Replicated and Distributed Layout Reference System in a DFS Design*

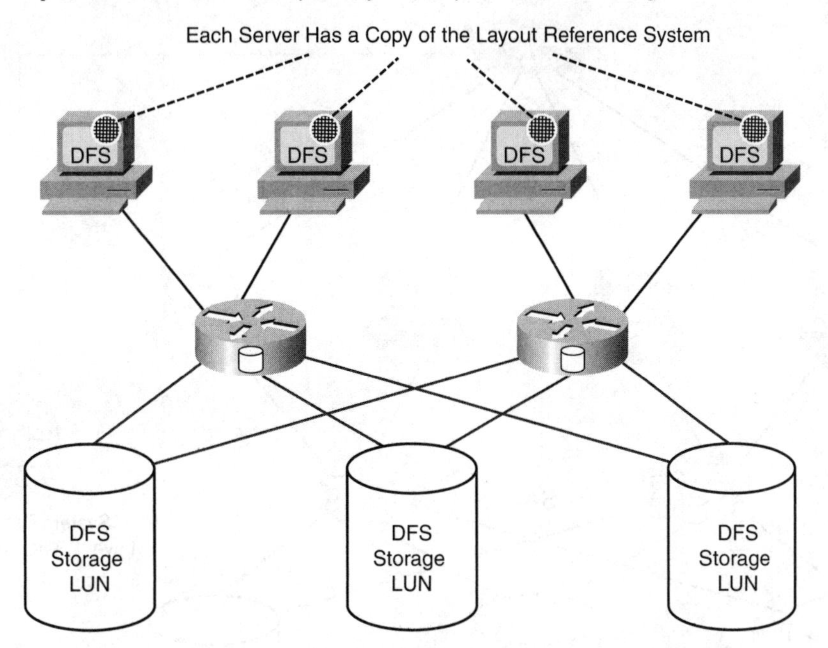

As changes are made to the distributed file system, the layout reference system in each server has to be updated too. This can be done a number of ways, including the use of an update protocol that is similar in function those used for network routing tables. The method that is used can have a significant impact on the capacity scaling of the file system. It is possible for a distributed file system like this to have hundreds of servers, although 8 to 16 servers are more commonly deployed.

Centralized Layout Reference System

Centralizing the layout reference system on another single system provides optimal administrative control over the layout reference system and other file system functions, such as metadata. Doing this establishes the layout reference system as a network service to the name space servers in a DFS. A basic, centralized layout reference system design is shown in Figure 16-9.

Figure 16-9 *DFS with a Centralized Layout Reference System*

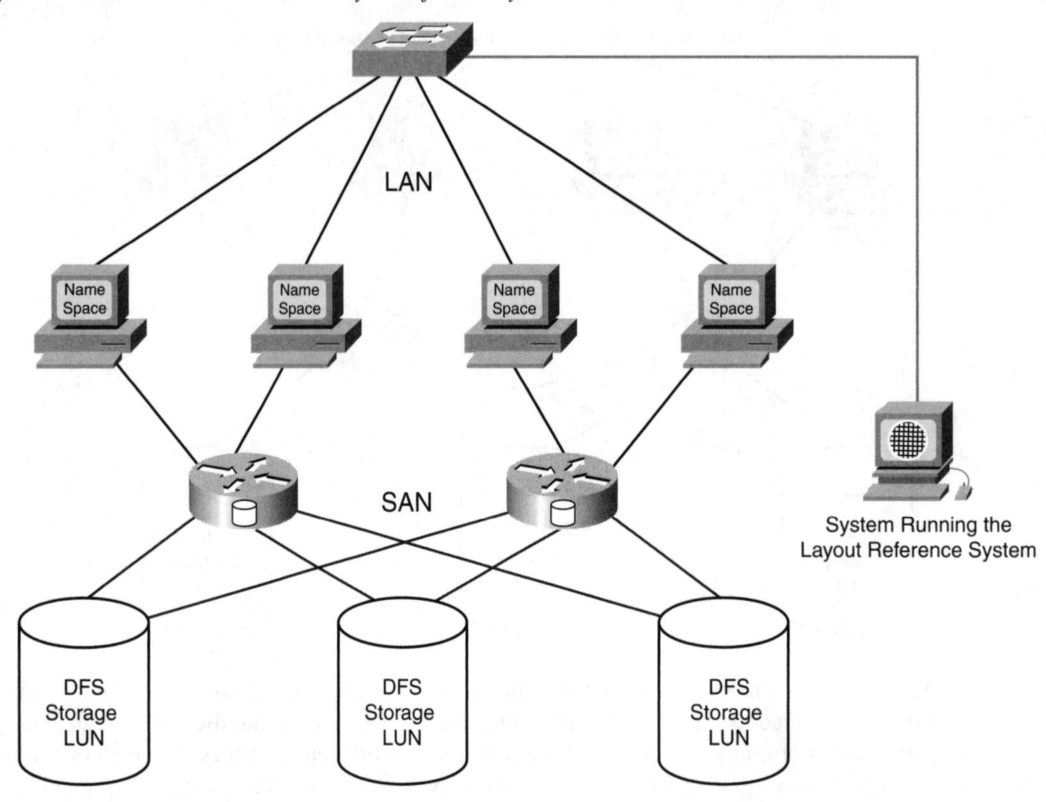

The network used for communication between the DFS name space servers and the layout reference server is shown as a LAN in Figure 16-9. The SAN could also be used by employing a messaging protocol in addition to serial SCSI.

However, the single system running the layout reference system is a single point of failure. For that reason, clustering is typically used for the systems running the layout reference function. These are tightly coupled cluster systems, not loosely coupled systems running as a farm.

Integrated Volume Manager

The layout reference system provides a way to locate data in the storage address space of the DFS. But before this can work as advertised, the DFS needs to assemble the various storage address spaces in the SAN into a complete address space. The assembly of multiple storage address spaces is traditionally not a file system function, but a volume management function. There is no implication of mirroring, RAID, or other traditional volume management features, although these could be part of the feature set of a DFS.

Distributed or Centralized Lock Manager

The lock manager manages all data locks in a DFS. With the potential of having tens or hundreds of systems accessing data in a DFS, locking is a critical function to enforce data consistency.

In general, the design choices for lock managers are similar to those for the layout reference system. The two options are either a distributed or centralized lock manager. Unlike the distributed layout reference system, the lock manager does not necessarily have to be replicated, as long as all systems can access the lock information they need when data access occurs. Designs with a centralized layout reference system typically run the centralized lock manager in the same system(s).

Expanded Metadata (Optional)

A DFS can accommodate expanded metadata to help administrators manage storage and data. Data could have many characteristics associated with it, such as a relative priority for backup or thresholds for minimal I/O performance. The ability to classify data for redundancy, performance, and management purposes could prove to be very helpful to administrators as the amount of stored data continues to increase. Expanded metadata can also be used to facilitate policy-based data management.

Advantages of Distributed File Systems

New distributed file system architectures have the potential to offer several key advantages over traditional file system designs:

- Modular scalability and performance tuning
- Storage quality of service (QoS)
- Dynamic address space expansion
- Storage migration
- Data snapshots

Modular Scalability and Performance Tuning

A distributed file system can be thought of as a modular file system with both system and storage modules. Understood this way, a DFS can scale its capacity or its performance or both by increasing one or more of its modules. The ability to add servers or storage in response to application requirements provides a way to tune the DFS.

For instance, a hypothetical web server farm with 25 web servers might store an enormous amount of static data that is rarely updated with only moderate I/O traffic. In that case, a DFS system for the web farm might need only three or four servers running DFS software but connect to 40 or more storage subsystems over a SAN. All DFS servers would be able to access all storage on behalf of the web servers. In this case, the DFS resembles a NAS head, but with built-in redundancy and data sharing between all servers.

Another DFS configuration could involve eight clustered database systems running a high-performance transaction application. Assuming there is not that much data in the database, this could be supported by two disk subsystems. In this case, each database system could have its own dedicated DFS server, which would have redundant access to each of the two subsystems.

In addition to the number of systems used in the DFS, the technology implemented in systems can change too. One obvious change involves upgrading the system/processor technology used in DFS server systems. For instance, each server in a DFS farm could be replaced one at a time by a newer, faster system. Eventually all the systems could have faster processors without interrupting the operations of the DFS at any time.

Storage for Tiered Storage

Distributed file systems with expanded metadata could indicate QoS levels to match data and storage requirements in tiered storage implementations.

For instance, a DFS QoS assignment could be used to select storage tiers for different types of data. It could also be used to determine the block size to be used for individual data files. This is not to say that each file could request a special block size, but it is certainly possible for a DFS to identify and use certain ranges of address spaces within the system that have different characteristics. This way, a single DFS could theoretically be used to accommodate both small block transaction data and large block multimedia streaming data.

A DFS could reserve specific storage tiers for certain applications. For instance, a specific application could have its data written to an optimized storage tier, while other applications would write data to a common storage pool.

Dynamic Address Space Expansion

A DFS can expand the size of its storage address space by adding storage to the SAN and assigning it to the DFS. New storage address spaces could be appended to the existing address space of the DFS without interrupting operations. Data could be spread over the new, larger address space, or the new address space could simply be placed in the free pool of the file system. The redistribution of data over the new, larger address space is not necessarily a requirement for all applications.

Storage Migration

The modularity of storage in a DFS facilitates storage configuration changes. However, unlike servers, which can practically be swapped out at will, data resides on storage and must be copied from the outgoing subsystem to the incoming subsystem. A DFS design can include the ability to transparently copy data from old storage to new and manage all I/O activity to prevent data consistency errors.

This capability allows storage administrators to deploy a variety of storage products and adjust to changes in their environment. The incoming storage could be newer, older, faster, or slower than the existing storage, which may be needed elsewhere or at the end of its useful life.

Data Snapshots

Chapter 17, "Data Management," discusses point-in-time data snapshots as a way of capturing historical versions of data for archiving and to comply with regulations for retaining data. Some DFS products offer this capability as an integrated feature.

Network Storage for Databases

Database systems can function either as filing entities in storage networks or as applications that use the services of a file system. The remainder of this chapter briefly discusses the relationship between databases and file systems.

Database Filing: Raw Partitions

Databases that provide their own filing functions are said to be running "raw partitions." A raw partition is a storage address space that is unoccupied by a file system. The way it is commonly used in the context of database discussions, raw partition implies a storage address space managed by a database system and accessed through its own internal layout reference system.

Until recently, database administrators (DBAs) favored using raw partitions for the performance advantages they offered. The rationale used for raw partitions was that the database system had the most efficient processes for locating its own data on disk and that working through a file system to locate data was too slow.

The other problem with storing database data in a file system was the risk that the file system would cache data in system buffers and not write it to disk immediately. A system crash that prevented data from being flushed to storage would result in the loss of data consistency and the ensuing long and costly work restoring the database to a functioning state.

Storing Databases on File Systems

The problem with using raw partitions is data management. All storage and data management processes with raw partitions must use facilities provided in the database, because there is no other way to identify database components in storage. These database internal processes tend to take a long time to run and can severely impact the performance of the database while they are running.

As it turns out, most DBAs run their databases on file system storage because it is much more flexible than raw partitions. In addition, data management applications like backup and recovery are much simpler if the database is being run on a file system. This is not a problem as long as file system caching does not risk data consistency by holding write data in system cache. A facility called *direct I/O* is used with some databases to ensure write caching is not used by a file system storing database data.

The storage software company Veritas has a technology called Quick I/O that creates a virtual raw partition within a special file in the Veritas VxFS file system. The Quick I/O file is mounted like a device by the database system, which accesses it like a raw partition. However, the contents of the file can be copied during backup or other data management processes just like any other file.

Oracle 10g Automated Storage Manager

The newest version of the Oracle database system, Oracle 10g, ships with a facility called Automated Storage Manager (ASM). ASM provides a volume manager function to create storage address spaces from available storage and then creates a proprietary Oracle file system to store database files, in accordance with Oracle database tuning algorithms. ASM assumes that storage management for its 10g database can be provided more effectively by an automated function in the Oracle database than it can by an Oracle DBA.

ASM is considerably different from the old raw partition method. Database administrators were responsible for configuring the raw partitions that formed database storage. Oracle had its own layout reference system that it used to locate data within a raw partition. In contrast, ASM is a complete automated storage environment manager, including low-level storage redundancy. The file system created by ASM is not mountable by the host operating system and is managed entirely by Oracle. It remains to be seen whether the remaining Oracle tools for backup and recovery as well as remote copy will compare with methods that use file systems.

Database Data Types

Databases create two basic types of data during their normal operations: log data and tablespace data.

Log Data

Database logs are similar to file system journals (actually, file system journaling was modeled after database logging designs). They write the intent of every I/O in the system, and they acknowledge their completion after the operation finishes. Logging I/Os allows a DBA to find the exact state of a database when an unexpected shutdown occurred and restore the database data to a consistent, reliable state.

Databases often employ multiple log files (three or more) and use them in rotation. After a log file has been actively logging I/Os for a prescribed amount of time, it is taken out of use and replaced by another log file. The deactivated log file can be copied by an archiving process for historical purposes. When the log file is needed again by the database rotation, it is activated and overwritten by the next logging session.

Log data files are unusual in two ways: they are used exclusively for writing (while they are active), and they are written to sequentially. Because every I/O must be logged, and log data must be written to disk and acknowledged, the log data storage is an obvious potential bottleneck for the database system. For that reason, many administrators elect to use mirrored storage for log files to avoid the RAID 5 write penalty. (See Chapter 9, "Bigger, Faster, More Reliable Storage with RAID," for a discussion of the RAID 5 write penalty.)

Tablespace Data

Tablespaces contain the data stored by the database system and used by applications. This is the data that most people think of when they think of a database. Tablespace data is used for transaction processing, reports, and many types of data analysis.

Tablespaces can be large and involve many concurrent I/O operations. The rule of thumb for tablespace data is to stripe the data across a large number of drives to reduce the likelihood of disk contention on a single disk drive.

Database Backup and Business Continuity

Backup and recovery of databases is normally a specialized task requiring the oversight and involvement of DBAs. Large databases are rarely backed up in their entirety, but instead are backed up in parts.

Database log files are sometimes used as part of the business continuity plan. The log files can be applied by a log file utility in the database to re-create the transactions and the state of the database. This is an application of delta, or difference, redundancy, which was introduced in Chapter 8, "An Introduction to Data Redundancy and Mirroring."

Databases and Network Storage

Databases can run in a variety of network storage environments, including SANs, NAS, and distributed file systems.

Databases and SANs

Databases can connect to SAN-based storage without much difficulty or trouble. They typically are implemented in SANs using a variety of fencing methods, including LUN masking, zoning, and virtual SANs (VSANs).

Databases and NAS

One of the more controversial topics in the storage industry over the last decade has been whether it is safe to store database data on NAS file systems. For the most part, this has been resolved positively for most applications. Many databases stored on NAS systems depend on clustered NAS for high availability.

In essence, the database system creates its files on NAS systems and processes transaction I/Os by making file byte-range requests for data in the NAS file system. Gigabit Ethernet and fiber-optic cables are recommended as the connecting network between the database and NAS systems. Transmission Control Protocol/Internet Protocol (TCP/IP) may be required, as opposed to User Datagram Protocol/Internet Protocol (UDP/IP), to guarantee in-order delivery of data. Just as direct I/O is used to bypass file system write caching on local file systems, direct I/O may be needed on the NAS system also.

Databases and Distributed File Systems

Distributed database systems can use a distributed file system for storing their database data. This is not much different from storing a database system on a NAS system, except the file system is provided by a DFS farm instead of a NAS cluster. Some DFS products, such as the IBM SAN File System, support direct I/O and can be used to store very large databases.

Summary

This chapter introduced a few more advanced topics in file systems used in network storage: cluster file systems, distributed file systems, and database systems.

Cluster file systems have to support the application and failover requirements of cluster operations. Two basic storage architectures are used with clusters: shared everything and shared nothing. Shared everything clusters provide the best performance and scalability, but shared nothing cluster storage is much simpler for the purposes of locking and memory mirroring.

Distributed file systems were then discussed as a way to implement the basic concepts of network file systems, but in a server farm environment. The chapter closed with a brief survey of the relationships between database systems and network storage technology. Several options are available for database storage controlled by a distributed file system.

Q & A

1. What are the two kinds of cluster storage designs?
2. Why is locking more important for a cluster file system than a traditional file system?
3. True or false: You typically do not have to worry about data in host buffers with a cluster file system.
4. Why are SANs valuable for cluster file systems?
5. True or false: NAS clusters are used primarily to increase storage capacity.
6. What is the main difference between a cluster file system and a DFS farm?
7. What are two ways to implement a lock manager for a distributed file system?
8. What is the purpose of direct I/O?
9. Database logs are an example of what kind of redundancy technique?

Upon completing this chapter, you will be able to

- Participate in meetings and discussions with coworkers regarding data redundancy methods for your organization
- Discuss point-in-time solutions within your organization and with vendors
- Participate in meetings and discussions about regulatory compliance for data storage and ILM

CHAPTER 17

Data Management

In many respects, the most challenging aspect of managing any storage environment is managing the data stored in it. Companies are inundated with data from many different sources, including office applications, databases, financial and accounting applications, e-mail, the Internet, and custom applications that support specific business operations. Once data is generated or received, it can be stored in any number of storage facilities, including e-mail storage, databases and data warehouses, file servers, and backup systems. The problem is that once data is stored it can become practically invisible and very difficult to find.

Regardless of how or where data originates, the IT organization is responsible for taking care of it. In fact, it can be argued that data stewardship is the most important responsibility for systems administrators today. As system hardware becomes increasingly commoditized, the relative importance of data continues to increase. If data availability is expected to be "five-nines" to support the business mission, data must be preserved without corruption and maintained to provide efficient operations.

NOTE I expect most readers have had the experience of looking for a data file and having trouble finding it. Heck, I had that happen more than a few times in the course of writing this book. Now that my laptop has a 40-GB disk drive, it is truly a cavernous hazard for my "no-nines" neuron-ball.

In the last several years governments around the world have created an astonishing number of regulations enforcing the long-term retention of data. This new legal environment has cast a confused light on the area of data management and inspired interest in the latest incarnation of corporate data management: Information Life Cycle Management (ILM).

This chapter takes a brief survey of data management technologies and practices used in storage networks today. Among the topics covered are point-in-time snapshots, historical versions of files and data archiving, regulations compliance, capacity management, and ILM.

Managing Data in Time

Data exists in time. It is originally created when it is first saved as a file or entered as a record in a database. From then on, the data may be actively used by applications and updated, or it may be static and unchanged. Many data management technologies are designed to recover or regenerate data as it was at some previous time. In general, there are two primary reasons for managing data by its time variables:

- To recreate a system state
- To access a previous version of data

Recreating a System State Through Point-in-Time Snapshot Technology

Business continuity is a discipline with the goal of resuming normal operations following some type of disaster. For many businesses, the primary responsibility of business continuity is making sure that data and data processing equipment are available and operating correctly. This means complete data integrity and consistency must be maintained in all copies of data that may be used to re-create a complete system state in the future.

Backup technology (see Chapter 13, "Network Backup: The Foundation of Storage Management") and remote copy technology (see Chapter 10, "Redundancy Over Distance with Remote Copy") are the primary applications that have been used to protect data from loss during a disaster. Backup allows companies to create copies of data on tape. Unfortunately, backups can take a long time to run, and maintaining consistency requires live backup operations using copy-on-write. This causes problems on production servers by overloading their CPU capacity.

Remote copy provides a way to transfer data between physically separated disk storage subsystems. Unfortunately, maintaining consistency is challenging with active applications where data is constantly being updated and transferred. Even though the forwarding and receiving controllers in a remote copy system may accurately monitor the communications process, there may still be unaccounted for data stored in host system buffers at any particular time, creating potential data consistency errors. It is necessary to periodically ensure data consistency by emptying host buffers and synchronizing data at local and remote sites.

The fundamental goal of business continuity is to be able to resume computing operations from a recent point in time where the data is known to be complete and consistent. A technology designed for that purpose is called point-in-time copy, also known as snapshot technology. Many companies use point-in-time snapshot products along with both their backup and remote copy applications in their business continuity practices.

Three common approaches are used to create point-in-time copies of data, as discussed in the following sections:

- Whole volume snapshots
- Volume delta snapshots
- File system snapshots

Whole Volume Snapshots

A simple concept for creating a point-in-time copy of storage is to detach (stop the connection) from one of the redundant storage subsystem logical unit numbers (LUNs), thereby creating a snapshot of the entire volume at the time the storage was detached. Sometimes the process of detaching is referred to as "breaking the mirror."

NOTE Remember that secondary storage can be physically located nearby or far away from primary storage, even though a "remote copy" application is being used to create the redundant data.

To be precise, the point-in-time copy is usually created immediately after the host system has flushed its buffers and when the host system has temporarily stopped writing and updating data. The remote storage subsystem is then disconnected logically or physically from the host system or the subsystem running the remote copy application, preserving the state of data at that point in time. This is also called *taking a snapshot* of the data.

The data snapshot that is created has a file system image complete with all on-disk file system components, including the superblock, metadata, and layout reference system. Other systems running the same file system software can connect to this storage, mount the file system, and commence operations.

A whole volume snapshot scenario is illustrated in Figure 17-1, where three storage targets are being used to store data for a host system. Primary storage targets A and A' are mirrored by a host process and ready to accept I/Os from the host system. The snapshot target, which had been receiving writes from a host-based process has been disconnected from the host system and now has a connection established with the data management system.

Figure 17-1 *A Whole Volume Snapshot with a Data Management System Accessing Snapshot Target Storage*

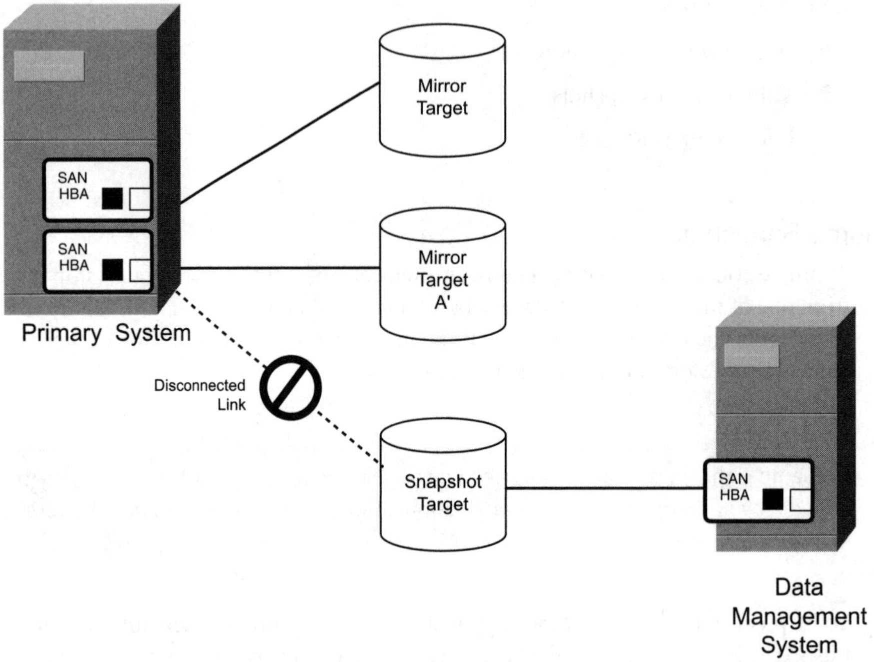

After the snapshot target is connected to the data management system and the file system in it has been mounted, the data management system is free to run any application against the data, including backup. The advantage of running backup on a snapshot target is that cold backups can be run at high speed without impacting the performance of primary storage and its applications. Another common use for point-in-time copies is for system testing. Many point-in-time systems were sold in 1998 and 1999 to help companies with their Y2K testing.

After the point-in-time copy has been processed by the data management system, the snapshot storage target is disconnected from the data management system and reconnected to the host or the primary subsystem. A process called *resilvering* is performed to populate the reattached target with any data updates that occurred after the snapshot was created.

NOTE The snapshot target in Figure 17-1 could be connected to either a host controller or a forwarding remote copy controller in a storage subsystem. It is even possible for the snapshot target to be located in the same subsystem cabinet as a primary storage target. Whatever. The important point is that the original connection for receiving data updates is re-established in order to resume normal operations.

Volume Delta Snapshots

A point-in-time copy does not have to keep a separate, whole copy of a target. Another approach is based on the concept of keeping all blocks that are overwritten when data updates occur and then accessing those older blocks as they existed at a certain point in time. In other words, it provides a virtual view of the former volume at the time the snapshot operation was run.

The former versions of changed data blocks are sometimes referred to as volume deltas. These volume deltas can be written either into special-purpose snapshot files or volumes. A virtual viewer interface, which is part of the point-in-time snapshot application provides access to point-in-time views of data by merging the views from the original volume and any volume deltas. The point-in-time snapshot application allows the administrator to select which previous version of data to view and then provides the selected version through the virtual viewer. Data management systems can use those virtual views to perform their operations.

Figure 17-2 shows a volume delta snapshot scenario with older-version blocks being copied to a snapshot volume before being overwritten by an update to the primary volume. A viewer application merges the view of data in the primary volume with the view of data in the snapshot volume, overlaying the view of the most recent updates with views of older data versions.

Figure 17-2 *Older Data Is Copied to a Snapshot Volume, Where It Can Be Viewed as a Point-in-Time Snapshot*

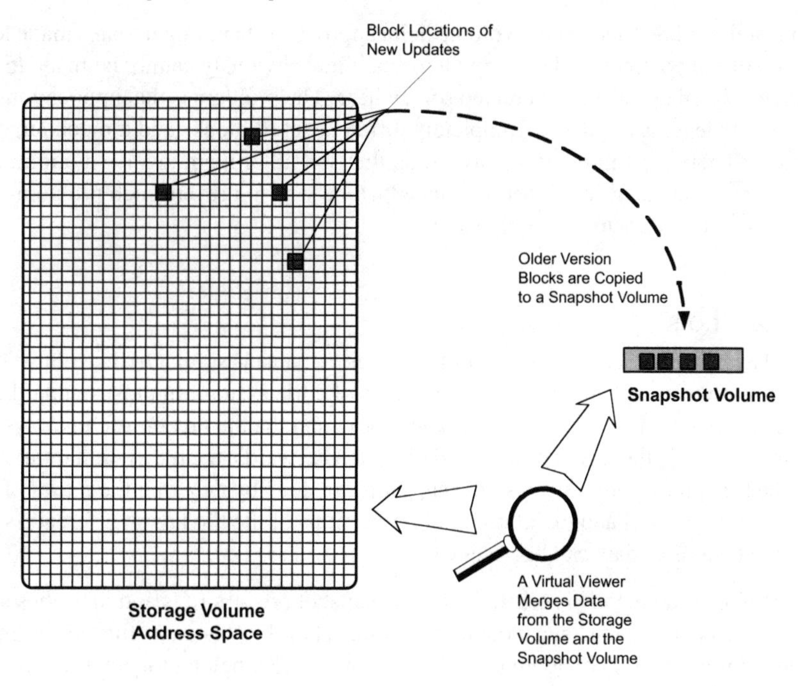

Creating this snapshot involves first flushing host buffers and then closing writes to the volume or file where old blocks are being written. This process is similar to copy-on-write used by backup applications, but this snapshot process copies the older-generation data to long-term snapshot storage instead of temporary storage. When the snapshot viewer is run, it merges the view of the primary storage volume with the view of blocks in snapshot volumes. Assuming that several such snapshot virtual views exist, multiple point-in-time views can be created by merging different combinations of volume deltas.

Notice that all file system components, including the name space and layout reference system, are preserved this way. As long as all the data needed to operate the file system is stored within the volume and snapshot volumes, the volume delta method will be consistent. In fact, updates and writes to data files are made to free blocks, as opposed to overwriting existing blocks. It is possible that the old-version blocks copied to snapshot volumes were never used previously by the file system to store data. However, these "mystery blocks" are not a problem as long as the layout reference system maintains its integrity.

Backup and other processes can be run against the virtual view of the volume. Depending on how the snapshot data structures are organized, and if the storage is located in a SAN, it might be possible for a second system to mount a virtual view of the data and process it with backup or or some other application, offloading data management tasks from the production system.

One of the subtle tricks in the volume delta approach is handling updates made to any snapshot views of the volume. Updates from a virtual view obviously cannot be made to the actual volume, but they have to be created somewhere. The problem is that applications working with a virtual view may update a completely different set of blocks and a much larger group of blocks. There are a number of ways to do this, but all of them involve a fair amount of complexity and additional storage capacity. One way to prevent such problems is to limit volume delta views to read-only status.

File System Snapshots

The last method of creating point-in-time copies of data is similar to the volume delta approach, but it is done completely within the confines of a file system. In most standard file systems, updates to files are made to free storage blocks and the the layout reference system is updated to locate data in those newly allocated blocks. Afterwards, the file system returns the old blocks to the free block pool. File system snapshots are done by delaying the return of old blocks to the free block pool and maintaining older versions of the the layout reference system so these older versions of data can be accessed.

The point-in-time copy is created when a snapshot process runs and identifies all data blocks that have been changed since the previous snapshot. For instance, file system metadata could contain information about which older versions of data belong together in a point-in-time group, allowing them to be viewed and accessed as a virtual, snapshot volume. Access to old files uses the exact same layout reference system that was used when the old file version was still current. Like the other point-in-time copy methods, backup operations can be run against the snapshot view of the file system.

The main difference between the file system snapshot and the whole volume and delta volume methods described previously is the fact that file system snapshot data can be accessed using network file system protocols like NFS and does not rely on storage connectivity over a SAN. While SAN connectivity can be valuable for systems administrators, it has limited applicability for desktop users whose systems are not connected to a SAN.

Practice Good Data Hygiene and Flush Data from Host Buffers

A necessary process to ensure data consistency for point-in-time data is flushing host system buffers before making the point-in-time copy. Data held in file system write cache buffers must be on disk before the point-in-time process begins. The process of flushing host buffers is sometimes referred to as synchronizing the file system.

Syncing the file system can be done several different ways, depending on the implementation details of the various products in use. It can be done manually at the system console, through scripts, and even through programmatic interfaces. One way to make sure cache buffers are flushed is to unmount the file system.

Synchronization may not be necessary if direct I/O is being used, as it often is with database systems. Just the same, it is probably necessary to stop processing briefly when creating a snapshot with data stored under direct I/O to make sure the disconnection process does not occur in the middle of any pending I/Os.

Continuous Volume Snapshots

An interesting variation of point-in-time snapshot technology borrows an idea from mainframe computing, where I/O operations are time-stamped for precision operations and diagnostics. Continuous volume snapshot technology is based on the concept of logging all write I/Os and assigning a time value to each. This approach is similar to file system or database journaling, but the journal is at the storing (block) level and includes fine-granularity time designations. In essence this is an extremely precise, small-granularity application of delta redundancy technology.

There are many possible ways this technology can be structured—none of them easy. That said, the capability provided could be very valuable to database administrators and systems administrators for other high-performance applications. By correlating time values with I/O operations and keeping accurate logs, it is possible to roll the software state forward and backward in microsecond intervals and find the most recent consistent data state to operate from.

NOTE Continuous snapshot is definitely an application that would benefit from the use of direct I/O to bypass host buffers. If the goal is to recover from almost any point in time, why would you prevent that from happening by holding necessary write data in cache buffers?

File Replication

Another technology used for business continuity purposes is file replication. File replication is a process where a software agent monitors file system activity and sends changed file data to another system, usually over a TCP/IP network. Replication can be scheduled to run at regular intervals or as a continuous operation. Replication transmissions can be done over LAN or WAN networks.

To differentiate from remote copy, where data blocks are sent without any knowledge of their context, file replication processes identify the file in which a change has occurred. A data transfer process sends either the entire file or just the byte range changes for the file. If byte range changes are transmitted, the receiving replication system applies them to the file to re-create the new version.

Replication does not communicate file system layout reference information; instead, the receiving system stores replicated files in its own file system. That means multiple sending systems can replicate data to a single receiving system that stores the data under a separate directory structure.

There can be communication cost advantages to using file replication. Only files that are selected for replication are transmitted, compared to remote copy, where all writes are transmitted. This allows systems that support multiple applications to have their highest-priority data transmitted to another system. Replication can also be used with backup to reduce the load on production servers. For instance, a system could replicate files for a high-availability application and back them up on the receiving system instead of the primary production system.

Historical Versions of Files

While business continuity may be the most pressing application of historical data management, there are several compelling reasons to keep copies of historical versions of files:

- Intellectual property documentation and protection
- Compliance with government regulations
- Human fallibility (protein robot malfunction)
- Multiuse applications

Intellectual property includes many different things such as patents, copyrights, marketing plans, corporate plans, and various other corporate documents and data files. Disputes over the rights to own, access, and control intellectual property are settled based on accurate records and documentation proving when a company or person invented or acquired it. There are many good reasons to keep all electronic documents related to a company's intellectual property.

Corporate tax law in many countries requires data to be retained for a number of years in support of possible tax audits and disputes. However, today new government requirements, such as the Sarbanes-Oxley Act in the United States, mandate the retention of electronic records of all kinds of corporate data, including e-mails and instant messaging. Other regulations regarding customer and patient privacy require stored data to be secure from theft and improper access. The full impact of these new requirements on IT organizations is not clear, but it is likely to create new practice areas in IT for data archiving or ILM.

Another reason to store historical versions of files is the fallibility of human beings (protein robots). It continues to be true that the largest risk to data is a person. When users make mistakes on files they are working on, they sometimes prefer to start over again from the last wayward point of departure rather than undoing that which they have wrought.

NOTE Of course, systems administrators never, ever make mistakes in the process of managing systems and data. But, *if they did,* their miscues might go unnoticed by the rest of the organization through amazing feats of skill in the operations of their snapshot or backup systems.

The notion of errors also applies to automated processes that may give disappointing results or have bugs. A process that modifies a data file improperly could be run again by starting over with the previous version of the data.

Creating Historical File Versions

Historical file versions are created when a storage process runs and makes a separate copy of a file. In other words, a spare copy is made and reserved for other purposes besides primary storage. Historical file versions are normally created through backup systems and point-in-time snapshot products.

Data Archiving

Unlike point-in-time copy applications, there usually is not a requirement to access individual files from a specific point in time. Instead, the particular *version* is what is wanted, regardless of when the file was actively being used.

Data archiving is the practice of making data copies solely for the purpose of accessing long-lasting historical versions of files.

NOTE There is no agreement on the definition of data archiving within the industry. Many people use the term *archive* to mean backup. This is a little bit like referring to a river as an ocean, but that's storage talk for you.

The problem is that—amazingly enough—there is no common term for the unnamed thing that makes long-lasting copies of files that can be easily accessed if they ever need to be. ILM seems to be emerging as a million-dollar acronym that encompasses the concept and extends it in a few similar dimensions.

So, I like to use terms like *historical version* or *archival copy* as opposed to the shorter term *archive*. Hopefully these work for you without getting in the way of your understanding.

Creating Historical Versions with Backup

One of the most common ways to create historical versions is with a backup system. Depending on the rotation algorithms and operations schedules, backups sweep file systems, backing up copies of files when they are changed and occasionally backing up complete volumes.

Snapshot products also create historical versions of files either by capturing the complete volume contents or by preserving older versions when they create point-in-time data sets.

But neither backup nor snapshot techniques can be relied on to create long-lasting (three to seven years) archival copies of files, because storage space in both systems is typically reused at some point. Backup tapes are periodically reused according to the tape rotation schedule. Snapshot disk capacity is eventually recycled as part of regular capacity management and system maintenance.

Currently the best way to keep file versions for an extended period of time is through backup technology where data can be stored off-line historical purposes. If it were not for maintenance problems, tape media would be perfect for the task. Tape has relatively large capacities, and multiple versions of a file can be stored on a single tape. Also, data stored on tape does not interfere with production online processing.

One way to create long-term archival copies of data is to make copies of backup tapes. The problem with this approach is that the backup metadata may be erased when the original tape is rewritten by the backup system. In that case, it is important to make sure a copy of the backup database is on each tape or is otherwise available to facilitate locating file versions on tape.

Another way to create long-lasting copies of files on tape is to create different pools for archival copies. These tapes can be managed separately, outside the normal rotation scheme, and could be created through tape-to-tape copy processes or could be separate, special-purpose backup jobs.

It is also possible to install separate backup software systems for archiving purposes. Normal day-to-day backup processes would use one backup system and archiving processes would run periodically with the archiving system. It is essential to practice diligent tape management if you do this to ensure the two tape systems do not become confused and mixed.

The backup system may be able to write to optical media in addition to tape. Storing historical versions on optical media is not a bad idea, but there may be problems finding optical media that is both fast enough and has the capacity for the job. Considering the relative lack of success the optical disk industry has had in its history, it is not clear that suitable optical systems and media will always be available, even though it would appear to be an excellent technology for historical data archiving.

Finally, historical versions of files can be accessed only if there is a device and a system that can use the device and software that runs on the system to use the device and read the media. That translates into archiving the complete backup system as well as the tapes. Either that, or copies must be made periodically from old media to new media as backup equipment is updated. This tape-to-tape copy approach has merit as a way to keep refreshing the media that data copies are stored on, but it is also likely to be the sort of work that is easily skipped or overlooked.

Creating Historical Versions with Snapshot Technology

Whereas tape is designed to sit on shelves or in libraries, point-in-time snapshots take up storage space in disk subsystems, which eventually leads to capacity-full problems, performance problems, or both. It could be argued that whole volume snapshots do not have this problem because they do not reside on production disks. However, the capacity needed for a whole volume snapshot can be enormous, and it is unrealistic to think that there would be many such versions spinning on disk drives within an organization.

One approach is to implement snapshots in a way that stores snapshot data on second tier storage. This could be using delta-volume snapshots, where the old overwritten data is written to a second tier storage subsystem. It also could be done with file system snapshots where the older, overwritten blocks of a file are relocated to second tier storage, so that their block locations in the primary file system can be returned to the free space pool.

Accessing Historical File Versions

Storage and retrieval are different but related processes. The following sections discuss techniques and technologies used to access historical versions of files.

Restoring Files from Backup Tapes

Traditionally, the most common way of accessing different versions of files is through a backup system restore process. This involves using an interface presented by the backup system and locating historical files on backup tapes. Most backup applications have a number of different views that are generated from information in the backup system metadata (database or log files). For instance, the administrator can search for files based on the day they were backed up or based on their location in the file system.

NOTE One of the more common requests is to restore a file that was deleted by mistake. When that happens, the process of finding the last file version is complicated by the fact that users will sometimes swear on a stack of religious books that the file was always located in a particular directory that actually never contained it. That's one of the reasons administrators prefer file system snapshots—users can restore their own files and waste their own time.

Once a particular file version has been identified, the backup software indicates one or more tapes that can be used to restore it. If a tape library is being used and one of the tapes is available in the library, this restore process can be mostly automated. File or path names will probably have to be changed to allow both the current version and the historical version to coexist in the same file system.

Accessing Snapshot Versions of Files

Point-in-time snapshot technology is also used to access historical versions of files. Unlike backup systems, which tend to be independent of operating systems and file systems, delta volume and file system snapshots can be closely integrated with operating system functions.

File system snapshot facilities allow users to view different versions of files from different virtual network volumes and select the one they want to work on. End-user access to snapshot data can be displayed through familiar name space interfaces, such as a mount point (drive letter) or folder.

Whole volume snapshot technology is the least useful for accessing historical file versions due to the size of the snapshot volume and the challenges in keeping multiple copies of the files available. Dedicated backup systems that back up whole volume archives could be used to locate data from tape and restore it.

Storing Data in Compliance with Government Regulations

The matter of complying with government regulations for retaining data is certainly related to the topic of historical file archiving, as discussed in the preceding section. However, under the microscope of audits and investigations, the matter of storage practices is likely to be opened to external scrutiny in a way that most IT workers are not necessarily comfortable with.

This section discusses some of the aspects of storing data in an environment that includes accountability to external auditors and investigators.

Risks of Noncompliance

There is a long history of government investigators using data records in their cases against corporations and individuals. The Enron securities fraud case, the Frank Quattrone obstruction of justice case, and the Martha Stewart insider trading case are all examples of court cases in the United States where e-mail records were gathered by federal prosecutors to build cases against the defendants.

The government also uses technology in investigations of its own operations, as evidenced in various 9/11 investigations, the Iran/Contra hearings, and even the Watergate scandal in the early 1970s, when tape recordings made and saved by President Richard Nixon became pivotal pieces of evidence against him.

Some regulations have heavy fines associated with the inability to provide information asked for in a timely manner. That means that retained data needs to be easy to locate—even after several years (something that most IT workers have limited confidence in).

IT workers should not make the mistake of thinking they will not have a role in possible legal proceedings against corporate managers who are being investigated. The unfortunate result of these new regulations for IT workers is that it opens the door for obstruction of justice charges for IT workers who do not execute data retention policies and practices properly.

NOTE The possibility of personal legal risk may seem a bit far-fetched, but unfortunately the risk exists. The regulations are public documents, but unfortunately, they do not come with a legalese interpreter. IT organizations should get legal opinions as to how to interpret the regulations. Like most legal language, there is significant room for interpretation. Whatever the case, there is a CYA factor to consider: ignorance of the law has been proven many times to be a lousy defense strategy.

Immutable Data

Auditors and investigators understand that data can be tampered with. Proving that stored data is immutable, or in other words, not altered after its creation is more difficult than it appears. The date and time stamp associated with a file can be falsified unless special provisions are taken to prevent the erasure and overwriting of historical data.

Write-Once Storage

Regulations may specify the characteristics of storage and media used, but they seldom specify the technologies that can be used. In general, it is likely that investigators will want to see proof that stored data has not been tampered with, especially if they have reason to believe that there was motivation for doing so.

Write-once, read-many (WORM) media has been used for many years for this purpose. WORM media and devices allow companies to create immutable copies of data that can be read but not overwritten. Recently, companies have developed other types of write-once technologies that can be used to prove data stored on them has not been altered. For instance, there are WORM disk subsystems that use file system technology that prohibit file updates after the file is written to disk the first time. There are also new WORM tape technologies that write data to tapes for permanent storage.

Content Addressable Storage

Another new technology that could be useful for government regulations compliance is content addressable storage (CAS). The idea of CAS is to create a unique identifier for a file that is generated from the contents of the file. One method to create this identifier is to use encryption, or hashing technology and create a unique identification key from the bit contents of the data. With a sufficient algorithm, a sufficiently large identification key can be created that ensures the identifier will be unique. That means changes to the file would generate a different key. A comparison of keys would indicate the data was changed.

Content addressable storage is useful as a way to prove data has not been altered. The trick is proving that a given key was created at a given time and was not fraudulently created. One way to do this would be to write key identifiers to WORM media and archive them.

E-Mail Archiving and Indexing

E-mail data is one of the primary areas of interest in regulations compliance. Backup companies may have specialized products or agents that work with particular e-mail systems for backing up and archiving e-mail data. More importantly, email indexing technology that facilitates the litigation discovery process (also referred to as e-discovery) will be extremely important to IT professionals in years to come. Once data has been extracted from an e-mail system, it can be stored using any storage techniques or technologies, including WORM storage.

Capacity Management

When filing systems fill storage address spaces past a certain point, system performance can become unacceptably slow. Also, the presence of old, unused data adds time to time-critical processes like backup, virus scanning, and system management practices. Capacity management is the process of relocating files from primary storage and placing them on second tier storage where they do not interfere with production operations.

One of the questions that eventually comes up is "Should capacity management be called storage management or data management?" Although it is often referred to as storage management, it is actually a filing-level process. The point is to return empty blocks to the file system's free space pool.

NOTE A storage address space is just a bunch of continuous blocks that are formed by virtualization and volume management. It is not always obvious, but a storage address space is already full of nonsensical bits when it is created. Writing data into an address space does not fill the address space; it creates a layout reference system within its boundaries. Over time, the layout reference system becomes increasingly convoluted as the free space pool becomes smaller and more fragmented. The best way to untangle a layout reference system is to remove files and return blocks to the free space pool. A defragmentation process finishes the job by restructuring the file layout within the address space.

The most common form of capacity management is simply to buy larger storage products and migrate data from smaller-capacity devices to them. This can become difficult in a data center environment if a lot of equipment has to be moved and storage components, rack spaces, and cabling all have to be juggled. Virtualization systems provide an excellent technology solution for these problems, as discussed in Chapter 12, "Storage Virtualization: The Power in Volume Management Software and SAN Virtualization Systems."

But purchasing more storage comes at a price. It is certainly possible to spend less money on storage equipment by managing the capacity of file systems more effectively. Three capacity management methods are discussed in the following sections:

- Storage Resource Management
- Hierarchical Storage Management and archiving
- Tiered Storage

Storage Resource Management

Storage resource management (SRM) is an application that maps file systems to LUNs and monitors file system capacity trends. The goal is to provide a proactive means to predict when capacity problems could occur, giving administrators an opportunity to take action before a storage crisis occurs. SRM products normally record a variety of statistics about the file system, including the characteristics of files within the file system. These can include the percentage of files over or under a certain size and those that are older or newer than certain dates. In some cases it might be possible to identify capacities used by certain applications and create trend analysis for them.

Administrators establish the thresholds and set the policies that an SRM system uses. For instance, a policy could be set that would identify all files that have not been accessed in the last 90 days and that are larger than 25 MB. The policies used for individual servers can vary according to the characteristics of the applications they support. For example, a multimedia server would have different policies than a database system. Some SRM applications provide automation tie-ins to other system tools that could perform maintenance actions. Alternatively, SRM systems may be able to create scripts that an administrator can edit and run.

Hierarchical Storage Management

Hierarchical storage management (HSM) is an automated system that moves files from primary to secondary storage but continues to provide (more or less) transparent access to data as if it were still stored on primary storage. Most HSM systems use policies similar to those just described for SRM systems. Files are identified by the HSM system as candidates for migrating to secondary storage based on their size, lack of activity, or both. A capacity monitor periodically queries the file system to determine its filled capacity. When the capacity exceeds the "high water mark," the files that were identified as candidates for migration are copied to secondary storage. As they are copied, they are replaced by a "stub file" that has the same name as the original file but fills a minimum amount of storage capacity. The migration of files from primary storage to secondary storage continues this way until capacity levels drop below the "low water mark" and migration stops.

Figure 17-3 illustrates three steps in a basic HSM migration process. In Step 1, capacity levels in a storage address space exceed the high water mark. This starts Step 2, which migrates files to secondary storage, in this case, tape. Migration stops in Step 3 when the capacity level drops below the assigned low water mark.

Figure 17-3 *An HSM System Migrates Data from Primary Storage to Secondary Storage*

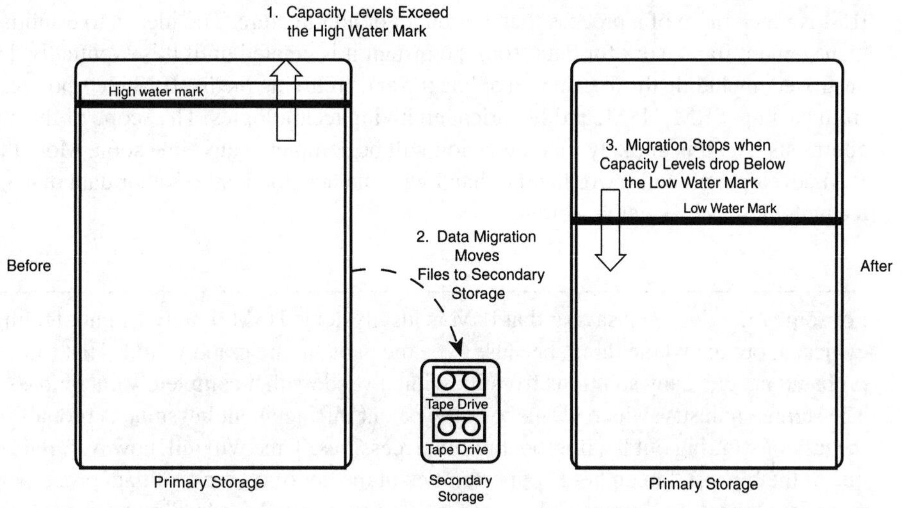

HSM depends on a process running in kernel space that intercepts the file-open process to see if it is a stub file. If the file is determined to be a stub file, the HSM system suspends the file-open task and reads the contents of the HSM stub file, which has information needed for the HSM system to *demigrate* the file. Demigration involves locating the file in secondary storage and restoring it to the file system. This process necessarily involves creating new layout reference data for the file. The speed of the demigration process depends a great deal on the type of secondary storage used to migrate files. For example, disk storage is quite a bit faster than tape storage. After the file has been completely restored, the file-open process is returned to the file system, which services the request as it normally would.

Tiered Storage

One of the most important new, trends in storage is tiered storage, which attempts to match the cost of storage with the importance of the data stored on it. Tiered storage is similar to HSM, but without the necessity to migrate and demigrate data. Determined by data management policies, the most important data is located on high performance, first tier storage, while less important data is located on lower performing, high-capacity second tier storage. Finally data that is not needed on-line, such as backup or historical archived data might be located on third tier storage. Tiered storage is an area that will see significant development in the years to come.

Information Life Cycle Management

ILM is much more of a process than a product or architecture. The idea is to establish a management framework for data from the instant it is created until it is eventually deleted or destroyed, including the destruction of backup and archiving media. ILM incorporates concepts from backup, SRM, HSM, and historical archiving technologies. The scope of the effort is enormous, and it is unlikely that the vision will be completed any time soon. More than likely, ILM development will move hand in hand with the development of other data management technologies such as tiered storage.

NOTE For some time I've been saying that ILM is just dyslexic HSM. Lately I'm not feeling quite as cynical about the whole thing, because I see the value in the grand vision. That said, there will probably never be any solutions from individual vendors that completely encompass its scope. The storage industry, which seems to enjoy patent infringement lawsuits, is probably not up to the task of working out the interoperability necessities. Time will tell, however. Because this is one of the biggest "green field" opportunities in the entire universe of data processing, it will be interesting to see if industry leaders find ways to create broad solutions or try to circle the legal wagons around proprietary intellectual property.

The basic ideas inherent in ILM can be summarized as follows:

- Identify file and derivative versions as belonging to the same information expression. (A file can be modified and given a different name even though its contents and usage are basically the same.)
- Identify and catalog the location of files and all derivatives within an organization, including geographic, system, and file system location.
- Create file copies and automate the dissemination and tracking of files within the organization to meet redundancy policies and guidelines.
- Determine an expiration date for each file and its derivative versions; confirm all deletions and destroyed media.
- Record all known file life cycle actions.

The points listed here represent an enormous effort for any organization. There is no doubt that new automation of filing-level functions will be needed to provide a comprehensive ILM solution some day. That said, many existing technologies could be used as part of an ILM practice. Most of the familiar storage technologies could be borrowed to fit specific roles. For instance, snapshot technology could be used to create virtual views that other processes would use to scan data key identifiers from content addressable storage could be used to identify duplicate files with different names, and WORM storage could be used to permanently store reference copies of files.

Summary

Data management will continue to be a challenging task for the foreseeable future. This chapter discussed four different perspectives on data management: managing data for point-in-time recovery using snapshot technology, managing historical versions of files using backup and snapshot technology, managing storage to comply with government regulations using WORM, and CAS technology and managing capacity with SRM.

ILM was discussed at the close of the chapter as an important area for IT organizations to develop. This is a big topic that the industry is just starting to understand. While some vendors are claiming to have ILM products, it seems more likely that organizations will end up building this capability piece by piece and platform by platform.

Q & A

1. What is point-in-time copy used for?
2. Can you use host write caching with point-in-time copy?
3. Which type of point-in-time copy requires the most storage capacity?
4. True or false: By default, backup systems automatically create historical copies of data.
5. True or false: File system snapshots create extra copies of data.
6. What type of media prevents data from being overwritten?
7. Is capacity management mostly a storing function or a filing function?
8. What is the file called in an HSM system that replaces the original file?
9. True or false: ILM is a major industry standard.

PART VI

Appendixes

APPENDIX A

Q & A Answers

Chapter 1

1. How much downtime is allowed per year to have five-nines availability?

   Answer: 5 minutes

2. Before SANs and NAS, what was DAS called?

   Answer: It was simply called storage; there was nothing else to compare it to.

3. DAS is used by which storage technologies?

   Answer: SCSI and ATA

4. True or false: DAS allows storage devices to be connected and disconnected while the system is operating.

   Answer: False

5. What is the relationship between host systems and storage using DAS?

   Answer: One to many

6. What is the relationship between host systems and storage using network storage?

   Answer: Many to many

7. True or false: Upgrading storage and servers is easier with network storage than it is with DAS.

   Answer: True

8. Where is data located in a data-centric architecture?

   Answer: In the middle

Chapter 2

1. What are the three primary components of storage networking?

   Answer: Storing, connecting, and filing

2. True or false: Buses guarantee the order of delivery.

   Answer: True

3. Which of the following is not part of the storing component: volume management, virtualization, zoning, host bus adapters, or block I/O?

   Answer: Zoning

4. True or false: Disk drives do not need a controller.

   Answer: False

5. What is the difference between initiator and target controllers?

   Answer: Initiators generate commands and send them to targets; targets respond to those commands.

6. What kinds of storage devices and subsystems create storage address spaces?

   Answer: They all do.

7. What are the primary three things filing is responsible for?

   Answer: Filing organizes where data is stored in a storage address space, and it presents that data to users and applications and it provides access control for files and directories.

8. Explain the different roles of file systems and operating systems.

   Answer: Operating systems manage time (when processes run), and file systems manage space (where data is located).

9. What is the application difference between SAN and NAS?

   Answer: SAN is the application of storing in a network, and NAS is the application of filing in a network.

10. True or false: Storing and filing have to use different networks.

    Answer: False

Chapter 3

1. What are the two main performance concerns in storage networks?

   Answer: Bandwidth and latency

2. True or false: DAS storage is less reliable than network storage.

   Answer: False. DAS has historically been extremely reliable.

3. Which of the following is not part of the software used in the I/O path: file system, volume manager, storage resource manager, multi-pathing drivers, or SCSI driver?

   Answer: Storage resource manager

4. What are the two layers most HBAs need?

   Answer: SCSI application layer driver and network driver

5. Name the host system hardware components in the I/O path.

   Answer: System processors, system memory, memory bus, I/O bus, and host bus adapter

6. What is flow control used for?

   Answer: It adjusts the data rate of data being transmitted by a network node.

7. Name the subsystem hardware elements found in the I/O path.

   Answer: Network port, storage controller, cache memory, storage interconnect, storage device, and storage media

8. True or false: Storage controllers in subsystems are the same as host system HBAs.

   Answer: False. They have different logic to handle different types of tasks.

9. True or false: File systems and operating systems do not have to be from the same vendor.

   Answer: True. Installable file systems have worked very successfully for many years.

10. True or false: The volume manager usually writes I/Os directly to disk device drivers.

    Answer: False. The operating system kernel does this.

Chapter 4

1. Which of the following is not part of a disk drive: platters, arms, controller, or fan?

   Answer: Fan

2. What is the flying height of modern disk heads?

   Answer: 15 nanometers

3. True or false: The clicking sound coming from disk drives is caused by the head touching the media.

   Answer: False. It's the sound of the actuator moving.

4. What does logical block addressing provide?

   Answer: Addressing by sector number in a flat address space, as opposed to having to use cylinders, tracks, and sectors

5. Where is disk throughput greater: inside tracks or outside tracks?

   Answer: Outside tracks

6. What is MTBF used for?

   Answer: MTBF is used to predict the failure rates for many disk drives.

7. True or false: Multiple applications can access different partitions on a disk drive without regard for performance.

   Answer: False

8. How often should tape heads be cleaned?

   Answer: Every 30 hours of operation

9. True or false: Data compression always cuts the time it takes to run backup in half.

   Answer: False. It depends on the data's compressibility.

10. What are the two major types of tape technologies used in UNIX and Windows environments?

    Answer: Linear and helical scan

Chapter 5

1. List four types of connecting technologies used in storage subsystems.

   Answer: DAS bus, Fibre Channel loop, system I/O bus, and switched connections

2. Name two types of device redundancy.

   Answer: Mirroring and parity RAID

3. True or false: Disk drives can have only a single connecting port.

   Answer: False. Fibre Channel drives are dual-ported and SATA, and SAS drives are expected to implement dual porting also.

4. How is battery backup used in a subsystem?

   Answer: It keeps power to volatile cache memory.

5. True or false: Temperature is never a problem for disk subsystems.

   Answer: False. Temperature should always be monitored.

6. What form of device redundancy does not increase capacity?

   Answer: Mirroring is a form of device redundancy that does not increase capacity.

7. Name two ways in which performance can be boosted in disk subsystems.

   Answer: Parallelism (overlapped I/Os) and caching

8. What is the difference between hot swapping and hot sparing?

   Answer: Hot swapping allows devices to be removed and inserted into a system without turning off the system. Hot sparing keeps a spare device available to be inserted in subsystem operations without having to remove and replace a device.

9. Explain the difference between a subsystem and an array.

   Answer: An array is a logical construct, and a subsystem is a physical collection of different components.

10. True or false: LUN masking blocks I/Os.

    Answer: False. It hides devices by not responding to initiator inquiries.

Chapter 6

1. The SCSI-3 standard is used for which SAN implementations?

   a. Fibre Channel

   b. iSCSI

   c. SSA

   d. All of them

   Answer: D

2. What is the standards organization for SCSI?

   Answer: INCITS T10

3. True or false: Target and initiator ports are part of the logical processing of SCSI.

   Answer: False. Ports are considered to be part of the underlying connecting technology.

4. True or false: SCSI guarantees in-order delivery.

   Answer: False. Delivery ordering is provided by the underlying connecting technology, such as a parallel SCSI bus or a SAN.

5. Where are SCSI logical units implemented?

   Answer: In storage subsystem and device controllers

6. Name the two main functions in a logical unit.

   Answer: Device server and task manager

7. What are queues in SCSI called?

   Answer: Task sets

8. What is the standard size of SCSI CDBs?

   Answer: There is no standard, prescribed CDB size. They vary according to the command and the action taken.

9. What is a SCSI nexus?

   Answer: The connection relationship between initiator and target entities

10. Explain how tagged command queuing (TCQ) increases performance.

    Answer: TCQ reduces seek time by restructuring disk access.

Chapter 7

1. Explain the difference between an interconnect and a SAN.

   Answer: An interconnect is used inside a cabinet to connect devices to controllers, and a SAN is used externally, between systems and storage subsystems.

2. What is the maximum distance of a parallel SCSI LVD bus?

   Answer: 12 meters

3. What is the highest-priority address on a 16-bit (wide) SCSI bus?

   Answer: ID 7

4. Why would you use parallel SCSI disks inside a server system connected to a SAN?

   Answer: For boot disks

5. True or false: Performance with an Ultra ATA/100 disk drive is independent of the type of cable used.

   Answer: False. It requires the 80-pin cable.

6. Name the two main performance shortcomings of ATA disk drives for storage network applications.

   Answer: No command queuing and no overlapped I/O

7. Which Fibre Channel topology is used as a device interconnect?

   Answer: Loops

8. Why isn't Fibre Channel used often for the internal drives inside system cabinets?

   Answer: They don't have off-the-shelf cables and connectors for use in systems.

9. What is the primary capacity scaling issue with SATA?

   Answer: There is only one drive per SATA connector.

10. List the four interconnects from slowest to fastest performance for storage networking applications.

    Answer: ATA, SATA, FC, SCSI

Chapter 8

1. Why is data redundancy important?

   Answer: It provides protection from data loss.

2. What are three different forms of redundancy?

   Answer: Duplicate, parity, and delta (difference)

3. What's the first step in using delta redundancy?

   Answer: Make a complete copy of the data.

4. List four locations in the I/O path that could contain mirroring operators

   Answer: Host software, HBAs, network systems, and subsystem controllers

5. Why can't two targets in a mirrored pair have different sizes (capacities)?

   Answer: File systems are designed to manage a single address space. This means that all storing (block) operations are duplicated within the boundaries of that address space.

6. How can mirroring improve system performance?

   Answer: Reads can be overlapped, providing parallelism.

7. Explain how a mirrored pair in a subsystem can be accessed through two different target addresses in a SAN.

   Answer: A single logical unit formed by a mirrored pair can be exported by the subsystem through different port/LUN pairs.

8. Mirroring is sometimes used for remote data protection up to what distance?

   Answer: 10 miles

9. If there are three layers of mirrors working in an I/O path, how many copies of data will be created?

   Answer: Eight

Chapter 9

1. What does RAID stand for?

   Answer: Redundant array of inexpensive disks

2. What kinds of storage entities can be members of a RAID array?

   Answer: Any storage address space: Devices, subsystems, SCSI logical units, and volumes

3. True or false: RAID members have to be the same size.

   Answer: True

4. What is the Boolean function used in parity RAID?

   Answer: XOR

5. What is the purpose of parity with RAID?

   Answer: Parity RAID provides efficient data redundancy.

6. Describe the difference between strips and stripes.

   Answer: Strips are written to individual members, and stripes are all the related strips with a common parity value.

7. What is the best possible MTDL in a RAID 5 array?

   Answer: MTBF + MTBF/2, using the MTBF specification for member drives in the array

8. Briefly explain the RAID 5 write penalty.

   Answer: The RAID 5 write penalty is the process of reading both old data and parity data from disk to re-create new parity data to go with new data being written to a member strip in the array.

9. What is the maximum number of member pairs in a RAID 10 array?

   Answer: There is no maximum.

10. What is the most common type of parity RAID used today?

    Answer: RAID 5

Chapter 10

1. What is primary storage, and where is it located?

   Answer: Primary storage is online disk storage used by applications and systems. It is local to applications systems.

2. What is secondary storage, and where is it located?

   Answer: Secondary storage is used by remote copy systems to hold redundant copies of data. It can be located at the primary site or at remote secondary sites.

3. What are the three primary objectives of remote copy systems?

   Answer: Provide ready access to data at remote storage sites

   Maintain data consistency

   Resume normal operations at the primary processing site

4. How can remote copy slow down application processing?

   Answer: Responses from write commands can be delayed, causing an I/O bottleneck.

5. What is the latency of signal propagation in a fiber-optic cable?

   Answer: 5 microseconds per kilometer or 8 microseconds per mile

6. How many signals have to be transmitted for each write operation in remote copy?

   Answer: Four

7. What is the difference between synchronous and asynchronous mode?

   Answer: Synchronous mode acknowledges each write before forwarding another. Asynchronous mode allows multiple writes to be forwarded without receiving an acknowledgment from the remote site.

8. True or false: The receiving controller never acts like a SCSI initiator.

   Answer: False. It acts like an initiator when writing to secondary storage.

9. Name three locations where secondary storage can be found.

   Answer: Local site or campus, bunker site, and remote site

Chapter 11

1. Is multipathing more of a connecting (network) technology or a storing (SCSI) technology?

   Answer: Storing

2. What is the minimum number of HBAs needed for multipathing?

   Answer: One if the HBA has more than one port

3. How many LUs can a single LUN be associated with?

   Answer: One

4. What is the difference between a WWNN and a WWPN?

   Answer: WWNN represents the system or subsystem, and WWPN represents the port name.

5. What three pieces of information define a path?

   Answer: Initiator, WWPN+LUN, and LU

6. True or false: Multipathing always uses active/passive configurations with static load balancing.

   Answer: False. Active/active configurations are also used, along with dynamic load balancing.

7. How long are typical timeout values for failing over?

   Answer: 30 seconds to several minutes

8. Describe the difference between mirroring, multipathing, and SAN routing.

   Answer: Mirroring creates redundant data, multipathing provides multiple initiator-to-LU paths to access it, and network routing determines where transmission frames are forwarded in a SAN.

9. What identifies the LU uniquely?

   Answer: A serial number or UUID

Chapter 12

1. What is the primary function of storage virtualization?

   Answer: To create upstream storage address spaces from downstream storage address spaces

2. What is the similarity between a SAN virtualization system and a storage subsystem?

   Answer: A SAN virtualization system is similar to placing the subsystem controller in the SAN instead of in a subsystem cabinet.

3. How do volume managers and SAN virtualization systems differ in their "view" of the network?

   Answer: SAN virtualization systems work with multiple hosts, and volume managers work with a single host.

4. Describe the difference between concatenation and striping.

   Answer: Concatenation appends a storage address space to another, and striping intertwines strips of different address spaces.

5. What is the difference between fan-in and fan-out of a SAN virtualization system?

   Answer: Fan-in is the number of simultaneous initiator/target connections available through a single port. Fan-out is the number of downstream LUNs used to form a single upstream LUN.

6. How can high utilization of storage lead to poorer I/O performance?

   Answer: It causes disk fragmentation, which leads to longer seek times and the creation of hot spots on disk drives.

7. True or false: Storage subsystems have more predictable connection environments than volume managers or SAN virtualization controllers.

   Answer: True

8. Starting with the filing system and looking downstream, name the elements of the I/O software stack in a host system.

   Answer: Filing system, volume manager, multipathing software, SCSI command driver

9. If a SAN virtualization system is a single point of failure, what can be done to improve availability?

   Answer: Operate two or more virtualization systems in a cluster configuration.

Chapter 13

1. Name four uses for backup technology.

   Answer: Disaster protection, historical archiving, system migration, data sharing

2. What is offline storage?

   Answer: Storage that cannot be accessed without an administrator's making it available

3. What does backup metadata do?

   Answer: It keeps data about backup operations and tapes.

4. What does tape rotation do?

   Answer: It determines which tapes to use and when.

5. Explain the difference between incremental and differential backups.

   Answer: Incremental backups copy data that has changed since the last backup. Differential backups copy data that has changed since the last full backup.

6. What is hot backup?

   Answer: Hot backup operates while the application system is running.

7. Name two advantages of backing up over the SAN.

   Answer: Excellent performance and centralized backup management

8. True or false: LAN-free backup requires backup data to move through the application servers being backed up.

   Answer: True. An application server reads data from a disk LUN in the SAN, stores it temporarily in memory, and writes it to tape drives in the SAN.

9. A data mover is used in what kind of SAN-based backup?

   Answer: Serverless backup

10. Why does disk capacity for backup scale and tape capacity not scale?

    Answer: Disk can use RAID and other virtualization techniques to create scalable capacity, whereas tape is limited to the capacity of a single cartridge.

Chapter 14

1. What is the file system's primary responsibility?

   Answer: To manage the allocation of storage addresses for file data

2. True or false: The operating system/file system interface is a clearly delineated abstract boundary.

   Answer: False. The interactions between a file system and an operating system are complex and not generally well known.

3. The layout reference system in most UNIX file systems is called what?

   Answer: The inodes

4. True or false: The directory structure and layout of data in the storage address space are closely related.

   Answer: False. They are completely independent.

5. What is the importance of the file system's layout reference system?

   Answer: It allows data to be located within a storage address space.

6. What is metadata?

   Answer: It is data kept by the file system that describes the data. Traditional file system attributes are an example.

7. True or false: Storage expansion by virtualization methods or volume managers is automatically detected by the file system.

   Answer: False. File systems must run special processes to recognize any increases to their storage address spaces.

8. What is the reason for using a journaled file system?

   Answer: To quickly identify and repair any data inconsistencies caused by unexpected shutdowns or failures

9. Why is file system caching more accurate than storing-level block caching?

   Answer: File systems have the layout references to know the precise blocks holding a file's data. Block storing-level caches have to guess.

Chapter 15

1. What are the two major transport protocols used in network file systems?

   Answer: NFS and CIFS

2. True or false: NFS was originally designed to run over UDP.

   Answer: True

3. What kind of locking does NFS provide?

   Answer: Advisory locking

4. True or false: CIFS is a published industry standard.

   Answer: False

5. What is the benefit of a stateful protocol?

   Answer: Processes interrupted by communications failures can be resynchronized.

6. Name one of the two primary applications for network file systems.

   Answer: Centralized data management and data sharing

7. True or false: Name space virtualization resolves naming conflicts from different clients.

   Answer: False. Name space virtualization allows different groupings of file system objects at client systems.

8. What is SAMBA used for?

   Answer: SAMBA allows Linux systems to function as file servers for Windows clients.

9. What protocol was developed for backing up NAS?

   Answer: NDMP

10. How does data management differ from storage management?

    Answer: Data management works with data objects such as files and directories. Storage management tends to work with block storage and storage address spaces.

Chapter 16

1. What are the two kinds of cluster storage designs?

   Answer: Shared everything and shared nothing

2. Why is locking more important for a cluster file system than a traditional file system?

   Answer: The cluster file system can have multiple systems trying to access the same data.

3. True or false: You typically do not have to worry about data in host buffers with a cluster file system.

   Answer: False. You have to account for all cached data.

4. Why are SANs valuable for cluster file systems?

   Answer: They are the easiest way to connect all systems to all storage.

5. True or false: NAS clusters are used primarily to increase storage capacity.

   Answer: False. They are used primarily for high availability.

6. What is the main difference between a cluster file system and a DFS farm?

   Answer: There is no failover in a DFS farm.

7. What are two ways to implement a lock manager for a distributed file system?

   Answer: Distributed or centralized

8. What is the purpose of direct I/O?

   Answer: To prevent host systems from caching data for database applications

9. Database logs are an example of what kind of redundancy technique?

   Answer: Delta or difference redundancy

Chapter 17

1. What is point-in-time copy used for?

   Answer: To re-create consistent data for business continuity

2. Can you use host write caching with point-in-time copy?

   Answer: Yes, but you must flush host buffers before detaching secondary storage.

3. Which type of point-in-time copy requires the most storage capacity?

   Answer: Whole volume snapshots

4. True or false: By default, backup systems automatically create historical copies of data.

   Answer: False. They make backup copies that are eventually overwritten. You should make separate tapes or tape pools for historical archiving.

5. True or false: File system snapshots create extra copies of data.

   Answer: False. They keep old data blocks from being returned to the free block pool.

6. What type of media prevents data from being overwritten?

   Answer: WORM

7. Is capacity management mostly a storing function or a filing function?

   Answer: Filing

8. What is the file called in an HSM system that replaces the original file?

   Answer: Stub file

9. True or false: ILM is a major industry standard.

   Answer: False

APPENDIX B

INCITS Storage Standards

The International Committee for Information Technology Standards (INCITS) is an American standards organization that is a vehicle for creating, publishing, and maintaining computer and communications standards. The "International" in INCITS refers to its role in working with other international standards groups to create worldwide technology standards.

Several storage standards are managed by INCITS committees. The T10 committee is devoted to Small Computer Systems Interface (SCSI) technology. While most of the T10 committee's activities relate to storage, a significant amount of nonstorage SCSI technology is described in T10 standards documents. The T11 committee publishes standards for various communications and storage technologies, including Fibre Channel (FC) and High-Performance Parallel Interface (HIPPI). Today, FC is the most active technology under development as a T11 INCITS standard. Finally, the T13 committee is dedicated to AT Attachment (ATA) storage technology.

Each of these committees has its own website describing the work it does with references to draft versions of standards documents. Draft documents are typically available as free PDF downloads, but finalized, published versions of the committee's standards must be purchased from INCITS. The casual reader can gather a great deal of insight into the standards without reading the final, published versions. Engineering organizations obviously need to see "the real McCoy" before embarking on any serious development efforts. The sections in this appendix are a listing of information available through the T10, T11, and T13 committee websites.

T10 SCSI Storage Interfaces

The INCITS T10 committee website is at http://www.t10.org/. Among the draft documents available at this website are excellent versions of the SCSI Architecture Model (SAM). A great deal of open-system storage operating theory can be derived by reading the SAM documents.

T10 Subcommittees and Working Groups

The following is a list of subject areas under development as T10 standards that have documents available on the T10 committee website:

- SBC—SCSI Block Commands (disk drive commands)
- RBC—Reduced Block Commands (simplified disk drive commands)
- SSC—SCSI Stream Commands
- SMC—SCSI Media Changer Commands
- MMC—Multimedia Commands
- SCC—SCSI Controller Commands
- SES—SCSI Enclosure Services
- OSD—Object-based Storage Devices
- MSC—Management Server Commands
- ADC—Automation/Drive Interface Commands
- ADT—Automation/Drive Interface Transport Protocol
- SPC—SCSI Primary Commands
- SAM—SCSI Architecture Model
- SPI—SCSI Parallel Interface
- SDV—SCSI Domain Validation
- PIP—SCSI Passive Interconnect Performance
- SSM—SCSI Signaling Model
- EPI—SCSI Enhanced Parallel Interface
- SBP—Serial Bus Protocol
- FCP—Fibre Channel Protocol
- SSA—Serial Storage Architecture Protocol
- SRP—SCSI RDMA Protocol
- SAS—Serial Attached SCSI
- CAM—SCSI Common Access Method

T11 Device Level Interfaces

The T11 committee develops interfaces for device communications and has a website at http://www.t11.org/. It turns out that most of the interfaces developed by T11 are storage-related, and this is where standards specific to FC technology can be viewed.

T11 Standards

Some of the standards in T11 are completed and are not undergoing further development, while others are continuing to be developed. The two areas currently under development in T11 are FC and Storage (Network) Management. The URLs for these subcommittees are as follows:

- Fibre Channel

  http://www.t11.org/t11/stat.nsf/fcproj

- Storage (Network) Management

  http://www.t11.org/t11/stat.nsf/smproj

Finished standards are mostly interesting for historical reasons. Readers wanting to look at older storage interface standards can visit the websites of the following T11 subcommittees:

- High-Performance Parallel Interface

  http://www.t11.org/t11/stat.nsf/hippiproj

- Intelligent Peripheral Interface

  http://www.t11.org/t11/stat.nsf/ipiproj

- Single-Byte Command Code Sets Connection

  http://www.t11.org/t11/stat.nsf/sbproj

Fibre Channel Subcommittees and Working Groups

The following list indicates areas of development in FC with downloadable documents from the T11 FC website:

- FC-AE—Fibre Channel Avionics Environment
- FC-AL—Fibre Channel Arbitrated Loop
- FC-AV—Fibre Channel Audiovisual
- FC-BB—Fibre Channel Backbone
- FC-DA—Fibre Channel Device Attach
- FC-FG—Fabric Generic Requirements
- FC-FLA—Fabric Loop Attachment
- FC-FP—Fibre Channel Mapping to HIPPI-FP
- FC-FS—Fibre Channel Framing and Signaling Interface
- FC-GS—Fibre Channel Generic Services
- FC-HBA—Fibre Channel HBA API
- FC-HSPI—Fibre Channel High-Speed Parallel Interface

- FC-LE—Fibre Channel Link Encapsulation
- FC-LS—Fibre Channel Link Services
- FC-MI—Fibre Channel Methodologies for Interconnects
- FC-MJS—Fibre Channel Methodology of Jitter Specification
- FC-MJSQ—Fibre Channel Methodologies for Jitter and Signal Quality Specification
- FC-PH—Fibre Channel Physical and Signaling Interface
- FC-PI—Fibre Channel Physical Interface
- FC-PLDA—Fibre Channel Private Loop Direct Attach
- FC-SB—Fibre Channel Single Byte Command Code Sets
- FC-SM—Fibre Channel Signal Modeling
- FC-SP—Fibre Channel Security Protocols
- FC-SW—Fibre Channel Switch Fabric and Switch Control Requirements
- FC-SWAPI—Fibre Channel Switch Application Programming Interface
- FC-TAPE—Tape Technical Report
- FC-VI—Fibre Channel Virtual Interface Architecture Mapping
- MIB-FA—Fibre Channel Management Information Base
- SM-LL-V—Fibre Channel Very Long Length Optical Interface

Storage (Network) Management Subcommittees and Working Groups

The following list shows areas of work in the T11 Storage Network Management subcommittee:

- FAIS—Fabric Application Interface Standard
- SM-AMD—SAN Management Attribute and Method Dictionary
- SM-HBA—Host Bus Adapter Application Programming Interface
- SM-MM—SAN Management Management Model
- SM-NSM—Storage Management Name Server MIB
- SM-RTM—Storage Management Routing Information MIB

T13 AT Attachment

The T13 INCITS committee is responsible for all standards related to ATA technologies, including Serial ATA (SATA). The website for the T13 committee is at http://www.t13.org/.

The following list shows areas of development in the T13 committee that are available on the T13 website:

- AT Attachment with Packet Interface (ATA/ATAPI)
- BIOS Enhanced Disk Drive Services
- 1394 to AT Attachment—Tailgate
- Protected Area Runtime Interface Extension Services
- Address Offset Reserved Area Boot Method
- ATA/ATAPI Host Adapter Standards (ATA Adapter)
- ATA/ATAPI AV Command Set Usage Guidelines

GLOSSARY

active. A component that is performing work or is waiting to perform work.

active/active. An architecture for high availability where all components are active and can assume extra work if another component fails.

active/passive. An architecture for high availability where one or more components are idle, waiting to take over for another that fails.

actuator. A mechanism in disk drives that rotates and moves disk arms across disk platters.

aggregation. The combination of storage address spaces, making a larger space from multiple smaller storage address spaces.

allocation. A file system process that selects the storage blocks to use in creating or updating a file.

appliance. A special-purpose server or device that is easy to install and use.

arbitration. The method of determining which initiator or target gets access to the bus or network. Used with parallel SCSI and Fibre Channel loops.

archive. A copy of data written to secondary storage for the purpose of making historical versions of files.

areal density. The ratio of storage capacity to area on magnetic storage media media.

arm. An assembly that connects disk drive heads to the disk actuator.

array. A logical structure of same-sized storage address spaces configured as a single storage entity with a composite storage address space. Can be manipulated by virtualization techniques. Usually operated as a RAID array.

asynchronous I/O. A method of I/O processing that allows unacknowledged I/Os.

ATA. Advanced Technology Attachment. An interface for desktop disk drives.

attribute. File system metadata that is used to manage data. Attributes indicate basic information about files, including file creation and access dates and times, size, access rights, and update indicators.

average seek time. The average delay incurred in disk I/O waiting for heads to be relocated from one track to another.

backing. The base layer of tape media, not magnetic.

backplane. The common rigid connecting circuit board that carries all I/O traffic in a subsystem or system.

backup. The process of copying data to secondary storage for the purpose of restoring it when it is needed.

backup engine. Backup management software and the system it runs on.

backup window. The amount of time in a 24-hour period in which to perform backup operations.

binder. The adhesive used to adhere the magnetic layer to the backing in tape media.

block. A granular unit of storage capacity used by a file system or database.

block address. A location of a block of storage within a storage address space.

buffer memory. Memory used in data transfers to temporarily store data.

bunker storage. Storage located in proximity to the main data center that allows high-performance copies of data to be made (either remote copy or mirroring). Bunker storage is typically used to "stage" data that will be transmitted to storage a longer distance away.

business continuity. A business practice to prepare for the resumption of IT operations following a disaster.

byte range. Contiguous data locations within a file, where bytes are used as the granular units of storage.

caching. Temporary storage of data to enhance performance.

CAS. Content Addressable Storage. A way to identify and manage data based on its contents as opposed to its name or metadata.

CDB. Command Descriptor Block. A SCSI command protocol data unit.

CFS. Cluster File System.

CIFS. Common Internet File System. The evolution of Server Message Block in Windows technology.

clusters. A high-availability architecture where more than one system can provide application services.

coating. A lubricating layer on tape media.

cold backup. A backup process that runs while applications are not running.

command. A granular unit of work in storage operations.

command queuing. A method of command processing that allows logical units to determine the order in which tasks are processed.

compression. A method of reducing the number of bits needed to convey data.

concatenation. Appending one storage address space to another to create a larger one.

connecting. Along with filing and storing, one of three main elements in storage networks having to do with buses or networks.

consistency. A complete recording of all related data on media as intended by the writing application and including layout reference data updates and metadata.

contiguous. Adjoining and in order. Usually used with blocks, as in contiguous blocks.

control path. A combination of hardware and software used to manage and control data transmissions.

controller. A system function that manages storage transfers. Usually a hardware implementation with firmware.

copy-on-write. A process that allows data management to be performed on files while they are being updated by applications.

cylinders. Multiple tracks used together on parallel platters.

D2D. Disk-to-disk backup.

D2D2T. Disk-to-disk-to-tape backup.

D2T. Disk-to-tape backup.

DAS. Direct Attached Storage.

data migration. The process of relocating data from one system or subsystem to another one.

data mover. An initiator that performs third-party copy processes.

data sharing. Multiple systems that can access common data.

degraded mode. A RAID array operating with a failed member.

delta/difference. A redundancy method where data can be recreated based on applying or subtracting change data to or from a known state.

device. A storage drive. A disk drive or tape drive.

device server. A component of a SCSI logical unit that is responsible for receiving and responding to commands from initiators.

DFS. Distributed File System.

differential backup. A backup operation that copies all data that has changed since the last full backup.

differential SCSI. An extended-distance SCSI bus technology.

direct I/O. A method of processing updates in host systems that bypasses host buffer memory and transfers writes and updates directly to storage.

directory. A file containing a listing of files and serving as an access point for those files within a name space.

disk drive. A granular component of disk storage; a device with rotating media platters.

disk platter. A rigid rotating medium coated with a magnetic surface and used in disk drives.

disk quota. A limit placed on the amount of storage capacity available to a specific user or application.

downstream. In the direction away from an initiator.

dual-mode controller. A storage controller with both target and initiator functionality.

duplication. A redundancy method where data is duplicated on two independent components.

dynamic expansion. A file system process that adds block storage capacity to an storage address space without stopping system operations and halting application processing.

exported drive. Virtual or real storage in a disk subsystem.

extended copy. *See* third-party copy.

failing back. The inverse of failover. Changing work from a redundant component back to a reinstated or replaced component.

failover. The process of changing work from a failed, active component to other active, redundant components. May involve the activation of a passive component.

fan out. The ratio of downstream to upstream entities in a network.

fencing. The logical segregation of resources and processes used in network operations.

Fibre Channel. A networking technology developed in the 1990s that was the first network used for SANs.

file. A data storage abstraction used by applications to store data by relative byte addressing.

file I/O. A type of storage transfer that is used between applications and operating systems.

file service. The server application that services client requests for file I/O in a network file system.

file system. System software that determines the location of files in storage address spaces and provides access control for files and directories.

filing. Along with connecting and storing, one of three main elements in storage networks having to do with locating data in storage address spaces and managing data objects.

firmware. Software that operates on circuit boards or adapters.

flow control. A method of governing data transfers in networks.

forwarding controller. A controller used in remote copy systems to transmit data to a receiving controller.

fragmentation. The natural progression in a file system resulting in shorter contiguous available blocks.

free space pool. Block addresses that are available to be allocated to files by a file system.

full path name. A filename appended to a complete directory path, beginning with the root directory.

global name space. A replicated, identical view of the file and directory structure of a cluster or distributed file system.

HBA. Host Bus Adapter. A system storage controller providing initiator functionality and acting as the storage interface between the system's I/O bus and a storage bus or network.

head. A microscopic electro-physical device responsible for recording and detecting data signals on media.

heartbeat. A low-latency message used in clusters to validate system availability.

helical scan. An alignment used in tape equipment where the heads make diagonal tracks across tape media.

high availability. A characteristic describing equipment and implementations designed for minimal downtime.

hot backup. A backup process that runs while applications are running.

hot spare. A redundant component available to replace a failing or failed component.

HSM. Hierarchical Storage Management. A data management application that attempts to match the priority of data with the cost of storage.

IDE. Integrated Device Electronics. The same as ATA.

ILM. Information Life Cycle Management.

immutable. Unchanged; impossible to change.

in-band. A process that runs in a hardware or software component of the I/O path.

incremental. A backup operation that copies only data that has changed since the last backup.

initiator. A SCSI architectural component that creates an I/O command.

inquiry. A command issued to discover storage resources accessible through a particular target address.

installable file system. A file system that runs as a "guest" using the interfaces provided by the operating system.

interconnect. A device connection method. Includes hardware, software, and cabling (bus or network).

interswitch link (ISL). Links between switches in a switched topology network.

I/O. A storage transfer.

I/O bus. A system bus used to connect adapters such as HBAs.

I/O path. A sequence of hardware and software components traversed in the transmission of data between systems and storage.

I/O redirection. A virtualization method for accessing data on a network file server. Runs in a client of a network file system.

I/O request. A SCSI command to read or write data.

I/O termination. Used with storage virtualization to identify the processes used by an in-path virtual logical unit where storage commands are managed and received.

JBOD. Just a Bunch of Disks. A disk subsystem that does not use RAID or mirroring.

journaling. A logging method in file systems that records all intended I/Os and their completion.

kernel. Operating system core processes that manage the execution of work in a system.

kernel space. A mode of system operation that is typically reserved for system services and is not used for application processing.

LAN-free backup. A backup operation in a SAN where data is not transmitted over a LAN.

latency. Delay in transmission or process.

layout. The organization of files in a storage address space.

layout reference system. The method used to locate file data within a storage address space; in UNIX, these are the inodes or vnodes.

LBA. Logical Block Addressing. Used by disk drive controllers to virtualize storage locations inside disk drives.

locking. A method of controlling the sequence of access and access permissions in a file system.

log file. A file maintained by a database system that records all intended I/Os and their completion.

loop. A ring topology typically implemented as a Fibre Channel device interconnect where disk drives and initiators share a single connecting path.

LU. Logical Unit. A SCSI architectural component that receives and processes commands on behalf of a storage address space.

LUN. Logical Unit Number. A SCSI architectural component that provides an access point for a SCSI logical unit.

LVD. Low-Voltage Differential. The most recent implementation of the parallel SCSI bus with high data rates, cable lengths of 12 meters, and backward compatibility with single-ended SCSI.

media. The materials used for recording data.

media management. A method of determining the usage of backup tapes.

media pool. Multiple media that are used for a common purpose, such as a pool of backup tapes.

media transfer rate. The performance of transfers on storage media.

member. A storage address space functioning as a component in a RAID array.

metadata. Data used to describe data.

mirrored cache. Cache memory belonging to a pair of storage controllers that are connected over a high-speed link. All updates and changes are reflected in both caches simultaneously.

mirroring. A technique of creating duplicate copies of data on different storage address spaces.

MTBF. Mean Time Between Failure. The statistical calculation of failure rates based on testing large numbers of products.

multipathing. The use of redundant connections for high-availability access to a single storage logical unit.

name space. A file system component that displays the logical organization of directories and files.

NAS. Network-Attached Storage.

NAS head. A standalone network-attached storage computer system without integrated storage.

NDMP. Network Data Management Protocol.

near-line storage. Secondary or tertiary storage that is not online but that can be quickly accessed through automated processes.

nexus. A relationship set of SCSI components made up of initiators, target, LUN, and LUs.

NFS. Network File System. The original network file system developed by Sun Microsystems.

offline storage. Storage that cannot be immediately accessed.

online storage. Primary or secondary storage that is readily accessed.

out-of-band. A process that runs in a hardware or software component not in the I/O path.

overlapped I/O. The ability to process multiple SCSI commands on multiple devices connected to the same physical interconnect.

parallelism. The ability to perform work in parallel.

parity. A redundancy method where multiple pieces of data are used to generate a single piece of data. In RAID, the parity algorithm is XOR.

parity rebuild. The process of re-creating data in a RAID array on a replacement member.

partition. A logical structure establishing boundaries of a contiguous storage address space in a disk drive.

passive. A component that is not used until it is needed to assume the work of a failed component.

path. The sequence of directory names, starting with the root directory, used to access a given directory.

PDU. Protocol Data Unit. Examples are frames, packets, and cells.

pending. An I/O command that was issued and is waiting for a response.

point-in-time copy. A physical or virtual view of data that existed in the system at some previous point in time.

point-in-time recovery. The re-creation of system data as it existed at a previous, particular time.

point-to-point. A line topology connecting two entities.

port. A physical connection to a network or bus.

primary storage. Storage used to support application and system processing.

provisioning. The process of defining LUs and LUNs in a subsystem, including interconnect, device, partitions, and RAID levels.

QoS. quality of service. A way to designate performance and service quality for systems or applications having designated priorities.

RAID. Redundant Array of Inexpensive Disks.

RAID 4. Parity RAID with a static parity location.

RAID 5. Parity RAID with a changing parity location.

RAID 10. A RAID array formed by striping data across mirrored pairs of storage address spaces.

RAID level. An indication of RAID algorithms used in a RAID array.

raw partition. A storage address space recognized by the operating system, but lacking file system management. Raw partitions are commonly associated with database storage where the database system provides its own layout reference system.

read. Data transfer from storage to system.

read/write channel. Data transmission electronics used inside a disk drive.

receiving controller. A controller used in remote copy systems to receive data from a forwarding controller and commit it to remote storage.

redundancy. The use of multiple components to create higher data availability.

reinitiation. Used with storage virtualization to identify the process of creating one or more new storage commands from commands received and managed by a virtual logical unit.

remote copy. A data management application that creates redundant data when a dual-mode storage controller forwards writes to a remote storage controller.

remote mount. The process of establishing access to a network file system with an I/O redirector.

request sense. A command issued to check the status of the SCSI target, LUN, LU, or task.

restore. The process of copying data back from secondary backup storage to an application system.

root directory. The top-level directory in a file system's hierarchy of directories.

rotational latency. The delay incurred in disk I/O while waiting for a sector to rotate beneath the heads.

route convergence. The process of determining a new network path based on network algorithms.

SAMBA. An open-source software initiative to provide Windows server message block support on Linux systems.

SAN. Storage Area Network.

SAS. Serial Attached SCSI. The serial version of SCSI server interconnect technology.

SATA. Serial ATA. The serial version of the ATA desktop disk drive interconnect.

scalability. The ability to increase the size of a system; in storage, this usually means capacity.

SCSI. Small Computer Systems Interface.

SCSI-3. A SCSI standard separating physical and logical components, enabling the implementation of serial SCSI SANs.

secondary storage. Storage used to support data and storage management functions to make redundant copies of data.

sector. A regularly sized subsection of a track on a disk platter.

semantics. Programmatic interfaces used by applications to access file system services.

semisynchronous. A method of I/O processing allowing up to two pending write I/Os.

serial SCSI. The implementation of SCSI protocols on independent communications networks.

server farm. A method of computing where multiple servers run the same applications and access the same data.

serverless backup. A backup operation in a SAN where data is not transmitted through a server system, instead using third-party copy.

shared everything. A cluster storage design where all systems can access all storage.

shared nothing. A cluster storage design where storage is accessed through its corresponding controlling system.

short-stroking. A method of establishing a single partition on a disk drive to limit actuator movements and hence seek times.

single-ended. The original bus technology used for parallel SCSI.

SMB. Server Message Block. A client/server protocol developed for Windows server systems in the early 1990s.

snapshot. The process of creating a point-in-time copy of data.

space allocation. A file system function that selects blocks in a storage address space for storing file contents.

spindle. A rotating shaft that spins disk platters.

SPOF. Single Point of Failure. Describes single components that compromise high availability.

SRM. Storage Resource Management.

start-stop. A mode of tape operation where tape is stopped and restarted.

stateful. A method of distributed processing where participating systems retain connection details following a communication interruption.

stateless. A method of distributed processing where participating systems do not retain connection details following a communication interruption.

storage address space. Contiguous blocks used to store data. Managed as a granular, complete storage container by a single filing system.

storage I/O. Transmissions of storage data and commands.

storage pool. Storage address spaces used for a common purpose, such as a pool of secondary storage or a pool of storage for disk backup.

storage pooling. A term used with virtualized disk storage. The aggregation and subdivision of storage address spaces to create storage address spaces.

storage router. A network device used to exchange storage transmissions across different types of storage connecting technologies, such as Fibre Channel and parallel SCSI.

storing. Along with filing and connecting, one of the three main elements in storage networks having to do with the methods and operations of initiators, devices, and subsystems.

streaming. A mode of tape operation for sustained high performance.

stripe. A composite storage entity in RAID arrays formed from the set of aligned strips (all strips have the same relative block addresses in their corresponding members).

stripe depth. The amount of storage capacity (in blocks) corresponding to a defined RAID stripe: (the number of blocks per strip) * (the number of members in the array).

strip. A granular unit of data written to a single member of a RAID array.

striping. The process of writing storage I/Os to multiple storage address spaces. Usually done across multiple disk drives to reduce disk drive contention.

subdivision. The segmentation of resources, making several smaller resources from a single larger resource. Partitioning a disk drive is one example.

substitution. Replacing the function of one resource with a different resource.

substrate. The rigid base layer of disk platters.

subsystem. An assembly of storage devices, power distribution, cooling, and connection technology operating as a single integrated product.

superblock. A private storage area used by the file system to store configuration and operating status information.

sustained transfer rate. The performance of transfer in and out of a disk drive.

switched. A hub-and-spoke topology using network switches where end nodes have dedicated links and interswitch links are shared.

synchronous I/O. A method of I/O processing that requires a response for each write command before the next command is issued.

system cache. Memory used by an operating system to temporarily store data during I/O activity.

tablespace. Files used by relational database systems to store user and application data.

target. The receiver of storage commands.

task manager. The component of a SCSI logical unit that is responsible for maintaining the order of the task (command) list.

tertiary storage. Storage used to make third-generation copies of data.

third-party copy. A method of making data copies where a managing process uses an initiator located on another system or subsystem to issue read and write commands.

tiered storage. A storage management approach that attempts to match the cost of storage with the relative importance of the data stored on it.

track. Circular storage entities on disk platters having a unique address and many embedded sectors for storing data.

upstream. In the direction of an initiator.

user space. A mode of system operation that is used for application processing.

utilization. The percentage of storage occupied by system and application data.

virtual drive. A storage address space made from a combination or subdivision of other storage address spaces. Typically accessed as a SCSI LUN in a SAN.

virtualization. The creation of a storage address space from a subset or superset of other storage address spaces.

volume. The operating system definition of a storage address space.

volume manager. System software that manipulates storage address spaces to create RAID, mirroring, aggregation, and so on.

WORM. Write Once, Read Many. A technology that is used to store data that is inteneded to never be changed.

write. Data transfer from system to storage.

write ordering. An I/O process that maintains the sequence of I/O write commands as issued by an initiator.

write penalty. The process of reading old data and parity data before writing new data and parity in parity RAID 5 arrays.

WWN. World Wide Name. A unique 64-bit identifier used in Fibre Channel networking equipment.

WWNN. World Wide Node Name. The WWN for a system or subsystem that may contain one or more ports, each with its own WWPN.

WWPN. World Wide Port Name. The WWN for an individual network port.

XOR. An exclusive OR algorithm used in parity RAID.

zoned-bit recording. A method of recording on disk drives that places more sectors in tracks as the radius of the track increases.

INDEX

A

B

C

D

E

F

G

H

I

J

K

L

M

N

O

P

Q

R

S

T

U

V

W

X

Z